Why Blacks Fear
'America's Mayor'

Why Blacks Fear 'America's Mayor'

◆

Reporting Police Brutality and Black Activist Politics Under Rudy Giuliani

Peter Noel

iUniverse, Inc.
New York Lincoln Shanghai

Why Blacks Fear 'America's Mayor'
Reporting Police Brutality and Black Activist Politics Under Rudy Giuliani

iUniverse books may be ordered through booksellers or by contacting:

iUniverse
2021 Pine Lake Road, Suite 100
Lincoln, NE 68512
www.iuniverse.com
1-800-Authors (1-800-288-4677)

Because of the dynamic nature of the Internet, any Web addresses or links contained in this book may have changed since publication and may no longer be valid.

photographer credit: AP Images/Gino Domenico

ISBN: 978-0-595-47657-2 (pbk)
ISBN: 978-0-595-71621-0 (cloth)
ISBN: 978-0-595-91920-8 (ebk)

Printed in the United States of America

for
My Mother Alice

You've told me, time and again, the story of my life, death, and rebirth. I was five years old when my caretakers at the General Hospital in Port of Spain, Trinidad, put me in a wooden crib in a desolate corner of the "infant ward" that, you said, was their *Lapeyrouse*, their almost-cemetery, where "little innocents" like me with killer diseases were consigned to die. That night, after all the other "innocents" around me had bawled, and peed, and died alone in their soiled diapers; that night after my doctor, my priest, my "seer man" had told you, "de boy go dead just now" from diphtheria; that night after they'd called Simpson's Funeral Home and told you that the white hearse, the one that took the "innocents," was on its way for me, you read the 91st Psalm. That night you said at my death-watch, "He's just a little boy with a K foot (knock-kneed). He still breathing, there's hope. He'll wake up and call for me. He'll cry, 'Ma! Ma! Ma!' That will be 'the sign.' And I will come back in the morning and take him home."

and in memory of
Juanita Samuel, my grandmother
Mama used to say: "Meekly wait and murmur not."

Contents

Acknowledgments

Black Advocacy Journalism (BAJ) is the journalism of outrage, the voice of the ideologue whose finger is firmly pressed on the pulse of popular black dissent. BAJ is tempered only by strictures, which, at my behest, my editors Utrice C. Leid and Richard P. Goldstein, skillfully have circumnavigated for this book. Any imperfections or errors of omission or commission are strictly mine. I am deeply indebted to these old friends whose graciousness and patience are more than I can ever satisfactorily acknowledge.

Utrice (my former editor at *The City Sun*), you were the first to recognize BAJ and encourage me always to seek to perfect the concept through solid investigative reporting and stylized feature writing. From raw copy, you honed and chiseled and brought to life the most riveting characters in my pieces. It was you—when I would loudly assert, "Seems like murder here"—who sifted through my mishmash of ideologies by, in the words of Adam Gussow, "contributing to an evolving discourse of black revolutionary violence in the broadest sense—which is to say, black violence as a way of resisting white violence"—then purified, as Jackson Browne put it, "the blood in the ink" of my headlines. I can never repay you for working the graveyard shift on this project, even with a bum leg; you've turned night into day and a once-incoherent rant into readable text.

Richard (my former editor at *The Village Voice*), you're a *mensch*. I've never met a more candid advocate of soulful militancy. Throughout the years, you improved on BAJ and crossed it over even to the harshest critic of "New Jack Journalism."

And for Don Forst, my former editor in chief at the *Voice*. You pushed my experimental reporting to the limit; thanks for sharing my vision and putting up with me all these years. I remember you with great affection and admiration.

I owe my life in journalism to my teacher and mentor Keith Smith (my former editor at *The Sun* in Trinidad.) Keith, you've remained my editor-at-large, the raconteur of "Lavantee" who first told me to look to my village of John John, to the people who live "behind de bridge," for "in dem proud and inventive people" I would find poignant chronicles and the greatest backdrop for journalistic expression. Keith, at 19, I was free-lancing, searching for a voice, a style, the kind of prose *you* would lay down to evoke change, praise, bacchanal—and condemnation. "Style and that voice," you said, "come with age and experience." Thanks for having first introduced me to Naipaul, Walcott and Lovelace, and for feeding my *Inward Hunger,* and for taking me on that journey *From Columbus to Castro.*

To my brother Michael: This brief acknowledgment cannot adequately recognize how much you've devoted to my career as a budding '70s journalist. Brother, you critiqued my short stories about growing up poor while lying on a thorny mattress or hanging precariously from a downs tree. Without you, they never would have seen the light of day. Thanks for introducing me to Robert Nesta Marley ("Soon we'll find out who is the real revolutionary"), and *Reggae Bloodlines.*

To Ken and Noel, beautiful brothers of mine; you protected me, you are humble and compassionate.

For Seaver and Sean, who Ma calls "the Golden Boys," you have the biggest hearts. Your unmatched generosity has kept the lights on, the kids in school, and our bellies full. Your constant support and encouragement helped me to complete the manuscript. Seaver, you're right: "Brothers gonna work it out." I am blessed to have you as my brothers.

To Lynette, who I acknowledge with great love, deep gratitude and abiding respect. You never doubted that I could do it, "Teacher Princess." You've been a steadfast companion and friend, the loudest voice in the cheering squad. Your incisive suggestions on which stories worked and which didn't were extremely helpful to me. Your trademark, rip-roaring laughter broke the drudgery of research. Lynette, you've raised two wonderful children, Karen and Herschel, and taught them humility; you continue to inspire me.

Paula, mother of my children Zanelia, Peter Jr. and Tevin, you've walked a long way with me in my chosen path and I honor your contribution to bringing this book to fruition. Since starting our book-writing team in 1979, you've never failed to share your skills—whether as a typist or as a word surgeon, cutting up early drafts and putting the pieces where they belonged.

Zanelia, Peter Jr. and Tevin, I love your zany politics and sense of humor; you're exemplary in character, in my blood, and I've learned a lot from parenting you.

To Kelene, my daughter, my "Olive Oil," you are the mirror image of your mother, sweet, innocent, and forgiving. Thank you for typing those hard to scan pieces.

For Robert Samuel, Robert Warner, Wilfred Tyrell, Don Grant, and Sam Hill; I am proud to call you brothers. In my darkest days, you were beacons of light, guiding this combative iconoclast to a steady berth.

And for Mikie Sookoo, my nephew, who is one of the most courageous and kindest people on this earth.

John Noel, the Emmy award winning journalist; man, you epitomize professionalism and cool under fire. I can only hope to be as good as you.

To that raucous band of intellectual sparring partners who duked it out with me and each other on KISS-FM's "The Week in Review," I say, "Thank you." Bob "The Navigator" Slade, James "The Third Answer" Mtume, Judge Robert Pickett, and Sanford "The Cut Man" Moore truly have been like brothers, giving me both time and space to express my often pointed opinions, and doing so with a mutually shared respect. Mtume, I depend on you and will remain a burden to you to the end. As you're fond of saying, "me and you."

To my KISS crew, Robin Williams, Kahlil Bess, and Fatyin Muhammad, you're experts at modulating black rage. I have benefitted also from the insights of Lenny Green, Jeff Foxx, Shaila, Talent, Felix Hernandez, Bugsy, Raqiyah, Kesha Monk, Mike Shannon, Julie Gustines, and Toya Beasley. I owe a special word of gratitude to Kamau Callender and Danilvia Ramos.

From my sister Vinette Pryce, I learned more about the art of the dogged pursuit than I did during my twelve years of ambulance chasing for the *Voice*. Your assistance in recalling details was crucial to my own recollection of the events in Crown Heights and other communities where we covered race, crime, and black activist politics. You are a veritable source, a reporter's spare backbone going into the back alleys and dank stairwells of Brooklyn's mean housing projects. I am lucky to be so close to you.

To my adopted grandma Ivy Green, you treat me like the son you never had.

To my auntie Monica Williams; you moved mountains for me when I stumbled.

For my sisters Maureen Samuel, Pamela Green Perkins, Casilda Roper-Simpson, Marlene Crosdale, Alyene, Wanda, and Nedra English, Glenda Cadogan, Yvette Noel-Schure, and Sabrina Lamb; you're strong, independent women who I can *always* lean on for moral support and spiritual guidance.

Paul "Paulie Paul" Eliacin, you're my confidant and doting big brother; your politeness and willingness to accompany me anywhere in the dead of night to pursue a lead is the hallmark of your altruism. When things appeared to fall apart, you were my balm in Gilead. I owe you more than you'd care to admit.

For Alton H. Maddox, my Godbrother and attorney at war; after watching you battle the enemy all these years, and savoring every victory, I now fully understand the meaning of no retreat no surrender.

To attorney Michael Wildes, I envy the ease with which you solve the most complicated problems; you're disciplined and compassionate. I'm happy to call you my friend.

And for attorneys Michael W. Warren, Hudson Reid, Ron Kuby, and Norman Siegel, who taught me how to navigate the criminal justice system.

Shmuley Boteach, you are God's man, a soul brother who taught me how to face my fear. Those hectic months we spent together on WWRL, just you and me, pioneers—a black man and a Jew repudiating the racialization of New York on a morning talk show—were lessons in tolerance. One day, after some callers in our mostly black audience had bludgeoned you over a controversial opinion, you won them over with one of Martin Luther King's leadership techniques: "Appeal to the sense of morality and decency of the people on the other side of the negotiating table." Shmuley, you're a skilled interviewer who would turn an uninterested observer into a witness to the conflict.

And for Debbie, who bore Shmuley eight loving children, you are a great confidence booster.

For my kid brother Phillip Browne, you've reinforced in me that I have the power to triumph over those who seek to tear me down; from you I've learned patience and the true meaning of dedication.

Clifford Benton, my friend and literary agent; no one has been a more ardent promoter of my brand of BAJ. You've left an indelible impression on my family and me and we will cherish your friendship forever.

For Benita Noel, my sister, an Emmy award winning writer who remains one of the hardest working people in American journalism. Benita, just watching you work makes me tired.

R. C. Baker, my friend, artist extraordinaire, writer, and book cover designer; I've put you through so many changes; but I'd be lost without your eye for artistic detail. I, however, bear total responsibility for the final product.

I am deeply grateful to Randolph Archbald, a big brother, master teacher, and highly regarded IT authority who gave freely of his computer skills and sound editorial advice.

And to Joseph Best, Steve "Dog" Willit, Joseph "Tally" Sookoo, Rickie and Ishmael Rouff, my childhood buddies; you're better politicians than you think.

For Jonathan Rieder, my former editor at *Common Quest* magazine); it was an honor writing for you and journeying back to a time "When Justice Was the Rage."

Lisa Evers, you're my "guruette."

Mark Claxton and Noel Leader, you guys are first rate detectives, truly blacks in law enforcement who care.

Joe Morgan and Vie Wilson; their friendship meter is off the scale. No one who encounters these exceptionally gifted and generous black folk walk away without a passion for politics or an appreciation for the art of clinching the deal. Joe, thanks for reading an early version of the manuscript and suggesting important changes: We rarely differ in our approach to racial justice.

I am forever grateful to Bryant Rollins, Ernie Johnston, Jr., Wista Johnson, Michael Caruso, and Jonathan Z. Larsen, my former editors in chief at *The New York Amsterdam News*, and the *Voice*. You showed your faith in me by asking me to interpret "the new black view."

I owe my deepest appreciation to Dawad W. Philip, my former editor at *The Daily Challenge*, who put me through a crash course in deadline reporting. Dawad, I thank you also for introducing me to reliable sources that to this day I call upon, and for fixing in my brain the old Marcus Garvey truism that "it takes the slave to interpret the feelings of the slave."

Special thanks to my former interns and personally motivated researchers whose additional reporting saved me from blowing many a deadline at the *Voice*. Among them are: Amanda Ward, Karen Mahabir (for her patient and competent assistance in transcribing taped interviews), Danielle Douglass, W. Michelle Beckles, Vicki Shiah, Linda DiProperzio, Kristen Nelson, and Skye McFarlane.

I am indebted to *NY 1's* Dominic Carter, Dennis Bernstein, host-producer of KPFA/Pacifica Radio's *Flashpoints*, Janny Scott, Ralph Blumenthal, Dennis Hevesi, Joseph P. Fried, David Habfinger, Robert D. McFadden, and David Firestone of *The New York Times*, and to *The Associated Press and United Press International*. I've drawn on their exclusive reporting to help me reconstruct events critical to an accurate account in my own reporting.

To the many people who have encouraged me over the years and made invaluable contributions: Cecelia Vincent, Fitzroy and Iris Harrington, Anthony and Lorna Alphonso, Earl and Jacqueline Phillip, Annmarie Lee, Jean and Christopher Griffith, Joseph Mikie Sookoo, Greg Tate, Nelson George, Cheryl, Susan, and Ann Peters, SherryAnn Pedro, Rennie Bishop, Hakim Al-Mutlaq, Johnnie Chisholm, Ian Gellineau, Anthony Ricco, Dan Jacobson, Martin Osei, Moktar, Lena Green, Samba Fall, Richard Black, Jannie Green, Wayne Gillman, Angela Applewhite, Curtis and Melvin Phillip, Allan Job, Yusef Salaam, Tony Morris, Willie Egyir, Bill Perkins, Adamma Ince, Georgina Knight-Alphonso, Brian Parks (thanks for digging successfully into the *Voice* archive), Frank Lombardi, Anita Petraske, and Ed Park.

But finally, to Frances Louise, my wife, mother of our daughter Kelene: For your patience and unswerving support, this book really belongs to you, my love. Your calming spirit, sweetness, and understanding all these months was reminiscent of the Biblical Job; it seemed I was married more to this project than to you. Thanks for growing intellectually with me, participating intimately in defining the elements of BAJ, and for fighting off my most vicious critics with your sharpened tongue and disarming attractiveness.

Prologue

♦

The Quality of Life … and Mercy

GIULIANI FOR NEW YORK
415 Madison Avenue
New York, N.Y. 10017

Mr. Giuliani:

Remember me? It's Air Hoodlum, "Sneaker Felon," G, your "quality of life offender." Me, the foul-mouthed, blind, crippled and sickinnahead menace to the city: The nappified, thick-lipped, stable-smelling, pimply, smarmy form of animal life you'd rather quarantine north of the 96th Parallel, consign to feudalistic labor or some muthafuckin' Alcatraz. Remember me? I'm the target of your fears and misplaced emphasis on blame. I'm the Section 8 mob coming to a ghetto near you. I'm Larry Hogue. I'm Miss America's homeless uncle. Remember me?

A friend of mine calls you "the Stephen King of politics." In truth, real or imagined, you scare the hell into me when you open your mouth. You fail to realize how Hitchcockian you sound. Two weeks ago, I heard your "Quality of Life Speech," a battology that, even by the acerebral standards of Beavis and Butt-Head, was obnoxious and riddled with class bias and hostility. You seem pitiless in your pursuit of that other New York; the speech was an act of meanness that justifies everything African Americans been saying about you. "Until you are willing," as Grandmaster Melle Mel says, "to eat rats" to survive, your understanding of the quality of life in New York City is zero.

In your speech, you quoted Cooper Union professor Fred Siegel, who complained about "the 'street tax' paid to drunk and drug ridden panhandlers," the "squeegee men shaking down the motorists waiting for a light," and "the swirling masses of garbage left by peddlers…." The views of this Professor Scrooge might have something to do with the disappearance of my friend Curtis Cuffie, the homeless man who turns street trash into art and festoons his creations along the fence of a parking lot in the shadow of Cooper Union, a couple of blocks from the Voice. I haven't seen Curtis in months.

In her profile of Curtis in June, my colleague Sarah Ferguson discovered that Cooper Union owns the parking lots where Curtis usually displays most of his work "and is largely responsible for the regular sanitation sweeps." Curtis never hurt a soul. Where's the compassion? Where the fuck is Curtis? Like you, G, the professor shows more respect for property rights than human rights.

You also highlighted the whining of Channel 2 reporter Marcia Kramer, who complained to mayor Dinkins that she moved out of the city last year because she "got fed up with ... a homeless person who took up permanent residence on my street corner, begging; who was very menacing." Every day, on her way to work, Kramer claimed she saw people pissing in the street and those pesky "squeegee people ... were aggressive in attacking" the miserly correspondent. Kramer acted as though her induction into "high society" would be threatened by hordes of the downtrodden.

Why can't she allow "the squeegee people" to make a living? Can't you see, G? Her flight to the 'burbs was driven by white guilt and a fear of unknown blacks. And since you have been quoting every brainiac dumb-dumb to make your points, let me introduce you to constitutional think tank Douglas Laycock, who argues that "the fear of unknown blacks is widely deemed racist." Okay? Laycock writes that "treating all unknown blacks with visible caution may be entirely rational to the risk-a-verse, but it is properly condemned because it imposes serious costs in racial isolation and ostracism on all blacks, the great majority of whom are law abiding." I can almost hear you shouting, "That's an alibi!" Why don't you—as you like to tell others—"Shut up!"

You vow that if elected mayor (which I believe is as easy as sneaking dawn past a rooster) you'd establish "swift and sure justice" courts in police stations to prosecute "menacing" squeegee operators, "aggressive panhandling," and "illegal vendors." Offenders will be sentenced to "quality-of-life duty," such as sweeping the streets. That's iron-handed, and maybe unmuthafuckinunconstitutional. *Your harsh measures are nothing more than the stopgap solutions of a pugnacious pol. For the past two weeks you've been waging war on the poor. Today the penalty and punishment for being homeless is 90 days in a shelter (of course, it can be extended one more day), after which, for example, a mother with child, or children, will be evicted—back into the streets. Your homeless-be-damned attitude, which you wear as a badge of honor rather than shame, can only incite popular hostility, particularly in the African American community.*

Another thing that pissed me off (sorry, Marcia) about the "Quality of Life Speech" was your scapegoating of Larry Hogue, the "Wild Man of 96th Street." It was very stupid of you to attempt to make Hogue the Willie Horton of this racially charged mayoral campaign. You reminded your audience of mostly white ethnics-Archie Bunker types, I presume-that Hogue was taken off the streets only after "he had assaulted women and children and terrorized the neighborhood." Though you mentioned that Hogue was mentally ill, you never bothered to explain who or what drove the brother mad.

Larry Hogue was a navy aircraft mechanic in the service of his country. In 1968, he was injured in a freak accident. "Working on an aircraft carrier, he was hit on the back of the head by a propeller," according to a confidential psychiatrist's report. "He suffered serious brain injury and was unconscious for three days. It took six months for him to recover. He was left with a seizure disorder." Although Hogue was discharged on 100 percent disability and received a substantial income, he continued working, holding down various jobs over the years. There are thousands of formerly mentally competent Larry Hogues roaming the streets. They need help, not to be used as political fodder.

Maybe, you need to have your head examined to determine where your coldblooded policies come from. Maybe you were smacked around one time too many by the Christian brothers and nuns at Bishop Loughlin Memorial High School. One suggestion (hey, take it or leave it): Be practical and less idealistic. You can't heal the wounds of urban society or re-invent government if you desire to make the permanent underclass invisible.

Remember me.

Peter Noel,
The Village Voice
September 1993

Introduction

✦

"Making the Historical Injustice Public"

I'm not gonna shut my mouth
I'm for the truth to come out
About the leader with the iron will
And his allegiance to the dollar bill
'Till I go down
'Till I go down
'Till I go down
I'm not gonna shut my eyes
'Till I go down

—Jackson Browne, *"Till I Go Down"*

I FIRST MET RUDOLPH W. GIULIANI in September 1993 while he was campaigning in Harlem to wrest control of City Hall from David N. Dinkins, New York City's first black mayor. Capitalizing on popular disenchantment with Dinkins over his handling of the 1991 Crown Heights riots in Brooklyn, Giuliani felt confident he didn't need a ghetto pass for a political foray into Harlem. For months I had been requesting a one-on-one interview with Giuliani to question him about his plans, if any, to include blacks in the highest levels of his administration, if he were elected. (The *Daily News* had reported a month earlier that "a tour of the Madison Avenue headquarters shows a staff that is overwhelmingly white.") His PR people ignored me; primarily because I had declared war against Giuliani death-bed defender, the mostly white Patrolmen's Benevolent Association (PBA), for their racist attacks on Dinkins. And in the wake of my open letter to Giuliani, baiting and cussing him out over that now infamous "Quality of Life Speech," tension between the candidate and me mounted. One "officious fool" in the GIULIANI FOR NEW YORK camp had urged me to keep my distance. But on this high noon, I dogged Giuliani's every move.

He wound up at the intersection of Park Avenue and East 116th Street, a bustling commercial strip in one of the poorest barrios, also known as Luis Muñoz Marín Boulevard. Giuliani stood on a podium of milk crates under the green and white street signs preening for the paparazzi. Seeing Giuliani up close and personal for the first time conjured the image of novelist Andrew Davis' *Mr. Devil*. "He didn't look much like the traditional Devil that everybody got all wound up about. All that stuff about horns and a pointed tail was idiocy, an attempt by the do-gooders in the world to keep humans under the repressive thumb of fear. In reality, he had a receding hairline where horns should have been, his vanishing hair now a ghost of its former existence. And his butt—where the tail should have been—was rather flat. The local joke was that God had flattened it when he 'booted the Old Man's ass out of Heaven.'"

There he was, peddling his "Confusion ticket"—Latino comptroller candidate Herman Badillo and public advocate candidate Susan Alter, a Jew, Democratic sheep gone astray—while hunting votes in this mostly Puerto Rican enclave, a Dinkins bailiwick. Giuliani was flanked by a throng of vocal Dinkins supporters, media gadflies, and bellicose white aides.

"Do you know who Luis Muñoz Marín is?" I asked Giuliani.

"Yes, I do," he snapped, looking me dead in the eye.

"Who *is* he?" I pounced, sensing I'd trapped Giuliani in a little white lie. He hesitated. I salivated. He exploded: "He's the first *governor* of Puerto Rico." In the last few weeks, Giuliani and his staff of control freaks openly berated other provocative journalists they didn't get along well with. An unidentified man muscled me out of the way. "Ask a real question!" he barked.

I lost it after that.

Frank Lombardi, the veteran *Daily News* reporter, who was shadowing Giuliani that day, reported what happened next between Giuliani and me to Linda Stasi, the tabloid's gossip columnist:

> … Frank Lombardi tells us that Peter Noel, a reporter for *The Village Voice* who often writes about race issues, has had it out with Giuliani, too. Rudy apparently gave Noel a tongue lashing after an East Harlem event last week when the journalist asked him a question the Republican-Liberal mayoral candidate found offensive.
>
> Noel … asked Giuliani about a recent article in *The Amsterdam News* in which a white cop was quoted as supposedly saying that when Giuliani is elected "he will kick your nigger ass." Since Giuliani can't prevent anything said by a cop, we'd be offended too. Giuliani told Noel that his writing in the *Voice* "divides people in this city … you report language that shouldn't be used … what you are doing is unfortunate for the city … It's a shame really

and you should be ashamed of yourself doing it." Noel, who loves a good fight, too, snapped: "You're talking about language? You used the word 'bull—'[at the police demonstration last year]." Noel also told Giuliani there is a perception in the African American community that if he becomes mayor "you're going to be oppressive" and that he was reporting the sentiments "of my people ..."

Giuliani had crossed the ethnic divide to drive a political wedge between Latinos and blacks, between the "Spanish" east and the "African" west. But in the end, the similarities between East and West Harlem would haunt him. He'd come to "El Hood," where people burn him in effigy and melt wax images of him; where the only handouts that trickle down are surplus cheese and pork with natural juices—salt added. He'd come Uptown, where blacks and Latinos historically have viewed cops as an occupying force, there not to protect them but to keep them under surveillance; to act as a buffer between *them* and Downtown society. "Giuliani comes here trying to fool us, because he thinks Puerto Ricans are ignorant," shouted Angelina Ortega, a school bus operator. Her message was clear: Latinos who vote for Giuliani could be left adrift in a stormy sea with neither rudder nor anchor, Giuliani would eventually toss them aside and they won't be able to turn to the black community for support. "Dinkins," she argued, "is the best thing that has happened to this community."

It was a mixed crowd of blacks and Latinos that greeted the visitor that day. What was supposed to be a cakewalk turned into a muddy dash, as Dinkins supporters harangued Giuliani and disgruntled former mayoral aide Willie Nieves. When Giuliani began to speak, 21-year-old Walter Torres interrupted: "Willie Nieves need to be put in jail." In his speech, Giuliani claimed the Nieves endorsement was "a devastating blow, as you can tell, to the Dinkins campaign." But his salvos only incited the mayor's supporters, who booed and shouted, "Four more years!" As Giuliani strained to be heard, Torres delivered the coup de grace: "We don't need more racists: Go home!"

Giuliani and I became bitter enemies after the confrontation. Riding a wave of outrage from Jewish and white voters, he went on to defeat Dinkins. As mayor, Giuliani balkanized the city, creating two distinct New Yorks—one white, one black. "I've got to get this city to stop thinking in categories, to stop thinking in terms of black and white ...," he told *The New York Times*. For eight years, I remained a committed commentator on this transparently false attempt to unite the two New Yorks: Our mutual contempt would fuel a feud that defined nearly a decade of my Black Advocacy Journalism (BAJ) that was hostile to the Giuliani mayoralty.

RUDY GIULIANI TODAY ENJOYS a remarkable reputation as a man of courage and conscience, an inspiration to millions of Americans. To the nation, he is best known as the ash-sodden mayor of New York City emerging defiantly from the rubble of the twin towers in the aftermath of the September 11, 2001 terrorist bombings. Oprah Winfrey dubbed him "America's Mayor," an honorific he has parlayed into a frontrunner campaign to become America's next president. Giuliani may have hoped that with the passage of time his post 911 celebrity would subvert unpleasant truths about his tragic history with New York City blacks. The truth is we fear him: Giuliani is to blacks what Osama bin Laden is to *all* Americans. I wrote this book vowing to make the former mayor's often-ignored record of oppressing the "other New York" a very public part of the 2008 presidential race. *If nothing else,* police brutality, his dirty little secret, should be front and center.

Media coverage of Giuliani has focused largely on whether evangelical voters might tolerate a White House hopeful who has been married three times; his support of a woman's right to choose an abortion; domestic partnership benefits for gay couples; gun-control; Bernard Kerik, his corrupt, ex-police commissioner and one-time nominee for Homeland Security secretary; and charges he was woefully unprepared for the terrorist attacks. *Rarely* in their pursuit of Giuliani's scandal-rich background do reporters dredge up "the historical injustice"—City Hall incited police crimes defined by serial killings, torture, maimings, and unlawful detention of the black citizenry. "Historical injustices," the eminent historian Elazar Barkan contends, "are those that have ended even though their consequences continue to impact on the survivors." And since "[a]mending such injustices [is] not on the political agenda" of presidential candidate Giuliani, I invoke Barkan's argument for "making the historical injustice public." I watched as black activists, hoisting aloft coffins at funerals, buried the bullet-riddled remains of police brutality victims in the graveyard they've dubbed "Ghouliani's Conscience." Shot after shot, blow after blow, I watched them lay bare the broken spirits of the survivors squarely in the mayor's bloodied hands.

Of course Giuliani has his legion of defenders, who argue that he should not be held responsible for police abuse of black citizens. ("Giuliani has publicly, and also in my presence, boasted, 'I run the Police Department,'" recalls former mayor Edward I. Koch. "… In the Giuliani administration … the Police Department is very much the mayor's creature.") And if you happen to die at the hands of "New York's Finest," *it's all your fault.* I clashed often with these Giuliani apologists regarding, what Barkan calls, "the morally and politically charged acknowledgment of guilt." *New York Magazine* writer Nina Teicholz captured one such encounter with "all-around bad boy of the black intelligentsia," author Stanley Crouch, during a debate about police violence on cable news station *New York 1* (NY1):

> Stanley Crouch is bobbing around like a heavyweight champion warming up for a fight. "I hope we see some blood," he says, gleefully shifting his stocky frame. "I'm going to get pilloried!" ... His opponent this evening is Peter Noel, the West Indian-born reporter who covers black politics for the *Voice*. Declining to jump on the anti-police bandwagon, Crouch tries to steer the conversation to black-on-black crime. "The issue is blue-on-black crime!" retorts Noel, growing heated. Noel accuses Crouch of being a Giuliani apologist and a front man for police-force bigots. "I know you voted for Rudy," Noel shouts. "That's the dirty little secret among boozhie black intellectuals like you."
>
> "That is just a bunch of bunk!" Crouch retorts. "The greatest threat to black life and limb is not the police; it's criminals in our community, and you, Peter Noel, know it."

New York Post columnist, John Podhoretz, a narrow-minded critic of the Dinkins administration, and me, argued that somehow I possessed the power to silence Giuliani at a time when the mayor should have been touting the real relationship between "minorities" and the NYPD. "The mayor honestly and truly does not believe that the NYPD is routinely abusive and horrible toward minorities, and so he doesn't say it," Podhoretz declared. "He has the facts on his side, tons and tons of facts. What has defeated him is that 'the facts don't matter,' as the Village Voice's Peter Noel has repeatedly said. What matters is that minorities are feeling oppressed, so obviously they are oppressed. In this circumstance the only thing a politician can possibly say is 'I feel your pain'—and Giuliani has come very close ... to uttering those Clintonite words."

Why Blacks Fear "America's Mayor" documents from an entirely black-eyed perspective how Giuliani's Afriphobic creature, the NYPD, spun out of control often with deadly consequence for blacks. The book—a compilation of my writings in *The Village Voice, New York Magazine,* and *Common Quest*—paints a classic portrait of grief expressed through the most compelling cases of police brutality ever investigated and reported in "Giuliani time." Politically, it takes you back to an era when justice was the cry, chronicling the resurgence of a '60s-styled black-led protest movement and civil-disobedience campaign reminiscent of the anti-apartheid rallies of the '80s. Both the Million Youth March, led by New Black Panther Party head Khallid Abdul Muhammad, and the weekly arrests of celebrities, orchestrated by the Reverend Al Sharpton following the police killing of West African immigrant Amadou Diallo, are covered in necessary detail.

Giuliani, who served as mayor of New York City from 1994–2001, treated black citizens as foreign occupiers of his beloved city. Under the guise of stamping out crime, Giuliani established "swift and sure justice" in neighborhoods most distrustful of police. Blacks were required to provide their names to cops, even if those officers had no probable cause that the person whose name they sought was completely innocent of any wrongdoing. "Some in our police department think it's OK if you violate the constitutional rights of 10 people if one of them happens to have a gun or contraband of some sort," said David Dinkins, referring to the stop-and-frisk campaign conducted under the Giuliani administration. "I say they're wrong. First of all, you're violating the rights of all 10. Worse yet, the bad guy may go free because the evidence is suppressed and not permitted to be introduced as evidence because it was secured unconstitutionally. These kinds of things are out there for everyone to see what some of us have been saying for a long time."

In the fall of 1996, months after an investigation by the City Council focused on cops' unauthorized use of black teens in lineups, callers to black radio stations WLIB and WWRL, continued to complain that police harass teens and haul them off to stand in as fillers without permission from their parents. According to the callers, cops randomly stop youths in black neighborhoods, often using strong-arm tactics when they refuse to produce identification. Usually "the suspect" is given a summons for resisting arrest, assaulting a police officer, or disorderly conduct. "It's not enough that a black kid has his hat on sideways and the seat of his pants are pulled down around his knees," said Dinkins on his now defunct talk show on WLIB. "Does that mean they can slam him against the wall and search him?" That year, the city doled out more than $15 million in settlements and judgments involving police brutality cases—$4 million in cases known as "no right to touch person" and $11 million for use of excessive force, false arrest and imprisonment, and malicious prosecution.

Amid vociferous calls to Giuliani to do something, the NYPD embarked on a bold campaign promoting CPR—Courtesy, Professionalism, and Respect for the public. Subway cars and city buses were plastered with the picture of a smiling black youth with dreadlocks in an oversized T-shirt shaking hands with a white police officer. Extra white cops were assigned to so-called "'hood patrol" and police cars sported a bumper sticker with the campaign theme: "NYC Needs CPR." But despite the NYPD's new "anti-dis" approach to community policing and Giuliani's vow that his administration would strive to overcome minority communities' distrust of police, the NYPD leaves a trail of law-enforcement tactics that blacks maintain are abusive.

"CPR breeds contempt," was the mocking response coined by Amen-Ra Jamal, founder of Citizens Against Police Brutality. "It [was] a public relations gimmick," he charged. Even disgruntled, mostly white cops ridiculed the slogan. In the midst of contentious city contract negotiations, the NYPD had a tough time policing the cops' scorn of the CPR campaign. Protesting officers on the street brandished placards declaring, "The NYPD Needs CPR." They said if Giuliani didn't take care of them, they were not going to enforce his policing strategies.

Most confrontations between blacks and police were not resolved with a simple apology and handshake.

On January 10, 1997, 19-year-old Lawanda Hallums, who was six months pregnant, interrupted six white police officers who were interrogating her brother, a cousin, and their friends in the stairwell of the Van Dyke Houses in the East New York section of Brooklyn. When Hallums asked the cops why the teenagers were on their knees, one officer allegedly "smashed my brother's head against the wall." Hallums said when she protested, a female cop struck her in the face. "I grabbed her by her hair and threw her on the floor. Then a male cop grabbed me by my leg and threw me flat on my stomach. They held my arms tightly behind my back." A cop allegedly threw Hallums's cousin on the floor and "busted his face" after he began yelling that Hallums was pregnant.

Despite telling the officers she was bleeding and experiencing abdominal pains, Hallums was taken to Central Booking, where she was charged with second-degree assault. A judge later dismissed the charge against her. A police department spokesperson said the department had no record of the incident.

Giuliani and Police Commissioner Howard Safir attributed what others said was a rise in police brutality to a more aggressive style of policing.

In February 1999, after the firing squad-style slaying of Amadou Diallo, rogue white cops sympathetic to their four indicted colleagues began reminding suspects and other innocent blacks they illegally stopped and frisked that they could wind up like Diallo if they resist arrest or mouth off. The cops implemented a tactic known as "rude-cop scenario." Contrived traffic stops would escalate into violence in which blacks usually wind up the losers. Police watchdogs contend that what happened to Bernadette Jeremiah and Elize Pierre-Paul is a classic example of racial profiling resulting in "rude-cop scenario."

A POMPOUS VOICE BOOMED over the loudspeaker of a patrol car that had tailgated a gray 1987 Cadillac as it pulled out of a gas station in the East New York section of Brooklyn, one airy December day about two months before Diallo was killed.

"Pull over!" Jeremiah remembered the voice, sounding more brassy and irritated, roaring a second time. Jeremiah, a 46-year-old West Indian beautician on her way to pick up her nephew from school, turned to her fiancé, Pierre-Paul, and insisted that the cops could not be summoning her since she was not driving recklessly, and neither of them had been in trouble with the law.

"Gray Cadillac!" the voice thundered. Jeremiah pulled to the curb. She says two white cops approached; one positioned himself on the driver's side, the other on the passenger side. Both had their hands on their gun belts.

When one of the cops demanded Jeremiah's license and registration, she protested, "What did I do?"

"Give me the license!" the cop barked.

"But why are you checking my license?" argued Jeremiah.

"That's the law!" she said the cop replied. "Give me the fucking license!"

Shocked by the officer's attitude, Jeremiah chided him for using obscene language. But sensing that he was growing impatient, she handed him the documents. "Instead of taking them, he grabbed my wrist, and he wouldn't let me go," she recalled. She said the cop warned her that if she didn't "get the fuck out of the car," he would arrest her. Pierre-Paul, 25, felt helpless. Diagnosed with polio as a child, the son of Haitian immigrants is unable to move his legs and relies on Jeremiah to get around. He broke into tears as Jeremiah screamed in pain after the cop allegedly grabbed her.

"Why does he have to twist her arm like that?" Pierre-Paul pleaded. Jeremiah claimed that her fiancé's rebuke angered the cop, who sucker-punched Pierre-Paul in the face, grabbed him by his collar, and attempted to yank him from the car. "Get outta the fucking car!" the cop kept shouting.

"He can't walk!" Jeremiah said. "He gotta use crutches!"

"I said, 'I'm not gonna open the door unless I see a negro cop come over here,'" Pierre-Paul recalled in an interview with NYI's Adele Sammarco. "There was a big one [white cop]," Pierre-Paul added in halting English. "He said, 'You think you're a king, motherfucker?' And while he pulling me, the other one keep punching me in my head...."

Despite the viselike grip the cop had on her arm, Jeremiah said she managed to reach into the back seat with her other hand to retrieve the crutches. "But they pulled them away from him and threw them back in the back seat." Pierre-Paul also told Sammarco that a cop asked, "The punch is not enough for you, mother-fucker?" and sprayed him with Mace. The cop then allegedly dragged him from the car and threw him on the ground. Backup cops arrived and, according to Jeremiah, joined their fellow officers in "kicking and punching and slamming" Pierre-Paul's head against the roadway.

"Please don't do that to him, he can't walk!" Jeremiah pleaded. She said two black cops also responded. One, a female, "kicked me, punched me, grabbed me by my ponytail, and slammed my head [against the ground] until I nearly shit on myself." Handcuffed and hoisted from the ground by the officers, Jeremiah looked frantically for Pierre-Paul. "I saw them punching and kicking my fiancé," she charged. "I was screaming so loud that the female cop took me and slammed my head against the trunk of my car." Pierre-Paul said that after the cops wrestled him to the ground, they rubbed his face in dog shit. Fearing it would get in his mouth, Pierre-Paul renewed his appeal for one of the black cops to intervene. "Somebody, please call a negro cop to come and save me!" he pleaded.

The female officer responded. "She come and she keep saying to me, 'Mother-fucker, get off the floor!' She kicked me five times in my face," Pierre-Paul lamented. Still, the cops had not realized that Pierre-Paul was disabled.

"Why the fuck won't you get up?" Jeremiah remembers one officer asking Pierre-Paul.

"Please don't beat me anymore!" Pierre-Paul begged. "I am paralyzed from my waist down!"

Reportedly, that declaration finally jolted the officers. "Oh shit!" Jeremiah said one cop remarked. "We just jumped a paralyzed person. We're gonna be in deep trouble." Jeremiah said the cops shoved them into the back seat of a patrol car and took them to the 73rd Precinct. According to Jeremiah, one cop said they'd pulled the suspects over for running a red light, but "they freaked out" and had to be restrained. She insists the cops beat them.

"The story is a lie," an NYPD spokesperson told *NY1*. The next night, they were arraigned in Criminal Court and finally released. According to a prosecutor's complaint filed in Criminal Court, all Officer John Marciano did was stop Jeremiah's car for running a red light. Marciano, prosecutors claim, approached her and courteously asked that she show him her license and registration, but Jeremiah "refused to comply and attempted to drive away." When the officer tried to arrest her, the complaint alleged, Pierre-Paul attempted to pull him into the vehicle and threw punches at him. Jeremiah "flail[ed] her arms" and "punched and kicked at" Marciano "and attempted to strike" him with Pierre-Paul's cane, causing the officer to "sustain a laceration to the finger [and] suffer substantial pain."

"Why the hell would I try to beat cops with a cane, and they have guns?" Jeremiah pointed out. "Am I out of my cotton-pickin' mind?"

"RUDE-COP SCENARIO" EVOKED so much concern after the Diallo shooting that it spawned another "while black" acronym in the category that has become synonymous with police mistreatment of blacks.

And so the fear of being "Dialloed While Black" (based on the phrase "Driving While Black") became a hot-button topic at anti-police-brutality rallies and on black talk radio.

"There's a poison goin' on," one caller declared on WLIB shortly after the release of a report by the state attorney general, who discovered that even in precincts that are 90-percent white, more than half the people stopped and searched are black or Latino. Some 175,000 stop-and-frisk forms were examined for the report. The forms are filled out by officers to explain the reason for a search, which is legally permitted if an officer has reasonable suspicion that someone is concealing a gun or drugs in his or her waistband. The report also found that the reasonable suspicion cited on the forms often was inadequate, meaning the officers had no justification for the stops.

A week later, Police Commissioner Howard Safir released the result of a poll commissioned by the NYPD that showed that 82 percent of residents questioned said they respected the NYPD and its officers. When broken down by ethnicity, 83 percent of whites, 75 percent of African Americans, and 83 percent of Latinos said they respected cops. When asked if the NYPD was working toward improving relations with minority communities, 59 percent of all respondents said yes. By ethnicity, 61 percent of whites, 51 percent of African Americans, and 58 percent of Latinos said yes.

The poll's most glaring flaw was that it contained no questions on police brutality.

What was striking, was the length some defenders of Diallo's accused killers went to portray the NYPD as an army of efficient lawmen unaffected by persistent accusations of brutality. "I don't hear lots of complaints about police misconduct," Commissioner Safir said at a City Council hearing. "What I do hear about is they want more cops. They want more cops doing what they've been doing."

In the WLIB caller's reference to "poison," he invoked a phrase by the rap group Public Enemy to dramatize how widespread the "DWB" threat had become. Public Enemy's summer release of "41:19," riddim warfare that targets the shooting of Diallo, remains the most popular rap commentary about the notorious stop-and-frisks that occur primarily in poor black and Latino neighborhoods.

"What you got?" asks Chuck D in the rap.

"Ratatat-ta-tat!" comes the reply, mimicking the staccato of the 41 shots fired at Diallo.

"Shot 41 only hit 19!" Flava Flav emphasizes.

The rapper later conjures the scenario of a routine stop-and-frisk: "[R]acist muthafuckrs mad 'cause they ain't with it," he says of the unfortunate victim. "Da poliz get out da car, searchin' him for nuthin.' If you got sumthin' then they got you for sumthin.' That's fucked up, the way they play dirty! Lock him up in jail until he's past 30. They don't give a fuck about you; they don't give a fuck about me, I'm past 33."

DURING HIS EIGHT-YEAR REIGN, Giuliani constantly harassed black leaders who spoke out against police brutality and tried to pry the mayor's iron-fisted grip from around the black body politic. Within the NYPD, Giuliani enforcers targeted activist cops like Eric Adams, the blunt-talking founder of *100 Blacks in Law Enforcement Who Care.*

A stocky, clean-cut figure with an imposing stride, the bald-headed Adams was sometimes referred to as "the laughing policeman" because of his ebullient giggle. Speaking as the head of *100 Blacks* at many of the racially charged NYPD controversies during the Giuliani years and addressing issues in crisp, articulate rhetoric, the charismatic Adams became a familiar figure to New Yorkers. He called friends and strangers "brother" or "sister" but was tough as nails on critics who branded him a maverick. The veteran cop railed daily about crime in black neighborhoods. His stock phrase is that black suspects, who, for example, rob and kill taxi drivers and who stash illegal handguns in homes that wind up in accidental, fatal shootings of children "are not representative of our community." The crime-fighting model, "Operation Take Back Our Community (Operation T Back)," which NYPD brass have imitated, was developed by Adams and his *100 Blacks.* Today, scores of black and Latino teens—designated "permanent suspects" by racial profiling cops during encounters—refer to the group's guidance on "What to do when stopped by the police."

But in the highest levels of the NYPD, Adams was considered a threat to the department and to the extremist views on policing enforced by the Giuliani administration. In 1998, the NYPD's Internal Affairs Bureau conducted two probes of *100 Blacks* and Adams for an allegation not related to his organization. The investigations were revealed during testimony by Deputy Chief Raymond King of Internal Affairs in federal court in Manhattan. King was testifying at the civil trial of Yvette Walton, a former officer who claimed she was fired because she spoke out at a City Council hearing on the Street Crime Unit following the killing of Diallo.

King made the statements under cross-examination by New York Civil Liberties Union attorney Christopher Dunn. He testified that from August to October 1998, Internal Affairs conducted "covert surveillances" of Adams and collected his phone records. King did not say why Internal Affairs was investigating Adams. "They said I was associating with a known felon," recalled Adams. "But the foundation of the investigation was bogus." He described the investigation of him as "straight out of COINTELPRO," referring to the acronym for the FBI's notorious investigations of black organizations and the civil rights movement during the '60s and early '70s.

Adams said he knew the "the dark side," a code name for Internal Affairs, was watching him because straight-arrow cops who protected him were watching the spies. "Someone has been calling me throughout my career, tipping me off," he said. "This is the same person who called me and told me Internal Affairs had cameras in my office. Sure enough, I found the cameras in my office. Then this person told me, 'They're monitoring your phone calls.' This person played back a telephone call I had gotten. This person said, 'They're trying to disrupt your home.'"

Adams told reporters there were no problems at work that would warrant an investigation, and added that during the time he was under surveillance, he was promoted from sergeant to lieutenant. The case was closed in June 1999 and deemed "unsubstantiated," meaning the charges could not be proved or disproved. In March 1999, Internal Affairs began a separate probe into *100 Blacks*. King did not say what the probe was about, but a police source, speaking on condition of anonymity, said it involved complaints from two black officers in the Street Crime Unit that members of *100 Blacks* were allegedly harassing them following the Diallo shooting. Adams's group allegedly wanted the Street Crime cops to tell them about alleged racist activities within the unit.

Adams said at the time that he was "bewildered and concerned" about the investigations. "Since our organization was put in place, we've prided ourselves in bringing about some type of harmony within the police force," said the activist cop who cofounded *100 Blacks* with Sergeant Noel Leader. "I cannot imagine what we have done in the last five years that would prompt this. We've held ourselves to a strict code, and expect our members to do the same."

Adams and *100 Blacks* criticized the department when they felt it gave out misleading information about controversial shootings involving fellow officers. Adams recalled how the department tried to cover up a so-called "friendly fire" shooting of a black officer during a drug probe in East New York. "Somehow it first leaked out that the shooting was [the work of] a sniper," Adams testified at a federal trial involving Yvette Walton's lawsuit against the department. "We knew that it was not a sniper and we [held] a news conference to inform the public that it was not a sniper." Adams also revealed that the department gathered information on officers' statements by sending undercover cops, who posed as reporters, to news conferences called by *100 Blacks*. The *100 Blacks* probe was closed and deemed unsubstantiated in March 1999. Adams denied that the group has ever intimidated anyone. Asked about the probes, Deputy Chief Tom Fahey defended the department's actions. "The investigation techniques used were consistent with an investigation of this nature, and subsequently the allegations were unsubstantiated," he said. Adams had asked the department for the records of the investigations, but later sued to have the documents released.

In September, 2001, a judge ordered the NYPD to reinstate former Police Officer Yvette Walton. The ruling was a victory for Walton and for Adams and his *100 Blacks*. It was Walton's association with *100 Blacks* that attracted the attention of her superiors. On February 14, 1999, 10 days after Diallo was gunned down, Walton (one of only three black women in the Street Crime Unit, and the only one assigned to street patrols) appeared at a news conference wearing a black leather jacket, gray hood, dark glasses, and a white and black scarf wrapped tightly around her face, and with her voice electronically altered. The entire affair, including putting Walton in disguise, was orchestrated by Adams. "It was my idea," Adams would later testify. "And after conferring with Sergeant Leader, we both agreed. But it was [at] my [insistence]."

With Adams at her side, the 12-year NYPD veteran charged that the racist practices of her unit led to the killing of Diallo. Two weeks later, Walton appeared on ABC's *Nightline*. The department took another beating when Walton, again in disguise, testified at a City Council hearing, whispering comments to Adams and Leader. At the time, Adams and *100 Blacks* were being investigated by Internal Affairs.

The NYPD, however, found out it was Walton doing the bashing and fired her the same day of the hearing, allegedly because she abused sick-leave privileges. After a nonjury trial, Judge Alvin K. Hellerstein found that Commissioner Safir had fired Walton in retaliation for speaking out. "I find that the Police Department knew that it was Walton who was the spokesperson of 100 Blacks criticizing the SCU for employing discriminatory policies that led to the killing of Amadou Diallo," Hellerstein wrote in a 36-page decision.

"The Police Department knew of Walton's role from their monitoring of 100 Blacks' activities, from their monitoring of incoming and outgoing calls to and from the 100 Blacks telephone, and from the ease with which Walton was identifiable behind her disguise," he stated. "The Department also knew that a female member formerly with the SCU, presumably the same female spokesperson, was to testify at the City Council hearing concerning the SCU...." The department's "denial of this knowledge is not credible," he added. The judge also noted that Walton "would not have been dismissed had she not spoken out publicly on behalf of '100 Blacks in Law Enforcement' on an issue of immediate and substantial concern to the Department."

IN ADDITION TO EMBARRASSING David Dinkins at the polls, Giuliani seemed to harbor a congenital hatred for the black former mayor. Only once, albeit begrudgingly, Giuliani acknowledged Dinkins in a positive light. "Mayor Dinkins, I salute your accomplishment for our city," Giuliani said during his first inaugural address in 1993. Even then he was compelled to pay homage to "Dinkins' special dignity and grace" as Dinkins sat among the invited guests. "Those endearing qualities "will also mark his governance of our city and it's something that we hope to call on in the future," added Giuliani. "And I know that we can and that we can count on it."

Giuliani never called on Dinkins for his advice on improving the city—on anything as a matter of fact. Instead he launched a campaign of blame that amounted to character assassination.

Giuliani never let go of his criticism of Dinkins' role in Crown Heights; he beat the issue irreverently to exploit Jewish and white angst, bringing the city to the brink of civil war during the 1993 and 1997 mayoral campaigns.

On August 19, 1991, violence erupted in the predominantly black and Jewish enclave after seven-year-old Gavin Cato, the son of Guyanese immigrants, was accidentally struck and killed by a car that was part of an entourage transporting the grand rabbi of the ultra-Orthodox Lubavitch sect, Menachem Schneerson. Cato's death sparked a rebellion in which rabbinical student Yankel Rosenbaum was fatally stabbed in a revenge attack. Giuliani and Ed Koch, sworn enemies, closed ranks and piled on, distorting even the basic fact about the duration of the tumult.

Like Dinkins, I scorn revisionist historians.

Both Giuliani and Koch attempted to tarnish Dinkins's legacy by promoting the image of him as a "murderer" and Jew hater.

It took an emotional toll on Dinkins every time we talked. "Yankel Rosenbaum got stabbed in the first few hours, and there was sporadic rioting over a period of time; it did not go on continuously for three days," Dinkins insisted. "It is not true that [former Police Commissioner] Lee Brown and I gave orders to hold back the cops and let blacks attack Jews. Giuliani and Ed Koch to this day blame me for that. Ed Koch calls it a *pogrom*, which is by definition a state-sponsored activity. But the courts have dismissed the lawsuits against me and Lee Brown. They found no such evidence...."

I will never forget Giuliani's public humiliation of Dinkins. Shortly after he took office, Giuliani set about to make good on an alleged promise to Crown Heights Jews that he'd bring Dinkins to his knees, groveling and apologizing for what he'd done to them. Giuliani allegedly encouraged legal efforts to force Dinkins to pay out of his own pocket millions of dollars in a financial settlement to 29 plaintiffs—Hasidic Jews, who had sued alleging that Dinkins "permitted, facilitated and effectively condoned" violent attacks on them by mostly rampaging black youths. For years Giuliani negotiated quietly behind the scenes with Jewish leaders. In 1998, after the talks came to light, a war of words erupted over Giuliani's ugly characterizations of Dinkins's stewardship and countercharges by Dinkins that Giuliani showed favoritism to the Hasidim of Crown Heights.

Being the statesman that he is, Dinkins ate crow but invited Giuliani to a private dinner at his home in Harlem. Giuliani unequivocally refused to sit down with his predecessor. Dinkins had considered the possibility that Giuliani would reject the "very large olive branch" he offered to him, but there was no longer any hiding the depth of the crisis, he told reporters—the dispute between him and the mayor was alarming the city. "What I did was the correct thing by seeking to ameliorate, as it were, what I feel is a very tense situation," Dinkins explained. "Giuliani's refusal to come to dinner further indicates where he is coming from, so I don't need to deal with him anymore in that regard."

Some black political leaders were caught off-guard by Dinkins's move. Even I questioned its political currency. Once regarded by blacks and Jews as the most popular black political leader in New York, Dinkins was caught in a desperate struggle to hold on to those two allies—both of whom he alienated in the firestorm over his reaction to the subsequent settlement and Giuliani apology to Jews on the city's behalf for its handling of the disturbance.

On one hand, black activists charged that Dinkins failed to call for the prosecution of the Hasidic driver who mowed down Gavin Cato after running a red light in the motorcade escorting the Lubavitch leader. On the other hand, the Crown Heights Hasidim believed that Dinkins withheld police protection, allowing the violence to go on for four days. For the beleaguered Dinkins there seemed to be no easy way out of the maelstrom. In a clear reference to his critics, a defiant Dinkins told me: "Those people who say, 'Why doesn't Dinkins just say he is sorry and let's get on with it?' don't want me simply to say, 'I'm sorry;' they want me to *confess*. They want me to say, 'I held back the cops,' but I did not do that. So I can't confess. I am sorry that people were injured. I'm sorry that Yankel Rosenbaum died as a result of those stab wounds. I'm certainly very, very sorry about Gavin Cato and Angela, Gavin's cousin, who was injured, but that doesn't mean that I am to blame for it."

After Giuliani rejected Dinkins' invitation to eat soul food, I remember attending a private meeting involving Al Sharpton and black nationalist Sonny Carson, former bitter foes, and attorney Carl Thomas (who would later play a key role in the Abner Louima police-torture case) at the Harlem headquarters of Sharpton's National Action Network, where they fashioned a response to Dinkins' surprise call for a cease-fire—a move that emboldened Giuliani's crude political posturing. "We are not gonna accept Dinkins speaking for the black community," said Carson, who headed the Brooklyn-based Committee to Honor Black Heroes, which was blamed for exacerbating the volcanic tensions between blacks and Jews in Crown Heights. Carson told me he was not speaking for Sharpton, whose reaction was less critical of Dinkins. "The black community feels insulted by what Dinkins has done," I recall Carson saying. "How dare this fallen darling of the Jews presume to be our leader?"

Carson's salvo, which I later reported, rattled the racial conciliator, who replied cautiously, illustrating how much the ex-mayor himself believed the black community's opinion of him had changed. "I did not make it the peace offering for black people," Dinkins told me. "I made it for myself. I have a right to my views, as Sonny Carson has to his." Then Crown Heights City Councilmember Una Clarke, a critic of Carson's unrelenting attacks on moderate black politicians, defended Dinkins' attempt to reach out to Giuliani. "It is the spirit of Martin Luther King, Nelson Mandela, and Mahatma Gandhi all wrapped up in David, which makes him think that everybody should be embraced," she told me.

The *New York Amsterdam News*, the city's oldest and largest black newspaper, in a front-page editorial, railed that Dinkins's invitation to Giuliani to "break bread" at his home and talk about their differences was "the final insult." Wilbert Tatum, the paper's outspoken publisher, wrote an editorial that equated Giuliani's snub of Dinkins to Hitler's refusal to shake hands with Jesse Owens at the 1936 Olympics. "There is nowhere to go from there," Tatum wrote. "David was misguided in the first place by inviting Rudy Giuliani, a polarizing bigot, racist and fool into his home.... We can only ask David, 'Don't you understand anything? Yet? Why did you have to compromise your dignity and ours by rolling over?"

In defense of Dinkins, I am always eager to point out that Giuliani's own bigoted politics is a throwback to the racial animus that was the hallmark of the Koch administration.

Dinkins defeated Ed Koch in 1989 after an election marked by outrage over the fatal shooting of Yusuf Hawkins by a gang of whites in Bensonhurst. Race relations were far better under the Dinkins administration than they were under Koch and Giuliani.

"I've taken a big hit because of Rudy," Dinkins said. "When rioting after the beating of Rodney King happened all over the country, we did not have rioting in New York City. Rudy Giuliani, Ed Koch, and [former U.S. Senator Alfonse] D'Amato publicly praised me for calming our city. Later on, they decided I was a bad guy."

Dinkins reminded me that, as mayor, Giuliani refused to meet with top black elected leaders like Carl McCall (then state comptroller and New York's highest elected official) and Manhattan Borough President C. Virginia Fields. It was only after the uproar over the shooting of Diallo that Giuliani seemed to relax his isolationist stance of not talking to his black critics. "Here's a guy who for five years refused to meet with Carl and Virginia—with whom he had not met since she was elected to office," Dinkins recalled. "When he finally met with them, some journalists wrote: 'The mayor is reaching out.' Reaching out? Ain't that a....? In my case, anything I said about Rudy during the first few years of his administration was 'sour grapes.' I was 'bitter' because I was a 'disgruntled former mayor.'"

The *Post*'s Podhoretz derided the claim that Giuliani "had somehow shown disrespect to the entire black community" by refusing to meet with the black pols. "Giuliani didn't want to meet with Fields and McCall not because they're black, but because he believes them to be enemies," he contended. "And is he wrong to think it? Both are partisan Democrats and strong supporters of his old rival, Dinkins. If you believe New York's mayor has a particular obligation to meet with the Manhattan borough president and the state comptroller, fine, attack him for that. But those who have been letting Giuliani have it on this point evidently believe that Fields and McCall deserve some kind of special treatment from Giuliani just because of their skin color."

Koch said it was black activists who shunned Giuliani, even though Giuliani himself made it clear in his 1993 inaugural speech that "each one of you has an equal claim on me to apply one standard of fairness." As far as Koch was concerned, the activists never gave Giuliani a fighting chance and had used the same divisive tactic against him. "[E]ven before his inauguration he was informed that the radicals would urge their political supporters and elected officials not to meet with him or shake his hand," Koch said. "Many of these people were those who sought to bring me down." Again in his 1997 mayoral victory speech, Giuliani vowed to try "endlessly and tirelessly" to reach out to everyone in the city. "We have to reach out to all of you. And if we haven't, I apologize," he said.

But many of Giuliani's harshest black critics were skeptical, and soon the hardline Republican was proving that "all of you" does not include black Muslims led by Nation of Islam Minister Louis Farrakhan.

During a speech in Harlem, Minister Benjamin Muhammad, formerly Ben Chavis, executive director of the NAACP, taunted the short-tempered Giuliani with an offer to meet and work out their differences. "With all due respect," Minister Benjamin said, "I plan to meet with the mayor and tell the mayor, 'This is not your city.... We're following God's man, Louis Farrakhan.'" In response to this challenge, Giuliani told *NY1*'s Dominic Carter: "I probably would not meet with him. I really would have nothing to do with people aligned with Mr. Farrakhan." It was the latest dismissive outburst from the mayor, a critic of Farrakhan.

CITY COUNCILMEMBER UNA CLARKE, a politician Giuliani eventually would reach out to, typified the dilemma black leaders faced when they felt dutybound to deal with the hated mayor. During a raucous televised debate in August 2000, on *NY1*, Representative Major R. Owens, who was fending off a challenge from Clarke in Central Brooklyn's 11th District, suggested that Clarke was a clandestine Giuliani supporter. Owens referred to "your good friend, the mayor" while addressing Clarke. He charged that it wasn't until Giuliani was in office that Clarke "started putting distance between herself and her political family," the Coalition for Community Empowerment. Clarke blamed Owens and the Coalition—Brooklyn's black political machine that had tried to dissuade Clarke from running against the eight-term incumbent—for spreading what Clarke called "that noxious thing in the air."

"I had no friendship with Rudy Giuliani," Clarke insisted. "I was too pissed with him to begin with for all of the programs that I needed that weren't being funded. They say, 'She supports him; otherwise she couldn't get so much for her district.' I do the business I need to do to help my district, and I don't think that an everyday indictment and badgering of the mayor gets to the point. If he's a racist, he knows it. I don't have to remind him of that."

But some of those same Democrats who criticized her for dealing with the Giuliani administration tried to enlist her help, and that of Congressman Edolphus Towns, in getting the mayor's support for a federally funded empowerment zone. "It was clear when [a well-known political operative] approached me that he had been sent by the Brooklyn Democratic machine. They thought that Ed Towns and myself had some strange relationship with the mayor, that somehow we could get him to sign on to the empowerment zone."

Clarke acknowledged that she talked often with Randy Levine, then deputy mayor for economic development, who was spearheading negotiations to bring Magic Johnson Theaters and other businesses to her district, which covers Crown Heights and Flatbush. "I had no direct contact with Rudy Giuliani," she reiterated. "I had had an ongoing relationship with Randy Levine to make sure the capital dollars that I put into the budget for those projects would remain in the budget." In fact it was during a ceremony at City Hall, in which Magic Johnson appeared to announce the joint project with the Giuliani administration, that Clarke said she had one of her rare encounters with the mayor. While awaiting Giuliani's arrival, Clarke said she cornered Johnson in a room and chided him for insisting on staying out of the uproar surrounding the police shooting of Diallo. "I told him that I was as angry as everybody else over Diallo. I said that the daily demonstrations at One Police Plaza was an indication of how angry people are about the way the mayor is handling the affair."

In walked Giuliani, Clarke recalled.

She said that after she scolded Giuliani, too, about his nonchalance, he asked her for advice on how to calm the racial tensions in his city. "He said he had held back for so long that nobody would talk to him," Clarke said. "I said to him, 'You probably thought that the [protest] was a black thing, but tomorrow morning some 11 rabbis are going to go over there and get arrested. How will you then handle that?'"

IN MAYA ANDREWS' TALE OF HARDSHIP AND INSULT, Giuliani was cast as Scrooge and her ailing 65-year-old grandmother as the Old Woman who lived in a cramped one-bedroom apartment with so many grandchildren she had no choice but to kick them out. "Giuliani [didn't] want us and my grandmother [would not]take us back," recalled Andrews, a homeless mother of three who lived in the city-run Powers House Assessment Center in the South Bronx for two months in 1996. "We became pawns in an urban refugee crisis," the 31-year-old Andrews cried one afternoon as advocates for the homeless mounted an assault against the Giuliani administration's "bed-of-nails" policy. "What do people like us do when the system and your own flesh and blood slams the door in your face?"

Everywhere Andrews turned in the bureaucratic maze of the Emergency Assistance Unit (EAU)—the notorious Bronx warehouse for the homeless which temporarily placed her family at Powers—someone kept changing the rules. Like the more than 5000 other adults with children who languished in city-run shelters, Andrews was trapped. In the summer of 1996, Giuliani directed employees to deem applicants for shelters ineligible if they had relatives with housing, regardless of whether space was actually available. On Thanksgiving eve, in the latest round of the struggle between activists for the homeless and Giuliani, State Supreme Court Justice Helen Freedman ruled that the city must prove a family had somewhere else to go before denying admittance to an emergency shelter.

In November 1994, Andrews had nowhere else to go. Two weeks after she was viciously beaten and raped by an acquaintance, she suffered from traumatic stress syndrome which left her in perpetual tears, disoriented, and terrified of going out: Andrews, who has a master's degree in early childhood education, gave up her $43,000 a-year job as a supervisor of youth services for a nonprofit agency, and her three bedroom apartment in Manhattan, and fled New York. A year and a half later, her anxieties somewhat abated, she moved back to the city at the request of her grandmother. Andrews, her 15-year-old daughter, and two sons, ages 11 and eight, at the time, slept on the floor. But the behavior of the eight year-old who suffered from attention deficit disorder, proved too much for the sexagenarian.

"Grandma yelled at him when he was loud and extremely hyper," said Andrews. "I increased my son's medication to help calm him down but it didn't seem to be enough for my grandmother," she recalled. "So she told us, 'Get out of my house; the kids are driving me crazy.'" Tossed out into the street one night, Andrews and the kids checked into the EAU, where the conditions and house rules were more draconian than grandma's.

"That's not gonna work," the nurse told her. "We have to give them a shot."

"Not only were my children going through the shock of being homeless and sleeping on the floor, but they wanted to give them a shot at 1:20 in the morning," said Andrews, welling with angry frustration. "I refused." According to Andrews, the nurse copped an attitude and punished the family.

When asked about the incident, Susan Wivott, a spokesperson for the Department of Homeless Services, which runs the EAU, told me, "I can't discuss specific cases."

"Later on that day, when I came back with the records, my whole file disappeared," she said. "And if your file disappears they log you out. You have to start the process of eligibility all over again. I felt it was punishment. He did something with the file." Andrews was in the process of being evicted when a sympathetic employee intervened. "We would have had to leave EAU and then call the hotline again—but only after 24 hours of the eviction. They expect you to sleep in the street for those 24 hours."

The first night, Andrews discovered the tactics EAU employees under the Giuliani administration allegedly us to declare a family ineligible for shelter. "The mothers don't sleep," she claimed. "We don't sleep at all because we have to sit up and listen for our names to be called. If you fall asleep and you don't hear your name, you're logged out. You have to start the process all over again." A family can be summoned at anytime and brow-beaten into accepting a "diversion," a process that determined that homeless applicants indeed had relatives who could put them up. "Basically when you go through diversion they sort of con you," Andrews explained. "They say, 'We'll give you $300 if you can find someone to stay with for two weeks.' They offered me $300. You can't get an apartment in New York for $300. I refused."

Again, the Department of Homeless services' Wivott would not talk to me about Andrew's charges.

The family slept on floors for two and a half days before they were shuttled to the Powers House Assessment Center. After 17 days at Powers, Andrews wrote a four-page letter to then Public Advocate Mark Green, chronicling a revolving door system she said was "forcing people to go back to emotional and abusive situations," and pleaded for his help. In the letter, she told Green that on her third day at Powers she suddenly was declared ineligible for shelter because EAU learned she had been staying with her grandmother.

"My grandmother told them that we could not stay there on all three occasions when they contacted her," Andrews wrote. "My appeal was denied and so we had to go back to EAU to start all over again, to once again sleep on the floor [for] three days and to be sent back to Powers—only to be found ineligible again. This time they said I 'failed to cooperate with agency guidelines to determine eligibility.'"

Andrews said the Giuliani administration's policies on dealing with homeless applicants for shelter contributed to overloading the welfare rolls. "Once you go to EAU you're forced to apply for public assistance; if you're not on public assistance, they will not process you," said the mother, who received $337 each month plus $244 in food stamps. "That's one of the reasons why I [was] not working."

But under Giuliani new workfare guidelines would force Andrews to work to keep her benefits. This was how she summed up her battle with the administration: "If I'm not on public assistance, they will either send us to hotel, where there are no cooking facilities, and my kids will have to eat out. I would be a working homeless person."

AS RUDY GIULIANI AND HILLARY CLINTON gear up for their likely history-making presidential race showdown, black voters should have deep doubts about being torn between the two candidates. Neither knows blacks. Neither deserves black support.

Throughout his mayoralty, Giuliani consistently viewed and treated blacks as though they were children—wild, undisciplined, and temperamentally unstable. Blacks were irresponsible wards who wanted things that were not good for them and rejected those family values necessary for proper growth and maturity. In Giuliani's world, these blacks needed a stern father figure who would give them that good, swift kick in the backside, throw their rowdy friends out of the door, and restore order in the household.

But Giuliani's ignorance of black life was total. He grew up surrounded by whites. He went to high school and law school with them, joined them in the stratosphere of the Reagan justice department, befriended them in private law practice, supervised them as United States Attorney, and hunkered down with them as mayor. Although Giuliani grew up during the civil rights era, the black struggle for equality had little impact on his sense of fairness and racial justice. Giuliani had no black friends and remarkably few black appointees (Only in Giuliani's small and often corrupt inner circle did he find peers). He was notorious for avoiding black audiences and openly contemptuous of black leaders. "It was as if from birth Giuliani was surrounded by a gauzy Caucasian bubble as he traveled across the political landscape," says Ron Kuby, a civil- and constitutional-rights lawyer, who was a former law partner of the late radical defense attorney William M. Kunstler.

On the crucial issue of crime and policing that marked Giuliani's tenure as mayor, his aggressive defense of the worst white police misconduct was legendary. It was in the crucible where race met crime that Giuliani's ignorance of and contempt for black people most defined him. While *all* New Yorkers wanted a decrease in crime and safer streets, blacks and whites split dramatically as to how this should be accomplished, and what trade-offs were acceptable to achieve it. "Whites and blacks had very different answers to the question of how many wrongful police shootings of innocent black people could be justified by the goal of decreasing crime," Kuby contends. "White people were perfectly willing to permit the black community to be subject to random sweeps, 'jump-out squads,' and brutality as long as crime fell. White people were terrified of blacks and blamed them for New York City's decay. They were more than willing to allow black people to pay the price, in lives and liberty, for lowering crime."

Giuliani viewed civil liberties in the black community as a luxury black people simply could not afford. And despite repeated proof that white cops had a different trigger finger for black and white suspects, Giuliani's faith in the essential goodness of the police was almost theological in its totality. Says Kuby: "Reflecting back on the Giuliani era a few years ago, I heard a black community leader comment, 'We asked for more police, jobs programs, drug rehabilitation centers, housing, and better schools, and all we got was more police.'"

Giuliani's belief that the most complex social problems could be solved by applying greater and greater doses of force, no matter what the collateral damage, defines his mayoralty. "Black New Yorkers experienced this for eight long years," Kuby lamented. "Now white America needs to ask itself whether this is what we want in the next president."

AFTER GIULIANI DISCLOSED IN MAY 2000 that he was battling prostate cancer and that his marriage was in shambles, I felt sorry for the mayor. I knew what I was feeling was not pity, a feeling that Giuliani and me, neither of us, had had for each other: this was a rush of raw compassion. At that point in my emotional maturity, I began to give credence to Dr. Martin Luther King's assertion that blacks like me had "acquired, as a result of [our] historical experience, a peculiar capacity to love their enemies, to endure patiently suffering, pain, and hardship and thereby 'teach the white man how to 'love' or 'cure the white man of his sickness.'"

I confided in black brothers like DeVry University computer science professor Randolph Archbald and Joseph Best, an electrical inspector for the city, that despite his notorious rap sheet on race *I* could teach a white man like Giuliani how to love and eventually cure him of *his* sickness—the cancer of racism. Randy and Joey concluded that I was a person with serious mental illness and threatened me with psychotherapy and indefinite confinement. Just as I was thinking about going public with my new-found "love" for Giuliani, I learned that he had showed none to my dear friend John Hynes.

Don't count John among the hordes of New Yorkers who disliked Giuliani, yet were rallying to his side in May 2000. Some like me, oddly, would have liked the prospective U.S. Senate candidate to remain in our political lives. Not John, a livery cab industry activist who suffers from Parkinson's disease and was scornfully depicted as a Neanderthal by Giuliani on his call-in show. John, who uses a wheelchair to get around, had been waging a one-man campaign to expose Giuliani's alleged insensitivity to the disabled.

"I regret that the mayor has cancer," John, then a forty-something, practicing Catholic, who was married and the father of two young boys, told me for a story I was doing on him for the *Voice*. "I hope that his children will suffer as little as possible as a result of the current turmoil in their lives," added John, graciously. "I sincerely wish the mayor a speedy recovery, but an equally speedy retirement and disappearance from public life."

Giuliani, he charged, was a pitiless politician. To those who watched the mayor's tough-as-nails exterior through the years, it was stunning to hear his public admission that he too was subject to common human frailties.

"Do you cry sometimes?" a reporter asked.

"Yeah, of course," Giuliani replied. "Of course I cry."

But to John, the pugnacious mayor might just as well have choked on his tears. "I have never despised an elected official as much as I despise Rudolph Giuliani," he confessed. "My family and others ask, 'Why do you hate Giuliani? Forget about him.' I say, 'It's bad enough that he does what he does to other people; that's enough for me to hate him.' I would have to do something, even if he left me alone. But when my disease was already robbing me of several hours a day and taking its toll on my family—when the mayor, through his underlings, robs me of more minutes of time I could be spending in the park or relaxing or doing whatever I want—then it's personal."

Their clash seemed almost inevitable. It can be traced to John's encounter with unfeeling bureaucrats in the Giuliani administration's Human Resources Administration (HRA). After John was diagnosed with Parkinson's in 1994, he quit his job as an MTA bus driver and enrolled in CUNY Law School. But the debilitating effect of his disease slurred his speech and left him crippled. No one would hire John. He depended on a monthly $1, 220 disability check and $300 in food stamps. "If I try to work, HRA takes every dollar," charged John, who devoted his time to advising the widows of slain livery cabbies that they are entitled to up to $30,000 in crime-victim's compensation plus $6000 for funeral expenses. In November 1999, the city agency launched an investigation of John, alleging food-stamp fraud. John, in turn, accused HRA of harassment. "Every time I have an issue with HRA they close my case, and I threaten civil disobedience; they always back down and reopen the case," he said.

HRA investigators notified John that they had discovered in his 1993 tax return that Citibank had sent him a check for $7000. "They had been asking me about this for several years in a row at recertification," John recalled. "I said, 'Yes, I am guilty. I had money in the bank before I got sick, before I ever thought I'd be in the welfare office.'" He summed up the attitude of his tormentors: "Why ask Mr. John to explain what this piece of paper is? Just open up a fraud investigation. Scare the shit out of him and maybe he won't answer, and we can close his case." The agency initiated a fraud probe. "So I get this letter telling me that I am the subject of a fraud investigation," John explained. "I call and 'Agent S' tells me I must come in. I tell him I can't travel easily—everything is explainable, right here and now, in 10 seconds, on the phone. No problem. If I can't come in, they will come to see me. Plus there is other stuff, which 'Agent S' cannot reveal to me on the phone. 'But, uh, Agent S, I am the accused.'"

According to John, Agent S also sought proof that his wife did not have a bank account in Florida. When John himself began to interrogate Agent S, the investigator allegedly said he'd already revealed too much to John, and he could have a lawyer present if he wanted. "Turns out the $7000 payment was a return of my pension contributions to the federal Thrift Savings Plan when I worked as an IRS officer," John said. "Then Agent S wanted proof that the $7000 was not a yearly pension. I gave him proof by fax and he never called back." In December, John said he called Agent S and was told by Agent S he believed that the case against him was closed.

"I am not a paranoid individual, but the investigation made me seriously think that they were harassing me even though I used to truly believe that the agency did not have it together enough to harass anyone, at least not deliberately," John said. "I confess that, for a moment, I was nervous. Not about being arrested—because I am innocent—but about being pushed too far. Parkinson's disease is not helped by stress. I have always managed to pay the rent and buy the food and pay the utilities. The thought of being unable to do that was not pleasant."

The investigation infuriated John, who unleashed his ire on Giuliani on January 7, 2000, on the mayor's morning radio show, *Live From City Hall With Rudy Giuliani*. John began with a hyperbolic attack, portraying the ex-prosecutor—who had set himself up as a tough-guy moralist—as a hypocrite.

".… The biggest thing you could do to reduce crime would be to resign, sir," John said in the taped conversation he had me listen to over and over to prove his point about Giuliani's hypocrisy and lack of compassion. "Crime would drop like a rock if you resigned. You're the biggest criminal in the city."

Giuliani laughed. But his trademark insult was not far behind.

"Hey, John!" Giuliani said. "What kind of little hole are you in there, John? It sounds like you are in a little hole. John!"

I thought John had missed the chance to confront Giuliani about the alleged harassment by HRA investigators when John suddenly jumped on Atlanta Braves pitcher John Rocker, who at the time was stealing headlines for his racist, homophobic, and anti-New York remarks.

"Why don't you accuse Mr. Rocker of being a convicted sodomite like you do your other opponents?" John asked.

"Are you okay there? You're breathing funny," Giuliani teased.

"No, I'm not Ok," John replied. "I'm sick, and you cut me off my food stamps and Medicaid several times; but I suppose you don't give a damn about that either."

Giuliani ignored John's complaint, preferring to engage the caller in more vexing rhetoric. "There's something really wrong with you there, John. I can hear it in your voice. Tell me a few of your other things you'd like to say."

"I'd like to say that my hero is [sidewalk artist activist] Robert Lederman, who paints you as Hitler. He should be mayor. He's the man!"

"Robert Lederman for mayor?" Giuliani smirked. "You gonna be his campaign manager, John?"

"I don't use words like fascist and racist loosely, sir, but I use them when I refer to you," John shot back. "You're the worst mayor this city has ever known."

Giuliani took the condemnation as a compliment.

"Now, why don't you stay on the line," he urged John. "We'll take your name and your number and we'll send you psychiatric help, 'cause you seriously need it. Sounds like you need it more than John Rocker."

After screeners cut off John, the mayor continued: "Man! Look, it's a big city, and you get some real weirdos who hang out in this city, and that's what I was worried about on, uh, New Year's Eve. I wasn't, you know—I figured, the terrorist groups and all that we could keep under control—worried, but who knows what, what's living in some cave somewhere. So, uh, and John called up. John calls up from Queens, but who knows where he's from."

Giuliani then took a call from a woman who identified herself as Victoria and said she was calling from Westchester.

"Hi, I'm so glad that I followed that jerk," Victoria said.

"He's not a jerk," Giuliani said, giggling. "Victoria, I spent a lot of years being a lawyer, Assistant U.S. Attorney, U.S. Attorney. I've dealt with a lot of disturbed people; sometimes you can just hear it in their voice...."

"Boy, you had him tagged ..."

"That's a seriously disturbed guy and I hope he takes up our offer of giving us his name and number so we can get him some psychiatric help 'cause, even more than John Rocker, he needs it."

I asked John why he openly baited the mayor. John said he felt Giuliani had declared war on poor and disabled people. "Mr. Giuliani showed a total lack of respect for all disabled people when he mocked me after I revealed that I was sick," he contended. "He could have had a field day laughing at my tremors and inability to walk or even speak at times had we met in person."

John conceded that he provoked Giuliani's harsh comments, "but that does not make such remarks by an elected official tolerable." Giuliani, he said, should have been aware of his illness.

"I did not make it personal," he insisted. "I called him 'sir' and 'Mr. Mayor,' yet he referred to me as a 'weirdo' in need of psychological help. Perhaps the most bizarre part of the conversation was when Mr. Giuliani stated that he was more worried about people like me coming to Times Square on New Year's Eve than he was about terrorism. That statement speaks for itself. I cannot make the point of the mayor's unfitness to serve any better than he made it himself."

John maintained that Giuliani was too wrapped up in defending his ego to acknowledge the serious aspects of his fight with the HRA. "At no point [on the program] did the mayor express concern for a constituent who was on the line alleging victimization by a mayoral agency under his direct control," John argued. "He did promise, interestingly, to attempt to help a recently arrived student who had overstayed his visa—that he would help him secure a green card. While I wish the best for the student, the fact is that Mr. Giuliani ridiculed a person he had the power to help and gave false hope to someone who probably stands a snowball's chance in hell of success in a federal jurisdiction over which the mayor has no influence."

After their on-air battle, John extended his war with Giuliani onto the Internet and TV. In a lengthy complaint he left on the viewer's mailbox for *NY1*'s Inside City Hall, John began by asserting that Giuliani tried to dismiss him as a nobody. "Look, uh, you know, man, I am indeed from Queens, and my name is indeed John," he said in his message. "I don't know where the mayor received his medical degree, but he misdiagnosed my condition. What he heard in my voice was one of the symptoms of Parkinson's disease, the occasional inability to speak. He mocked me after I told him I was sick."

While some speculated that Giuliani secretly did not really want to run for the Senate and was sabotaging himself so he could drop out, John envisioned Giuliani self-destructing in an absurd political trap he had set for his adversary. "I [would] call the mayor for a photo op for his senatorial campaign," he fantasized. "Rudy laugh[s] at me as I stride down a Manhattan street looking well and I suddenly freeze and need my wheelchair. Or we could do an ad showing me falling in front of a subway train while the mayor rolls on the platform in uncontrollable laughter. I need not be the star in this ad. How about a three-part ad? In Part One, city attorneys whoop it up in court after winning the right to take home health attendants out of the homes of people with Alzheimer's. In Part Two, an elderly woman dies of a heart attack, or maybe in a fire, because she is unaware of the 911 alert button that was hung around her neck in place of the aide. Part Three shows a smiling Mayor Giuliani the next day leading and chairing the annual Alzheimer's Walk. The possibilities are endless."

HILLARY CLINTON IS A DISAPPOINTMENT to black New Yorkers. She has waffled on the question of police brutality and abandoned blacks during the Giuliani reign of terror. Perhaps, black Democrats will vote for this two-faced political hack, who has taken them for granted before on the lesser-of-two-evils theory of Negro politics. Don't be fooled this time! I've come to the conclusion that blacks should *not* vote for Mrs. Clinton. Indeed, I've joined the anti-Clinton campaign, but not the vast conspiracist subculture found in right-wing populism. I still believe, as essayist Ralph Melcher put it, that "the right wing has succeeded in doing what it set out to do.... make Bill and Hillary into political monsters."

For me, it's all about Mrs. Clinton's brand of racial politics.

Isn't it odd that Mrs. Clinton has never participated in a grassroots demonstration in support of victims of police brutality? What is her excuse for not showing up at the 2000 "Redeem the Dream" rally in Washington, D.C., to protest racial profiling?

She always seems to confound black people.

First, she described the police killing of Amadou Diallo as a "murder," then pulled back after Giuliani characterized her comments as "a significant rush to judgment." She said she misspoke. Then, in what seemed to be an attempt to recover, she criticized the mayor's release of police shooting victim Patrick Dorismond's sealed juvenile record—adding the admonition that it would be just as wrong to taint the reputations of the police officers involved by dredging up stains in their past before the facts were in. In the face of mounting evidence that the NYPD is out of control, Mrs. Clinton refused to join the call for a federal monitor of the department. She supports the release of convicted spy Jonathan Pollard, who gave America's top secrets to Israel, but she won't question the controversial conviction of Mumia Abu Jamal, the black journalist who is on death row in Pennsylvania in the shooting death of a white cop.

Who in the grassroots community could brush aside Mrs. Clinton's attack on Lenora Fulani, the formidable, left-leaning black activist who ran for president in 1992 as an independent? On April 29, 2000, at a candidates' forum in Buffalo sponsored by the Independence Party (the state wing of the Reform Party), Mrs. Clinton condemned the group for allowing itself to "become defined by the anti-Semitism, extremism, prejudice, and intolerance of a few shrill voices of both the right and the left." She later emphasized that she was referring to Reform Party presidential candidate Patrick Buchanan and Fulani, who had become an important force in the Independence Party. "I've known Lenora Fulani for many years and she is a fighter for civil liberty, community empowerment, and the dissolution of economic injustice in our country," Sharpton told the *Amsterdam News.* "I do not share Mrs. Clinton's reported views that Fulani is an anti-Semite or a bigot in any form." (For her part, Fulani said that Mrs. Clinton and her advisers "feel completely secure that they have the support of New York's black leadership and that they can single me out for abuse.")

Despite her dismal record of championing meaningful black causes there was no great outcry coming from Mrs. Clinton's prominent black supporters. For several months during the 2000 U.S. Senate race, Randy Credico—an in-your-face comedian and progressive agitator—feuded behind the scenes with Sharpton about his muted criticism of the Democratic nominee. With his populist appeal and constant, outspoken presence in the political life of black New Yorkers, Sharpton can expose vulnerabilities in the candidate that no one else can. But Credico charged that Sharpton had not gone far enough in explaining to voter-rich black constituencies that they should be upset with Mrs. Clinton. Credico pressured Sharpton to criticize Mrs. Clinton more consistently—and harshly—about some of her controversial positions. Black voters, Credico thinks, should have known about political skeletons in the First Lady's closet. For example, are blacks aware that:

- During the 1992 presidential race, Mrs. Clinton supported the decision by her husband, then governor of Arkansas, to allow the execution of Ricky Ray Rector, a brain-damaged black man, for killing a police officer? Despite pleas for leniency from the Reverend Jesse Jackson and other black leaders, Bill Clinton stopped campaigning and returned to Arkansas to oversee the execution. Why didn't Mrs. Clinton speak out in defense of a retarded man who was so baffled by the process that he decided to save his last meal, a pie, until after the execution? Says Credico: "The death penalty, which Hillary Clinton supports, is the ultimate act of racism. If Hillary had her way, Mumia Abu-Jamal would be dead."

- Mrs. Clinton supported her husband's welfare-reform initiatives, which, Credico insists, "gave Giuliani the power to put poor people of color on the streets, working for 35 cents an hour under workfare." President Clinton twice vetoed welfare reform before signing a Republican-passed bill during his 1996 re-election campaign.

- Mrs. Clinton passed up the opportunity to speak out against the Confederate flag flying atop South Carolina's statehouse. Public pressure and an NAACP boycott of South Carolina's tourist attractions combined to strike a blow against racism. "She lived under a flag in the Arkansas capitol with some kind of reference to the Confederacy and never said anything," Credico charges.

- Mrs. Clinton has not attacked the so-called Rockefeller drug laws, the backbone of New York's brutal mandatory drug-offense sentences, which were pushed through by Governor Nelson Rockefeller during his last term. "Why," asks Credico, "has she not said anything about the 2 million people in prison who are overwhelmingly people of color?"

- Mrs. Clinton has not spoken out about lifting economic sanctions against Cuba.

Credico says he told Sharpton's aides that the minister "looked unsavory and unsophisticated when he sucked up" to Mrs. Clinton during her historic King Day visit to his House of Justice in Harlem. "She should be begging him for a forum," he rails. "He looked too eager."

Apparently some of Sharpton's closest advisers had warned him that Mrs. Clinton is evasive and insincere. Within hours of Giuliani's withdrawal from the 2000 Senate race, Sharpton was poised to emerge as a threat to Mrs. Clinton's political legitimacy in the black community. Just before one of his weekly Saturday rally, Sharpton told me he had planned to caution Mrs. Clinton against taking black voters for granted. The minister theorized that without "a volatile, polarizing opponent" like Giuliani to inspire maximum black turnout at the polls, Mrs. Clinton's coronation by blacks would be imperiled. To ward off apathy, he told me, she must break her silence about key concerns that Giuliani's controversial stewardship has propelled to the top of the black activist agenda.

Sharpton vowed to upbraid Mrs. Clinton publicly over her alleged reluctance to call for the Justice Department to seize control of the NYPD and demand that federal civil rights charges be brought against the four white cops who were later acquitted of killing Diallo. "Hillary Clinton must aggressively campaign to earn the black and Latino vote," he said. "With Rudy Giuliani as an opponent, she was about to be awarded the largest black and Latino turnout in the history of the state."

Sharpton also promised to press Mrs. Clinton to admit that she, too, had made a mistake by not visiting the family of Patrick Dorismond to personally express her condolences. "Hillary Clinton didn't call the Dorismonds either," Sharpton fumed. He confided that Haitian community leaders like Dr. Jean Claude Compas, who treated police-torture victim Abner Louima, were perplexed by Clinton's absence, and had demanded explanations from him. "Dr. Compas asked me, 'Why hasn't she reached out?' I said, 'I do not understand.'"

Mrs. Clinton later would dance around, duck under and sidestep all or most of Sharpton's concerns. But in time, Sharpton predicted, she will be reined in by a slew of complaints, including the ones lodged by Credico. "She has not been as aggressive as some of us want her to be," Sharpton acknowledged.

Mrs. Clinton's campaign appearance at St. Luke AME Church in Harlem on October 7, 2000 is a glaring example of the chicanery black voters have become accustomed to. *The Associated Press* provided this account:

> As booming gospel music dies away, a jam-packed audience focuses its attention on Mrs. Clinton standing in the pulpit. She's talking about Harriet Tubman in a narrative she's perfected in visits to black churches after initially confusing Tubman with Sojourner Truth, then correcting the error after *Our Time Press*, a black monthly, demanded an apology. It's the story of a runaway slave who returns to the South to lead others to freedom, but in Mrs. Clinton's telling, it becomes a metaphor for how she views herself: Hillary the persecuted woman who won't back down. It's a theme her campaign can't get enough of, and it's a message that plays well today. "If you hear the dogs, keep on going. If you hear gunfire, keep on going. If you hear shouts and footsteps, keep on going," intones Mrs. Clinton, evoking Tubman urging on the slaves. Then, as cries of 'Yes!' fill the church, the first lady reverts to politics. "I will not turn back, no matter who's behind me, or what they're saying, or what they're doing!" she declares, her voice rising and falling with a preacher's cadence. She pauses, then adds emphatically: "There is one thing you know about me: When I tell you, 'I'll stick with you,' I'll stick with you.'" Like other audiences in churches and union rallies that have heard Mrs. Clinton use this line from her stump speech, this one explodes with applause.

But think about it: This Al Jolson act could have been left on the cutting room floor of Spike Lee's movie, *Bamboozled*. Couldn't she have applied the allusions to "gunfire," "shouts" and "footsteps" to a more relevant period in modern black history—like "Giuliani time?" Had she invoked the names of Abner Louima, Amadou Diallo, and Patrick Dorismond, her message truly might have resonated with *all* blacks. But apparently Mrs. Clinton did not feel it was imperative to point out *that* reality and stand firmly with the black community on *that* crucial dispute.

The very next day, during a televised debate with Rick Lazio, Giuliani's replacement in the U.S. Senate race, Mrs. Clinton passed up the opportunity to point the finger for police misconduct at Giuliani, who was in a front-row seat. In her response to a question about racial profiling, she never mentioned Giuliani, whose police force had been found by the U.S. attorney in Manhattan to have engaged in the often deadly practice. Instead, Mrs. Clinton, replying to a question about Giuliani's plan to build a stadium on Manhattan's West Side, chuckled softly as she acknowledged the mayor, while declaring she would not support it. Giuliani laughed. She had let him off the hook.

I was fantasizing Mrs. Clinton parodying Giuliani's trademark tantrums, dredging up his divisive rhetoric to illustrate his lack of compassion. I was fantasizing Mrs. Clinton using her bully pulpit to lay into Giuliani with the same fervor Giuliani attacked Fidel Castro, who he called "a despicable, horrible human being." I was fantasizing her taking her cue from Giuliani: "You should always make that point every time you get a chance to make that point." Giuliani felt justified in calling Castro, a head of state, a "murderer." What then should we call the former head of a city whose police department has claimed so many innocent lives?

I was fantasizing Mrs. Clinton picking up a copy of Gerry Boyle's *Cover Story*, a thriller about a fictional crime-fighting mayor of New York City (any resemblance to actual persons living is entirely coincidental), and reading aloud Boyle's whodunit, which picks up with a news bulletin from anchorman Dan Rather:

> Intones Rather: "CBS News has learned of new developments in the murder of Johnny Fiore, the beloved mayor of New York, who single-handedly, his supporters say, took this city from the criminal elements that had plagued it, and handed it back to the law-abiding residents. As he so often put it, 'the real New Yorkers.'"
>
> The crowd was silent. The woman in front of me shook her head and listened.

"As you probably know by now, Mayor Fiore, in one of history's more astounding ironies, has become a crime victim himself."

Rather turned and held his arm out toward the facade of the Algonquin. The camera zoomed in on a somber cop, then back to Rather.

"To cap this historic and tragic and so very discouraging story, the mayor of New York City was killed here sometime around midnight last night, stabbed to death in the restroom of this famous New York landmark, authorities say. One man is in custody ..."

PART I
The Politics of Fear
(1993)

1

Why Blacks Fear Giuliani

[There is a city] chapter of the Ku Klux Klan, who are individuals who hate African Americans and all those who are not, like them, white Anglo Saxons. They're individuals you have to fear. The group is small, but I imagine that to give Giuliani a vote gives power to this type of people.... I speak to people who talk badly about African Americans, who talk badly about Jews, some who even talk badly about Puerto Ricans. And every time I ask them who they will vote for, they say Giuliani.

—Dinkins campaign official José Torres

It's not a hate vote, it's a fear vote. I was brought up in a city that was a white city. We ran it. And there are a lot of people around—and not just people my age, they're younger than I am—who feel that city is being taken away from them. Whether we're talking about crime, welfare, drugs, guns—all of those have a black coloration. They want their city back, and that's what Rudy Giuliani represents to them.

—Professor Andrew Hacker

IN AN EFFORT TO CALM AMERICANS at a poignant period in history, Franklin D. Roosevelt declared, "The only thing we have to fear is fear itself." In November 1993—at a crucial juncture in the political history of New York City—the mayoral candidacy of Republican-Liberal Rudy Giuliani struck enough terror in the psyche of blacks to make "fear itself" a campaign issue.

There were two opposing realities: One was the image Giuliani projected in his TV commercials, where he was depicted as a son of the city in a baseball cap, strolling through urban parkland, wife and kids in tow. The other image was evoked by the *Amsterdam News,* in a jarring front-page story by J. Zambga Browne under the headline GIULIANI TO TEACH NIGGERS A LESSON. For blacks, it illustrated the fear that Giuliani generated: "A Guyanese mother, trying to make an honest living as a street vendor on the East Flatbush Avenue

3

commercial strip ... said she was badly beaten last week by four white cops, who invoked the name of ... Rudolph Giuliani as they hit her repeatedly." One officer reportedly told the woman, Jean Luther, "Just wait until Giuliani takes over this town and we will teach you niggers a lesson." Underground economists like Luther were part of what Giuliani called "the proliferation of illegal street vendors." Under his program, she would be re-classified as a "quality-of-life offender" and jailed.

By an appropriate coincidence, three weeks after the incident involving the black woman and the white cops, Bernard Cawley, a beefy, six-foot-tall officer, told the Mollen Commission investigating links between police corruption and brutality that a sergeant in his Bronx stationhouse nicknamed him "The Mechanic" because he used to "tune people up"—police jargon for indiscriminately assaulting bystanders. Blacks who watched the rogue cop's testimony on TV envisioned Giuliani dispatching his own mechanics into Harlem, Washington Heights, or East Flatbush to tune people up.

It was easy imagining "Giuliani saying to New York City's Finest, after arming them with bazookas, 'Go forth and fight crime in the black community,'" said Betty Dopson, co-chair of CEMOTAP, the Committee to Eliminate Media Offensive to African people. For weeks, the black press was ablaze with headlines like these in *The City Sun*: GIULIANI PROMOTES RACIAL HATRED AND 'OPEN FIRE ON BLACKS,' SAYS CHIEF CARUSO. There were more than fatuous conspiracy theories and hysteria mongering in these banners. Behind the need to rouse the black electorate into voting its fear was a perception gap as wide as the distance between Harlem and Giuliani's boyhood Brooklyn home.

Whites were tempted by Giuliani's emphasis on "re-establish[ing] civilized behavior in our streets and in our public spaces." They saw this rhetoric as an aggressive response to crime. But to black people, who have a direct knowledge of how the police can be used to control their everyday movements—whether or not they seem "menacing"—such statements had the ring of bigotry unleashed. Even blacks who professed no fealty to Mayor Dinkins considered Giuliani the city's most dangerous white hope. To them, the man *The New York Times* dubbed the "Wonder Bread son of the '50s," is fear itself: an iron-fisted former federal prosecutor with a predilection for gun-butt diplomacy.

The Giuliani fear factor had much to do with the candidate's abettors. First there was the dangerous liaison between badass white cops and Afriphobic talk show hosts. Consider this exchange of merrythought between WABC radio's Jay Diamond and Pat, a caller who identified himself as a member of the NYPD.

"Your job," Pat said, "is to stay there and be ticked off to satisfy the political appetite of a lowlife like Dinkins."

"Well, that's why we pray for Rudy Giuliani," said Diamond. "We pray for him. Go forth and pray for the empowerment that Rudy Giuliani will hand the police in New York."

"You realize, Jay, that every 30 hours a New York City police officer is either shot, stabbed, bludgeoned, or beaten severely."

"Be too bad if a lot of those people doing that ... were to commit suicide in police custody," Diamond responded.

Cut to Rego Park, Queens, where hundreds of whites rallied for Giuliani two weeks before the election. Black free-lance reporter Debbie Officer heard children as young as nine screaming, "Dinkins Stinkins," while their parents bellowed, "Blacks go back to Somalia," "Bunch of fucking animals," and "Niggers on welfare, we're not."

Meanwhile, secessionist Staten Islanders like Borough President Guy Molinari were telling whites Giuliani would bring back the death penalty, end welfare, and keep jails and homeless shelters out of their neighborhoods. "Do you want 4 more years of David Dinkins as your mayor?" Molinari, a Republican loyalist, asked in a four-page leaflet he circulated throughout the island. "Some of our finest residential communities were listed as potential shelter locations including one across the street from a public grammar school." This was the kind of code that passed for politics in this campaign. Was it really about curbing drug dealers and welfare cheats or was it a covert way of affirming what the "Dinkins Stinkins" crowd believed?

Giuliani never repudiated Diamond and Pat, not to mention the racists in Rego Park and polite proponents of apartheid such as Molinari. Blacks feared these were the people Giuliani would empower if he won. How else should a man like the Reverend William Augustus Jones, a senior black Baptist preacher who marched with Martin Luther King, describe this fifth column of bigots? "Elements that can best be described as fascist seem to have grown up and flowered around Mr. Giuliani's campaign," Jones warned. Is that "astounding," as Giuliani would later claim, or was Jones just speaking truth to power?

Giuliani claimed that Dinkins' allies had "a deliberate political strategy" of demonizing him, but anyone with intimate knowledge of the role white supremacists desired to play in the Giuliani campaign would empathize with José Torres' fear that Giuliani had become a "magnet for the worst elements."

If Giuliani's rhetoric weren't fearsome enough, there was also his dossier on race. As U.S. Attorney in the Southern District, he had a poor minority hiring record and prosecuted no civil-rights cases. He is best remembered as the Reagan administration Justice Department official who certified that "Baby Doc" was not brutal to Haitians. He cast himself as the "fusion candidate," but his campaign employed few blacks. As the *Daily News* reported in August, "31 of 37 aides on the payroll [are] white—including all of his senior advisers." What would a Giuliani administration look like?

With such a record, is it any wonder that Giuliani ignored pleas by Sharpton and other prominent black activists to launch civil-rights investigations into the fatal shooting of 66-year-old Eleanor Bumpurs by a white cop; the gunning down of four black teenagers on a subway train by Bernhard Goetz; the murder of Michael Griffith by white teens in Howard Beach, Queens; and other racially motivated attacks that, as Sharpton put it, "terrorized the black community" during the '80s? "What is just as bad as murder is to scream murder to deaf ears," Sharpton told me. "That's a terrifying experience, and that was our experience with prosecutor Rudy Giuliani. He cannot now expect black people not to have fears about him possibly becoming mayor."

But it was the cop violence at City Hall on September 16, 1992—when, as Dinkins would later put it, Giuliani "played chief cheerleader and angry master of ceremonies"—that triggered the worst fears in blacks. This was an act so reminiscent of the Jim Crow South that it raised serious questions about whether Giuliani cared how he'd be viewed by a community he's long alienated. What message was he sending?

Near the anniversary of the police riot, *NY1* released a poll entitled "The Giuliani Profile." The poll found that 77 percent of black voters agreed with the statement that, "If elected mayor, Rudolph Giuliani's sharp temper could make problems worse by adding fuel to the fire rather that calming tensions." Only 11 percent thought otherwise.

"Our aim should be to restore our common-sense notions of civility and tolerance that once characterized this city," Giuliani said in his controversial "Quality of Life" speech. It seemed obvious to blacks that the darling of the Patrolmen's Benevolent Association speaks the language of force. As the late revolutionary Frantz Fanon put it in the context of colonialism, "All these esthetic expressions of respect for the established order serve to create around the exploited person an atmosphere of submission and of inhibition which lightens the task of policing considerably." Giuliani, as Fanon also might have argued, "[did] not lighten the oppression, nor seek to hide the domination; he show[ed] them up and put them into practice with the clear conscience of an upholder of the peace; yet he [was] the bringer of violence."

The Fear That Hate Produced

UNA CLARKE, THE WILLOWY former lawmaker from Brooklyn's mostly West Indian 40th Councilmanic District, came face to face with the violence, fear, and street justice Giuliani brought to the steps of City Hall on the morning of September 16, 1992.

There he was, cheek by jowl with Patrolmen's Benevolent Association (PBA) honcho Phil Caruso, courting what *Newsday* columnist Murray Kempton called the "Creatures of Chaos"—more than 15,000 mostly white off-duty cops who'd stormed City Hall to protest Dinkins' proposal for an all-civilian Civilian Complaint Review Board (CCRB). Most of the cops were violently drunk and armed. Some seized the Brooklyn Bridge, while others, calling Dinkins a "nigger" and chanting, "dump the washroom attendant," broke through police barricades at City Hall, stomped on cars, and assaulted reporters and photographers. Giuliani claimed he was trying to calm the crowd, but the tactic he chose was bellowing "Bullshit!" into a bullhorn. Said Clarke, "He became a part of mob rule."

Not since her civil-rights pilgrimage through the Deep South, where she encountered hardline "segs," had Clarke been confronted by such blatant racism. "It was fearsome," recalled the Jamaican-born reformer, referring to that lawless morning when she had to run a gauntlet of menacing cops to get to a City Hall hearing on the "Safe Streets, Safe City" program. "Please, excuse me," Clarke, a prime sponsor of the bill to revamp the CCRB, told a white cop with a crew cut. Other than his blue uniform shirt, the cop was in civilian clothes; his back was turned and he had a beer bottle in one hand. "I am Councilmember Una Clarke. I have a meeting to attend." The cop spun around and eyed her scornfully. Clarke had seen that look before—the one that required blacks, as the historian Leon F. Litwack writes, to "cringe in the presence of whites or … respond obsequiously to their whims and petty humiliations."

"Above the din of Giuliani's rabble-rousing, the cop, who blocked her path, turned to a fellow officer and barked with the ferociousness of one of Bull Connor's dogs, "This nigger says she is a councilmember; should we let her in?"

"It was jolting, revolting," Clarke recalled, her voice, even now, cracking, "I was angry. But all that kept going through my mind was, 'You are an elected official, not a street activist anymore. People are depending on you, don't go off on him. You're never gonna win.' If I had reacted negatively he would have done something to me."

To this day, Clarke holds Giuliani responsible for what happened to her. She expected an apology or some gesture of empathy from him. Giuliani, according to a 1993 campaign commercial featuring his second wife Donna, was supposed to be "someone to whom professional, independent women can relate." But why should Giuliani wash himself in the blood of a bleeding-heart liberal to allay a black woman's fear? Though Giuliani subsequently mentioned the incident, "I never heard from him," Clarke said.

Like vendor Jean Luther, Clarke was living proof of the Giuliani fear factor. "My fear of him is based on experience. If in broad daylight *I*, who have reached the status as one of the people who help to run this city, can be called a 'nigger' by an officer he was whipping into a frenzy, how do you think this officer, especially if he was drunk, would have reacted in East Flatbush or Crown Heights? How would he have reacted if he'd confronted a Haitian American who did not understand English? My fear [told] me that if Giuliani [were to be elected] mayor I [could] look forward to a police state where cops would be given carte blanche to run through poor communities and mistreat and disrespect their residents, solely on the basis of their skin color."

Why Black Youths Are Afraid

IT IS ABOUT 1:45 p.m., less than two hours after some creatures from the blue lagoon tried to eat the city's black mayor. Five white men—who'd later turn out to be cops—are seated aboard a crowded Brooklyn-bound M train guzzling beer. The train stopped at the Myrtle-Wyckoff station and in walked Yunas Laroche Mohamed. The 18-year-old Mohamed straddled the car, recalls Miguel Matos, a passenger and eyewitness. Suddenly, one of the cops "puts out his leg and trips" Mohamed. According to Matos, "the kid turns around and said, 'Why'd you trip me?' and the cop said, 'You stepped on me, boy.' He was pointing his hands in the kids face, and the kid pushed them away, and then the cop threw the first blow and hit the kid in his face. Closed fist."

Rogue white cops trip up and step on black youths all the time as if they were cockroaches. But Yunas Mohamed was no squash bug. Mohamed "hit the cop back and [the cop] started bleeding ...," according to Matos. Mohamed had slashed police officer John Coughlin across the face with a box-cutter knife, cutting him to the bone. The witness recalls that the four other cops jumped on Mohamed and began to gangbang him. "I didn't realize how far they were going to beat him down." Matos recalls Mohamed being toted off "spread-eagle" by police.

Mohamed had been brutally beat down. He lay flat on his back. The left side of his face was bruised and bloated in the image of Rodney King, his left eye, the size of a billiard ball, was swollen shut and his bandaged right arm shackled to the railing of his bed in Brooklyn's Woodhull hospital. Although his jaw was held together by wires, Mohamed—according to former defense attorney Lynne F. Stewart and her private investigator Ralph Poynter—spoke through gritted teeth, painfully recalling for the first time what had happened. "I tripped on this guy's foot. I apologized. He punched me. I cut him," Mohamed said in a statement.

Mohamed said he was shoved into the back seat of a car, two cops on each side of him. "One cop said, 'Hold his hand,' and he bent back my middle finger," Mohammed recalled in the statement. "Another cop punched me in the jaw and they spit in my face all the way to the precinct." Officer Coughlin received more than 100 stitches to close his facial wound. Now, Mohamed, charged with attempted murder of a cop and criminal possession of a weapon, faced the possibility of life in prison.

The more serious charge seemed incredible to Mohamed. "He kept on asking, 'Attempted murder?' They charged me with attempted murder? Am I going away?'" Stewart said.

In 1991, at the age of 16, the criminal-justice system refused to put Yasun Mohamed away. He and three friends were arrested in Buffalo for possession of four $20 glassine bags of cocaine. The case was dismissed. Shortly thereafter, Mohamed and some friends were arrested for an alleged robbery in a Brooklyn subway. He was given youth-offender status and placed on five years probation. The troubled teen, who had not seen his mother or father in three years, lived with his guardian, Clara Garner, a devout Pentecostal, in the Bushwick section of Brooklyn.

Mohamed had decided to turn his life around. He enrolled in the Bushwick Outreach GED program. By his own account, he was going straight until his tragic encounter with an allegedly lawless cop. "A rogue cop has robbed this teenager of his education, his right to a future," Stewart said. Mohamed said that the man who tripped and punched him never identified himself as a police officer. None of the men who beat him ever did. Asked whether he would have retaliated if he knew Officer Coughlin was a cop, Mohamed replied: "I don't let nobody punch me in the face like that ... Nobody steps on me. I'm not a cockroach."

"These kids out here today are social dynamite," said Poynter, a former high school teacher. "They are armed for self-defense. A white cop has learned about this the hard way." Lynne Stewart rebuffed suggestions that Mohamed, knowing of the cops' raucous behavior at City Hall, might have gone into the subway spoiling for a fight with officers. "He had no idea that there had been a demonstration at City Hall or as a matter of fact why the cops were angry."

SEVEN MONTHS AFTER THE RIOT, the beleaguered Dinkins administration braced itself for another brazen assault. In an attempt to jump-start stalled contract negotiations with the city, combative PBA's Caruso began running newspaper, radio, and TV ads claiming that Mayor Dinkins treated cops "worse than garbage" because cops allegedly earn less than sanitation workers. Dinkins complained that the ads were designed "to personally and, probably, politically bludgeon" him. Who was Caruso really appealing to? In 1990, the city paid a then record $13.3 million to the victims of police misconduct: Money that could have been used to place the cops' annual pay on par with sanitation workers.

Mimicking the layout of their full-page newspaper advertisement, I wrote the following response to the PBA's campaign, which ran in the *Voice* on May 4, 1993:

As the PBA Begins Contract Talks

There are two types of police officers you encounter each day in the City of New York:

The good cop, who is illustrated in an artist's sketch as a uniformed police officer holding the hand of a black child donning a baseball cap, which tilted to the left side of his head, and wearing a tee-shirt with an emblazoned X.

Then there is the PBA cop, who is also depicted in a sketch as two uniformed officers pummeling a dreadlocked man with their nightsticks.

There are a few good cops in the PBA with a commitment to the community rather than the "Patrolmen's Brutality Association." But they are the exception. The good cop is relatively easy to get along with. He displays a monumental degree of sensitivity in African American, Latino, and Asian neighborhoods, even when he hears da mad wunz shouting: #@&*, #@&*, #@&* da poliz. The good cop stops the reign of the TEC. He's got Slick Rick an' Gangsta Bitch on da run. Give "props" to the good cop.

The PBA cop is "da Five-0," or "da DT." He's a rookie from Massapequa who jack bruthas on the corner for kickin' the Geto Boys's "Crooked Officer." Every day, the PBA cop scapegoats African Americans and Latinos for the ills of society. He sees struggling neighborhoods as battlefields rife with guns, drugs, and extreme violence. The PBA cop is always "in hot pursuit" of jeep-azz niggaz boom-bashin' an' illin' from da chronic. He suspects that every glass-tinted Benzo was carjacked by a Nuyorican. He gives $55 tickets to "Mira" and to "Salsa" and to "Loco" for frontin' on da man in a no-fly zone.

Ain't A Damn Thang Changed

The PBA cop is media-hype active. He watches *The Rush Limbaugh Show, All in the Family* reruns, and reads the *New York Post* with racist gloating. He believes, as the raptivist group The Coup put it, that your little black boyz 'n girlz are: "Niggas, thugs, dope dealers, and pimps/Basketball players, rap stars, and simps/Sluts [and] broads [who] pop that coochie ..."

With these condemnatory stereotypes in mind, the PBA cop harbors his fear of unknown blacks. In fact, folks—unknown black males, particularly—have been begging the PBA cop to "keep it good in da hood." They've been calling, "Hip Hop to CPOP." But the PBA cop squelches. His words are hollow and insincere. Any black male in tribal grunge, or sagging Karl Kani-jeans with hat to the back, is a permanent suspect. He's a potential Cop Killer programmed by Ice M.F. T. Mothers, don't believe da hype. Black kids ain't really "hot" and "want police shot."

Body Count

The PBA cop's productivity is measured in blood. His trigga gotz no heart. He bucks the black cop and calls it "friendly fire." Did his "intelligence [and] extensive training" require him to shoot dead Eleanor Bummer? Did Yvonne Smallwood, Federico Pereira, and Bonnie Vargas have to die? Oh, the victims. You know them so well.

Our Reward?

In 1990, two years after "the Lower East Side ... was rocked by one of the most serious and shocking outbursts of police violence in New York City's history," the New York Civil Liberties Union released a report entitled "Police Abuse: The Need for Civilian Investigation and Oversight." The report called for an effective Civilian Complaint Review Board ... independent, powerful, and worthy of public trust."

Nowhere Else on This Planet Would the PBA Be Given Another Black Cent
PBA Doubletalk

The PBA cop swears he's not above the law but there's a tremor in his blood. He runs to Phil Caruso immediately after he's been involved in controversial police behavior, such as the "fatal shooting" of an "unarmed black youth," or the "hogtying death" of an alleged EDP (emotionally disturbed person). The PBA cop won't speak to the district attorney for another 48 hours. Meanwhile, Caruso ad hominem defends the killings with phrases like "justifiable homicide" and "within police guidelines." The PBA cop is a riot when it comes to law and order. He stormed City Hall protesting the creation of a civilian-controlled board. Apart from invoking the "48-hour rule," the PBA cop refuses to break the code of silence. The PBA cop is no Serpico. That's why the Mollen Commission is investigating the corruption of the PBA cop.

Lopsided Priorities

Only wackos shoot cops. "There are weird people in our society who have no … respect for humans …," says Douglas Haycock, a constitutional commentator. "We call them psychopaths, and when they act on their impulses and we catch them, we lock them up." So why does Phil Caruso conjure up the image of Dodge City every time cops are shot, injured, or maimed? He calls for the death penalty. What about the death penalty for the PBA cop who unjustifiably kills? Caruso bellows for more firepower. He's been pushing for the approval of the 17-shot 9mm Glock, a weapon that former Police Commissioner Lee Brown argued would do more harm than good in this densely populated city because of its deadly ricochet. Caruso obviously places a higher priority on a Robocop arsenal and gives pure lip service to the notion of Safe Streets/Safe City.

Who da real gangztaz? Would you support the PBA if it treated you worse than garbage?

SHORTLY AFTER DAWN ON SEPTEMBER 16, 1993, the anniversary of the City Hall police riot, Robert Earle, a 25-year-old dispatcher at a securities house, stepped into a breezy morning on his way to work. Though he had a flat-top haircut, Earle was dressed like any other Wall Street suit on his way to take over a Fortune 500 company. As he walked along an East Flatbush street in Brooklyn, a patrol car from the 67th Precinct with two cops, one white, one black, cruised by him. "Come here," commanded the white cop, who was the driver. "We have a problem in the neighborhood and I need to take you back to the precinct. A lady just got mugged and she described a black man, your height, your age."

"Sir, look at the way I'm dressed," Earle replied. "I'm wearing a suit and tie." It didn't matter now that he'd read George Marlin's *Bond Buyers Guide to Municipal Bonds* or understood the ups and downs of the stock market; as a young black man venturing into the still darkened morning, Robert Earle was a permanent suspect to cops on the heels of a criminal.

"If you didn't do it you'll be out of there in five minutes," the cop told Earle. He complied. He had no choice. To ignore a cop and walk away would play into the old police story: "We had to subdue the prisoner because he resisted arrest."

"That's him!" a white woman shouted, pointing at Earle as the youth was led into the 76th Precinct stationhouse. "You just robbed me," she insisted.

"I *cannot* rob anybody," Earle protested. "I'm dressed up in a suit."

Despite his explanation, the woman pointed out another black youth who was thrown into a lineup. He, too, had a flat-top haircut, but unlike Earle, he sported gold-plated teeth, several rings on his fingers, and a jogging suit. "They're friends, both of them," Earle remembers the woman saying. Shortly after he was brought in for questioning, police picked up a suspect who confessed.

When Earle argued that the cops had stereotyped him because he was black, the white cop said, "All blacks fit the description." The only concession he got was the promise of a courtesy call to his job to explain why he was late. The call was never made.

Two weeks ago, Earle sat in the living room of Roy Canton, a Brooklyn school head custodian, recalling the incident to a group of attentive neighborhood teens. Earle was relieved that he escaped being brutalized by the cops. He was convinced he was released unharmed because Dinkins was the mayor.

"They know he wouldn't stand for it. If Giuliani was mayor, I think they would have done me harm. They realize they are the law. They have a badge; it's a badge to kill. You heard what that cop said at the hearing, 'Who's gonna catch us? We're the police.'"

Canton nodded knowingly. His son Darren, a 12th-grader and major-league baseball hopeful, was walking through Crown Heights with friends on the second night of the disturbances, unaware of the violence nearby. A group of white cops spotted them and gave chase. They ran up the stairs of a building where they were protected by a man waving a camcorder in the cops' face. The cops backed off. "If all this was happening under Dinkins," says Darren, "imagine what it would have been like under Giuliani—worse, since he is pro police," Canton said. "The police is my biggest fear when I leave home. I don't worry about getting shot by posses. Walking late at night, police rolling by you, you always have to watch out."

Nadine Nader, 22, a City College graduate, said at the time that Giuliani "exploits situations" and is "a kind of race baiter," a flaw that is "very reminiscent of Koch, who was very partisan." The city, she told me, bubbled with race hate. "Someone likened New York City to not a melting pot, but a boiling pot. The fire has to be kept going in order for New York to have its flavor, but if you raise that temperature too high or add the wrong ingredients, it will explode."

Giuliani And 'W(hAte)BC'

EVERY TIME RUDY GIULIANI WAS HEARD ON WABC RADIO, the temperature of New York City neared boiling point. But that didn't stop the candidate from making frequent appearances on shows hosted by Bob Grant and Jay Diamond, who earned themselves the sobriquet Air Fascists in the black community. Is there a better way to describe a man who would react to the fatal stampede at City College of New York (CCNY) as Grant did?

"While I was away I heard about the news at CCNY. And I knew where the incident at CCNY had occurred. I knew the occasion which had inspired the crowd of savages to convene. And therefore I must tell you in all sincerity, I was not at all surprised. Because we have, in our city, we have in our state of New York, we have in our nation, not hundreds of thousands but millions of subhumanoids, savages, who really would feel more at home careening along the sands of the Kalahari or the dry deserts of Eastern Kenya. People who, for whatever reason, have not become civilized. Am I the only one who makes that observation? No, certainly not. Perhaps I express it more directly, more candidly, far less euphemistically than politicians would."

James McIntosh is co-chair of CEMOTAP. A key mission of the group is to monitor talk radio, record offensive remarks, and bring them to the attention of the black community. McIntosh wrote a series of articles in the *Daily Challenge*, the city's only black daily, attacking WABC for trafficking in "hate radio."

"A W(hAte)BC host urges the sending of cyanide to the Reverend Al Sharpton" and "A W(hAte)BC host calls a listener … a 'black bitch,'" the activist wrote. McIntosh's catalogue of abuses prompted WABC Program Director John Mainelli to fax an angry letter to the *Challenge*, attacking the paper for publishing Diamond's home phone number. But he did not deny McIntosh's charges.

On October 6, 1993, CEMOTAP wrote to Giuliani to complain about Grant's attacks on Haitian refugees. Attached was a list of eight statements referred to as "Bob Grant's War Against Haiti." CEMOTAP called on Giuliani to "speak out on your position regarding Haitian immigrants [and] to denounce these despicable anti-Haitian statements."

For example:

"I'm too upset over the fact that these Haitian scumbags are allowed in the city because of Sterling Johnson (U.S. District Court Judge for the Eastern District)."

"You know what? The ideal situation would be if they drowned. Then they would stop coming in."

"I wonder if they've figured out how they multiply like that. You know, it's like maggots. You know, on a hot day, you just, you look one minute and there's so many there. Then you look again and wow, they've tripled!"

Giuliani, of course, was the Reagan administration's enforcer of interdiction laws against Haitian "boat people" fleeing the bloody Duvalier regime. Haitians captured in U.S. waters were either returned to the island of fear or warehoused in squalid detention centers. Giuliani did not respond to CEMOTAP's petition, nor did he repudiate Grant or Diamond. Indeed, his campaign invited Grant to make a "special appearance" (as advertised in *The Jewish Press*) at the rally in Rego Park.

It puts one in mind of comedian Jackie Mason, who touched off a furor in 1989 by calling David Dinkins "a schvartzer with a moustache" in the pages of the *Voice*. Mason had stayed on the sidelines during the campaign, but eventually he leaped into the fray: "Giuliani sees the opportunity to prove that he has great compassion for black people, so he makes me out to be a bigot. He has no conscience about lying. He's a common pig. I'd like to take a walk in Harlem with him. When I walk down the street, I get nothing but love from black people." Jackie Mason has yet to play the Apollo to prove his point.

Crime And Punishment

TWO CITIES, TWO REALITIES. For Rudy Giuliani, David Dinkins treated drug dealers as benign Robin Hoods. For many in the black community, that statement made no sense. But like so much Giuliani rhetoric about crime, the real message was hidden. Was this Giuliani's way of implying that Dinkins was indifferent to boyz robbin' 'da hood?

Former mayor Ed Koch, wanting to rid the streets of low-level drug dealers during the '80s crack epidemic, jailed hundreds of petty dealers, most of them black. Only when some of them wound up on barges floating in the Hudson did the courts rule that warehousing these mostly nonviolent offenders was cruel and unusual punishment. Comes now Rudolph Giuliani with his solutions: mass arrests, jail, more jail.

Under Dinkins, fewer blacks went to jail. And it's not because, as Giuliani claimed, "the police ... made 75,000 fewer drug arrests." It's because community policing focused attention on the dons and drove petty dealers underground. In fact, Thomas A. Coughlin III, former state commissioner of corrections, credits Dinkins for the significant drop in inmates entering the prison system. "With 70 percent of inmates coming from New York City, any changes that it makes in policing policies has a direct impact upon us," Coughlin wrote in a 1992 agency newsletter. "For example, we were receiving a net increase of more than 4,000 inmates annually during the mid- to late 1980s. Then a new mayor was elected in New York City, who exercised his right to make new policies toward policing. Instead of a net 5,000 in new commitments next year, we are expecting 1,500 to 2,000."

Coughlin predicted that if this approach continues, "arrests will remain flat at their current levels." Giuliani warned: "We'll change that by once again arresting people who sell drugs."

Did the Republican really understand the nature of crime in this city? Taking out nickel and dime dealers won't solve the problem; the dealers never have more money than what is allotted to them by their dons and these dons find it easy to recruit new "slangers" because of high unemployment in the ghetto. Unable to arrest unemployment—the true culprit that's keeping young blacks and Latinos fixed on lawlessness—Giuliani declared war on "menacing squeegee operators," whom he charged double as drug dealers. But many of these folks were homeless and unwilling to check into overcrowded city shelters. One can understand their fears, knowing that when Giuliani looks at them all he sees are criminals.

But even a stockbroker like Robert Earle, a college graduate like Nadine Nader, and a high school student like Darren Canton feel implicated in the fate of "quality-of-life offenders." What happened to Jean Luther, the "illegal street vendor," could happen to them.

The fear of being tuned up by mechanics was at the heart of the '93 mayoral contest. As Sharpton put it, "Giuliani's image as a ruthless prosecutor in an unfair criminal justice system is the worst nightmare of any urban black." This palpable fear turned into an intense hatred of Giuliani. And when a people, as Machiavelli saw it, are "hostile and hold [a politician] in hatred, then he [too] must fear everything and everybody."

2

The Deposition of Rudy Giuliani

REPORTER'S NOTE: *The hotly contested election was less than ten weeks away. If Rudy Giuliani had wished the Crown Heights rebellion would come back to haunt Mayor Dinkins and boost his own standing among Jews, a crucial voting bloc, that wish would be granted in an unusual way. On August 24, the Hasidim of Crown Heights cornered Dinkins like an elusive rat, in, as one reporter put it, "his own house." The Hasidim had sued Dinkins and Police Commissioner Lee Brown alleging that the mayor allowed violence against Lubavitch Jews to go unchallenged. Now they sat face to face with Dinkins outside the ballroom of Gracie Mansion, badgering and interrogating him during a court-ordered deposition. "For the sitting mayor of New York City to be forced to sit here and be accused of withholding police protection from a group of citizens is an outrage," Dinkins' attorney and close adviser George Daniels would protest later to reporters.*

Pool reporter Alan Finder, representing excluded colleagues like me, depicted Dinkins as "stubborn, focused and direct as he answered questions," from Franklyn Snitow a lawyer for the Hasidim and the estate of Yankel Rosenbaum. Dinkins was "tight-lipped and combative, quietly sincere and sarcastic" at times "as he endured five hours of harsh questioning" said Finder, a reporter for The New York Times. *The mayor repeatedly denied that the police were told to take a hands-off approach during the violence. Frustrated, Snitow asked Dinkins if he knew what a yeshiva was. "You are being insolent now, sir," Dinkins shot back. "Asking me if I knew what a yeshiva is." It was obvious what Snitow and the Hasidim were trying to accomplish. "During a break in the questioning ... the Mayor suggested that the lawsuit had been brought, in essence, to do him political damage by keeping questions about Crown Heights alive as he seeks re-election," reported Finder, who quoted Dinkins as saying, "They seek solely to embarrass me and my administration."*

Indeed, after all David Dinkins had done for Jews in this city, he was now being portrayed as something akin to a Nazi sympathizer. I watched as Dinkins tried to salvage his reputation and his administration. In June, about two months before the deposition, he asked me to accompany him as part of a 34-member delegation to Israel. It was a last-ditch effort to prove to Jews he had been a loyal friend; it was a move, he prayed, might play well to the Hasidim back at home. On July 8, I filed my story for the Voice *in the form of an entreaty to God by following a popular ritual—stuffing a script, "a phat Beatitude rolled like a Phillies Blunt," through a crack in the Wailing Wall, the holiest shrine of Judaism.*

The following is an excerpt:

I'm here on the last leg of my four-day, pilgrimage to Israelity. Homeboy has come to pray in this land the Reverend Al Sharpton called, "hell." G, you're the God of compassion; save the lightning bolt for some other blaspheming negro. The pursy preacher really didn't mean it. It was a rage of the mouth. He'd come to Israel and stayed only four hours, searching for the Hasid who fled here after his car accidently struck and killed Gavin Caro. The truth is he had no illusions of nabbing "the fugitive" and hauling him back to America. He'd made a symbolic journey for justice, which ended in his humiliating rejection. But that was almost 30 months ago.

Now, see that elegantly raw-boned gentleman with the silvery hair and guileless pop-eyes set in a furrowed, well-scrubbed, hollow-cheeked face standing about a foot away from me in kicks and sweatin' the technique of ritualism at the Wailing Wall? His name is David N. Dinkins, the would-be "healer" of the City of New York, another black man come to Israel seeking justice. Can he clear his name in the murder of Yankel Rosenbaum? Look at him, G, moving solemnly, silently, comfortably in the company of the Rabbi of the Wall. Look at this native son with the tears welling in his eyes. Pray tell, is he some politician pandering to ethnic emotionalism?

Who is that gangly grandfather with the two boys, yelling at Dinkins, "Tell us about Crown Heights"? G, it's been like that for three days, hecklers demanding that the mayor do *tshuva*—atone—for Crown Heights. Yesterday afternoon, I went to Kfar Habad, a Lubavitcher village about an hour's drive from Jerusalem. There in the shadow of a stunning replica of 770 Eastern Parkway, headquarters of the Lubavitchers in Brooklyn, Rabbi Tuvia Bolton reasoned that Dinkins was supposed to be a leader but didn't lead.

"There was a lack of leardership and all of a sudden comes this Reverend Sharpton and he says to the people that the answer to all your problems is the Crown Heights Jews," the rabbi told me. "What was obviously the thing to do, with the police standing there, is to fire a couple of buck shots in the air and show 'em that you mean business and all the black people would start saying, 'This guy Sharpton is not where it's at. He's out to kill us. He doesn't care about us.' But they see no one there and they say, 'Oh, Sharpton is a true-prophet. *He* told us to come here. We're having a good time.' How could Sharpton have known the right thing to do?' Then there was one day and another day and another day. We were lucky: Black people, in my estimation, could never do what the Germans did."

Niggaz ain't as Nazi as they wanna be—'n' you know that, G. This was the message Dinkins tried to get across to Israelis: that African Americans in Crown Heights did not rise up in fear that Jews were going to get in their cars and kill all our children. Later that evening, Dinkins, Shimon Peres, and Teddy Kollek, the mayor of Jerusalem, dedicated New York Place—a tiny traffic Island on a busy street with a metal sculpture of the Statue of Liberty that looked more like the Terminatrix. "Dinky" was how the *Jerusalem Post* referred to it—a perfect setting for Rabbi Avi Weiss and his "dignified" protest to humiliate Dinkins. At the very least they want him to "do a Janet Reno"—take full responsibility for Crown Heights.

Weiss and his supporters are also upset with Dinkins for inviting a Syrian delegation with "American blood on their hands from Pan Am 103" to take part in a parade honoring Gulf War veterans. But imagine, G, for one hot flash; these people are illin' over the fact that a black mayor had the *kishkas* to host ticker tape parade for Nelson Mandela and shake his hand after he'd embraced Yasser Arafat. G, Avi and his lieutenants say "it was not the appropriate thing to do" in a city of more than a million Jews. Bullshit! (Sorry, G, I'll do my penance later.) Mandela is a symbol of black pride, as if you didn't know. He's *my* Homie, G. What would you have done? Aren't you also the God of Yasser Arafat? And the Syrians? Yeah, I know, but Avi Weiss never came to his senses. He seemed surprised and dismayed by the warm reception the mayor received from Tel Aviv to Jerusalem—busloads of kids shouting "May-ah Deenkeens," grandmothers coralling him to pose for a picture.

Look, G, in case you've been busy in Bosnia, Somalia, or in some other part of the joint, David Dinkins is at the crossroads of black-Jewish relations back home. He had to come to Israel, G. Forget what the official reasons were; the man was up to his neck in politics on this trip. Clearly, the mayor has begun to absorb the true dimensions of his political dilemma. There was strenuous opposition to him coming here from the Reverend Calvin Butts and other powerful black activists who have nothing but contempt for Dinkins' relationship with the Jews. But the Jewish alliance is something he could not afford to alienate or lose. The stated purpose of the trip seemed to vanish as the '93 mayoral elections moved to the forefront. On more than two occasions he told audiences, "I'm in trouble." He's asking for help, G.

Upon our return to New York, the Hasidim of Crown Heights, were unimpressed by Dinkins' bended-knee appeal and went full tilt with the deposition. I suspected that the Giuliani campaign had something to do with this take-no-prisoner attack on Dinkins but I lacked strong evidence to expose the alleged dirty trick. Dinkins, however, accused Giuliani ally Rabbi Joseph Spielman, the head of the Crown Heights

Jewish Community Council, of conspiring to run him out of office. Spielman "and others have set forth what they feel their goal is," he said.

"One of Mr. Dinkins's lawyers, O. Peter Sherwood, then cited a … newspaper article in which, he said, Rabbi Spielman was said to have talked about a strategy that included the lawsuit, a Federal investigation of possible civil-rights violations during the unrest and a challenge to the Mayor's re-election campaign," Finder reported.

I was angry: I could see Giuliani sitting back and licking his chops, waiting for Dinkins to self-destruct with the bombshell admission he was "out of touch during four days of interracial violence" in Crown Heights, and as a concession, as a way of doing tshuva, *he would drop out of the mayoral race.*

After the first day of the Dinkins deposition, I fantasized about would-be mayor Giuliani's response if he were to be deposed by a black lawyer representing black and Latino citizens of the city in a counter lawsuit. What I romanticized about was entirely a work of fiction.

IT WAS THE MORNING AFTER RUDY GIULIANI'S Quality-of-Life speech. It was also the day that a lawyer for "Cuffs on the Cops," a coalition of black civil rights groups, was set to grill the renegade mouth in a court-ordered deposition of his role in inciting the police riot at City Hall.

That morning, the press was buzzing with the revelation that minutes before Giuliani was to deliver his now controversial speech, the former prosecutor yanked an even more shocking proposal that would forbid black and Latino women from bearing a second child within four years of their first. Patterned after China's draconian one-child policy, third children would be aborted at conception if Giuliani—at the time, the father of a six-year old boy—had his way.

Somewhere beneath Giuliani's cold-blooded exterior lay a cold-blooded interior. Under his policy, leaked to reporters by a disgruntled campaign staffer, "the husband or the wife of a couple that have two or more children would be sterilized" to enhance the quality of life in New York City. "We should implement thoroughly our policy on sterilization primarily in African American and Hispanic communities and resort to abortions when dealing with pregnancies that do not comply with planning," Giuliani proposed. "If an unauthorized baby is the second, third, or subsequent child in a family and sterilization has not been accepted, the family will be denied welfare, primary health care, have their water and electricity cut off and eventually evicted from their apartment."

After hours of last-ditch wrangling, federal judge Rena Raggi, who ordered the city's first black mayor to submit to a similar deposition by the Hasidim, ruled that it would be "too emotional" for Giuliani to answer questions regarding the one-child policy but that Giuliani must develop a cogent position paper on "Pseudo-Scientific Engineering" before the November elections. The judge ordered the lawyer for the blacks to question Giuliani only about his conduct at the September 16, 1992 police riot.

"Cuffs on The Cops," charging that Giuliani failed to hold back the rampaging cops who desired to lynch Dinkins, filed a class action suit against Giuliani, the NYPD, and PBA President Phil Caruso on behalf of 50 black and Latino victims. The suit alleged "conscious pain and suffering, assault and battery, false arrest, abuse of process, violation of civil right, conspiracy to cover unlawful acts by law enforcement officers, intentional and negligent infliction of emotional distress, and negligence in the testing, screening, hiring, training and supervising controlling, and disciplining of persons employed" by the NYPD. Each plaintiff stood to collect $35,000, a figure representative of the hordes of workers Giuliani promised to fire from city rolls if he was elected.

Only two pool reporters, Columnist Murray Kempton and me, were allowed to cover the deposition. Observing the proceedings were Giuliani supporters Councilman Noach Dear, Assemblyman Dov Hikind, and Senator Al D'Amato. Representing the black community were Al Sharpton and Sonny Carson. Having waved a reading of the allegations against him, Giuliani reluctantly submitted to interrogation by the lawyer for "Cuffs on the Cops."

Q: Now Mr. Giuliani, were you present at the demonstration at ... (Snide murmuring by Councilman Dear interrupted the lawyer. An Orthodox Jew and foe of Dinkins, Dear was predictably combative.) "This is a distracting sideshow," he sneered, pointed, and wagged his finger in the direction of Sharpton. As Sharpton was poised to respond, Carson whispered in his ear, "It's a set up, Jack" and muzzled the porky preacher with a debilitating jab to the gut. Sharpton bowed breathlessly, apparently pained by the infliction of corporal silence.

But Dear's tantrums grew more threatening. Suddenly, Giuliani, an impressionist who became his own characters, sprang from his chair, pounded his fist against the table, and shouted, "Shut up, Noach! Just shut the fuck up and sit down!" Giuliani confronted his black inquisitor with tears in his eyes, "Why are we wasting the voters' time with this cop-baiting bullshit? Imagine asking me if I was at the bloody riot."

Q: Mr. Giuliani, do you recall giving any speeches at the "bloody riot?"

A: Yes, I gave a rousing speech; it takes a lotta tough talk to run a tough city.

Q: Could you tell us exactly what you said?

A: Uh (Giuliani, looking in the direction of his adviser Franklyn Snitow), I don't recall.

The usually poker-faced Giuliani couldn't bear to look the black lawyer straight in the eye. It was then that Murray Kempton reminded me of a passage in Creatures of Chaos; a piece he wrote two days after the riot. The old sage whispered in my ear, "The text of Rudolph Giuliani's speech to these demonstrators is unavailable and would perhaps be unprintable since its published shards pulsed with obscenities." The lawyer pressed Giuliani.

Q: During your speech, did you say that David Dinkins was trying to "Protect his political ass?" Wasn't this invective designed to whip the cops into a frenzy?

A: Never! Never!

Q: Did you bellow the word "bullshit" into a bullhorn?"

A: It was an excited utterance, the triumph of reality over squeamishness. 'Bullshit' was the word the conceited, whining David Dinkins used talking to police officers at the 34th Precinct when he tried to explain why he paid for the funeral of a drug dealer. Guy Molinari quoted him. I was quoting Molinari, for crying out loud.

Q: Were there any discussions between you and Phil Caruso, who columnist Mike McAlary called, "a lawbreaking hypocrite," prior to attending the rally, such as whether he would endorse you for mayor?

A: Of course we talked, Phil promised to endorse me. I promised to make him police commissioner if I'm elected mayor. That's no secret.

Q: Who paid for the 40 cases of beer, the $13,000 beers the cops consumed before they went wilding?

A: I did; I picked up the $2,700 tab.

Q: Mr. Giuliani, can you describe the mood of the crowd at the time of your excited utterance?

A: Mood? What do you expect from a buncha pissin' drunk cops? There was a lot of yelling, "No Justice! No Police!" and that sort of thing.

Q: Mr. Giuliani, one of these "pissin' drunk" cops, with a beer bottle in his hand, accosted Una Clarke, the first Jamaican woman ever elected to the City Council, and blocked her entrance to City Hall. This drunken cop told another drunken cop, "This nigger says she's a councilperson." Should he be punished?

A: Well, is she or isn't she?

Q: The thought of all these white cops having guns and drinking beer and calling blacks "niggers" didn't horrify you?

A: The cops were there to prevent burglaries, robberies, muggings, rapes and murders and insure domestic tranquility. They were fulfilling one of their primary functions as set forth in the preamble to the United States Constitution.

Q: Did you see any signs that the crowd held up?

A: What signs?

Q: Well, Mr. Giuliani, did you see a sign in which David Dinkins was portrayed as a "washroom attendant?

A: So?

Q: Did you see a sign that said, "Dump the Washroom Attendant?" Did you see that sign?

A: I saw a sign calling him "N-I-G-G-E-R."

Q: Speak up! What?

A: David Dinkins is a nigger. A nigger, all right?

Q: What went through your mind when you saw those signs? Did you feel that your comments were going to cool the situation or incite the angry cops?

A: I really didn't give much thought to what I was saying. I reacted in the tradition of four of my uncles who were cops and …

Q: Mr. Giuliani, the primary mission of police officers is to prevent crimes, protect, stores, schools, the elderly, children, and everyone else against criminal behavior, as well as littering and disorderly conduct. Well, do you think that someone speaking before a crowd of angry, lawbreaking cops, who don't give much thought to racist signs, should be elected mayor of the City of New York?

A: Ob-fucking-jection! Look, I was caught up in the excitement. There were TV cameras and reporters shouting questions at me, "Rudy! Rudy, are you losing it."

Q: Mr. Giuliani, it maybe your contention that you got carried away but do you recall the mayoral election of 1989?

A: Hell, yeah! I was robbed.

Q: Do you recall the speech you made on the night of your defeat?

A: Some of it.

Q: And you were in front of another unruly mob at that time, weren't you?

A: Yes, I was.

Q: And in fact, wasn't that unruly mob yelling and screaming and wouldn't even let you speak?

A: That's correct.

Q: And isn't it true, Mr. Giuliani, that you yelled at them at the top of your lungs "Shut up! Shut up! Shut up!"?

A: Things had gotten *waaaaaay* too emotional.

Q: Would you say that your loud and grating response was behavior typical of a temperate, judicious, you know, would-be chief executive or the words of a rabble rouser?

A: I have a confession to make. At the time, I was suffering from severe depression. Apparently, the president's assistant counsel suffered from such a malady.

Q: Mr. Giuliani, do you in fact have a problem controlling your temper?

A: It is still too difficult to be social and the days are terribly difficult. My own kid calls me 'The Self-Demolition Man.' Why don't you get the fuck off my back with this temper tantrum bullshit?

Q: It's happened more than once, Mr. Giuliani. At the very least do you not agree that your actions and statements were out of character for a person who wants to calm a racially tense city like New York?

A: Asked and answered.

Q: So you're saying that it is in character for a mayor to yell and scream at his constituents? To go over the edge?

A: David Dinkins lost his cool during the Crown Heights deposition.

Q: Well, Mr. Giuliani, if you, a friend to Jews, who had denounced Louis Farrakhan, gone to Bittburgh to protest Ronald Reagan's visit there, and faced Skud missiles in Israel, were asked an insulting question like, "Do you know what a yeshiva is?" Wouldn't you lose your cool?

Giuliani stared at Murray Kempton then answered the question.

"Despite the bizarre assertions of one of this city's leading editorial writers, David Dinkins had no constitutional right to relieve himself that way," Giuliani said.

Q: Do you know what a Ujama is?

A: That's stupid!

Q: Stupid? What about the time when you and Al D'Amato, TV cameras in tow, went Uptown Harlem to buy crack? Wasn't that a stupid thing to do? Wasn't that stereotyping? Wasn't the journey to Harlem designed to foster the view of you as being tough on "niggers?"

A: That was my fucking job!

Q: Why didn't you go to Bensonhurst?

A: The Mafia would kill me, fool.

I have no further questions.

3

Giuliani, Voodoo Justice, and Me

Mr. Noel, this is Dr. St. Fleur speaking. I do not know you. Now, I see by your last name you seem to be Haitian.... I do not know who sent you to speak to me, and I'm not going to take this lightly. I'm extremely upset, but I'll tell you one thing, and I'm gonna spell it out for you, in Kréyôl.... B-A-F-F-I-M M-A-M-Y-A-N. You will have to answer to Baffim Mamyan. You don't know what I mean, you will know.... This is the last person in your life you are going to ... treat like this, abuse like this, verbally, socially.... Baffim Mamyan will have to answer with you. And I'm not joking. I'm from Haiti. I was born in Gonaïves, and Gonaïves people NEVER, NEVER *play with people. I'm scientific; you may laugh as much as you want. But spiritually, you and I, we have a rendezvous. Never forget that in your life.*

AFTER LISTENING OVER AND OVER to the message that Dr. Guirlaine St. Fleur left on my voice mail on the evening of October 5, 1993, I remember what Paul Theroux wrote to Salman Rushdie shortly after the Ayatollah Khomeini handed down his *fatwa* regarding Rushdie and *The Satanic Verses:* "I swear I thought it was a joke—a very bad joke, a bit like Papa Doc Duvalier putting a voodoo curse on Graham Greene for writing *The Comedians,* but a joke nevertheless, in the sense of being no more than an example of harmless flatulence—just wind."

My sin was that I'd learned about St. Fleur, a graduate medical student who claimed to be the strategist behind a quietly run campaign to recruit Haitian immigrants to come out publicly in support of, or vote for, Rudy Giuliani. Giuliani was to *Lavalas*—followers of former Haitian President Jean-Bertrand Aristide—what Ivan the Terrible was to Jews. *Lavalas* held Giuliani, former associate attorney general in the Reagan administration, responsible for the detention program that imprisoned some 2,200 Haitian "boat people" in inhumane conditions at the Krome Detention Center near the Everglades swamp in Florida. I discovered that the "Haitians for Giuliani" scheme operated out of Giuliani-backed

25

comptroller candidate Herman Badillo's Manhattan campaign headquarters at 909 Third Avenue.

And now, I, a former wannabe altar boy from Trinidad, had to "answer to *Baffim Mamyan*"? Who is this bogey? Ruminating on her fatwa, I faced the prospect of being doomed to some wilderness for muckracking villains where the ghosts of those afflicted by my satanic verses would exact retributive justice. Although I have long been emancipated from my belief that voodoo, a dominant religion among Haitians, is evil, the tone of St. Fleur's voice suggested something dreadful might befall me at our spiritual rendezvous.

I began to think that this woman truly possessed the power to make things happen.

My brother Michael tried to shake the spell. "Don't be a believer," he warned. "'What a fool believes, he sees,'" he said, quoting the Doobie Brothers. But I needed a less secular sort of assurance. That evening, I called my spiritual adviser, whose name I will not reveal. If I believed what the Apostle Paul told the Ephesians—that "we wrestle not against flesh and blood, but against principalities, against powers, against the rulers of the darkness of this world, against spiritual wickedness in high places"—then I would have shattered the illusion of evil, defeating whoever or whatever, this *Baffim Mamyan* was.

For investigating St. Fleur's operations, I was erroneously portrayed on *Page Six* of the *New York Post* as "the 200-plus-pound *Village Voice* writer" who got into Badillo's campaign headquarters by claiming to be a cop, "there to do a background check" on St. Fleur. None of this was true—not even my weight. But according to the *Post*, Badillo's press secretary, Sherman Jackson, kicked me out of the office after he discovered me "harassing" St. Fleur. She had denied talking with me a day earlier—though I kept a tape of our hour-long conversation—inviting me to the Badillo camp for a face-to-face meeting with her. Based on that tape, I can now report the truth about our initial conversation and why she is so vilified by Haitians.

On October 4, a Giuliani gadfly told me that St. Fleur can often be found at Badillo's campaign headquarters, and that pretty soon the doctor and a group called Caribbeans for Giuliani (composed mostly of Haitians similar to Caribbeans for Koch in 1985) would be announcing its endorsement. This was a typical ploy of political campaign strategist David Garth: Posed pictures of "minorities" on the steps of City Hall. "But Haitians for Giuliani?" I asked the source. Like Theroux, I thought it was a joke, a very bad joke.

That afternoon, after insisting for several minutes that "no Dr. St. Fleur works here," a Badillo fugleman gave me a number where she could be reached. St.

Fleur answered the telephone at her parent's home and inquired as to how I got her number. From the outset, I made it plain to her that it had come from an unidentified campaign source at Badillo's headquarters. She agreed to talk, "honestly." But even after I'd identified myself as a *Voice* reporter—and she claimed that she was "more or less" familiar with the newspaper—the woman seemed confused or naïve. "Oh, but I need to talk to you; that is very nice. We met today?" St. Fleur, who was amicable and giggled a lot, would interrupt the interview several times to verify that I worked at the *Voice*. At times she was satirical: "By the way, it's not the Haitian side of the Dinkins [camp] that send you after me?"

GUIRLAINE ST. FLEUR WAS A WELL-EDUCATED, twice-divorced mother of two young children. By her own account, she emigrated to the United States at the age of 13 to join her parents, self-exiled members of the Haitian elite who'd become disaffected with dictator François "Papa Doc" Duvalier. Throughout the years, as she aspired to be a medical doctor, St. Fleur lived in several cities, including New York; Seattle; Washington, D.C.; Atlanta, and Fort Myers, Florida.

Because she spoke Kréyòl, English, and five other languages, St. Fleur landed a job as a security guard at the infamous Krome Detention Center. She began to speak out, but not about the squalid conditions in which illegal Haitians were being detained. On radio talk shows, St. Fleur bragged about her training at the Georgia Bureau of Investigation, where she studied forensic medicine, but that, she told me, only made *Lavalas* "paranoid." Some called in to denounce her as a member of the Tonton Macoutes. "I have no association with Haitian government," she said.

St. Fleur was eight when Duvalier ordered the Tonton Macoutes, his secret police, to execute her uncle and cousins. "When they call me that name, it makes me sad because it reminds me of how they happen to kill my cousins. So many little school friends I had … I could not find them to play doll with because they disappeared. How can I have bad memories like that and be Macoutes?"

In May 1993, she left her job as an assistant physician in Fort Myers and came to New York City. St. Fleur said she joined the Badillo campaign party to repay a favor to a lawyer and Badillo associate who helped her parents buy a house when they first moved here almost 50 years ago. After hooking up with Badillo, she became a part of the Giuliani mayoral campaign. "It was a decision I took after I [became] very disappointed with the Aristide people."

St. Fleur claimed she tried to get to Aristide. "I have sent message that I want to speak to him; he did not want to see me because these people are strongly with Mr. Dinkins. The only Haitians who are really interested in Mr. Giuliani are people mostly in the opposition, and some of them are part of the elite.... The only thing the [*Lavalas*] people told me is that Mr. Dinkins helped them whenever they want to make their march for Aristide. They say he has given the key to Aristide and I ask, 'Which key?' I still don't know which key.

"I do not know exactly what Mr. Dinkins have really done for my people in terms of jobs, in terms of placement. I'm not a dictator either. They have the right to choose. But what I don't understand is the amount of people to be so much for someone like this. I don't know what it is."

The *Lavalas* faithful adorned Dinkins with garlands because he was a staunch defender of their rights as refugees fleeing a repressive right-wing regime. For the eight years that the "Haitian Program" was in effect, about 19,000 "boat people" were seajacked and forcibly returned to Haiti by U.S. Coast Guard vessels. After a 1982 meeting with Jean Claude "Baby Doc" Duvalier in Port-au-Prince, Giuliani, in a memo to Undersecretary of State Lawrence Eagleburger, reported that Baby Doc "gave me his personal assurance that Haitians that returned to Haiti are not, and will not be, persecuted." Other Haitian government officials "appeared to be amused by our statement that Haitians in the United States are claiming that they are subject to political persecution in Haiti." To shore up the Reagan Administration's policy that "interdiction was an effective deterrent" to the "boat people," Giuliani ended his seven-page memo to Eagleburger by claiming, "Though most people live in extreme poverty, they seem to be left to their own devices with little government interference."

Haitians captured in U.S. waters were jailed, their families separated; hunger strikes and uprisings were the order of the day. Ira Kurzban, an attorney for the Haitians, said that Giuliani, who personally argued the government's case before the 11th Circuit Court of Appeals, "went after the Haitians as a zealous prosecutor would go after anyone committing a crime."

Despite Giuliani's troubling record regarding the fleeing Haitians, St. Fleur believed his election "would be good" for them. "I honestly think so," she told me. "He did make a mistake. He was [following] orders. I don't think because of the decisions that he took he hates my people.... If Rudy had something wrong with him and something evil, I would see it and I would feel it. And you better believe that."

I believed St. Fleur was not just running off her mouth about her close ties to the Giuliani and Badillo campaigns. Although Badillo spokesman Bill Holtzman insisted that Badillo did not know who St. Fleur was, she claimed to have campaigned with both candidates on numerous occasions. ("Mr. Giuliani, himself; I have walked several weekends with him. When I go out with Mr. Badillo, I do go a lot with Mr. Giuliani.") St. Fleur then confirmed what my source had already told me. A group of Haitians, Trinidadians, and Indo-Guyanese, calling themselves "Caribbeans for Giuliani and Badillo," had been formed. St. Fleur told me that I'd be "shocked" to learn the level of support for Giuliani, particularly among Haitians. "A lot of professionals are going to vote for Giuliani, but the problem is they don't want to come out in the public because of their business. Who come in their business? The *Lavalas* people."

St. Fleur said she feared that her Haitian enemies would try to hurt her. "I find my own people too violent," she said, adding that just a week earlier, she was threatened "on the radio."

I ENDED THE INTERVIEW WITH ST. FLEUR and we agreed to meet at 2 p.m. the next day in Badillo's campaign headquarters. Ten minutes later she called me back at the *Voice* to verify that I worked there. Part two of our conversation ended with her consenting to have her picture taken by a *Voice* photographer. "I'm not upset about that, my God, something I wanna do."

The next day, St. Fleur called me. In an unrecorded conversation, she told me she was upset that someone in Badillo's office had given out her private number and that she'd briefed Badillo about our conversation. (Badillo's spokesperson denies that any such conversation between St. Fleur and Badillo took place). She still wanted to meet me. I called her back a few minutes later and asked her to reschedule the appointment to 2:30. I showed up at the office at 2:15, identified myself, and prominently displayed my press credentials. About three minutes later, a plump, *en bon point* woman dressed in a black business suit strolled into the reception area. "I'm Dr. St. Fleur," she announced. "See, I'm not a monster." She led me to a conference room in the back where we engaged in small talk for about 20 minutes. Linda Rosier, a *Voice* photographer, showed up shortly after and was getting her equipment ready when St. Fleur told me she was going to copy her resume for me. No sooner had she left the room than the press secretary, Sherman Jackson, stormed in and demanded to know how I got into the office. He kept throwing questions at me. "Dr. St. Fleur invited me here," I yelled, rising from my seat. Pushing his hand against my chest, he asked: "Who's Dr. St. Fleur?" She was now standing in the hall, and I heard her say, "I don't know you. I never spoke to you before."

Three men escorted me and the photographer to the door. The next thing I knew, I was the latest *Post* hoax. Someone had called Page Six to plant the story that I had invaded the Badillo offices and harassed the very person who invited me in for an interview. I had been transformed into a gorilla more grotesque than *Baffim Mamyan* might have done. This was the eternal damnation not even my spiritual adviser could protect me from. This was the curse of the satanic tabloid.

4

Why Giuliani Won

There are campaigns and there are campaigns, and there are two [kinds of] campaigns to look out for in New York. There's the ground war that takes place in the people's branch, the legislature, where we have seen much progress. And then there's the more symbolic, fuzzy, operatic performance that takes place in citywide campaigns that are more driven by media and polling and fundraising and posturing—playing above the rim, while the folks back in the neighborhoods and on the ground are eking out territory on a district-by-district basis.... And I personally believe that the best campaigns are the ones that utilize both sets of tactics. Being personally involved in a number of races, the '93 mayoral election is one where I believe ... the Dinkins and Giuliani campaigns traded places, and what the Giuliani campaign learned between '89 and '93 was to sharpen up its ground war tactics. What the Dinkins campaign did was spend a lot more focus on media, and that was the big sucking sound of millions of dollars going out on the tube instead of fueling a ground war in the neighborhoods. [I]t boiled down to a very small margin, the closest of margins that decided the outcome of that election.... I think it was because of the ground war and get-out-the-vote [campaigns] on election day.

—John Flateau, former Chief of Staff, Mayor David Dinkins

AT 12:27 ON THE MORNING OF NOVEMBER 4, 1993, Rudy Giuliani was announced as the 107th mayor of the City of New York. In what some activists later would call "the mourning after," referring to Giuliani's victory, black politics in New York definitively changed. The old schism—between Manhattan and Brooklyn, between the clubhouse and the street—had lost its sting after what, to even veteran black politicians, was a slap in the face by the city's Democratic establishment.

For black ultranationalist Sonny Carson, Dinkins' penchant for playing to white fear of black power was the major cause of his downfall. Ten months prior to the elections, Carson told a trusted street lieutenant that officials in the ill-fated campaign asked him not to do anything to further aggravate the mayor's sore relations with Jews and Asians, as well as capricious white liberals. As Carson put it, "They held my loyalty hostage for too long."

A polarizing figure to whites, Robert "Sonny" Carson co-chaired the December 12th Movement, a group composed of numerous separate cells with a five-member council called The Leadership Five. Despite the fragile accommodation of power sharing, the Movement was personified by a single leader. And that was Carson. During the '60s, he was one of the leading agitators in the school-decentralization battles in the neighboring Brooklyn communities of Ocean Hill and Brownsville. In 1990, Carson—although never proven—was identified as the shadowy mastermind behind the boycott of Korean greengrocers in Brooklyn's Flatbush and Bedford-Stuyvesant sections. Tension between Korean merchants and community activists erupted after a Church Avenue Korean store owner accused a Haitian woman of shoplifting. Carson would emerge at the center of the Crown Heights racial disturbances a year later.

Carson, a field operative in Dinkins'1989 mayoral campaign, wanted to get involved again. He approached senior Dinkins aides with an ambitious plan to register at least 100,000 tenants in city housing projects who felt abandoned by the administration and seemed apathetic about voting. Carson did not want to go on the record but permitted Akeem, his trusted lieutenant, to speak freely with me. Akeem said Carson told Dinkins campaign manager Bill Lynch that "the way to win this shit" was to bombard the projects, particularly those in Central Brooklyn, with popular rappers like X-Clan, Public Enemy, Heavy D, Big Daddy Kane, MC Lyte, and Poor Righteous Teachers.

MC Lyte, because of her summer hit "Ruff Neck," could have played a crucial role by appealing directly to "ruffnecks" in the Red Hook development, where, as rapper Joe Sinister put it, "they draw chalk around ya body." Carson proposed that the rappers take their message about the importance of voting to the "Temple of Boom," meaning they would saturate the airwaves with hiphop commercials. "We had laid out a master plan," Akeem claimed. "We were going to put rap artists on sound trucks and march the people out. You can't get nobody out to vote unless you put music, 'Ain't No Stopping Us Now,' *loud,* all day long. You embarrass the muthafuckas and make them listen to you, and then you put them on the trucks or walk them down there."

Carson had established the Malcolm X Voter Registration Project in Bedford-Stuyvesant. "We went and hired brothers; got our place and everything. They [the Dinkins campaign] gave the first payment up, and then in April they started to double cross us. All of a sudden these niggers are acting funny. So I said, 'What the fuck is this?' We don't hear from them anymore because, of course, Sonny is not supposed to be seen near anybody." Carson, Akeem asserted, was caught in a Catch-22. "He knew the campaign was going to be pressured by questions about Crown Heights and the Korean boycott. And whenever you say that, you say Sonny Carson next."

After the Dinkins campaign abruptly cut off communication with Carson, the activist, Akeem said, asked one of his advisers, a prominent local intellectual, to intercede. The adviser, who requested anonymity, said he met with Dinkins' aides "a number of times" to ascertain why the campaign was reneging on its arrangement with Carson. "There was an agreement in principle," the adviser recalled, "but there was no follow through."

"They brought in Jesse Jackson and Al Sharpton," Akeem recalled, "because they thought they could get by without getting down with the nationalists. That's how they also lost the election. How are you going to send Sharpton and Jesse to the Fort Greene projects and tell the brothers down there they need to come out and vote? It ain't going to happen." Carson's street warriors also objected to the presence of "freedom riders" from Mississippi, who came to New York City at the behest of the NAACP's Ben Chavis to help get out the vote.

"Freedom riders?" Akeem asked. "That's a joke! You need *freedom fighters,* not freedom riders. How the hell are you going to send freedom riders into the most notorious developments in the country and get the people's undivided attention?"

Jitu Weusi, chair of African Americans United for Political Power, a Brooklyn-based pressure group, was banished from Dinkins'1989 campaign when it was revealed that 20 years earlier he'd written a poem with anti-Semitic overtones. Weusi backed Carson's claim that the Dinkins campaign, fearing a firestorm from Jews and other whites, adopted a "deliberate strategy to muzzle black activists" and any talk of black power.

"In the last 10 days, when they began to get panicky, they brought in Sharpton and Jackson and who else they could put their hands on," Weusi said. But Weusi distanced himself from the claim by Carson's lieutenant that Sharpton and Jackson, two Baptist preachers, had no juice in the projects.

Weusi, too, had a plan to pull out the black vote as far back as 1989. "I was given resources to carry out the strategy," he explained. After press reports that Dinkins was not enjoying enthusiastic support among blacks, Weusi was summoned to meet with Bill Lynch, and "several key borough coordinators came out of my recruitment strategy." But four years later, they had no use for him, and, as a result, Weusi said, "This time, the Bronx did not have an African American coordinator until after the primary, OK? The Queens person, a very nice person, I don't think had the political capability to do that job. They were trying to play it so safe they neglected grassroots leaders who knew what was going on."

As for Lynch, who tried to achieve the impossible—reconciling the passions of black activists with the fears of whites—he mused about "the mourning after."

"There's frustration and concern out there," he sighed, his voice still hoarse from the grueling battle. "I take full responsibility for not having a winning strategy." Not everyone thought Lynch's strategy was the reason for Dinkins' defeat. "It was not the failure of black power. No!" said the Reverend Timothy Mitchell, pastor of the Ebenezer Missionary Baptist Church in Flushing, Queens. "It was the assumption that white power wouldn't be as racist as it is." Weusi called for a people's tribunal into "why this defeat took place." But the major task of black leaders, he insisted, was the formation of an "independent party that is controlled by progressive elements of the African and Latino communities." Whites, he said, should not be excluded.

"No!" Akeem objected. "Fuck a rainbow party! We ain't down with no rainbow."

"A rainbow, a rainbow," urged Percy Sutton, the former Manhattan borough president, who tried unsuccessfully to become the city's first black mayor in 1977. You need a rainbow because the minute you label it a black party, some people will feel unwelcome. And we don't need to frighten anybody away. There are people who think like us who are not us. Not too many of them—but those that are there must not be frightened away."

Did whites betray Sutton in 1977 because he was black? "Let's be honest and admit it," Sutton told me. "Instead of writing about me like they did—'He does not have a constituency'—what they meant was that whites wouldn't support me. We moved in 1989, when we got enough [white] friends supporting us to elect David. Four years later, an additional number of [white] Democrats find themselves unable to support David Dinkins. While in Harlem and Bed-Stuy, all over this city where African Americans reside in large numbers and form a voting bloc, they voted for Mr. Hevesi and Mr. Green, who are white candidates. But somehow Mr. Hevesi and Mr. Green were unable, or unwilling, or just negligent in not persuading many Democrats in their communities to vote for David Dinkins."

The day after his good friend lost, Sutton spewed his bitterness all over the city's dirty little secret. "What did we get? We got nothing. What did they get? They got two elected officials. This is so similar to the Dixiecrats. What we are finding is that we know how to join other parties as well. And it may well be that we need to examine, here in New York state, New York City, the possibility of establishing a third party more meaningful than this shabby little thing called the Liberal Party. Let's be sophisticated like the Democrats are."

The debate over whether blacks should defect *en masse* from the Democratic Party as political retribution for how whites treated Dinkins did not get any simpler. "I think we will have to withstand the efforts to fragment us into pockets of personal interests that rob us of the full impact of our collective engagement," said Dr. James A. Forbes Jr., senior minister of Riverside Church. "It appears to me that there could be a kind of 'ethnic party,' where race and culture and religion come together to revolutionize the significance of Democrats, Republicans, Liberals, and Conservatives. Those old lines seem not to hold. If there is a way for certain people of ideological convictions to come together above and beyond the two-party system, we have to consider that as an option. I would tend, since I'm a lifelong Democrat, to see if the party is salvageable as a standard-bearer for the values I hold and the needs I perceive our people have."

Look to Fannie Lou Hamer, who formed the Mississippi Freedom Democratic Party in 1968, Reverend Mitchell offered. "We have historical precedent. I am not saying that name [of the party] should be emulated; I am saying that the same racism and exclusion that motivated the initiation of that party is operative in New York City. Too many people, black and white, have been under the delusion that this is a liberal city."

Even Brooklyn's Al Vann, a black career politician, was galvanized by the election. "Maybe this kind of trauma will force us to do something we don't ordinarily do," he said. But Vann seemed to shun the idea of an all-black party. "I don't know if that alone is the answer." To which Akeem replied: "We are going to run candidates against all them niggers!"

Though Sutton tiptoed around Carson's claim that he could have won the election for Dinkins, he seemed to address the issue when he appeared on WLIB's *The Mark Riley Show*. "The question is could a supermilitant have gotten all these various groups? If you can do that, yes, be supermilitant. And do I think a more militant person may come along, and will there be a more militant, diverse group that will support him? Maybe so."

The Giuliani victory was a wake-up call to black-party politics, whatever its ideological roots. Leroy, a Brooklyn resident who called in while Sutton was on the air, put it this way: "All the grassroots organizations—the United African Movement, the December 12th Movement, the National Action Network, the Lost Nation of Islam, the Nation of Islam, and the Patrice Lumumba Coalition—I think it is incumbent upon each of them to come together right now, to put together a platform and ignore, forget, and resolve our silly egos."

Giuliani's election evoked mixed feelings in Carson. "Sonny is glad he won because now we can get busy," Akeem said. "We have to watch Giuliani because we know who he is. Remember, he was the prosecutor who put the New York 8 under surveillance and then indicted them. He's the enemy of the movement and there is no way we can work with him." Even Sutton seemed to back Akeem's fear about Giuliani's threat to the black activist movement (after all, he was Malcolm X's lawyer). "What I think will happen is that Mr. Giuliani will produce militancy within the black community, within the Latino community, within the liberal community," Sutton said on WLIB. "A more militant person may be selected the next time, but you have to have a more militant electorate."

Leroy, the caller from Brooklyn, was a supermilitant who voted for supermilitants. "I may be criticized by others, but I did not vote for Mr. Marlin, Mr. Giuliani, or Mr. Dinkins," he declared. "I went Independent. For mayor, I wrote in [former Tawana Brawley attorney] Alton H. Maddox. I did that because there have been some unfortunate strategic errors Mr. Dinkins made, and I don't feel upset today because I did not give my vote away."

SUTTON, FORBES, AND MITCHELL were less than gracious toward Giuliani after Dinkins' defeat. "I am frightened personally because I still see this angry, tightened face," Sutton said. "This man screaming with rioting police officers—that makes me very uncomfortable. I remember the code words about 'one standard,' the indication being that blacks who get ahead don't have to meet that standard of competency."

Reverend Mitchell drafted a letter to fellow ministers in the Eastern Baptist Association calling on them "not to allow Mayor-elect Giuliani access to our sacred fortresses" unless he answers a series of questions "to our satisfaction" regarding his relationship with the PBA and the future of the all-civilian complaint review board. Mitchell asked his colleagues not to consider his call for a ban on Giuliani "an arrogant statement" because the new mayor will preside over "a divided city" with half of its citizens having "increased tension, anxiety, and apprehension" over his election.

Giuliani's 1993 victory, some like Akeem maintain, damaged any hope that a new political party—black and proud—would emerge from rapprochement between dissenting black activist organizations. "What the fuck do we have?" Akeem snarled. "We haven't really implemented black power because the Negroes who orchestrated this thing sold black power out."

PART II
Dividing the City
(1994)

in memory of
Willie "Spanky" Woods

5

Fools Rush In

◆

The Police Raid on Malcom X's Mosque

I want to know who the men in the shadows are
I want to hear somebody asking them why
They can be counted on to tell us who our enemies are

—Jackson Browne, *Lives In the Balance*

IT WAS A DARK, BONE-CHILLING EVENING ON JANUARY 9, 1994, merely seven days after Rudy Giuliani was installed in his long-sought-after job as mayor of New York City. Apart from a howling, fierce wind that scattered about shards of ice and slammed loose pages of the Sunday papers against clogged sewer drains, there was a sense of disquiet, almost foreboding, in the air. Outside of a nondescript building on the corner of 125th Street and Fifth Avenue in Harlem, a cadre of solemn-faced black men nattily attired in gray and tan business suits, bow ties, and Stetson hats, stood watch at the front door. Three flights up at Muhammad's Mosque No. 7, the storied temple once headed by Malcolm X, Nation of Islam Minister Conrad Muhammad was preaching to the converted.

Conrad's "instruction" that day to the jam-packed temple easily could have become a rant on Giuliani's inaugural address, suffused as it was with the kind of veiled threats the minister had become accustomed to hearing from the rookie politician. (Giuliani by then had had a contentious relationship with the Nation of Islam (NOI). Just before the mayoral election, NOI leader Minister Louis Farrakhan had tried to hold a "Stop the Killing" rally in Yankee Stadium. Giuliani openly opposed the gathering, declaring that if he were mayor, he would not allow it.) Unmasked, Giuliani's avowal that "the era of fear has had a long enough reign" *was* about blacks walking a straight line from then on; it *was* about

39

Giuliani sending a strong message to blacks, now that he firmly was in charge at City Hall. Who else could Giuliani have been talking to when he announced that "change in many forms" was coming to the city, and that it "must be built around respect for the law and justice?"

Respect for whose law? Whose justice?

Blacks like Conrad were wary of that kind of rhetoric. "First of all, one could not put his hand in his pocket without getting shot by the New York Police Department," he said. "You knew you couldn't fight them and not get killed."

It was against this backdrop—a taut atmosphere fraught with uncertainty about an impending law-and-order crackdown by Giuliani—that black Muslims ventured out to worship. Conrad, however, would say nothing to provoke the new sheriff in town. He stuck to his scripted homily, calling on the 400-strong followers of Farrakhan to remain true to his teaching of nonviolence—the *only* pathway they *must* seek to a glorious Paradise.

But that Sunday afternoon, "someone decided to test the cops and Rudy's support of them," as former Mayor Ed Koch put it. At 3:57 p.m., an anonymous call came in to 911:

OPERATOR:	Police Operator 1817. Where is the emergency?
CALLER:	2-0-3-3 Five Avenue. Minister Farrakhan Mosque …
OPERATOR:	What is the emergency?
CALLER:	You have a male black, light skin, making a pickup …
OPERATOR:	What is he doing?
CALLER:	He's sticking up the Muhammad's Mosque. He has on blue jeans, black jacket, and he's also selling crack.
OPERATOR:	Is he a male black?
CALLER:	Male black, light skin or brown skin.
OPERATOR:	He's light skin?
CALLER:	Brown skin is a better description …
OPERATOR:	OK. Brown skin. What is he wearing?
CALLER:	He has on blue jeans and a black jacket, wearing a knit hat and a hood.
OPERATOR:	A knit hat? I can't hear you.

CALLER:	A knit hat and a hood.
OPERATOR:	What color hoodie?
CALLER:	A black hood. And he has a gun and he's with another male …
OPERATOR:	OK. Give me a description of him.
CALLER:	He's 5-feet-10, dark skin, graying hair. He has on a bright pants and a black parka.
OPERATOR:	Dark skin and he's got on a what?
CALLER:	Blue jeans and a black parka. Yeah. Blue jeans, a black parka, black knit hat.
OPERATOR:	A black parka?
CALLER:	Yes, a blue knit hat.
OPERATOR:	A what, sir?
CALLER:	A black knit hat.
OPERATOR:	I can't hear you.
CALLER:	He has on a black knit hat.
OPERATOR:	A black knitted hat.
CALLER:	Yeah. And a gun, he has a gun.
OPERATOR:	And he has a gun?
CALLER:	Yes ma'am. Thank you for your time.
OPERATOR:	And what are they doing? They're robbing what?
CALLER:	The Minister Farrakhan Mosque.
OPERATOR:	The Farrakhan?
CALLER:	Mosque. It's called the Muhammad Mosque Incorporated …
OPERATOR:	OK. So it's a mosque.
CALLER:	Have a Happy New Year to you, OK?
OPERATOR:	OK.

Police were dispatched to the mosque to check out reports of "a man with a gun," a robbery in progress. "In unknowing violation of a longstanding police protocol, two unsupervised uniformed police officers engaged in a heated exchange with persons ... near the mosque building," trial judge Howard E. Bell would later determine.

The call turned out to be bogus. The caller knew exactly what he was doing by luring the officers to a building that had been designated a "sensitive location." An angry Giuliani aide described it as "a place that's dangerous to police."

Truth be told, Giuliani's promise of "much greater emphasis on stricter enforcement of the law" and "changes in policing" to rid the city of "guns, the handguns," was clearly evident by the overzealousness of the two cops who responded to the report of an armed stickup man. According to a prosecutor's complaint, at about 4:20 p.m., Officers Wendy Jarvis and Paul Palombo were blocked at the door "by numerous males" and "prevented from investigating." When Jarvis and Palombo tried to push their way past the men—conscripts in the Fruit of Islam (FOI), the NOI's elite guard who are a mosque's first line of defense—they "punched and kicked" the cops and "forcibly ejected them from the building." Meanwhile, Officers Francis Ortiz and Wilfredo Quiñones, who also responded to the 911 call, tried to help Palombo and Jarvis storm the building. The FOI quickly fortified its ranks and held its ground. In the battle for the front door, Ortiz, authorities claimed, was "punched about the face and body by numerous males, who also attempted to take his gun from him."

A steady wail of sirens and blasting horns from police vehicles captured the attention and curiosity of the worshipers. Still, Conrad stayed on his message. "But then I noticed the sirens kept getting louder and louder, like something had happened downstairs," he said. "It was distracting. Some plugged their ears, but I just kept on preaching." Suddenly, a platoon of high-ranking FOI soldiers appeared in the sanctuary. Instead of handing a note to the minister—longstanding security protocol to alert him that something needed his urgent attention—Anthony Hollis, the mosque's 29-year-old local captain, reportedly emptied a back row of brothers and led them out. James 14X then approached the lectern and, again in violation of procedure, whispered in the cleric's ear: "Brother Minister, the mosque is being attacked by the police."

Conrad told his flock, "Apparently, there is a situation downstairs." He ordered them to remain calm; he'd be right back with an explanation. As he left the podium, his "blood ran cold"—not in dread of the turmoil he'd be walking into, but because he remembered what Farrakhan had told him only a few months earlier. Farrakhan abruptly brought up the subject of the 1973 police raid on the historic Mosque No. 7, which was on 116th Street in Harlem at the time. Bob Drury recalls the incident with now-disgraced NYPD Detective Lou Eppolito in *Mafia Cop*, a book they co-wrote:

> Answering an anonymous '10:13,' or officer-in-distress telephone call, Patrolman Phil Cardillo entered [the] mosque and in the melee that ensued was fatally wounded by shots fired from what was believed to be his own revolver. The weapon, however, was never recovered. No one was ever charged with the homicide. And the unorthodox investigation into Cardillo's murder was viewed by many—most especially the Department's rank and file—as so shoddy as to be a rollover to the political pressures brought by the city's black community, particularly the mosque's fiery spiritual leader, the Reverend (sic) Louis Farrakhan.
>
> I was in the second or third squad car on the scene after the Muslims attacked and killed Cardillo in the mosque. That day was one of the toughest in my life, because it was a massacre and it was a one-way deal. The brass botched the investigation and that poor cop died in vain. If the incident taught me anything, it taught me about the politics of the Police Department. If my bosses were going to back down every time there was pressure from a special-interest group, then my policy would be to shoot first and ask questions later. In truth, that had always been my policy, but now it was, like, official.

If Farrakhan had a premonition about trouble at Conrad's mosque, he surely didn't make it plain to his disciple. Instead, in typical NOI doublespeak, the minister recalled his own role in the tragic event. "I remember him saying that when the mosque was attacked, the brothers came and got him and tried to get him to go under the desk. 'Brother Minister, you hide,' they said. He said, 'No, I will not run and hide.' He said he went down to the scene and he saw the smoke from the policeman's gun. When he rounded the corner [and faced a phalanx of cops], he asked, 'Who's in charge?'" Farrakhan told Conrad "it was a good thing he stood up" because when he later reported to NOI spiritual leader Elijah Muhammad in Chicago what had happened, Muhammad asked, "What did *you* do?"

Twenty-one years later, the circumstances surrounding the police attempt to storm Mosque No. 7 a second time reverberated with uncanny similarity as Conrad hesitantly headed toward the battleground. "I felt somebody was going to die that day and I thought it was going to be me," he told me. But there was no turning back. He imagined—if he were ever to make it through this crisis—Farrakhan would ask him that question: "What did *you* do?"

"I had no choice," he said. "I had to go."

AT 29 YEARS OLD, THE HOLLYWOOD-HANDSOME Conrad Muhammad was like the lone star beside the crescent moon—the Muslim symbol representing justice, freedom and equality, as well as Islam. He became known as the "hip hop minister," an up-and-coming firebrand who one day might replace Farrakhan at the helm of the frayed black-separatist theocracy. Conrad was Farrakhan's emissary to feared street gangs like the Bloods and Crips. Even as a militant student leader at Wellesley College in Connecticut during the 1980s, Conrad seemed to have it all. "I remember we went to Connecticut with Minister Farrakhan some years ago, and there was a young brother there … who told me about a brother named Conrad, who was kickin' slam-butt up there at Wellesley College," Eric Muhammad, executive director of the Black African Holocaust Council, recalled in a 1994 speech. "And they wanted to expel him … because of his anti-Semitic—his pro-black—stand. He supported Brother [Jesse] Jackson's Rainbow Coalition—a whole litany of stuff."

Conrad studied under men like Khallid Muhammad. "Brother Khallid was one of my teachers," he acknowledged. "He was one of the first brothers to teach me into the knowledge of Islam. I was one of those students right by Brother Khallid's side because I saw in him a man that loved black people." Eric and Conrad toured the nation's college campuses together. Conrad, Eric recalled, would deliver fiery speeches in his bootlegged Farrakhan cadence, and would recruit young black radicals who saw no future at their "institutions of lower learning." In 1985, the tag team helped organize Farrakhan's controversial appearance at Madison Square Garden. Conrad then went to the University of Pennsylvania, but left shortly after to join Temple No. 7 and become national student representative.

In 1990, Farrakhan passed over Conrad and appointed Khallid as minister of Mosque No. 7. Both Conrad and Kevin Muhammad, the mosque's interim minister, had campaigned aggressively for the post. "This is not a demotion for Brother Kevin, and it is not a demotion for Brother Conrad," Farrakhan said as he introduced the new leader. "It gives to them a more mature, experienced guide to speed up their development." The following year, Khallid was promoted and became Farrakhan's national assistant. Conrad at last won the prize he'd long coveted. As minister of the mosque, Conrad reached out to Harlem's black elected officials, who admired the always-polite NOI official dressed in the dark suit, crisp white shirt, and signature bow tie. When Conrad persuaded two Harlem Democrats to support an NOI fundraiser, it laid the groundwork for the formation of black political-empowerment groups such as the influential African American Leadership Conference.

CONRAD'S MOSQUE WAS UNDER SIEGE. Making his way to the vestibule, he was overcome by fear he was walking into a death trap. "It felt like I was walking in slow motion down this long corridor," he recalled. "All around me sirens, voices, shouting—it felt like I was walking to certain death. You had the long corridor I was walking down, then you had a view of a precipitous drop, all the way down to the vestibule. It was like looking into Death Valley."

As he descended, several FOI wounded in hand-to-hand combat with cops were being carried up the stairs by their brothers to a makeshift triage unit in the mosque. "It was like a war zone," Conrad said. The FOI might have incurred far more casualties had it not been for Muhammad Abdul Aziz, a fire-in-the-belly soldier some in the NOI had hoped would guide scores of wayward Muslims back to the sect. As Norman 3X Butler at the time, Aziz was one of three men convicted of the February 21, 1965 assassination of Malcolm X, cut down by 16 bullets as he spoke at a rally at Harlem's Audubon Ballroom. He served 19 years in prison before being paroled in 1985. Aziz was "part of the council that gave advice" to Conrad, a keeper of the faith told me, and his military training came in handy after cops tried to overrun the mosque. Aziz and his men blocked the entrance.

"I knew that if we fought those cops, eventually they were going to pull out some guns and reinforcements would show up," Conrad said. "What was so frightening and terrifying to me was that it all had to come together in that tiny vestibule. As I rounded the corner, I said to myself, 'With your bad luck, the shooting would start right now. I was just waiting for the gunshots. I asked God to bless me."

Reaching the vestibule, Conrad's heart sank. The holy mosque was crawling with SWAT sharpshooters and angry cops; it had become an armed camp.

"Who's in charge?" he bellowed, asking the same question a young Farrakhan asked of the fools who rushed into his mosque on that fateful day in 1973. An in-your-face answer came from a burly white cop who collared Conrad and knocked and pinned him against a wall. Several of the officers locked and loaded shotguns and aimed them at his head.

This is it, he thought, this is how he would die.

"That's the minister!" a black cop shouted.

"What the hell are you doing down here?" Conrad demanded, his back pressed against the wall but still fighting back. "We're in the middle of a religious service! *What the hell is going on?*"

Only "by the grace of God" did the black cop step forward, Conrad told me. His intervention caused the SWAT team to lower their weapons. But the cops were visibly upset. By their own count, eight of their fellow officers had been injured. The Muslims had hurled several of the invaders down three flights of stairs, taking one officer's gun and another's radio, and ignominiously ejected them from the building. Soon every able-bodied Muslim male in the mosque that evening joined the FOI, blocking any further encroachment by the police. The cops warned they'd use force if he did not step aside, but Conrad in a test of wills took a deep breath and stiffened, bringing the confrontation to a hair-trigger standoff.

The cops said no one would be allowed to leave the building.

"Where's Commander Leake?" he asked testily, referring to Joseph Leake, head of the NYPD's Manhattan North Division, who was black. Leake had befriended the newly minted minister; they had an excellent relationship. As police tried to contact Leake, Conrad negotiated a fragile truce: There were children among the restive worshipers. He would go upstairs to the main hall and calm things down; no one would leave the building; and the cops would not attempt to breach the FOI's human wall.

Upstairs, Conrad put to test the bond he'd developed with some of Harlem's top politicians. He reached out to State Senator David Paterson, a former prosecutor in the Manhattan district attorney's office. Paterson, Leake and David W. Scott, first deputy police commissioner, who also was black, rushed to the scene. After several hours of negotiations, Conrad and Commander Leake agreed on one thing: They had a problem.

"I got a problem," Leake said. "Eight of my officers were injured."

"*We* got a problem," Conrad retorted. "We were in our religious service. We weren't bothering anybody."

By this time, the entire city was astir with the news of the cops-and-Muslims faceoff and anxiously awaited the outcome of Rudy Giuliani's first official skirmish with the black community. Who would blink first? "It was getting dark, it was about 7 o'clock," Conrad recalled. "People in the mosque were feeling like hostages; they were growing more and more agitated."

Both sides cut a deal that included the Muslims' promise to surrender a suspect in the attacks on the officers. "The deal was that everyone could leave," said Conrad. "We gave them our word that we would hand over any suspect that they had identified. They would watch everyone that came out. Whoever was a suspect, they would not arrest that night so as not to inflame an already volatile situation."

Two hours later, under the watchful eyes of detectives, worshipers filed out of their embattled mosque into the hoary weather and dispersed. The cops wasted no time tracking down suspects. "Officers from the 25th Precinct detective squad canvassed the area during the period immediately after the incident and made a list of the license plates of cars parked in the vicinity of the mosque," Judge Bell noted. "These lists were fed into the Department of Motor Vehicles computer and cross-referenced to the names and addresses of their owners. As a regular part of their investigation, the detectives began to call car owners in search of possible witnesses or participants to the incident."

THE NEXT MORNING, THE NEWSPAPERS' REPORTING about the melee seemed to confirm what blacks had been saying all along about Giuliani: He was a trigger-happy authoritarian spoiling for the ultimate showdown with them. Giuliani reiterated to the media that the city had to give the marauding cops the benefit of the doubt. He sternly advised the NOI to hand over its members who attacked and beat the officers. Arrests, he made it clear, were a top priority of his fledgling, zero-tolerance regime.

"There are no negotiations here; the law is violated," the mayor decreed at one of his news conferences. "Now it's time for the people who were responsible for it to turn themselves in, and the courts can resolve what happened. We have a system of laws in this country, a system of laws in the city. I'm committed to them, and this is the same view that I would take, no matter where it happened, at any time that it happened." Then as if there were any doubts about whose side he had taken in the dispute, he said of the cops, "They acted correctly and properly, and I support them."

In his report to Farrakhan, Conrad insisted worshipers did nothing to instigate the brawl. But the mosque leader's explanation of his own role did not satisfactorily answer that burning question, "What did *you* do?" Right after his briefing from Conrad, Farrakhan dispatched Leonard Farrakhan, his son-in-law and chief of staff, and Supreme Captain Abdul Sharieff Muhammad from NOI headquarters in Chicago to take over Conrad's investigation of the near-fatal fracas. "Chicago was acting like I had organized some type of publicity stunt," a stung Conrad said. (The NYPD had entertained that hunch, too, but "officials familiar with the Nation of Islam" told reporters at *Newsday* it was "highly unlikely the phony 911 call came from anyone connected to the mosque.")

Word spread quickly about the deal to allow the Muslims to leave the mosque without handing over suspects in the beating of the officers. Through back-channel discussions, Giuliani conveyed to the Muslims he would publicly denounce negotiated justice and slam the agreement as irresponsible. And in a meeting with newly appointed Police Commissioner William Bratton and Commander Leake, Giuliani expressed his disdain for the agreement. "The mayor made it quite clear to me and to Chief Leake that as he looked at it, he [felt] an arrest should have been made," Bratton told *The New York Times*. The day after the clash was Bratton's first official day on the job. Bratton also intimated he "defended Chief Leake's power to make a decision as the commanding officer on the scene."

"Joe Leake prevented a bloodbath, but Giuliani made it seem like he was incompetent for negotiating with us like that," Conrad said in the commander's defense. As far as Giuliani was concerned, his police officers were assaulted and his administration would never negotiate with people who beat up his officers.

Meanwhile, Conrad was sensing that Farrakhan also wasn't happy about the deal, but he refused to be hobbled by nagging doubts about his stewardship; until the arrival of the NOI heavies from Chicago, he still officially was in charge. In an attempt to marshal support, he convened a morning meeting on January 10 of his lieutenants and other well-known community activists at a Harlem brownstone owned by Sister Captain Kareema Muhammad, who hosted Farrakhan whenever he came to town. After a news conference at Abyssinian Baptist Church, led by the outspoken Reverend Calvin O. Butts III, Conrad went back to Sister Captain Kareema's home, where he met Leonard Farrakhan and Supreme Captain Sharieff.

There they strategized further.

"What I immediately didn't like about Chicago was that they came in and right away started pooh-poohing the deal I had negotiated," Conrad told me. "They started passing blame and Leonard Farrakhan said, 'We ain't turning over no suspects.' Keep in mind that I had guns in my face, we got vengeful police officers in our place of worship, and the commander of Manhattan North Division, and a state senator had tried the best they could to negotiate in good faith to diffuse the situation. The best we could come up with at the time was, 'Don't arrest anybody tonight, otherwise we're gonna be here all night.' Commander Leak and Senator Paterson deserve tremendous credit for using wisdom. They showed tremendous courage."

The "always super nervous" emissaries from Chicago signaled the NOI's determination not to give in to Giuliani's and Bratton's demands. "'They would think we're [Uncle] Toms,'" Conrad quoted one of the Muslim leaders as saying. "We ain't turning over no suspects."

As the Muslims dug in their heels, their ranks of volunteer advisers began to swell. Al Sharpton called Conrad to say that the incident was no longer a "Muslim problem," but one that had engulfed the entire civil-rights fraternity. He and others had embarked on a course of action of their own, Sharpton said. Activist attorney C. Vernon Mason—a nemesis of Giuliani, who as U.S. Attorney in Manhattan tried to entrap him, fellow attorney Alton Maddox and Sharpton in a wiretapping fiasco during the '80s Tawana Brawley scandal—also jumped into the fray. "[T]here was a meeting at the mosque, at which some members were informed that a prominent attorney, C. Vernon Mason, had been retained to represent the mosque in its dealings with the police, and that he would be available to represent them individually," Judge Bell found. "Thereafter, out of some 75 persons at the mosque meeting on January 10th, Attorney Mason distributed his business cards to twenty clients ... who indicated a desire to retain him." At that meeting, according to Conrad, Mason angrily declared, "We ain't turning over a damn suspect."

Complaining that mosque leaders reneged on a promise to turn in suspects, the NYPD released a composite sketch of a man they said they were interested in questioning. "The damn sketch looked just like me," Conrad recalled.

Later, at a private strategy session back at Sister Captain Kareema's, Leonard Farrakhan and Supreme Captain Sharieff began to call the shots. After several hours of talks, they told Conrad that the official position of the NOI was not to cooperate with the police investigation identifying a suspect. Although Conrad himself was not eager to surrender anyone, the battle cry was not what he had expected. "Senator Paterson was putting pressure on them," said Conrad. "He said, 'Look, I put my credibility on the line to ensure the safe passage of your people.' But, of course, Leonard and the supreme captain don't live in New York; they hadn't negotiated that agreement in good faith. They saw what was happening as larger political theater. They didn't give a damn about any agreement I'd made."

Conrad's discussions with the out-of-towners were at an impasse until Farrakhan's representatives suggested calling on Boston-based Minister Don Muhammad to intervene. Minister Don, the NOI's former East Coast regional representative, knew Bratton when he was chief of police in Beantown. "Don and Bratton had been very tight in Boston," Conrad told me. "Don knew all those Irish cops and politicians in Boston; he had enormous political clout." They approved a strategy to authorize Minister Don to establish contact with Bratton to bring an end to the stalemate.

Flanked by a throng of black leaders at a news conference on the steps of City Hall the next morning, Minister Don called the invasion of the mosque an act of disrespect toward the black community. Publicly he demanded an apology from the Giuliani administration. "We don't believe that this would have happened at a Jewish synagogue [like] Temple Emanuel [or] a Catholic Cathedral [like] St. Patrick's," Minister Don told reporters.

Sharpton went on the offensive, warning, "If this is the first showdown between Giuliani and the black community, he will not limit it to one religious sect." NY1's Dominic Carter asked Giuliani what he thought of Sharpton's statement. "That isn't even worthy of a response," the mayor shot back, at first appearing to bite his tongue on the topic of engaging the reverend in a public debate. "That's an attempt to politicize what is in fact an incident that involves the police and a particular mosque," he said.

But Giuliani couldn't pass up the opportunity to marginalize his old foe.

"There are some people [who] would prefer to continue to divide us," the mayor told Carter. "I think those are the voices you would do well to ignore for a while in this city. Instead, let's listen to the voices of reason and calm." Bratton, Carter reported, rallied to his boss's defense, claiming, "This has nothing to do with Mayor Giuliani. To characterize it as such is way off base."

Following the news conference, Minister Don reached out to his old friend as planned. Bratton agreed to a meeting and assured Giuliani that its focus was on bringing in a suspect who injured officers, a man involved in the assaults. Later, in a telephone interview with Ralph Blumenthal of the Times, Minister Don "confirmed that the meeting with the commissioner was set up at his urging. He said he had held Mr. Bratton in high regard since Mr. Bratton's days in the Boston Police Department." Minister Don told Blumenthal he expected the same kind of "working relationship and mutual respect" he and Bratton had to anchor their meeting at One Police Plaza, the NYPD headquarters in Manhattan. As a good-faith gesture, the NOI official said he'd already "pledged cooperation in the search for those who police officials say assaulted the officers."

On January 12, Bratton confirmed media reports he'd agreed to meet with Minister Don on the mosque incident. He chastised some reporters whose questions implied that the Muslims appeared to be controlling the negotiations, saying there was no "harm [in] sitting down and discussing it." But skeptics in Giuliani's inner circle remained suspicious about the Muslims' role in the bogus 911 call. "At a closed-door meeting at City Hall," Newsday reported, "top aides to Mayor Rudolph Giuliani … raised the specter of a setup, saying the 911 caller might have wanted to draw the police into a confrontation with the Muslims to test the new [A]dministration, according to senior Giuliani [A]dministration officials. A close aide to Giuliani, however, said the mayor does not believe that to be the case." Insisted Bratton: "We don't know what the motivation of the call was." Other senior Giuliani aides privately complained to their media contacts that the Muslim leaders believed the NOI was above the law. "It's just outrageous they could get away with beating up a cop and think they would not get arrested," one official said.

THOUGH GIULIANI HAD ANGRILY REJECTED SHARPTON'S prediction of an NYPD crusade against black religious groups in the wake of the attack on Mosque No. 7, he was thrust into a new controversy with the police killing of an unarmed 17-year-old, Shu'aib Abdul-Latif, the son of a prominent Sunni imam.

"The police officer reacted both properly and bravely," Giuliani said of Officer Kevin Sherman, a black cop who was shot in the leg in an alleged scuffle that police said led to the shooting of the teenager in the East New York section of Brooklyn on January 11.

"I feel our son was murdered," said a distraught Al-Amin Abdul-Latif, president of the Islamic Leadership Council of New York and leader of Mosque Al-Muminin, located in the Bedford-Stuyvesant section of Brooklyn.

Shu'aib was portrayed by relatives as a "painfully shy" young man who lived on his own as part of a Muslim rite of passage. Though he had dropped out of school, he was being tutored four times a week by an uncle and working toward obtaining his General Equivalency Diploma. He dreamed of being a carpenter. One of ten children, the "humble, jolly kid"—not a "belligerent or aggressive person," his father insisted—also would help out at the family's food-distribution business. "This boy ran away from violence at any cost," his uncle, Ismail Abdul-Karim, said. "He was not one to mix it up."

But Shu'aib was ill-prepared for the unforgiving streets of East New York. On March 27, 1993, while on probation for jumping a subway turnstile, he was arrested for possession of 22 vials of crack that cops said he intended to sell. Shu'aib was convicted of a felony, but because he was only 16 and a first-time offender, he was sentenced to five years probation. Friends of Shu'aib told a reporter that he was not a drug user or dealer, but worked as a courier for a neighborhood pusher to earn money. "That's irrelevant," the imam was quoted as saying about Shu'aib. "It has nothing to do with the murder of my son. If a man is in possession of drugs, you arrest him for that. The coldblooded murder of my son is not justified."

Even as the NYPD conceded it was still wading through the murky circumstances of the shooting, officials gave reporters unfettered access to the "labyrinthine layout" of the crime scene—a dank, dimly lit basement at 499 Williams Avenue, where Shu'aib lived and was gunned down.

This account by David Firestone in the *Times* was based partly on the NYPD's self-serving reconstruction of the alleged scuffle, it said, caused Shu'aib's death:

> Inspector Lawrence F. Loesch, a Police Department spokesman, said that 11 police officers, including a sergeant, had entered the building shortly after 9 P.M. in response to a 911 call reporting a dispute involving a gun. The caller left a name and number that turned out to be false, he said. After the officers descended an unlighted staircase, they entered a 'dark, dingy basement, with one light bulb hanging from a wire,' he said. The basement was divided into six cubicles, which may have been rented out as individual apartments. Reporters entering the basement ... saw a bed and some clothes in one open cubicle, as well as a communal kitchen area and bathroom. Officer Sherman entered the cubicle area while the other officers were still descending the stairs, Inspector Loesch said. The other officers then heard someone say, 'Police! Don't move!' and heard a scuffle and then one gunshot. But they could not see what was happening.
>
> Suddenly, [Shu'aib and Sherman] tumbled through one of the rickety walls of the cubicles and into the view of the other officers, the inspector said. He said the officers realized that Officer Sherman had been wounded and could not get up. When Mr. Abdul-Latif tried to stand, 'additional shots were fired,' the inspector said, and he fell to the ground. The three other officers had fired a total of four bullets, two of which apparently struck Mr. Abdul-Latif, said John Miller, the Deputy Commissioner for public information. One bullet struck Mr. Abdul-Latif in the arm and the other in the left side of the chest. Inspector Loesch said Officer Sherman's .38-caliber service revolver was recovered from the basement, although he said the department did not know if the officer had lost it in a struggle. Shooting an unarmed civilian is within police guidelines if it takes place during a struggle for an officer's gun, the inspector said. He said the bullet that struck Officer Sherman apparently entered his leg through the top of the thigh and moved down, a trajectory he said could be consistent with a shot fired during a struggle.

Firestone also interviewed Alane Thompson, who said she knew Shu'aib and was an eyewitness to how cops really ended the teenager's life: "Ms. Thompson ... said [Abdul-Latif] ran into the basement out of fear when officers entered the building, and was found by them crouching behind a stove in the kitchen area of the basement. 'He came up from behind the stove with his hands up, and then they started shooting,' said Ms. Thompson, who accompanied the officers into the basement. 'All the shots came all at once as soon as we got into the basement.'"

Bratton discredited Thompson's account, saying that at best it was shaky: He would rely on the findings of the NYPD's investigators. But a second woman, Dariel Johnson, backed Thompson's story. Johnson told Firestone she was the only full-time resident of the basement apartments and that shortly before the shooting cops had cleared her to enter that area of the building. "She said she walked past officers with their guns drawn," wrote Firestone, "and as she reached her door at the end of the basement hallway, she turned and saw Mr. Abdul-Latif come out from behind a wall at the other end of the hall. She said she then heard two shots and saw Mr. Abdul-Latif fall with his hands up. Frightened, she ran into her room and heard two more shots and recalled saying to herself, 'Oh my God, they just shot him for nothing.'"

The NYPD later would amend the shooting scenario, claiming that Shu'aib was shot after he stood up, broke loose from Sherman, and ran into two other cops who were heading in his direction. "He actually bumped into the first officer, and reached the second, and both fired one shot," said a law-enforcement official.

Cops said they retrieved more than 20 crack vials and $83 from Shu'aib's basement hovel. No gun was found on the premises or on Shu'aib. "He would not pull a gun on anybody and definitely not the police," his father insisted, speculating that Sherman might have shot himself accidentally in the foot. "A lot of the police today are not as professional as they ought to be. Many of them are racist [and] fearful of young black and Hispanic men. And when they see one, they think right away that he has a gun."

DESPITE MOUNTING OUTRAGE OVER THE SHOOTING and pleas by some callers on black talk radio not to meet with the NYPD, the NOI leaders began making preparations for their private January 13 summit with the police commissioner. After consulting with Farrakhan, it was decided that only Ministers Don and Conrad would meet with Bratton.

Promptly at 7 o'clock the next morning, the NOI leaders met at Sister Captain Kareema's for a final briefing of the two-man delegation. According to Conrad, out of nowhere Sharpton and Mason "showed up, offering their services." Stunned by the eleventh-hour intrusion, the Chicagoans and Minister Don retired to a separate room and hastily discussed the pros and cons of including the uninvited guests. Conrad said he overheard the men finally agreeing to discourage Sharpton and Mason from attending the meeting. "They didn't want them to go," he said.

But none of Farrakhan's emissaries had the nerve to break the news to the activists. "We're getting ready to leave for the meeting and none of these Chicago Negroes had the balls to say to Mason and Sharpton, 'You can't go to the meeting.' They didn't have the courage to tell Sharpton and Mason, 'Brothers, we appreciate you, but we need to go on our own.'"

Even when black activists like Sharpton and Mason and black Muslims came together, as they occasionally did in New York City, they were suspicious of each other. At first glance they seemed like natural allies, both having experienced systemic discrimination. But that is not the reality.

For example, it took years for black politicians and black Muslims to see eye to eye on the direction of blacks in America. In the early '60s, at the height of the attraction to black nationalism and black power, black politicians and Muslims grew wary of each other. But some, like Harlem Congressman Adam Clayton Powell Jr., maintained a mutual though fragile relationship with the Muslims. The audacious Powell was singled out by Nation of Islam patriach the Honorable Elijah Muhammad as one politician deserving of Muslim support.

"To my knowledge, the strongest politician of our kind, or the one who comes nearest to giving you political justice in the white courts (if he had our complete backing) is Congressman Adam Clayton Powell Jr.—though he is not a Muslim," Elijah said in a 1964 speech *The Time and What Must Be Done.* "A Muslim politician is what you need. But Congressman Powell is not afraid and would not be easily bribed, for he is not hungry.… We must give the black politician, who is for us, the total backing of the 22 million. He must be under an oath to do for you, as near as possible, what you elect him to do or die, if necessary."

Black Muslims began to ask a lot of questions of black politicians like Powell's successor, Charles Rangel, who was often in the company of Malcolm X. Rangel also knew Louis Farrakhan. "I knew young Farrakhan, so we go way, way back," Rangel told me. In the heat of the 1993 mayoral race, when Giuliani spoke out against Farrakhan holding his anti-black-on-black violence rally in Yankee Stadium, Rangel worked behind the scenes to ensure the NOI's rights were protected. "The interesting thing is that while the newspapers were so busy saying that the Muslims were coming to Yankee Stadium, I was on the phone talking with Chicago and working out something, because the last thing they wanted was to get involved in the mayor's race," Rangel recalled. "They wanted to have a rally and what happened was that the contract said that they could have this space unless there was a sports event. The scheduling then went back to the city and they gave the date to the Department of Parks. They were blaming them for try-ing to upset Dinkins, but I had never met with anyone who was more dignified and courteous than the Nation of Islam. In the eye of a tornado created by the press, they never got involved in that."

In citing examples of the distrust some black activists harbor for black politi-cians, one Harlem community leader, who spoke to me on condition of anonym-ity, offered political analyst Manning Marable's searing critique of how David Dinkins "fucked over" some in the grassroots community on his historic journey to City Hall. "[H]e made several strategic political compromises to secure the support of the white upper-middle class, and especially Jewish voters who had supported neoconservative mayor Ed Koch in the Democratic primaries," Marable contended in a 1990 article entitled *Black Politics and the Challenges for the Left.* "Dinkins distanced himself from Jackson politically, and reminded white voters that he had denounced black-nationalist leader Louis Farrakhan. Dinkins' lieutenants shunned efforts by Brooklyn's Arab-American Democratic Club to hold a fund-raising event, for fear of alienating the Jewish electorate."

Marable claimed that Dinkins' campaign manager, Bill Lynch, "told Arab-American leaders not to seek to be visibly associated with the candidate," but the campaign would still accept their financial contributions. "In effect," Marable added, "New York City's Arab-American community of 100,000 was disavowed by a 'liberal' who had worked closely with them in the past. After his election, Dinkins and his associates refused to honor promises of appointments to several black progressives and nationalists who had been pivotal in mobilizing African-American voters."

THE ARRANGED MEETING AT ONE POLICE PLAZA was doomed from the start. Bratton would later reveal that he first learned that Sharpton and Mason were going to attend the meeting when Mason called to say the delegation was caught in traffic and would be a couple of minutes late. But an examination by the *Times* of Bratton's schedule that day suggested that he didn't allocate enough time to the thorny issue that was dividing the city. And upon learning that Giuliani's enemies were accompanying the Muslims, Bratton wasn't sticking around to break the mayor's campaign promise of not meeting with racial huck-sters like Sharpton and Mason.

"The timing was off," the newspaper reported. "The meeting had been set for 4 p.m. in Mr. Bratton's office. But the visitors, saying they had been caught in traffic, did not arrive until 5:15 p.m., pulling up in three cars to enter Police Headquarters' restricted underground parking garage as V.I.P. guests. In addition to Don Muhammad and Conrad Muhammad, Mr. Sharpton and Mr. Mason, there were five others from the Nation of Islam, including someone said to have been a top aide to Minister Louis A. Farrakhan. But by that time Mr. Bratton had already left to attend the swearing in of District Attorney Charles J. Hynes of Brooklyn. Caught himself in heavy traffic, aides said, he hopped the subway to speed the trip back to Manhattan for the swearing in of District Attorney Robert M. Morgenthau at 5 p.m. By the time he walked across the street back to his office, the visitors, saying they had agreed to wait only to 6:30, were departing."

While the group was waiting for Bratton, they were greeted by First Deputy Commissioner Scott. That session solved nothing; there was arguing about "who was supposed to be at the meeting, as well as the meeting's scope and scheduling," the *Times'* Blumenthal wrote. Bratton complained later to the reporter that the group was "larger than he had expected, and that the focus of the meeting was different from what had been agreed." But that was Bratton's way of rationalizing his refusal to meet while hinting he would not cross his boss.

"It was inappropriate to have that meeting with a larger-than-intended group and get into areas I was not prepared to discuss," the commissioner reiterated. Mason, Bratton suspected, would use the occasion to interrogate him and gather information that would be helpful in his defense of possible clients arrested for the assault of the officers. "I was not prepared to discuss criminal aspects of that case," he said.

Minister Don bared his disappointment over Bratton's snub of the delegation. "We came all the way from Boston prepared to discuss the incident," he told reporters gathered outside of police headquarters. Then in a face-saving gesture, he said, "Friends can always disagree."

Sharpton and Mason were less conciliatory. Giuliani, Mason said, had "sent a clear message" to blacks on how he intended to govern them: "We have a dead young man who was murdered, and a mosque desecrated, and now we have an insult." Sharpton called Bratton's move "an affront to our community" and "clearly a political decision" that was a Giuliani-engineered power play.

Conrad remembered how Sharpton reacted to Bratton's snub. "Sharpton was looking all crazy," he said. "I was angry because I know what happened. I was *pissed.* I was worried about my men who I was trying to keep out of jail."

The Muslims and their would-be advisers headed back to Sister Captain Kareema's. There Conrad described the mood as awkward, embarrassing, almost defeatist. "It was like a morgue," he said. "Everybody knew there was a white elephant in the room was, but nobody wanted wants to say it. Chicago was being political as they always were, not saying anything. Sharpton and Mason were sitting around, knowing damn well they were the cause the meeting didn't take place."

Leonard Farrakhan called a meeting of his Muslim brothers, including Supreme Captain Sharieff, Minister Don, and Conrad. They went into another room, out of earshot of Sharpton and Mason, and broke the news to Farrakhan. Conrad's recollection of the phone call that night was that "the Minister kicked a new hole in Leonard's backside about the meeting not taking place. The Minister's position was, 'I sent you all to meet with the police commissioner; we've got a mosque and some believers in harm's way. We've got to resolve this, and you all are playing politics. *What do you mean Sharpton?* He's not critical to this! *I sent Don down there to meet with that man!*'"

The top aides still couldn't muster up the courage to jettison the excess baggage. Instead, they relied on Conrad to play the heavy—to tell Sharpton and Mason to back off. "They asked me to tell Sharpton and Mason, 'Brothers, we got to have the Bratton meeting without you,'" he said. "Don, Leonard and the Supreme Captain sat back. By letting me fight Sharpton so aggressively, they were able to play it like it was me who didn't want Sharpton in the meeting rather than expose a decision that the Minister himself had made."

Conrad didn't mince words.

"Rev, we got to have this meeting with Bratton," he told Sharpton in the presence of Mason. "The Minister said we *got to* meet, and *you* ain't going."

Conrad said Sharpton "took offense" to taking orders from the Muslims. That tiff created the first crack in a solid alliance of grassroots activists who had coalesced against the storming of the mosque and the police killing of Shu'aib Abdul-Latif, and came out swinging at the Giuliani administration. Sharpton contended that excluding them was a Giuliani ploy to discredit black unity and, ultimately, destroy it. "I knew what he was doing," Conrad asserted. "He (Sharpton) was making himself the issue, and it was not about him." Sharpton retorted that the young minister was naïve and inexperienced in the crass warfare of New York City politics. The Muslim preacher-turned-political hit man for Chicago countered Sharpton's every nuanced putdown, cutting to the quick with an old gripe about Mayor Dinkins' isolation of the Nation of Islam and Sharpton's many broken promises to act as a go-between.

"I reminded Sharpton that he'd met with Dinkins many times and we couldn't go in the door with him," Conrad said. "I told him, 'You never made it an issue with Dinkins; you didn't tell him you ain't gonna meet with him if he don't allow us to be in the meeting.' I said, 'This is ridiculous; you're not critical to *our* meeting.'"

Sharpton stormed out.

Bratton finally did arrange a secret meeting with Ministers Don and Conrad. ("They turned around the next day and went and met with Bratton without my knowledge," a sour Sharpton told me, adding that "many people in the community said that was a sellout.") At the meeting, Bratton and Minister Don reminisced about policing in Boston and the improved relations between blacks and the police under Bratton's leadership. "They both talked about how things just spiraled out of control so quickly," said Conrad. "They said if this was Boston, they could have resolved this by now."

Then Bratton dropped a bombshell. "He alluded to the fact that he and Giuliani didn't see eye to eye on how this thing should be handled," Conrad recalled. Nevertheless, they had a pressing problem. "Bratton said they had a suspect, and we made an agreement and we didn't live up to that agreement. He said Don's credibility was on the line, and his credibility was on the line."

TWO DAYS AFTER MEETING WITH BRATTON, Detective Robert Stewart of the 25th Precinct stationhouse in Harlem placed a telephone call to Mosque No. 7's local captain, Anthony Hollis, at his home in Westchester County. The call was not based on any leads Ministers Don and Conrad provided to the police commissioner.

In their preliminary search for at least seven suspects, Detectives Stewart and George Forni, his partner, wrote down the license plate numbers of several cars parked near the mosque on the night of the incident. They called the owners to question them. Next on their list was Hollis. A run on the license plate number of a '93 black two-door Honda revealed the car was registered to him. An account of the cops' investigation—contained in a Manhattan Supreme Court decision issued by Judge Bell—confirmed that the Honda was "parked near the mosque on Sunday, January 9th at about the time of the crime the detective was investigating." But what happened next would seal Hollis' fate as the only cop-beating suspect the NYPD would round up, and it would raise troubling questions about police tactics that allegedly violated Hollis' constitutional rights against self-incrimination.

Stewart said in the court document that when a man at the address listed in Hollis' name answered the phone, he asked the man to speak to Anthony Hollis. The man told Stewart he was speaking to Hollis, and Stewart introduced himself and told Hollis why he was calling. Stewart said he then asked Hollis if he was at

Mosque No. 7 at the time of the melee and whether he was a witness to the assaults on the officers. Hollis allegedly blurted out he was at the "the nearby Apollo Theater that night." When the detective asked, "What was playing at the theater?" Hollis allegedly replied, "I have nothing further to say," and hung up on Stewart.

On January 18, Forni said he showed six head shots to Officers Wendy Jarvis and Wilfredo Quinoñes and that both officers, separately and "at different times," identified Hollis as "one of the individuals who was punching [Officer Francis] Ortiz." Ortiz claimed that as a result of the pummeling by Hollis, he suffered "substantial pain to his right shoulder, hand, jaw, head, back, nose, and a cut and swollen lip." During the scuffle, Jarvis lost her radio, suffered a broken nose and bled considerably. Palombo lost his revolver, and other officers sustained scrapes and bruises. (*NYT*'s Dominic Carter reported that police conceded "some of the injured officers may have just slipped on ice" and that the cops' gun and radio were "later returned after negotiations between the police and the mosque.")

The next day, a detective went to Westchester and brought Hollis back to the 24th Precinct stationhouse, where he was paraded in a series of police lineups, supposedly under the watchful eye of his attorney, C. Vernon Mason. The police insisted that witnesses who had not seen the lineup be separated from those waiting to view the lineup. Two witnesses identified Hollis as an assailant. A grand jury indicted Hollis on second-degree assault and second-degree obstruction of governmental administration.

THE ATTACK ON THE MOSQUE and calls for Farrakhan to repudiate his hothead lieutenant Khallid Muhammad (On January 16, as tensions between the NOI and the NYPD escalated, the Anti-Defamation League of B'nai B'rith took out a full-page advertisement in *The New York Times* denouncing an anti-Semitic speech made by Khallid in November 1993 at Kean College in New Jersey. In the speech, Khallid referred to Jews as "bloodsuckers" who "deserved Hitler," called for the genocide of white people in South Africa after the fall of apartheid, called Pope John Paul II a "cracker" and demeaned homosexuals.) were major—and often linked—news stories by the time the Nation of Islam leader came to New York on January 23 to deliver an urgent speech calling for an end to black-on-black crime. He also was slated to participate in a long-awaited sitdown with the city's black clergy. The Muslim and his Christian cohorts met at the Abyssinian Baptist Church. The Reverend Wyatt Tee Walker, a fellow traveler with Dr. Martin Luther King Jr. and staunch ally of Sharpton, chaired the summit.

At times the assembly took on the vehemence of a witch-hunt. According to Conrad, one of the preachers openly charged Farrakhan with shamelessly promoting himself as the black messiah. "There were a number of theological issues they raised with the Minister," Conrad told me. "A top preacher told the Minister, 'I'm with you on how badly Giuliani and the NYPD are handling the mosque issue, but this thing about you saying you are the Christ bothers me.'" Farrakhan tactfully warned his critics they were not qualified to conduct an inquisition.

The final order of business was mending fences with Sharpton, who'd demanded a face-to-face meeting with Farrakhan to complain about how shabbily the minister's underlings had treated him.

Conrad believed that the meeting of the clergymen was hijacked by a Sharpton cabal and turned into a bash-Farrakhan session. "Sharpton stacked the deck," he said. "His handpicked people got up and said, 'We can't have our leader disrespected.' I'm sitting there. I'm the Minister's representative in New York and I'm pissed because they had sandbagged the Minister at a time when we needed unity. But Sharpton was exacting the Minister's call for unity at a price. It was not so much about him helping people, it was about him being the central figure in this fight with Giuliani. It was about him showing the Minister how important he was."

Farrakhan, Conrad remembered, was "diplomatic and contrite, and uplifted Sharpton" in the eyes of his fellow clerics. He said the decision to meet privately with Bratton a second time was wrong and summarily reprimanded Ministers Don and Conrad.

The public censure of the NOI officials would "guarantee Sharpton a larger role" in the politically charged negotiations in the mosque incident, Conrad said. "I was relieved that the tension with the police was diffused; it was our hope," he told me. "To be honest, the thing that really broke the stalemate was Don's relationship with Bratton, because that immediately gave us an in to an otherwise very hostile Giuliani administration. That was a stroke of genius to think about Don. He was our trump card, really. We had to solve this problem so that the police didn't come in there the next Sunday and raid our mosque looking for suspects."

ANTHONY HOLLIS WASN'T TAKING THE FALL for anyone. The NOI and the NYPD had made their peace, but now it was left up to him and him alone to prove his innocence. For him, Bratton and Giuliani would have to prove they got their man.

At a pretrial hearing, Hollis challenged the admissibility of the statements attributed to him by Detective Stewart during their phone conversation. He asked Judge Bell to throw them out on the ground that the NYPD knew he had hired Mason as his lawyer but Stewart proceeded to question him anyway. (The rule is, once an attorney enters the proceedings, police may not question a defendant in the attorney's absence). Hollis was among the more than 70 Muslims "who indicated a desire" to retain Mason when he visited the mosque the day after the incident.

On January 11, Conrad "met with Commander Leake and other upper-echelon police officials, and informed them that Mr. Mason represented the entire mosque and its members," Judge Bell wrote as a finding of fact in his decision. "Based on later conversations with Minister Conrad, Mr. Mason (who was not at the meeting) believed the minister had informed Chief Leake of the specific names among mosque members whom Mason had been hired to represent. Minister Conrad testified that he had no recollection of having passed to the police a list of names that Mason had agreed to counsel. And Chief Leake stated that, while he was informed of Mr. Mason's general representation of the mosque and its members, and had so informed his detective personnel, he could state that he never was provided a list of Mason's clients or told specifically that Hollis had retained an attorney."

In admitting the statements into evidence, Judge Bell reasoned that if Hollis had told Stewart he was a member of Mosque No. 7 and was represented by Mason, Stewart "would have been compelled to cease questioning" Hollis. "That he chose to maintain a façade of innocence by asserting his presence at a location other than the mosque cannot now be voided by his assertion of a right to counsel he failed to assert at the time," the judge ruled. "Similarly, if Mr. Mason had specifically informed the police of his representation by forwarding to them a list of his retained clients at any time after his retention on January 10th and before the phone call on the 16th, the detective would have been constrained not to place the call to Hollis. However, since neither of these events transpired, the actions by Detective Stewart in calling [Hollis] and in following up [Hollis'] initial response by asking what [Hollis] had seen at the Apollo was entirely proper."

As for Hollis' claim that the lineup was flawed and led to the misidentification of him by witnesses, the Judge Bell ruled that "the police made every effort to avoid suggestiveness in the identification process." On December 21, 1994, Hollis was convicted on the two felony charges. He was sentenced to five years probation. In April 1995, the judge denied Hollis' motion to set aside the verdict.

After an investigation into the bogus 911 call that sparked the confrontation, officials concluded that the operator and the police dispatcher failed to alert the cops that the mosque was a listed "sensitive location," and that they needed supervisors' approval to enter. Both the operator and dispatcher were disciplined.

6

The Politics of Reconciliation

Dogs who make no reply to the greeting of other dogs are guilty of an offence against good manners which the humblest dog would never pardon any more than the greatest.

—Franz Kafka, *Investigation of a Dog*

CRISIS AFTER CRISIS INVOLVING HIS BLACK constituents marked Rudy Giuliani's first eight months in office. In separate incidents during a one week period, his cops had attacked a Nation of Islam mosque and shot dead the son of a Muslim imam. Instead of calming the city, which he insisted is what he tried to do, Giuliani waxed white-hot under this baptism by fire. He began to lash out, in unambiguous rhetoric, at his legion of critics—black leaders and civil libertarians—whom he vowed would not tell him how to govern. By August of 1994, the mayor was embroiled in two new crises that once again pitted his mostly white administration against blacks and tested the limits of racial tolerance in New York City.

On August 22, transit police officers responding to a report of two black youths with guns, converged on the platform in the subway station at 53rd Street and Lexington Avenue in Manhattan. One youth dropped a shotgun, which went off. Peter DelDebbio, a white off-duty police officer, who was on his way home, saw undercover cop Desmond Robinson, who was black, and mistook him for an armed suspect. DelDebbio fired five shots. The first two crippled Robinson, sending him, as one report said, "face-down and defenseless" on the platform. DelDebbio followed up with two more shots.

David Thompson, Robinson's partner, later told investigators that DelDebbio's face was full of anger as he fired repeatedly into Robinson, adding, "I would never have thought in my wildest dreams that he was a police officer." Thompson described DelDebbio as "very angry, violent, psychotic." DelDebbio, he said, kept firing like he was shooting at "a terrorist, a bank robber," adding that the cop was "shooting with a vengeance. It wasn't like he was shooting to run for cover, like he was shooting for someone to go down. He wanted to kill that person he was shooting."

In a more damning account, reported by the *Associated Press*, Dennis Kearns, an unemployed banker from Maplewood, N.J., told police that he saw DelDebbio make Robinson lay down on his stomach, then stepped back and fired at least three shots into his back. Police Commissioner Bratton rallied to DelDebbio's defense, insisting that DelDebbio did nothing wrong. According to one report, Bratton described DelDebbio as, "highly distraught over the incident." He said DelDebbio and Robinson were "two good cops that got caught up in an awful situation."

As black cops and civil rights activists like Sharpton argued that the shooting was symptomatic of a racist overreaction to black men with guns, Rudy Giuliani signed off on a novel PR stunt to blunt the stinging criticism. Three days after the shooting, Giuliani, DelDebbio and Bratton paid an unannounced visit to Robinson in his hospital room. Some critics said they brought along the *Daily News*, which published a bedside photo of the visit with an article claiming that Robinson had forgiven DelDebbio. The stunt backfired. Robinson's lawyer, Brian O'Dwyer, accused Giuliani of staging a reconciliation with a heavily sedated Robinson, adding that Robinson barely remembered the encounter. Robinson organized his own photo-op, surrounding himself with reporters who gathered around his hospital bed. There was no forgiveness in his heart, he swore. "I couldn't see myself forgiving someone who shot me in the back."

The so-called reconciliation would be mired in controversy. Who wanted it? And Why? What really happened in that hospital room?

I never got the full picture until I read an account by Janny Scott of *The New York Times*. Scott sorted out the undisputed players in what some civil libertarians charged was a carefully orchestrated plot by Giuliani to discredit black outrage over the shooting:

> The first bedside encounter between Officers Robinson and Del-Debbio took place early Thursday in Officer Robinson's room at Bellevue Hospital Center. Three childhood friends who had been keeping Officer Robinson company said they had arranged the meeting at his request, after he had asked to see Officer Del-Debbio. Two of those friends are New York City police officers, like Officer Del-Debbio; the third is a police officer in Coral Gables, Fla. All three are white. In accounts of the bedside meeting given afterward by Officer Robinson's friends, he and Officer Del-Debbio wept and hugged. One wore a

cast, the other a hospital gown and tangle of tubes. One apologized; the other reassured. In the privacy of that room, Officer Robinson's friends said, there were no hard feelings.

Then a second meeting occurred just a few hours later. As Officer Del-Debbio was leaving the hospital to go home, he stopped by Officer Robinson's room shortly after noon. Mayor Giuliani also showed up for that encounter, as did a photographer and a reporter for *The Daily News*. When word of that meeting got out, news organizations that had been trying for days to see Officer Robinson complained to the Police Department, which then tried to organize yet another bedside visit. Mayor Giuliani was to return in the early evening and a photographer for *The Associated Press* was to capture the encounter.

But Officer Robinson's doctors stepped in. Lieut. Pete Berry, a spokesman for the Police Department, said yesterday that the photo opportunity was canceled at the last minute because a doctor had said that the officer had been sedated and was not up to another appearance. Criticism of the events came yesterday from Officer Robinson's lawyer, his family and the Guardians Association, an organization of black police officers that has said from the beginning that Officer Del-Debbio mistook Officer Robinson for a criminal because he was black.

"We witnessed a very sad day in law enforcement yesterday when the Mayor and police brass smuggled a reporter into a room of a police officer who was just removed from life support and was heavily sedated with medicine," said Eric Adams, an association official, at a news conference at City Hall.

"This is a sad day to use propaganda just to have public relations, without concerning yourself with the well-being of the officer," he said. "How far will we go just to have the right photo opportunity to send a message that everything is all right?"

Mr. O'Dwyer, the lawyer for the Robinsons, also asserted that one participant in the meetings denied reports that Officer Robinson had "forgiven" Officer Del-Debbio. A law-enforcement official identified that participant as Ray Garcia, one of the two New York City police officers, friends of Officer Robinson, who had set up the first meeting.

But Commissioner Bratton and Mr. Miller, the chief spokesman for the department, insisted yesterday that the impetus for the encounters had come from Officer Robinson. Commissioner Bratton recalled what he had seen—tears, laughter and a kiss from Officer Del-Debbio on Officer Robinson's head. Mr. Bratton said he and Mr. Miller happened to attend the first meeting simply because they were visiting Officer Del-Debbio in the hospital when Officer Robinson invited him in.

As for the second meeting, Mr. Miller had told reporters late Thursday that that he had played no part in getting the reporter and photographer into the hospital room. But yesterday, a hospital spokeswoman said that Mr. Miller had asked her early Thursday to get Officer Robinson's consent for the reporter and photographer to be present. "This was not our doing," said Vicki Ciampa, the spokeswoman. She said Officer Robinson had consented. "He knew a reporter would be there but he didn't want to be interviewed," she said. "John Miller, the Police Department, that group said he had agreed to do this."

Mr. Miller said yesterday that he had helped obtain the permission only after Officer Robinson's friends from the department told him that Officer Robinson was willing to be photographed. Mr. Miller insisted that he had not taken the initiative in getting the reporter and photographer in. Yesterday, access to Officer Robinson was severely restricted, said Lieutenant Wheeler of the transit police. He said he had been authorized by top transit police management to supervise the officers guarding Officer Robinson's room. Detective Bill Nolan, who with Officer Garcia had arranged the first bedside encounter, said at the hospital yesterday that he had found himself barred from entering by a transit police officer, who said city police officers would no longer be let in. Commissioner Bratton dismissed suggestions that tensions were developing between the transit and city police, and said the investigation into the shooting was a joint one. Neither Officer Robinson nor Officer Del-Debbio has been interviewed yet.

After the reconciliation fiasco, critics viewed Giuliani more as a conniving, manipulative, and polarizing figure rather than a racial healer. Before long, his administration would intervene in a long-running dispute between West Indians and Jews not as a mediator seeking reconciliation but as a staunch behind-the-scenes upholder of one very powerful ethnic lobby.

EVERY WEST INDIAN AMERICAN DAY CARNIVAL in New York City has its demons: There are arrests for drunkenness, brawling, and, in recent years, for scrimmages between West Indian masqueraders and the ultra-Orthodox Hasidim. In the summer of 1994, a nervous Giuliani and his administration would have been relieved if only those events occurred. The confluence of Carnival and the start of Rosh Hashanah, one of the holiest days in the Jewish calendar, ignited tensions that had been smoldering since the Crown Heights disturbances of 1991, and there were factions within both the West Indian and Lubavitch communities that were stoking the cinders for a new conflagration on Labor Day.

"There is a certain anti-Semitic element within the Caribbean parade," claimed Rabbi Joseph Spielman, influential head of the Crown Heights Jewish Community Council, the Lubavitch group who sued Dinkins over the Crown Heights rebellion and gloated over his crushing deposition. "A lot of them actually look for a synagogue to urinate on it." But Spielman feared the worst from members of his own community, whose "sensitivities will be even more acute," he said with the recent death of the sect's revered leader, Menachem Mendel Schneerson. Added to that, on Labor Day, thousands of Hasidim would be making the pilgrimage to Crown Heights, a way station for mourners heading to Montefiore Cemetery in Springfield Gardens, Queens, where the grand rebbe was buried. "We are having a lot of people, and they won't take very kindly to someone urinating on a synagogue, a house of worship," Spielman warned.

Spielman's scenario was shared within the West Indian community, whose leaders feared clashes between members of the militant Jewish Defense Organization (who said they would be present as self-appointed observers) and black nationalists grandstanding among the masqueraders. Fired NAACP head Ben Chavis, who blamed his downfall partly on "right-wing" Jewish groups, was to be one of the leaders of the parade. And among the revelers would be rude-bwoi posses, roughnecks mobilized by rumors that the Hasidim would harass wining (lasciviously gyrating) West Indian women; battle-scarred veterans of Crown Heights' '91 race war; pro- and anti-Aristide Haitians, who were threatening to bring the civil strife from Port-au-Prince onto Eastern Parkway; and activists like Sonny Carson, who had railed in '91 that it was "a shame before God that people had the audacity to party on Eastern Parkway" three weeks after a Hasidic driver had struck and killed Gavin Cato. Carson planned to lead a contingent of militant young men from the Fannie Lou Hamer Collective and the Committee to Honor Black Heroes in protest. They'd decided to unfurl banners across the Parkway in support of Lemrick Nelson, the son of Trinidadian immigrants who was accused and later convicted of killing rabbinical student Yankel Rosenbaum.

How would the Hasidim react to such placards, including slogans demanding the prosecution of Yosef Lifsh, who fled to Israel immediately after running down Cato and his cousin Angela. "It will give us a reason to have more disrespect for the black community," Spielman told me at the time. "Let's say Lifsh comes [back] and he stands trial and he's acquitted, the Caribbean community won't be happy anyway. They want to see blood."

For Spielman, this rainbow of identities and ideologies converging on Eastern Parkway was, as he put it, "another Rwanda" in the making. "You're asking for anarchy," he told me. "No rules? No law? No order? Anyone can do what they want? They can murder, loot, rob, and we should say, 'Thank you?'" The rabbi's convictions, tinged with racism, led the Hasidim to demand that Giuliani restrict Carnival, both in duration and route. Entire sections of Crown Heights where Hasidic families lived were to be off-limits to the revelers. Instead, they would have to assemble on designated side streets and proceed down the center of the parkway. Most important to the Hasidic leadership, the revelers were to be off the streets by sundown, the start of Rosh Hashanah, when thousands of members of the sect would converge at their World headquarters at 770 Eastern Parkway.

As the Hasidim's demands were leaked to the press, the masqueraders reacted as they have for centuries in the West Indies whenever authorities try to repress Carnival: They vowed to fight (In 1994, "estimates of the Caribbean population in New York City [ran] as high as 500, 000," *The New York Times* reported, adding that "the Department of Planning reported that from 1982 to 1989 153,000 people from 23 Caribbean countries moved to the city. In the 1980's, the department said, more immigrants came to New York from Jamaica than from any other country except the Dominican Republic.") As early as December 1993, Jamaican-born City Councilmember Una Clarke warned Governor Mario Cuomo that "unless immediate steps are taken to resolve this issue, our community could be plunged into a highly volatile confrontation."

Giuliani, fearing the sort of disturbances that toppled his predecessor Mayor Dinkins, sprang into action. After a series of shouting matches that stretched through summer, both sides reached a controversial agreement; Carnival, a New York tradition since the 1930s, would go on as planned, proceeding down the Parkway unimpeded, except for a small buffer zone around the Lubavitch headquarters, but would end promptly at 6 p.m. Beyond that, there was no written agreement, and police declined to say how they planned to clear an estimated 2 million festive black folks from the area by sundown. A popular refrain police would hear around quitting time was the entreating chorus of calypsonian Swallow's big hit, "One More Jam, Mr. Officer"—"People want to jump up/People want to wail/We come here to mash up/We not in jail." Deputy Mayor Fran Reiter, Giuliani's representatives in the negotiations, didn't return my phone calls, but her assistant, Marty Algaze, would say only that the mayor was "working with both communities to ease tensions and make everyone happy." Meanwhile, both sides remained dissatisfied. West Indians on black talk-radio blamed Carlos Lezama, president of the West Indian American Day Carnival Association, for agreeing to any restrictions on the parade.

"I never backed down," Lezama swore to me.

"He's telling the truth," Spielman confirmed. "Carlos gave us zilch."

Giuliani's newly-appointed Police Commissioner Ray Kelly made a call to Lezama. What Kelly wanted to talk to him about couldn't be discussed on the phone. Kelly would either come to Lezama's home in Brooklyn or send his driver to pick Lezama up and both men would meet privately in Kelly's office at One Police Plaza. "What did the police commissioner want with [me]?" Lezama remembered asking himself all the way to Kelly's office on that brutally cold day.

There was no reason not to meet with Kelly, who Lezama considered a friend of the West Indian community. The previous year, when it appeared that some masquerade bands wouldn't make it in time to the judges' reviewing stand, Lezama asked and received permission from Kelly to go an hour beyond the normal six o'clock wrapup. "Carlos, I want you to do me a favor," Lezama remembered Kelly saying. "You are going to clash with a very important high holy day in the Hasidic community. I would like you to shift the date of the parade from Labor Day, the Monday, to Sunday, so as to give the Jewish community enough time to prepare for their holy day on Tuesday."

Kelly's request wiped the puzzled look off Lezama's face. "Commissioner," he said, recovering his trademark expansive smile, "this is a very heavy weight you are putting on me right now." He paused, then asked Kelly, "Which judge in his right mind will tell our committee that we have to shift Carnival because the Jews are having their high holy day?" Shortly after their meeting, Lezama learned that a delegation from the Anti-Defamation League was the first to approach Kelly officially about the brewing conflict. Kelly responded by twisting Lezama's arm. Lezama raised the issue of shifting Carnival with his organizing committee, which emphatically rejected Kelly's request. On November 22, 13 days after their meeting, Lezama wrote a strongly worded letter to Kelly, saying that the "unprecedented request" was "reflective of the kind of blatant disrespect and utter contempt" powerful city officials have for West Indians. The request only "reinforces the prevailing perception" among the West Indians of Crown Heights that police "afford preferential treatment" to the Hasidim.

Lezama was not surprised. After all, there was a certain history with this. Three days before Carnival '91, he learned from an official within the U.S. Justice Department that Lubavitch leaders, fearing "another pogrom," quietly had explored the possibility of a court injunction against the festival. Having failed to block the celebration, the persistent Shea Hecht, another influential rabbi with whom Lezama had forged a mutual respect, and Baruch Bush, a professor of law, arrived at Lezama's doorstep early one Sunday morning, on the eve of the Labor Day Carnival. The emissaries suggested that their Hasidic security patrol, which had been involved in brutal skirmishes with black residents of Crown Heights, might help to "marshal" the massive crowd.

Citing "the behavior" of his guests and the appearance of interference in the affairs of his organization, Lezama testily refused. "I am not chasing you, but we have nothing else to talk about," he recalled telling Hecht and Bush, who left to report back to their elders. Later that evening, Lezama and one of his advisers, Bill Howard, met with a council of rabbis, "the big boys." They talked. Lezama was adamant. No Hasidic patrols at *his* Carnival. He assured them, however, that no harm would come to Jewish residents, and that Hasidic leaders, if they cared to, could meet him and the corps of West Indian community leadership at a goodwill breakfast at a bank's office on the Parkway prior to the start of Carnival.

And what about Kelly? Had he forgotten that on Carnival day, amid catcalls of "Uncle Tom" and "traitor," Lezama had pulled off one of the great feats of ethnic unity in a city that was on the verge of another racial upheaval? Carlos Lezama had saved New York City. And he reminded Kelly of that in his letter: "Our organization, acting responsibly in the immediate aftermath of the 'accidental killing' of ... Gavin Cato, and the resulting disturbance which ended the life of Yankel Rosenbaum, extended an effective olive branch to the Hasidic community ... by inviting them to march with us ... as a gesture of helping to heal the wounds, and it worked. Displacement of the parade with Rosh Hashanah ... would destroy the impact of the olive branch with dire consequences."

After Lezama's letter was published in the black press, Rabbi Spielman wrote to Kelly asking that "consideration be given to the concerns of the Jewish community" in issuing a permit to the West Indians. Carnival was under siege.

Beginning in January '94, with Giuliani in control of City Hall, Lezama would meet frequently with an interracial coalition in Brooklyn Borough President Howard Golden's office, which was trying to broker a solution. Giuliani's gung ho Deputy Mayor Reiter and black and Jewish City Councilmembers were present at one of the meetings. Also present was Spielman, spokesman for the Hasidim. "He figured that Carnival was becoming a nuisance to the Jewish community. Then he began to talk about 'the ugly things' he [said] go on during the parade," Lezama recalled. But Lezama had heard enough racially coded tough talk from the rabbi.

"Do you own Eastern Parkway?" he remembered asking Spielman.

"No," Spielman replied.

"Well, we either coexist, or forget it," was Lezama's offer.

According to Lezama, "bad blood boiled." A month later, he organized a town meeting at nearby Medgar Evers College. That meeting aroused fears with the largely West Indian audience that Lezama somehow might bow to the Hasidim's political pressures. But the old man of Carnival only hardened his resolve to play mas on Labor Day, "regardless of who vex." Other key sessions involved College President Edison Jackson and Rabbi Hecht. "But every time we met, the answer was no," Lezama recalled.

On June 17, 1994, Spielman, on behalf of the Crown Heights Jewish Community Council, wrote an inflammatory letter to Reiter, demanding the Giuliani administration regulate the parade and suggesting how to do it. One proposal was to have the city cordon off large sections of Crown Heights in Hasidim strongholds so that people attending the parade wouldn't be able to move freely in their neighborhood. The Hasidim argued that it would be easier for their guests to get to and from Montefiore Cemetery where they would pray for their departed leader. "A 'clear corridor' should be established leading from Crown Heights to the intersection of Linden Boulevard and Kings Highway, so that residents and visitors can get in and out of the community to the cemetery and the airports," Spielman urged. "Whichever route is chosen, no parking should be allowed along the route on the day of the parade.... Further, police officers should be stationed at every intersection to control and direct traffic. In doing so, they should give priority passage to vehicles traveling to and from the Jewish community."

Lesly Lempert, then president of the New York Civil Liberties Union (NYCLU), called Spielman's "clear corridor" an "ethnic corridor" that would only lead to trouble. In Jerusalem, she pointed out, where certain areas of the city regularly are closed to non-Orthodox drivers of cars and buses on the Sabbath, there had been repeated public disturbances such as stonings and riots when these vehicles attempted to drive through. Lempert warned that the Hasidim's attempt to create "ethnic corridors" would be "profoundly offensive," not only to West Indians, but to all New Yorkers. Such corridors, she said, would "establish precedents that would inevitably cause social strife," and "the demand that police differentiate between cars belonging to disparate cultural groups is simply unreasonable.... Rabbi Spielman is unfortunately confusing Brooklyn with Sarajevo where a vital city has become segregated into ethnic enclaves."

Giuliani did not agree with the NYCLU. After denying the Hasidim's request for city-owned buses and jitneys "to ferry Jewish residents" from the city's two airports to Crown Heights and to the cemetery, Giuliani, according to Spielman, acquiesced to his request for "a guaranteed route that we can get in and out." Spielman rejoiced, "We got our corridor." Said Norman Siegel, then executive director of the NYCLU, "If they do that, [it] will only exacerbate tensions."

While the Carnival leadership was preoccupied with negotiations, Giuliani's NYPD were moving on the mas camps and pan yards. For years, about a dozen of these jerry-built workshop and rehearsal spaces had been operating without interference from police. But in 1994, things changed dramatically with Giuliani's quality-of-life campaign. Cops armed with noise meters began monitoring and cracking down on the mas camps and pan yards.

Chief Michael Markman, Commander of Patrol Borough Brooklyn South, that covered the 67th Precinct, called the mini raids "Strategy Number Five." Barbecue grills were doused by fire trucks, West Indians were rounded up for urinating in public, and the three largest mas camps were briefly shut down. "We'd been operating for the five years under the same conditions, with the same noise levels, trying to make a dollar," said Kevin "Fuzzy" Davis. "We never had a problem with Lindsay, Beame, Koch or Dinkins. "Now every mas camp had a problem."

In the early-morning hours of July 29, John Findley, an official of Borokeete U.S.A. who was given two summonses for blasting calypso music, saw several fire trucks pull up at the corner of Church and Nostrand in the Flatbush section, a hub of the West Indian community. "They put up flares. They issued a summons. They arrested the president of Borokeete"—all to douse the barbecue grills, Findlay recounted. The firefighters came in for plenty *mamaguy* (heckling) from the angry crowd. The police and firefighters were responding to what detectives at the 67th Precinct claimed were complaints from unnamed elected officials about massive crowds and noise. What they didn't understand was the purpose of the late-night *liming* (hanging out). It's a pre-Carnival ritual.

"[W]ith Carnival coming," as Trinidadian Earl Lovelace explained in *The Dragon Can't Dance,* a novel about the politics of Carnival in an urban ghetto of Port of Spain, "radios go on full blast, trembling these shacks, booming out calypsos, the songs that announce in this season the new rhythms for people to walk in, rhythms that climb over the red dirt and stone, break-away rhythms that laugh through the groans of these sights, these smells, that swim through the bones of these enduring people so that they shout: Life! They cry: Hurrah! They drink a rum and say: Fuck it!"

Cecil Mitchell, coordinator of Hawks International, another huge mas camp, said that membership, normally around 3,000 when people would come out to preview the costumes, had dwindled because of "intimidation" by Giuliani's police. "They made us shut the music down," Mitchell said. "They wanted nobody on the sidewalks, everybody should go home. It was rough. The people got scared of being arrested and stopped coming out. A lot of them were convinced that there [wasn't] going to be Carnival [that] year." Another target of the police was J'Ouvert City, an organization representing the steelbands, the first icons of Carnival to appear on the streets, sometimes as early as 3 a.m., to herald the start of J'Ouvert, the dawn opening of Carnival.

Since there was no way to tone down the scintillating sound of live steelband music, police impounded some of the drums. "They didn't understand the meaning of the J'Ouvert celebrations," said Earl King, president of J'Ouvert City. Other problems persisted. Liability insurance was hard to come by and costly, jumping from $6000 to $67,000 in 1993—prompting Lezama himself to call a bluff: No Carnival. That would have meant more than $50 million in lost revenues to the city and a tremendous political backlash. Mayor Dinkins and Governor Mario Cuomo intervened and Carnival went on as scheduled.

Thinking that the uproar over Mosque No. 7 and the killing of the Imam's son had subsided, Giuliani ventured out for the ceremonial walk of politicians and dignitaries prior to the start of Carnival. As planned, Giuliani, along with Sharpton (who was running for the U.S. Senate), Cuomo, other political hopefuls, and more than a hundred leaders of the Caribbean community, crowded a pre-parade breakfast at a social club at Utica Avenue and Eastern Parkway, *The New York Times* reported. Giuliani's attempt to waylay Carnival was a crushing personal defeat; his very presence at the breakfast spoke volumes: It was a desperate attempt to reconcile, testimony to the burgeoning political clout of West Indians in Crown Heights. "It's true we have to get to know each other better," said Giuliani, embracing West Indian leaders while not betraying his own hand in trying to disrupt their Carnival. "My success as mayor has a lot to do with your success as a community," he added. Amid jeers and boos and chants of "Giuliani, you can't stop Carnival!" and "You want to give Crown Heights to the Jews!" Giuliani led the parade, smiling, waving, and shaking some outstretched hands.

With the Carnival controversy behind him, Giuliani once more focused on existing tensions between his NYPD and the black community: Could relations get any worse?

ON THE MORNING OF OCTOBER 1, 1994, Rudy Giuliani, under heavy police escort, strode somber-faced into Herbert Daughtry's House of the Lord Pentecostal Church in the Boerum Hill section of Brooklyn. To ensure a smooth welcome, Giuliani had called ahead, pleading, not with Daughtry, but with the family of Nicholas Heyward Jr., a 13-year-old boy who was gunned down 12 days earlier by another one of Giuliani's police officers. The family gave Giuliani the all clear to attend the funeral.

A church matron ushered Giuliani into Daughtry's office, where the mayor took notice of an imposing portrait of his predecessor on a wall festooned with other revered political and spiritual leaders. "You don't have to worry," quipped Daughtry, breaking the solemnity with a touch of levity. "You're not dreaming, you really are the mayor." Giuliani said Dinkins' photo didn't bother him; he was just in awe of Daughtry having posed with Pope John Paul II and Jesse Jackson. "At that point he had not met with the Pope or Jesse," Daughtry said.

Then the activist pastor's history with the federal prosecutor came flooding back. "I reminded him that when he was the U.S. Attorney for the Eastern District I'd come to him to seek indictments of police officers who had violated the civil rights of black people," recalled Daughtry. "I told him that I remember asking him to look into the case of Michael Stewart, the graffiti artist who was choked to death in a subway station by white cops, and the case of subway vigilante Bernard Goetz, who shot those four black boys." Daughtry told me that Giuliani was "always cordial, always accessible," but never did anything to help his cause. "I reminded him that I had been on this pursuit of justice for many years," added the preacher, who recalled Giuliani nodding in agreement. "I said, 'I'm still on the case, still pursuing justice for people unlawfully killed.'"

On the night of September 20, while on patrol in the Gowanus Houses in the Boerum Hill section of Brooklyn, housing Police Officer Brian George allegedly responded to several reports of shots fired from rooftops in the housing development. Police said George encountered Nicholas, an honor student, who was in the 14th-floor stairwell of a building, playing cops and robbers with friends. George, reportedly mistaking Nicholas' toy gun for the real thing, pumped one shot into the boy's abdomen. Brooklyn D.A. Charles Hynes, concluding that the shooting was not intentional, did not present the case to a grand jury. George was not charged in Nicholas' death.

"It was first told to me that the ... stairwell was dimly lit; the officer heard a clicking sound in the stairwell; he fired into [the] dimly lit stairwell and he hit Nicholas in the abdomen," said Nicholas Heyward Sr. in an interview with Carl Dix of the October 22nd Coalition to Stop Police Brutality, Repression and the Criminalization of a Generation. "Nicholas died 8 hours later. My son was playing with a toy gun, a plastic cork pop gun. It was called pop gun; it was one [of] them plastic guns you put the corks into it. You cock it and you squeeze it, and the corks pop out of it. And it looks nothing like a real gun. It was plastic with orange stripes."

Heyward said that on learning that Nicholas had been shot, Angela Heyward "ran up 14 flights of stairs to try to comfort her son." He said she was prevented from seeing him by a cop who doubted her relationship to the victim. "They rushed Nicholas out the other exit while the officer was talking to my wife and they took Nicholas not to the hospital six blocks away, but [to one in] Manhattan," Heyward charged. "He died there. The district attorney ... basically blamed the killing on a realistic looking toy gun and said that the officer feared for his life."

Appearing to head off criticism he was too quick to defend cops involved in alleged police brutality, Giuliani tried the softer approach and reached out to the Heyward family. Dennis Hevesi of *The New York Times* said about 1,000 mourners packed into Daughtry's historic church and didn't seem to mind or care that the symbol of their fears was among them:

> The mourners seemed to have come to the church more with bewilderment than bitterness, and the Mayor was welcomed politely at the service. "I just ask you to consider that Nicholas's death now says something to an entire city," the Mayor said. "It says that the prejudices and stereotypes of youngsters are exactly that, prejudices and stereotypes." Speaking first as a father, the Mayor turned to the boy's parents, Nicholas Sr. and Angela, and said: "All New Yorkers share your pain, grieve with you. But it is particularly parents who understand some of what you are suffering."
>
> The fear of losing a child "renders parents speechless and senseless," he said, "because when you give complete love you are completely vulnerable."
>
> "I share with you the unifying belief that the only solace of this loss, if there is any, is the recognition that all of us are children of the same God," Mr. Giuliani continued. "Sadly, we live in a nation that is riddled with guns. Getting the guns off the streets is critical. But most of all, we need to pray to God to find a way to love each other more."
>
> With the light of a misty morning reaching through the stained-glass windows and playing off the dark green sheen of the casket before him, Mr. Daughtry said he found "something just incredibly strange, unreal, about children being killed by the people we pay to protect us."

It didn't matter to Daughtry that the cop who killed young Nicholas Heyward was black. "I told the mayor directly in my speech that day, 'I am still pursuing cops who unjustifiably kill," he said. The Heywards sued the city. "In a deposition done on the officer about two years after the killing," recalled the father, "the officer stated that he was not on [a] 911 call; that he was just basically on routine patrol; that the stairway was not dimly lit; that he was able to see very well, and that things did not happen in a split second, which was all of [D.A.] Charles Hynes' reasoning for closing the case and not presenting it to a grand jury."

PART III

Giuliani-Style Justice and the Return of Black Rage (1995–1997)

in memory of
Carl W. Thomas

7

A Time to Kill

When a political leader calls a mass meeting, we may say that there is blood in the air. Yet the same leader very often is above all anxious to "make a show" of force, so that in fact he need not use it. But the agitation which ensues, the coming and going, the listening of speeches, seeing the people assembled in one place, with the police all around … demonstrations, arrests … all this hubbub makes the people think that the moment has come for them to take action.

—Frantz Fanon, *The Wretched of The Earth*

THE PEOPLE, SOME 300 OF THEM, BEGAN TO MASS IN THE streets of East Flatbush a little shy of 4 o'clock on the afternoon of June 13, 1996. By 6 o'clock a surging crowd had converged on Church Avenue between East 34th and East 35th streets—a square block crammed with Haitian dollar-van taxis, West Indian roti shops, Korean fruit stands and Chinese restaurants—listening to ghetto disturbance rhetoric, thinking that the moment had come to take action. Word on the avenue was that three white undercover cops had gunned down a "foreign" (West Indian immigrant) like a rabid dog in his 1991 white Honda Accord outside of Chen's Kitchen. In the rapid-fire orgy of Glock 9-millimeter revolvers, 18 bullets had riddled the man's body.

As darkness descended, scores of residents from this largely West Indian working-class community in Brooklyn came wearily up from the subway station at Church and Nostrand only to be greeted by grim-faced newsmongers weaving a tale of summary execution and directing those fascinated by death to gawk at the killing ground. By 7 o'clock that night, "hoodshock"—the psychological trauma a black community experiences after violent conflict with authorities—had progressed to a tense standoff with cops poised to cosh their tormentors.

Feeling the pressure, Assistant Chief George Brown, commanding officer of Patrol Brooklyn South, reached out to City Councilmember Una Clarke, a warm, unpretentious woman with powerful emotions. When she got the call from the 67th Precinct, Clarke, a Jamaican-born naturalized American, was in the studios of *NY1* in Manhattan railing against the Giuliani administration's draconian budget cuts. Cops knew that black elected officials like Clarke could play an important role, especially in a crisis: Can she come to the Snyder Avenue stationhouse at once? She studied the implications of the commander's harried briefing, at times flashing back to the 1990 boycott of Korean greengrocers on Church Avenue.

Bitterness lingered on, but East Flatbush was infinitely more complicated. A younger generation of Jamaicans, the dominant immigrant population, had come to view police as a symbol of a repressive political state, now that the number of illegal Jamaican refugees and convicts being rounded up and sent back to their homeland had increased. ("Ruud bwai an' poliis a no fren," reggae dancehall ruler Shabba Ranks puts it.) Clarke knew the situation had to be addressed soon. Events surrounding the shooting in her district, which also covers Flatbush and parts of Crown Heights, were moving like a runaway train and the fuel that fed its engine was the combustible rhetoric of Black Rage.

At the 67th Precinct, Clarke was met by Assistant Chief Brown, other high-ranking officers from One Police Plaza, and the captain of the stationhouse. Police told her that the victim she would come to know as Keshwan Aswan Watson was suspected of carjacking the Honda at gunpoint on May 20 in Forest Hills, Queens; that when three undercover cops from the 67th's anti-crime unit spotted the car, they waited for the perpetrator to arrive; that when Watson got in, they blocked his car with theirs, got out, identified themselves and approached; that two of the three cops fired 24 shots into the vehicle when Watson reached under the seat; that the cops opened fire because they thought he was reaching for a gun; that after the shooting, they discovered Watson was wanted in the February 1 murder of a friend, Rory Ridley; and that Watson's photo had been published in the *Daily News* in April in a story on New York's most-wanted suspects; and one other thing, the gun they thought he was reaching for turned out to be a Club anti-theft device.

"Show me what you have to prove that it was a stolen car," Clarke recalled demanding of the authorities. Clarke said police told her that they ran a check on the Honda's license plate to prove that the vehicle had been reported stolen and followed up with a check of the address on the California license Watson had on him. "There was no such address in Los Angeles," she remembered a cop telling her. That's when Clarke concluded that Watson's bogus address "gave them license to promulgate a story about the car itself." But she kept that opinion to herself.

The smug-faced law-enforcement officials intimated to Clarke that there were many opinions about who was to be blame for the shooting, but their preliminary investigation—although stymied by a police union rule that rendered the officers mute for 48hours—showed that the undercover cops killed the fidgety suspect in self defense. Clarke understood the inference to mean that Watson committed "suicide by cops," meaning that he forced police to shoot him. She felt she could no longer maintain her role as an impartial listener and offered a purely common-sense argument: "If this was two bullets, or three bullets, I could justify it to the community that one was a [stray bullet. But not 24 bullets. Cops are trained to take escapees. They've stayed in Montana for 81 days to get the militia (Freemen) out. What is the difference between this and that? It's uncalled for. It's unnecessary."

In an awful rush to calm residents, some of the brass, hands knotted around their stomachs, nodded in agreement. Reports were filtering in: the rage had peaked on Church Avenue. Clarke interrupted the debriefing and left the stationhouse troubled by what she viewed as inconsistencies in the police version, but more concerned that she might not be able to stop violence. With all the talk of blood in the air, how could she walk the scaffold without a safety net?

The brass tagged along as the councilwoman and four aides raced to Church Avenue, a mere four blocks away from the stationhouse. "Here is Una Clarke! This is our Una Clarke! Tell the people what you're gonna do!" an excited protester in tatty clothes shouted. The Klieg lights of the TV cameras put the spotlight on her, panning the crowd only briefly to illuminate taut faces on the threshold of violent expression. "The people were really in a rage," Clarke recalled. When her appeals for calm were drowned out in a cacophony of angry voices, a sidewalk evangelist, seeing the people assembled in one place, pressed a bullhorn into her hands and hoisted the heavyweight politician on his shoulder.

High above the fray, she bellowed: "I am Una Clarke! I'm one of the representatives for this community, and whatever justice we're seeking we're gonna get!" What happened next to the councilwoman might best be described as a nonviolent moshing, a ritual at rock concerts in which, according to a *People* magazine article, frenzied fans "are plucked off their feet and sent soaring above the crowd. Then, just as suddenly, they are dropped to the floor." The mosh pit on Church Avenue was an impenetrable circle of intoxicated individuals who acted more like they were on a "red-rum" high. "When I leave here, I'm gonna call the Civilian Complaint Review Board to look into the background of these cops," Clarke vowed, starting in motion a moshing that sent her "body-surfing on a wave of extended arms." ("For about 20 minutes they were passing me from shoulder to shoulder," she recalled.)

When Clarke announced that she would contact Brooklyn District Attorney Charles Hynes, a top police official shouted that Hynes' assistants were already on their way to the 67th. "I wanna make sure that he remains independent of what the police is going to do," Clarke shot back, engaging the police in a colloquy. Clarke demanded that the cops involved in the shooting never return to East Flatbush because their presence would "enrage the people [even] more."

Some hotheads were arguing that Clarke was being too diplomatic with the police and threatened to trash and set afire the stinking Dumpsters left outside the shuttered stores. "Una-bummer! Una-suspect!" they chanted. Clarke counterargued that the community was beginning to see a black-inspired economic revival and cautioned the protesters against jackassery: "This is our community. Our people have come when everybody else abandoned [it]. We have bought these old buildings, we have reconstructed them. This is our home." (Clarke was alluding to the lack of affordable housing in the East New York section of Brooklyn and a rash of arson fires there that she suspected were set by black activists who had Jewish landlords of jacking up rents.)

"The people you thought you burnt out are still in Florida enjoying their retirement. Same thing with these cops," she shouted into the bullhorn. "When you have all your rage and tear up your community, they will be going back to Orange County, Suffolk County and Nassau County, where they come from. Tomorrow morning they will be watering their lawns and laughing at you and a burnt-up community, knowing that we may never get the money to fix them again. So think about it."

WHEN THE DEMAND FOR SWIFT JUSTICE IN THE KILLING OF Aswan Watson became mired in a foot-dragging analysis of when Black Rage is justified and when it is not, a number of the city's black community activists began to inquire openly about how far blacks were willing to go in their response to lethal police violence. Leaders of two black ultra-nationalist groups, the December 12th Movement and the New York Black Panther Collective, advocated that blacks should consider armed struggle if the NYPD continued to trample their constitutional, human, and civil rights.

The jingoism intensified on June 19, when police shot and killed 37-year-old Steve Excell, a Jamaican Rasta, as he fled from his home while being chased by cops in Queens. Police from the 103rd precinct were responding to a 911 call alleging that Excell had assaulted his wife with an electrical cord. Family members and neighbors said that after Excell was captured, a police officer shot him in the back of the head when he attempted to run away barefoot and handcuffed. The medical examiner determined that Excell died from "a bullet that entered the right side back of the head."

Sixteen days later, on Independence Day, Police Officer Paolo Colecchia shot 26-year-old Nathaniel Levi Gaines Jr. in the back of the head on a Bronx subway platform. A woman had complained to police that Gaines, a Navy veteran and part-time highway toll taker, was stalking her. As in the case of Aswan Watson, all of the victims were black and unarmed. All of the police officers accused of cold-blooded murder were white.

"'Kill a nigger a day' is the secret code," the December 12th Movement charged in a July 17 communiqué purporting to explain the anguish that ultimately drove black nationalists to consider armed struggle against the police. "Death squads speak to our existence in a state of war," the communiqué said.

Amnesty International, the London-based human-rights watchdog group, had issued a report in late June that fell short of comparing the NYPD to a Third World death squad. The report, titled, "United States of America: Police Brutality and Excessive Force in the New York City Police Department," seemed to corroborate what the black nationalists and other civil-rights monitors had been alleging all along: Police killings and ill treatment of black, Latino and Asian suspects had reached intolerable and epidemic proportions. The report detailed about 100 alleged cases of abuse, including deaths in custody and excessive use of force and unjustified shootings by police, from the late 1980s to early 1996. The vast majority of victims were black or Latino; the vast majority of alleged offender-cops were white.

"Amnesty's report only touches the tip of the iceberg," the December 12th Movement communiqué said. "The NYPD has been running amuck for years—harassment and intimidation, illegal searches and seizures, drug selling and gun running, criminalization of our movement, beating of Black women, helicopter night surveillance, rooftop sharpshooters. Overkill is the order of the day in Black and Latino communities."

Despite an investigation by the City Council in March that year, cops allegedly continued to pounce on black teenage boys and haul them off against their will to stand as fillers in police lineups without permission from their parents. They also had been accused of illegally stopping and interrogating West Indian immigrants in Brooklyn and sassing prominent black New Yorkers. The Reverend Calvin O. Butts III, pastor of Abyssinian Baptist Church in Harlem and an adviser to Governor George Pataki, complained of being pulled over by a discourteous uniformed cop and often being menaced by undercover police in black Chevy Impalas while driving late at night in the inner city.

"You don't really know if they are police or not, because oftentimes they jump out of the cars and don't identify themselves," said Butts, referring to the plainclothes officers. "You can have any group of white men driving around Harlem who may not be police jump out, call you nigger [or] any name [or] curse at you. They'd push around some black kid, who [might] not be a drug dealer, or a criminal, under the guise that they're protecting the community and nobody will challenge them."

Cries of outrage also emanated from the Grand Council of Guardians, a fraternal organization of black police officers, who had asked then-U.S. Attorney General Janet Reno to launch a federal investigation into the killing of Aswan Watson and Steve Excell, and the wider issue of police brutality.

"They are shooting us down in the streets," Guardians chair, Charles Billups, charged. "What's next? Are they going to kill our babies as we carry them down the street?"

"This is the daily reality facing Blacks," the December 12th Movement communiqué asserted, adding that "nothing short of a hostile armed conflict between a fascist occupying police force and two million ex-slaves who have yet to heed the call of 'Freedom or Death'" in New York City will stop the killings and brutality.

Their call—at a time that black militia groups were in the news—ignited the hottest debate in black communities from New York City to Dallas since the quarrel over Nation of Islam-led Million Man March.

Chants like—"Burn, Baby, Burn!" "By Any Means Necessary!" and "Black Power!" the most popular rallying cries of black liberation groups in the '60s and '70s—were enjoying a revival. But some, Butts, were accused of throwing gasoline on smoldering embers from their moral high ground. Butts said he was only articulating the moral precepts of self-defense.

"About 20 years ago or more now, the Black Panther Party was established for self-defense," he explained. "And I think that the Panthers, because of the growing and vicious incidents of police brutality, served notice on police departments in New York, California and especially Chicago, that our community would no longer tolerate the verbal and physical humiliation of our people. This in my mind was not a bad thing—when you consider what some police officers were doing. Until the mayor, the [district attorneys] and the police commissioner set some examples on the issue of police brutality, we have no other alternative but to defend ourselves, the honor of our women, and our young people."

A crackdown on "quality-of-life" crimes—begging, graffiti, turnstile-jumping, urinating in public, playing loud music, littering, loitering—had led to an increase in complaints of overzealous law enforcement. While Butts said he wasn't "one who is soft on street ruffians" and other hard-core criminals, he wouldn't condone the flagrant use of brutal force to get rid of them. "When people who are innocent are randomly subjected to this kind of force [and] the authorities won't police the police, then organizations like the Black Panthers and others would not only rise and become prominent, but unfortunately they would be necessary," he told me.

The Black Panther Collective, operating of a storefront in Harlem, claimed it represented "a resurgence of interest in the Black Panther Party." The Collective said it was "committed to both self-defense and armed struggle"—the true legacy of the Black Panther Party.

"We absolutely have to prepare ourselves to defend ourselves against our protectors. We've said that since the time of the Black Panther Party," Kwame Ture, the late leader of the All African People's Revolutionary Party, often told me. In the '60s, Ture, then Stokely Carmichael, coined and popularized the slogan, "Black Power." Ture was a leader of Student Nonviolent Coordinating Committee from 1967 to 1969, when he quit in protest of the organization's willingness to ally itself with white radicals. Shortly afterward he left the United States and went to live in Guinea.

In New York City undergoing treatment for prostate cancer that would later claim his life Ture explained to me that with or without armed struggle, the masses always are ready to combat police tyranny. The "seasoned leadership" of the December 12th Movement, he said, "have chosen the path of revolution, which means it's going to be difficult and bloody." But surprisingly, one of the first moves against police tyranny would come from black cops. That August, the Grand Council of Guardians, the *New York Post* reported, "threw down the gauntlet to City Hall and the Police Department." From then on, any its 30,000 members statewide witnessing acts of brutality would arrest fellow cops, the organization said. "We have hearing after hearing and nothing is done. It's time now, whether you [are] white or black. Lock that cop up if he commits brutality," urged spokesman Ozzie Thompson.

Angry black masses storming One Police Plaza with rifles and shotguns was self-deluding, some said. Nation of Islam leader Louis Farrakhan rejected armed confrontation outright as a solution and urged people to shun controversial figures he believed were inciting violence and racial hatred. Farrakhan was referring to one of his own, Khallid Abdul Muhammad, his former national spokesman who he rebuked in 1994. Snubbed by moderate civil rights activists who denied him a platform to advocate his Pan Africanist and Black Power views, Khallid aligned himself with the December 12th Movement, urging "a summit or a sacred covenant with all the militant, radical niggas in America, the ones who don't give a damn about the white man."

His call for a "state-of-the-race conference by the NAABP National Association for the Advancement of Black People)" would include former gang leaders of the Vice Lords, the Disciples, the Crips, the Bloods, the Five Percent Nation and the Black Hebrews—"the ones that stand on the corner of 44th and Broadway and call a cracker a cracker."

Khallid recently had returned from Dallas where he was advising a group called the New Black Panther Party in their dispute with the local school board. Blacks there were complaining bitterly about white leadership of the board, which controlled a predominantly black district. The dispute came to a head at a May 23 board meeting, when three NBPP members were arrested for refusing to sit down. Khallid was invigorated by the boldness of the '60s-style radicals who would walk around with loaded shotguns and rifles to protect themselves and their communities from undue police interference. But Farrakhan reportedly became furious when he learned that that a small group of Nation of Islam members, flanked by the NBPP and led by Khallid, had stormed into the Texas town of Greenville, pledging to protect black churches after two arson fires there.

Farrakhan reportedly confided in a tight circle of Fruit of Islam bodyguards that Khallid was gaining momentum and won't back down but "the enemy is blood-thirsty and there could be a bloodbath. If he's not careful, the brother could lose his life, and those Black Panthers, Crips, Bloods, whatever gang members that are coming up around him could lose their lives."

It was a different Louis Farrakhan in 1990, who rallied to the defense of radical Milwaukee Alderman Michael McGee. The black activist politician had established the Black Panther Community Militia to use violence if conditions for blacks in Milwaukee did not improve by 1995. "People have focused on his words and tried to make it seem as though he's radical and crazy rather than focusing on the conditions that caused him to speak such words," Farrakhan said about McGee at the time.

A Brooklyn community leader, and ally in several black activist camps invoked the Reverend Martin Luther King Jr.'s philosophy of nonviolence, asserting that it was a tried and tested method of achieving civil rights for blacks.

"But the overriding experience of the black American has been grief and sorrow and no man can change that fact," William H. Grier and Price M. Cobbs argued in their book, *Black Rage*, published in 1968.

The black psychiatrists explored the consequences of anger they detected in blacks after years of racial stress. "We want to emphasize yet again the depth of the grief for slain sons and ravished daughters, how deep and lingering it is," they wrote. If a black man harbors grief as a result of racial injustice, his rage, allowed to fester, will boil over and implode.

"As grief lifts and the sufferer moves toward health," Grier and Cobbs discovered, "the hatred he had turned on himself is redirected toward his tormentors, and the fury of his attack on the one who caused him pain in direct proportion to the depth of his grief. When the mourner lashes out in anger, it is a relief to those who love him, for they know he has now returned to health."

When Colin Ferguson allegedly purged himself of the pain of experiencing white racism in the United States, the unemployed Jamaican immigrant opened fire on a Long Island Rail Road train on December 7, 1993. Six people, mostly whites, were killed and 19 others wounded by hollow-point bullets from Ferguson's semiautomatic weapon. Although he admitted, "I've done a bad thing," Ferguson became the poster boy of Black Rage but rejected the theory as an insanity defense at trial.

The debate keeps coming back to a central question: How much more pain must blacks endure?

The answer engulfed, if not pitted against each other, attorneys Ron Kuby and Norman Siegel, two of New York City's staunchest civil-rights advocates, who happen to be white.

"At this point, I am so frustrated that I almost think it's going to come down to a Los Angeles-type of situation before there's any real change, I really do," said Kuby.

"That makes no sense," said Siegel a relentless critic of the NYPD. "The way to combat police brutality is through the legal system, to hold police accountable for their wrongdoing. Any options of using violence should be totally rejected."

Although groups like the Black Panther Collective would use "revolutionary propaganda tactics to expose and neutralize the enemy's current 'Pro-Police,' 'Hero Cop' and 'Officer Friendly' promotions" (tactics similar to the Black Panther Party's campaign to discredit the cops' "Pigs Are Beautiful" and "Hug A Hog Today" campaigns in the '70s), a "Black Death" for "the White Pig" remains not an option, but a rite of black nationalist retribution.

White KKKops Are The Enemy, a 24-page pamphlet issued by an anonymous militant group, called for a bloody uprising against the NYPD. It was as virulent, if not more explicit, than *The Turner Diaries.* "It is to be that whenever a cop comes into our community a sniper is to go upon (sic) top of a roof and have a long range shooting camera with a silencer, aimed at the head of the officer(s)," the pamphlet instructed. "If they kill someone, they must be taken on the spot. If they hurt someone, they must leave treated twice as bad. We must be cruel to those that have been cruel to us. Let us all help to remind them that what goes around comes around."

In this apocalyptic vision of armed struggle, white sympathizers of brutal cops would cower in fear of the brutality of the black avenger. "The streets of Amerikkka will overflow with the blood and stench of white men, women and children," the authors of the pamphlet predicted. "Many whites will start committing suicide because the suffering and pain that will be issued upon them will be too much for them to bear. Imagine Amerikkka in chaos, terrorists placing bombs in every city and large buildings, poisoning the water source that quenches their thirst, taking white pregnant women and plunging knives into their stomachs, burning their children at the stake, hanging their old men on branches of trees, cutting off their limbs, and beating them bitterly, just wanting to wipe them off the face of the earth."

The city's ultra-nationalist black movement was considered dormant after the FBI-inspired dissolution of groups like the Black Panther Party, the Revolutionary Action Movement and the Black Liberation Army in the '60s and '70s. But a fierce wind of revolution blew over the city on October 18, 1984, heralding the advent of the New York 8. The eight were arrested in a predawn raid when some 500 FBI agents and police officers swept through their Brooklyn safehouse, seized weapons and rounded up suspects who allegedly were plotting crimes as a continuation of criminal activities of an earlier group that committed a Brinks armored car robbery in Rockland County on October 20, 198. A guard and two police officers were slain.

A federal indictment charged that the eight were associated "for the purpose of committing prison escapes." But the black radicals argued that they were only involved in constitutionally protected political activities and that extensive surveillance of them did not turn up any criminal activity. In 1985, all eight were acquitted of racketeering, conspiring to commit murder, kidnapping, arson, bank holdups, armored car robberies and bombings to free fellow radicals from jail. All but Viola Plummer, the svelte queen mother of "Black Rage" and a key lieutenant in the December 12th Movement, also were convicted of weapons-possession charges.

In 1987, after the New York 8 joined forces with the Black Men's Movement Against Crack (BMMAC), Benjamin Ward, the city's first black police commissioner, accused some of its members of plotting to assassinate him. The anti-drug organization, led by Sonny Carson, is a quasi street-fighter brigade who gave riot cops an Excedrin headache the last time they clashed in the summer of 1989. The group was leading a "Day of Outrage and Mourning" in Brooklyn that shut down subways and the Brooklyn Bridge. More than 40 cops were hurt in a confrontation when they tried to prevent about 10,000 protesters from marching onto the roadway leading to the bridge. That march was held to protest the racial killing of 17-year-old Yusuf Hawkins in Bensonhurst section of Brooklyn and the "assassination" in Los Angeles of Huey Newton, former minister of defense of the '60s Black Panther Party.

The December 12th Movement remained adamant about the ultimate throwdown with the nation's largest police force and its former commander in chief Rudy Giuliani, the former federal prosecutor who'd sought to convict them. Giuliani had been suppressing usual accusations of police oppression of blacks more boldly than ever before. "We've noticed that Mayor Giuliani cares more about these murderers (kkkops) than he cares about Black people," the militants behind the mystery pamphlet said. "We have no love or respect for him, so f—k him and his kkkops, they'll all suffer in due time." Ironically, the self-avowed coldblooded cop killers are not threatening Giuliani with assassination: if he must die, it would be by the ballot, not the bullet. "The mayor is a hypocrite, thus we must make sure that his days are cut much shorter than he had planned when election time comes. We have studied his actions and reactions. We have judged him like God, and he must be put out of office for intentionally ignoring the crimes that white kkkops have done to our people," the widely circulated pamphlet said.

Basking in the enormous national spotlight that accompanied back-to-back arrests of some of the city's most wanted felons, Giuliani and Police Commissioner Safir, seemed emboldened about touting an assault on disruptive black dissent.

The New York Times reported at the end of May that Chief of Department Louis Anemone on April 29 wrote a memo detailing an ambitious plan to "flood" Harlem's busiest thoroughfare, 125th Street, with cops and federal agents to fight crime. Anemone's plan, which Giuliani and Safir denied approving, also was intended to "blunt criticism of the administration by black politicians."

"With [his] prosecutor mentality, we might wake up one morning in a police state—nobody's got any rights, and you got a dictator ruling your city," said Butts. "I'm very serious about this thing. I don't like the tone of it," the preacher added.

"In some quarters of the Giuliani administration black dissent is a euphemism for crime," said Sharpton, Giuliani's main black political nemesis at the time.

The December 12th Movement competed with Giuliani for the black community's attention. Well-placed black nationalist sources told me the December 12th Movement had begun to offer self-defense training to black youths. The recruits were to be trained by the Odinga Carson Brigade to be a new breed of so-called "shocktivists," the shock troops of militant action.

In the '60s, blacks were committed to one solution to winning respect "and that was 'burn baby, burn!' "according to Carson. "It wasn't a rare sight to turn a corner and see an automobile on its back, burning, with the tires revolving," he recalled.

Carson, whose autobiography *The Education of Sonny Carson*, a story about his rebellious life that was made into a movie in the '70s, said that there was "no other alternative but to return to the movement that caused police and everybody else to show respect for us in the black community."

Some elements within the black nationalist community favored the reactivation of the feared Black Liberation Army (BLA) as a warning to the NYPD that blacks would not tolerate any more attacks. ("Our soldiers must find every white KKKop that has killed a black youth, make examples out of them and their families," the unidentified black nationalists argued. "This is drastic, but it will make us heroes in the eyes of our people and avengers of our ancestors.")

In the 1970s, the Federal Bureau of Investigation, which had launched a counterintelligence program (COINTELPRO) against "black nationalist hate groups," warned the NYPD that the BLA planned to kill one cop every month. Black liberation leaders insisted they had moral reasons for targeting cops. From 1970 to 1973, 248 alleged suspects were killed by New York City police. Seventy-three percent of them were black (52 percent) and Latino (21 percent), and 10 percent were white, according to a 1974 study conducted by the Metropolitan Applied Research Center (The MARC Corporation). White cops killed a total of 96 blacks and Latinos during this period; 27 black and 12 Latino victims were under the age of 21.

"There is a permeating racial and ethnic discriminatory pattern in these police killings," the late sociologist Kenneth B. Clark complained in a September 17, 1974 letter to Mayor Abe Beame and Police Commissioner Michael J. Codd. Clark's letter introduced the officials to The MARC Corporation preliminary report, "An Analysis of 248 Persons Killed by New York City Policemen: 1970–1973."

"Something must be done immediately to reverse this outrage," Clark pleaded. He ended his letter with the prediction that the shootings would "contribute to that level of frustration and rage in the minority community which increase the chance of collective destructiveness; increase the possibility of mind-less, even though self-destructive, crimes; and retaliations against the police."

But the police killings of blacks and Latinos continued disproportionately. "From 1979 to present, there have been twenty-seven killings perpetrated by the NYPD which were under suspicious circumstances," Dave Walker of the Black United Front wrote to Governor Hugh Carey on March 6, 1981, pleading for the appointment of a special prosecutor to investigate the alarming trend. "Twenty-six of these killings were of blacks or Latinos by white officers.... Six people have been killed in the last five months. This year to date, 22 civilians, eight of them fatally have been shot by city police. Last year 126 persons were shot, 28 of them fatally."

Based on cases researched by the now-defunct New York City chapter of the Black United Front, a House judiciary subcommittee held two hearings on police brutality in New York City in the fall of 1983. Black community leaders pressed for the hearings, alleging, as the subcommittee put it, "questionable arrests by police, use of racial epithets and unwarranted use of physical force were becoming the norm."

GARY YEUNG, AN IMMIGRANT FROM HONG KONG, was the co-owner of Louisiana Fried Chicken, which in less than two years had become one of the more popular fast-food joint in East Flatbush. Yeung had hired Aswan Watson in June 1995 as a $6-an-hour general laborer. Watson worked 10 hours a day and was never late. Though he "acted, one or two times, stupid," Yeung knew that Watson wasn't the dope-dealing, gangsta-type. "Why would he want to work here for nine, ten hours a day? For what?" He trusted Watson enough to work the cash register on busy days. "I could depend on him," he said.

When Watson told Yeung he'd enrolled in a G.E.D. program to get his high school equivalency certificate, Yeung, who had a master's degree in business administration, promised to help pay Watson's way through Medgar Evers Col-lege. "Just do your job here; keep up the good work," Yeung advised his employee. The businessman treated Watson like a member of his own family. "We have a small operation here, about six employees. I know everybody's family and I go to their houses," he told me.

On the morning of June 13, Watson showed up for work as usual, but left sometime in the early afternoon to get a haircut at a nearby barber shop. Twenty-three-year-old Rachel Murray was leaving a store at the corner of Church and Nostrand just as Watson ambled out after his haircut. The sidewalk was crammed that afternoon with schoolchildren, bargain hunters and people like

Myriam Pierre, a hairdresser's apprentice, who was standing outside of the Romeo and Juliet Beauty Salon smoking a cigarette and watching passersby.

As she headed off to her job as a home-health aide, Murray kept an eye out for her 16-year-old brother Adrian, who was inside Chen's Kitchen, a takeout a few doors away, waiting on an order. Murray still doesn't know what caused her to fixate on the activities of a neatly dressed stranger with a low top haircut, bopping nonchalantly toward a Honda Accord. She remembered that he got into the car, and she heard the engine turn over and then sputter into an eerie, syncopated screech. As the man was about to pull out of the parking spot in front of Chen's, she saw three plainclothes officers drive up on the wrong side of the street, banging their unmarked, dark blue Caprice into the front of the Honda. The officers quickly scrambled out of the vehicle, the nozzles of their 9-millimeter Glocks trained on the driver.

"Stop!" commanded one of the cops as people clambered out of nearby stores in wide-eyed astonishment. Murray quickened her pace, heading curiously toward the affray that looked like a scene straight out of the Crown Heights rebellion.

"I kept asking myself, 'Is this for real?' because when I first stumbled onto it, I really thought maybe I was walking into a movie."

The three cops, deploying themselves in a triangle, inched toward the car. Murray got close enough to see Watson's hands on the steering wheel, stretched out before him and clamped to the dashboard.

But Myriam Pierre was hypnotized by the fear she saw in Watson's eyes.

"He knew he was dead," said the then-25-year-old daughter of an upstate police.

The lead cop with the "reddish-brown," she said, hair approached the Honda stealthily, positioning himself on the passenger side.

"'Freeze, nigger! You're dead!'" Pierre quoted the officer as shouting before squeezing off a round.

"He shot once, and it hit him in the head, and the guy just, like, slumped over," Murray told me, recalling that she was screaming hysterically, asking herself over and over in disbelief *"Is this for real? Is this for real?"*

"Don't kill him! Don't kill him!" a woman standing next to her was bawling.

"She was banging on her chest so hard that she was scraping the skin off," Murray remembered. "She was bleeding, and that's when I knew it was real."

The shooter looked back at his partners and they all muttered some words, Murray said "Then he opened up the car door and they all just start shooting."

"The impact of the bullet dropped him in the passenger seat," Pierre said. Watson's hands, as she described it, slid leadenly from the dashboard as if "sleep-dozing," she said. His body jerked again. "He went back up and they just continued. They went on and on and on."

"You fuckin' *mur-da-rah!*" Myriam Pierre yelled at the cops. "Oh my God, look what the fuck you did! You killed him!"

Pierre began to interrogate the cops on the spot. "How the hell you're gonna empty a whole clip on him and continue to fire again?" she screamed at them.

"Shut the fuck up, you black bitch," she said one of the cops barked at her.

"Yeah, that's OK. I'm a black bitch, but you're a fuckin' *mur-da rah!* You just killed a black brother on Church Avenue!"

Some horrified witnesses scampered away, but others advanced toward the cops like a vengeful mob. "Three white officers, mind you, just killed a black guy. And black peoples coming? I'm getting to hell out."

Trotting back to their unmarked car, two of the cops holstered their weapons and one kept his drawn as he screamed into his radio for backup. Then they sped off. "They left him at the scene," Murray said.

There was only one way Pierre could describe the body that they left in a twisted heap.

The bullet-riddled Watson "was curled up, like when a dog is sleeping and all his legs are underneath him," Pierre said.

Murray noticed that an ambulance that had been parked on Brooklyn Avenue for more than one hour. "If it was on Nostrand Avenue I wouldn't pay it no attention. But an ambulance on Brooklyn Avenue is unusual for our neighborhood," she said. "They drove right up and took the body."

Shortly after Watson was placed in the ambulance, the EMS technicians and some uniformed police officers who had been summoned to the scene allegedly broke into a mocking laughter. "They was congratulating each other, patting each other on the back," recalled Pierre, who again confronted the police.

"Oh, today, you went nigger hunting, right?" she asked of no one in particular. "But it wouldn't be funny if we go pig hunting."

"I remember one of the EMS workers had blood on his hands so he couldn't give a high five, but what they did [was] knock elbows," Murray said. "They was laughing like it was a big joke, like they was having a ball. They was happy—a job well done."

The frivolity infuriated the stunned onlookers.

"Pigs! Pigs! Pigs!" some in the crowd of about 50 witnesses yelled repeatedly.

UNA CLARKE KEPT HER PROMISE TO THE ANGRY demonstrators for swift action on the cops' killing of Watson. She remained in the street talking with enraged neighborhood people until 3 a.m. the following morning. Later that day, she faxed a letter to Jene Lopez at the embattled Civilian Complaint Review Board, laying out the details of what sparked the protest and providing the names and phone numbers of five witness to the killing.

"I have received two different versions of this one story," wrote Clarke, who also notified Lopez that her office was assisting D.A. Charles Hynes in his investigation. The councilwoman also offered Hynes the use of her district office to interview witnesses who might be intimidated by the prosecutorial environment of the DA's office. That evening, as a crowd of about 100 chanting demonstrators gathered for a rally, Clarke canvassed the block, urging business owners and their workers to talk to investigators in their shops or at her office.

Sonny Carson rebuked Clarke for making an extraordinary effort to help the authorities maintain calm. He led a group of about 30 people in a march on the 67th Precinct, carrying makeshift signs that read, "No Justice, No Peace." The December 12th Movement radicals castigated Clarke for defusing what they saw was the making of a righteous rebellion. Carson and Clarke traded barbs in the black press and heatedly debated the pros and cons of armed resistance on black-owned WLIB-AM. Carson The ultranationalist declared that any black politician who did not support the call for militant action and legislation to protect black males from police violence should leave town. He considered it meaningless that, at Clarke's urging, Representative Major R. Owens had written a letter to U.S. Attorney General Janet Reno asking for a Justice Department investigation into Watson's death.

"Instead of him storming into her office and saying, 'I want some change, lock me up,' he's writing a letter," Carson said derisively of Owens and his petition. "They (Clarke and Owens) represent the system that's responsible for what's happening to us. They have not made a difference; Una and all the rest of them better get out the fuckin' way." (Carson at one time suggested that the black community deal with its "Uncle Toms and Tomasinas" the way freedom fighters in South Africa dealt with those suspected of collaborating with the white-minority apartheid regime—by putting tires around the traitors' necks and setting them afire, a brutal practice called "necklacing."

"Maybe we can take a page from their book. There's a lot of tires around this city," the controversial Carson once said.)

"If they were worth a dime to me, I would be nervous and shaking," was Clarke's defiant retort to the radicals.

The December 12th Movement then announced that it would conduct something of a war-crimes tribunal, with defendants Mayor "Adolph" Giuliani; Watson's alleged killers, Officers James Gentile, Keith Tierny and James Olson; the NYPD; D.A. Hynes; and "the New York mainstream media and others" to be tried in absentia on charges of "coldblooded murder, conspiracy to cover up the murder, and conspiracy to violate the human rights of Black and Latino people."

Traumatized by Watson's violent death, Rachel Murray testified as a key witness at "The Peoples Street Tribunal," set up on a sidewalk a block away from where the shooting occurred. "I know they have in the news that he was reaching for something," she told the plaintiff crowd, described in the "indictment papers" as "the grassroots people of New York City."

"Anyone on Church Avenue would tell you he wasn't reaching for anything; his hands were on the dashboard," she testified. Other witnesses were afraid to come forward because they are illegal immigrants who feared retribution from the cops.

Clarke derided the tribunal as a "mock trial" and "child's play." Unlike the World Court in The Hague, the December 12th Movement-convened tribunal had neither the power nor authority to indict, try, convict, sentence and imprison police officers it deemed guilty of committing crimes against blacks. Any tribunal that does not have a jail to lock up a convicted war criminal "gives the white man more ammunition [to portray] us as shallow, narrow and ineffective," Clarke said.

The Brooklyn district attorney, the Justice Department, even the NYPD's Internal Affairs Bureau are the skilled triers of facts in police-brutality cases, Clarke maintained, adding that the tribunal should hand over any evidence of the defendants' wrongdoing to those agencies. Carson and his cohorts fired back that it was naïve of the politician to think that by playing the role of establishment agitator, and according to the rules of the system, Clarke could assure justice for Aswan Watson.

"Justice only comes from within the system," Clarke said. "We don't have any court of law [or] any jails. I think street action has its place, but as an elected official I am the person who is supposed to agitate within the system."

It is the same system that keeps denying justice to black victims of police brutality. "In the 11 years that I'd been at the NYCLUF, to my knowledge—and this is very startling—not a single police officer in New York City who'd fatally shot a citizen had ever been convicted in the New York courts," Siegel told me.

But in the people's court, all the defendants charged in Watson's killing were found "guilty beyond a shadow of a doubt." A "sentencing" document said that

Officers Gentile, Tierny and Olson, "who are presently fugitives, are to be arrested on sight, [and] are banned from entering any Black/Latino community for the rest of their unnatural lives."

The sentencing document of the people's tribunal also demanded that the "convicted" officers and commanders of the NYPD "submit themselves immediately to investigation and trial" by the United Nations Special Rapporteur on Summary and Arbitrary Executions and Extrajudicial Disappearances in Geneva, Switzerland. In that world court the defendants would face charges of murder, maintenance of membership and participation in an NYPD death squad, and other human rights abuses.

As for Giuliani, "the leader of the conspiracies," the Grassroots People of New York City demanded that he "resign immediately or be subject to impeachment."

On learning that Amnesty International's report on brutality by cops in the NYPD was about to released, Giuliani announced that New York's Finest would be following a new "respect program" dubbed "CPR"—for courtesy, professionalism and respect. Not surprisingly, the December 12th Movement and other radical groups said they'd heard that talk about sensitivity training before. They wanted all white cops out of black neighborhoods. "We know that the response to that [demand] would be, 'You're crazy!' But we mean that shit!" said Carson, a regular bungee jumper off the edge of radical politics. "We're gonna retaliate. We have to retaliate!" he vowed. We're just sitting ducks."

HAD ANYONE IN THE VAN DYKE HOUSES read the anonymously circulated *White KKKops Are the Enemy* pamphlet urging sniper-style assassinations of cops? Two months after the killing of Aswan Watson, two white cops on bike patrol in the sprawling courtyard of the housing development in the Brownsville section of Brooklyn pedaled over to a group of tenants sitting on a moss-green park bench. On this humid Friday night in mostly black East New York, Officer James Sullivan and his unidentified partner were on the prowl for the brazen sniper who'd shot an undercover narcotics detective, David Joseph, three times as he talked on a pay phone near the drug-infested housing project.

When a cop is felled by a bullet in the inner city's most violent enclaves, police usually would storm the 'hood expecting nine out of 10 times to hear the denizens retort, "I didn't see nothin', didn't hear nothin', don't know nothin'" to their questions. It had been almost a month since Sullivan's fellow officers on foot, bike patrol and in a COP-SHOT flatbed snitch truck began combing the stronghold of cocaine and crack drug lords in search of a woman named Sheila. They'd been telling residents that Sheila knew where the would-be cop killer might be hiding out. Their dragnet had pulled in potential informers, but didn't produce any results.

Witnesses hanging out in the courtyard that Friday night said they saw Sullivan use his nightstick to rattle a litter of empty 80-ounce beer bottles strewn about under the bench. He singled out and zeroed in on Richard Holder, they said, accusing him of drinking alcohol on the building grounds in violation of Housing Authority rules. Sullivan then demanded that Holder produce some form of identification, the witnesses said, but the 31-year-old Holder refused, telling Sullivan he hadn't been drinking.

"Get up!" Holder said the cop barked at him several times.

"He's blind. He can't go nowhere!" shouted 16-year-old Darryl Handy, who said he was promptly handcuffed by Sullivan's partner and isolated from the group. Unknown to Sullivan, Holder was declared legally blind two years before their encounter; a playful pit bull he was training pawed him in one eye and destroyed the retina. He later lost vision in both eyes. Angered by the mounting resistance, witnesses said Sullivan grabbed Holder by the arm and tried to yank him from the bench.

"I can't see!" Holder bellowed.

When Sullivan's partner failed to persuade Holder to cooperate, he threatened to arrest him.

Chauncey Williams, Holder's childhood friend, intervened. He said the cop ignored him, but when he tried to complain to the officer's partner, Sullivan flew into a tantrum.

"The officer just picked me up by my neck and started choking me," said Williams, an asthmatic. "I was spitting up. I was trying to catch my breath."

With his back pressed against a chain-link fence and fearing he would black out, Williams pried Sullivan's hands from his throat. "He just kept pushing me back to the fence," he said. "I got marks all over my neck."

Because he touched the cop's hand he was charged with resisting arrest, Williams said. He was handcuffed and ordered to stand against the fence.

"You're next, if you don't move off this bench," Sullivan reportedly told Holder.

"What you want me to do, walk out in the middle of the street?" the blind Holder said. That's where he said Sullivan threatened to take him and leave him to the mercy of cars speeding by.

Then, for the first time since initially accosting the tenants, Sullivan chastised them for being so cavalier about the shooting of Detective Joseph, who owed his life to a high-tech bulletproof vest. It's "not our problem one a y'all's officers got shot," Holder quoted one of the tenants as saying.

"I'll lock all you motherfuckers up!'" one of the cops announced. Handy and Williams were taken into custody. Holder was not charged.

At the 73rd Precinct, detectives questioned the teenager about the shooting. It was part of the NYPD's "just ask" policy that encouraged detectives to expand their interrogation of suspects beyond the scope of a specific crime—Did he know how to use a gun? Did he belong to a street gang? Did he like cops? Handy answered no, and emphatically no to the last question. The cops charged him with disorderly conduct and released him.

Williams said interrogators in the same stationhouse took turns poking him in the ribs with their nightsticks. Give them the scuttlebutt on the Brownsville sniper, they demanded. "You know you know something," he said one officer pressed him. "Who did it?" Williams denied he had any street intelligence on the shooting. Even if he knew something, he would keep his mouth shut for fear the cops would pin the crime on him. At 2 a.m. the next day, Williams was mugged, fingerprinted and taken downtown to Criminal Court for arraignment. He was released after more than 48 hours in detention.

In their zeal to capture the sniper, outraged residents said that police made no effort to differentiate law-abiding citizens from suspects. As they chased dead-end leads, the cops became less tolerant of those freely expressing their views about excessive force, false arrest and imprisonment, and malicious prosecution.

THE BLACK PANTHER COLLECTIVE had another secret weapon trained on cops all along. The group and its allies in communities in the North and South Bronx had been demanding changes in police policy following the December 1994 choking death of Anthony Baez. Officer Francis Livoti, who claimed he was trying to arrest Baez for disorderly conduct, was acquitted of criminally negligent homicide. Heavy-handed tactics by police after Baez' death, including the frisking of hundreds of young black and Latino men, fanned tensions in the city.

The Black Panthers felt cornered and fought back. They began to scour the city with Hi-8 cameras in search of cops meting out street justice. They put police on "Black Panther Camera" videotape surveillance—"shoot[ing] with 8-millimeter instead of 9 millimeter," they said—and distributed literature castigating the impunity the NYPD enjoyed under the Giuliani in mostly black and Latino neighborhoods.

On the evening of September 11, 1996, Shepard McDaniel, a 42-year-old member of the organization, attempted to monitor the conduct of two 41st Precinct cops who had arrested a teenage Latino drug suspect at the corner of Garrison and Manida streets in the borough's South Bronx section. Two women began to plead with them to let the suspect go, but the officers put the youth in their car and called for backup. Four cops, led by Sergeant James Caban, responded.

As McDaniel jotted down the identification numbers of the squad cars, Caban dashed over to him, asked why he was standing there, and demanded that he show ID. McDaniel said he was about to retrieve his ID from his briefcase when Caban snatched his pen and read his notes. McDaniel said the sergeant threw away the notes and "forcefully grabbed" him by the arm. McDaniel protested. Caban "then punched me in the face," he said. Caban threw a second punch at him, McDaniel said, and as he blocked it and backed away, three more officers charged him and rained blows on him with their fists and nightsticks.

"I then spent the next 15 seconds or so protecting myself from the physical assault of all four police officers, who repeatedly swung on me while yelling, 'Get down on the ground!' and 'He's a crazy fucking nigger.' I was forced to go down … to give better protection to my head, kneecaps and private parts," McDaniel wrote in a report on the incident.

His self-defense tactics only infuriated the officers. "It was then that one officer put his shoe on my neck while another one cuffed one of my hands," McDaniel recalled. He said he feared one of the cops was about to use an illegal chokehold on him.

"With my windpipe [in danger of being] crushed, I used my free hand to dislodge his foot from my neck," he said in his report. "Others began kicking me in the back and punching me while yelling for me to give them my other hand. They then suddenly ceased the attack in order to give attention to another officer who had screamed out in pain after breaking or dislocating one of his fingers apparently during the attack."

Eventually subdued and handcuffed, McDaniel was shuffled off to a squad car by Caban. He said he pleaded with Caban to secure rare books he was carrying and his briefcase with money, a passport and other important documents. "Fuck you and your briefcase!" McDaniel said Caban shouted as the officer slammed McDaniel's head into the roof of the cruiser. "Get in the fucking car!" McDaniel said he called out to a woman who witnessed his arrest to get his briefcase. "If you don't shut the fuck up, I'm gonna spray this Mace right in your big fucking mouth!" McDaniel said Caban told him.

A misdemeanor complaint charged McDaniel with "being unruly, causing a crowd to gather ... swinging at the officer (presumably Caban) [and] refusing to be cuffed."

"I never interfered with the arrest process [of the drug suspect], spoke to any of the officers, or even attempted to obtain any badge numbers," McDaniel said. "In fact, I never came within 30 feet of the scene of the incident."

McDaniel maintained he was illegally detained and harassed for 28 hours at the 41st Precinct stationhouse and at Bronx Central Booking. He also said the cops tried to lose him in the system. "My first set of 'good' fingerprints was allegedly lost, and despite my protests the second set was deliberately done incorrectly in an attempt to keep me locked up," he claimed. He said a sympathetic black cop working the overnight tour "caught the 'bad' prints and had me do a third set so that I would be able to see the judge [the next day] and go home." But McDaniel's ordeal in police custody was far from over. He charged that "during transport to and from Central Booking, the escorting police officers deliberately attempted to cause me further injury and discomfort by putting me cuffed in the back seat of the police van without a seat belt while they recklessly drove at high speeds through the streets with their sirens and lights flashing. On the return trip to the 41st, one officer [mentioned] that he was an 'excellent shot,' [in case] I or the prisoner I was cuffed to made any attempt to escape."

POINTING OUT THAT THERE HAD BEEN three separate fatal shootings of unarmed black men by white cops within a 30-day period, black activists led by Sonny Carson began to promote a new slogan: "Know the Code." The killings weren't just a series of unfortunate accidents, the militants charged they were part of a murderous pattern by racist cops confident that their acts would go unpunished. To the nationalists, this wasn't just police brutality, but genocide, and the only way to stop the killings, they said, was to arm groups like the Odinga Carson Brigade, patterning the fighting spirit after the ultraviolent Zulus in South Africa's Inkatha movement.

They were ready to strike.

Never mind, said Carson, that armed struggle conjured up horrible images—body bags; burning and looting; tear gas and fire hoses; snarling dogs; white supremacists marching through the 'hood with rifles and under police escort; COINTELPRO; bloody communiqués stapled to the bellies of killer cops; black radicals swinging from trees with their tongues cut out; Black Power funerals; cop killer trials; and Giuliani himself throwing the switch that would send bolts of deadly current surging through the black body politic.

"White people died in that scenario," I told the outspoken and opinionated militant.

"So did Malcolm X, Martin Luther King Jr. and Medgar Evers!" he snapped. "And whatcha call 'em three niggers white folk always talk about?"

"Goodman, Schwerner and Chaney (the three civil-rights workers in the Mississippi Summer Project who were murdered by segregationists in 1964)?"

"Yeah, 'em niggers."

"Goodman and Schwerner were Jews," I reminded Carson, a frequent target of integrationists who repudiated his frequently anti-Semitic views.

"The niggers dead, ain't they?"

"So who's going to lead this black liberation struggle against the police?"

"A Black Moses, brother. Who do you think?"

"Are you that Black Moses?"

"I'm that last angry nigger!" said Carson with a scowl, his self-deprecation a reflection of the rage within.

8

The Killing of Kevin Cedeno

No one can say/As they step delicately around/The red rivers you have so inconsiderately left/On all the sidewalks of New York/No one can tell/The always overburdened shoppers/That Rudy's angels/Shot you in self-defense/In the back/Sleep well, my brother, sleep well/The city is clean and safe

— From "Lament for Kevin Cedeno" by Leonard Cohen,
a retired civil-rights activist

ROMA CEDENO AND HER MOTHER JOYCE were huddled in a back office of the Community League of West 159th Street, Yvonne Stennett's multi-service agency that ran the five-story walkup where Roma rented an apartment. Agonized by Giuliani's "rush to judgment" after the killing of her son, Roma had been pondering Stennett's suggestion that she talk to me about Kevin's short life as a youthful offender. "What good would that do, Ro?" the grandmother asked. "It would bring about closure," offered Stennett, the bespectacled neighborhood voice of reason some credited with preventing Washington Heights from exploding over Kevin's controversial death. Since the shooting, everyone—including Al Sharpton, who knows exactly what you do when a black suspect dies—had been advising Roma Cedeno on the posthumous vindication of police-shooting victims.

While crowds of people were calling her by name, others were referring to her son as "the machete-wielding kid" and "convicted felon." They painted Kevin as a neighborhood thug who loved hard-core gangsta rap, grew up fast, and died young. From Mayor Giuliani's words, one would think Kevin Cedeno was one of the city's most violent criminals. But his death was a reminder of how black suspects are dealt with by police. "To this mayor and his enforcers every black suspect wears a rap sheet on his back," said Sharpton, who committed to leading protests every Saturday in front of One Police Plaza until Officer Anthony Pellegrini was indicted for Kevin's "murder."

As outrage over the shooting intensified, Manhattan District Attorney Robert Morgenthau hired a top forensic expert to examine a bullet hole in the long-sleeve T-shirt Cedeno was wearing the morning Pellegrini shot the 16-year-old in the back. Giuliani's newly appointed Police Commissioner Howard Safir "erupted after learning what Morgenthau had done," a well-placed insider confided to me. According to the source, Safir felt the move suggested that the D.A. was leaning more toward the theory that Cedeno was not lunging at officers when Pellegrini cut him down.

Cedeno was shot about 3:30 a.m. on April 6, 1997, at l63rd Street and Amsterdam Avenue in Washington Heights, after Officers Pellegrini and Mike Garcia responded to 911 calls about a disorderly group with knives and sticks. Some published reports said Pellegrini shot Cedeno because he thought the teenager, who was running along 164th Street with a 22-inch machete in his hand, was turning to pull a shotgun out of his oversized, long-sleeve T-shirt. But Cedeno's friends said he was shot as he ran from a group of Dominican youths he'd been fighting with. They insisted he never menaced Pellegrini or any other officer.

Safir said Pellegrini was 10 to 15 feet from Cedeno when he fired a single shot, mortally wounding him. The police commissioner at first said that Pellegrini shot Cedeno in the stomach when he threatened officers with the machete. Then an autopsy showed Cedeno was shot in the back. One officer at the scene told investigators he thought the machete was a gun. Morgenthau would rely on the findings of Peter DeForest, a professor of forensics at John Jay College of Criminal Justice, to bolster the case he intended to present to a grand jury.

(DeForest demonstrated different scenarios for the shooting. He was best known for his testimony in the 1987 attempted-murder trial of Larry Davis, a South Bronx drug dealer who shot six white cops on November 19, 1986. Davis claimed he was selling drugs for a ring of dirty cops and was about to expose them when they raided his sister's Bronx apartment and tried to kill him. At trial, the cops maintained they opened fire on Davis after he shot at them. But after a careful examination of the apartment, DeForest showed that police fired the first bullet, which landed in a dresser drawer. Davis was acquitted of attempted murder. "You can take Dr. DeForest to the bank," Davis' controversial defense attorney, Lynne Stewart, told the jury in her summation. "They brought doctors in here to refute other doctors, but they couldn't bring anybody in who could lay a glove on Dr. Peter DeForest; that's how good he is." Safir may have disapproved of

DeForest because of his testimony in the Davis case. But the expert also had testified successfully on behalf of the prosecution in some of the city's most controversial cop-shooting cases.)

Barbara Wolff, an independent pathologist hired by the Cedeno family, examined Kevin's body for about two hours. Wolff, employed by former New York
Chief Medical Examiner Michael Baden, "did not find any gunpowder residue"—which meant that Kevin was shot from a distance of more than three feet,
Michael Hardy, the Cedeno family's attorney, told me. Hardy said that preliminary toxicology tests showed a trace of marijuana residue in Cedeno's bile. "Dr.
Wolff said he may have smoked marijuana days or weeks previously, but he was
not under the influence of pot the night he was shot," said Hardy, adding that
Cedeno also had a blood alcohol level of .14, indicating he may have had about
eight beers prior to the shooting.

Wolff also may have clarified questions surrounding an EMS crew's decision
to transport Cedeno to Harlem Hospital instead of Columbia Presbyterian just a
few blocks from the shooting. Kevin's sister Roxanne, who said she witnessed the
shooting, claimed that emergency-room attendants at Harlem Hospital told her
some three hours after Kevin was brought in that he was alive and stable. "Dr.
Wolff said hospital and EMS reports indicated there were no vital signs at the
scene," Hardy said. "Kevin was essentially DOA at the hospital." The records
show that Cedeno was brought to the hospital at 4:15 a.m. and was pronounced
dead about 45 minutes later.

Peter DeForest's involvement in the Cedeno case came on the heels of a forced
meeting between the Cedeno family and Charles Hirsch, the city's chief medical
examiner. The family refused to claim Kevin's body until Hirsch handed over a
copy of the official autopsy report. Hirsch insisted his hands were tied because of
a law that prohibited him from releasing the report until a grand jury examined
it. But two days later, Sarah Scott, general counsel to the medical examiner,
invited the family to the morgue to have Hirsch explain his findings to them.
Mayoral hopeful Al Sharpton, who had been an adviser to the family since the
shooting, put together a delegation that included Cedeno's mother Roma, his
grandmother Joyce, Stennett, Hardy, and his law partner Terence Scheurer. At
12:30 p.m. Scott ushered the group into a conference room and introduced them
to Hirsch and Dr. Yvonne Milewski, who performed the autopsy.

Sharpton was no stranger to the morgue, and Scott reminded Hirsch that, in
1989, it was she who escorted Sharpton and Patricia Garcia to the basement mor-
tuary to identify the body of her son Richard Luke, who died in police custody.
(Protesters led by Sharpton accused the cops of beating Luke to death, but an

autopsy report released five days later concluded that Luke died of acute cocaine intoxication.) Sharpton later would tell me that, while sitting at the conference table, he vividly recalled Hirsch's testimony in the 1987 attempted-murder trial of subway vigilante Bernhard Goetz. On the stand, Hirsch, then chief medical examiner for Suffolk County, rebutted former New York Chief Medical Examiner Dominick DiMaio, who had said the four black youths Goetz shot could not have been seated or running away when Goetz fired his gun at them. Hirsch said that Darrell Cabey, paralyzed by Goetz' bullet, could have been standing directly in front of Goetz when he was shot, and could have fallen backward into a sitting position.

Using himself as a model, Hirsch asked Milewski to show the group how Kevin Cedeno could have been shot in the back. Pointing to the center of Hirsch's back below the waistline, Milewski tracked the trajectory of the single bullet she said followed a horizontal path and ruptured a major artery. Sharpton, Stennett and Hardy cut to the chase: Could Hirsch tell what position Cedeno was in when he was shot? "It (the autopsy) doesn't tell us anything about his absolute position," Hirsch said. "There is no way for us to determine his position." Hardy asked about the abrasions on Cedeno's right shoulder, right knuckle and right forearm. Witnesses had told the attorney that, before handcuffing Cedeno after he fell to the ground, a police officer used his foot to restrain the dying teenager. As the meeting broke up, Hirsch used the Goetz case to demonstrate that there were no hard-and-fast answers to what Cedeno was doing at the exact moment he was shot. "There were universal possibilities," she said.

With the autopsy showing that Officer Pellegrini shot Kevin in the back, a staunchly supportive Giuliani said he would always give cops the benefit of the doubt when their actions are called into question unless there are facts to prove he should do otherwise. He demanded that reporters shift their attention from Pellegrini to the dead teenager, suggesting that no good mother would allow her son to run around the streets at 3 a.m. with a machete. "I wish he doesn't call me, because I would spit in his face," said Roma, a Yoruba-Orisha Baptist who prayed with Jesse Jackson the night after her son died. But she could no longer resist answering the question that Giuliani seemed to put to her: How does a person between the ages of 14 and 16 have six arrests for robbery, almost all of them armed?' After several hours of careful consideration, the mother of six agreed to talk about two of the incidents. Her sing-song voice almost at a whisper, she talked for the first time about life with Kevin.

ROMA CEDENO EMIGRATED from Trinidad in 1982, when her identical-twin boys, Kevin and Kern, were seven months old. She settled in the Bedford-Stuyvesant section of Brooklyn, where her mother had lived for 10 years. Three weeks after her arrival, Roma took on odd jobs as a clerical worker at J.C. Penney and Lord & Taylor, and as a bank teller. The twins were inseparable and there was one incident that bound them even closer when they were about two years old. A pot of hot water scalded Kern and complications from the injury required him to stay in the hospital for quite a while. Kevin dressed himself one morning and was about to walk out. He told his mother he was going to see his brother in the hospital.

"He missed Kern so much that I had to lug Kevin every day to the hospital or one day I'd come home and my son would be gone," Roma recalled. When the boys were eight years old, Roma relocated to Harlem and moved into her rent-subsidized apartment on West 159th Street. The twins first got into serious trouble at J.H.S. 136, where teachers accused them of starting a fire. "It was one of the worst experiences I had with them, but to this day no one really knows if Kevin or Kern did it." Detective James Gilmore, a black cop who was assigned to the 33rd Precinct, befriended Kevin at a time when his childhood pranks were turning into criminal mischief.

Gilmore had a knack for turning troubled kids around. "A lot of fathers aren't home in that area, and kids picked up a lot from their peers as they searched for their identity," said Gilmore. "It's what you know that defines you as a man in Washington Heights." Gilmore had enrolled some neighborhood teens in youth-leadership workshops and rite-of-passage programs with the theme "Stop the Killing." Kevin, the detective recalled, "didn't come to those, but I would sit down and kick it to him about being aware of how friends would try to get him to do alcohol and drugs." But friends said Kevin would hang out late, drinking beer and getting high on marijuana. "I never liked it when he didn't call to say where he was," Roma said.

The man-child, she added, was "quick to cry" when she admonished him for being part of a gang that jumped a neighborhood teen and stole his videotape. "If I caught Kevin doing something he knew he shouldn't be doing, it was always, 'Aaaight, Officer Gilmore. Sorry, Officer Gilmore,'" the detective said. "He never had a major problem with the law."

Until February 1995.

At the age of 15, Kevin and several accomplices were arrested and charged with robbing a man at gunpoint. Roma said details of what really happened were sealed because Kevin was a juvenile at the time. But a source familiar with the case said some of Kevin's friends robbed the man and passed his wallet to Kevin. When Roma got to the precinct to inquire about Kevin, she recalled a cop asking her: "Where is your other son?"

"What he got to do with this?" she wanted to know.

"I heard he's in Florida," the cop said, according to Roma. "We heard that he was there when the incident happened." Roma said the officer threatened to arrest Kern when he returned to New York. "My sons had nothing to do with that robbery, and everybody in the neighborhood knows that," she claimed. Kevin was remanded to the custody of the Spofford Juvenile Center in the Bronx. "Every week I went to court I saw my son cry," she said. After five and a half months at the detention center, Kevin reluctantly pleaded guilty.

"I remember clearly at first Kevin pleading not guilty and crying. He forgot that he had to lie and say he was guilty." Roma said, insisting that Kevin pleaded guilty to spare the family additional pain. He was sentenced to six months time served at Spofford, and ordered to report daily for the next six months to CASES (the Center for Alternative Sentencing and Employment Services), located above a Popeye's fast-food franchise on 125th Street. Released in August 1995, Kevin went back to school from 7:30 a.m. to 3 p.m., and then reported to CASES, where he stayed until 7 p.m. "That was his routine for six months," Roma said. But the rigid rules of the program were taking their toll on Kevin. "He was going through a lot of emotional stress," his mother said. "If he walked out of our building and he saw the cops, he would run back upstairs. He'd say, 'Ma, the cops are downstairs.' And I would say, 'So what! You can't live like this.'"

Shortly before his stint at CASES ended, Kevin was arrested for robbing another teenager of $10 on Edgecombe Avenue in Harlem. "This kid said Kevin and another boy jumped him from behind and kicked and punched him, and that this happened between 5 and 5:30 in the afternoon," said Roma. Kevin was sent back to Spofford. A Family Court judge later dismissed the charges after CASES provided proof that he was in the program at the time of the alleged robbery.

Roma Cedeno found herself disliking New York City; Kevin had come to loathe cops. She sent Kern to California and (just before Kevin's death) found a home "with a big back yard and flowers" in a residential section of Baltimore, where her mother and siblings had relocated. Kevin, an asthmatic, thought it would be a nice place for him to look after his five-month-old son Kevin Jason Cedeno Jr. and his pit bull. Roma needed permission from a Family Court judge to move Kevin out of state. At a hearing in February, she pleaded with the judge to let her son go. "I told the judge, 'Let him come with me and every three weeks

I will take a day off and return to the city with him.'" Roma recalled the judge asking Kevin if he wanted to move with his mother: "He said, 'I just wanna get outta here. I just wanna go to Baltimore and live.'" The judge scheduled an appointment for April 7, and Roma returned to Baltimore. She told Kevin she would be back in New York on the morning of April 6 because they had to meet with his probation officer before the hearing, at 8 a.m., and had another appointment with a social services agency.

"Everything was falling into place," it seemed for Roma. But shortly before dawn on April 6, she received that dreaded telephone call: Kevin was dead.

"Go home!" the lone white man walking briskly past the 33nd Precinct on 165th Street in upper Washington Heights one Saturday afternoon shouted at the 100 or more people protesting peacefully across the street. David Sell, a community activist who fought against school segregation in the Jim Crow South, was directing most of his anger at Sharpton. It was Sharpton who organized the protest four days after a grand jury decided that the single bullet Officer Pellegrini pumped into the back of Cedeno was "justified under the law."

The 62-year-old Sell had moved into the Washington Heights neighborhood just five days before Cedeno was gunned down. The low turnout of demonstrators, said Sell, was proof that Sharpton "may represent one or more individuals" but not the entire district from which investigators were able to round up 36 witnesses who told a different story than the one Sharpton had been projecting in the media. "He has no business to come up and organize a community demonstration in a Zip code that's not his or in an area he certainly couldn't carry an election," asserted Sell, who grew up in a segregated community in Daville, Va. Though Sell insisted his disdain for Sharpton wasn't politically motivated, the mayoral candidate, he charged, was "trying to get some support for a doomed political run."

Sell pointed out that "the local people handled the whole situation rather well at the time because there was no immediate hysterical response" to the shooting of Cedeno. "The following Saturday when Sharpton and his crew came up here and started making a lot of noise, I told him, 'Go home!'" Sell told me. "I told him he was a fraud. He was taunting the police."

If Sell's views echoed those of Sharpton nemesis Rudy Giuliani—who was marginalizing the civil rights leader by not answering reporters' questions about his involvement in the Cedeno case—the similarity ended there. Sell was not on the reelect-Giuliani bandwagon, either. "I wouldn't even support him for husband of the year," he said about the martially challenged mayor.

Politics aside, Sell felt there shouldn't have been a "complete vindication" of Officer Pellegrini. "I've worked on a grand jury and it's a farce," he said. On this, he and Sharpton stood on common ground.

Sharpton went to Washington and hand-delivered a letter to U.S. Attorney General Janet Reno from the family of Kevin Cedeno, formally requesting that the Justice Department investigate whether Pellegrini violated Cedeno's civil rights. "I thought the shooting should have been investigated—probably a departmental trial, probably the feds," Sell said. But he wasn't holding out much hope: Independent investigations might only buttress the grand jury's conclusion that Pellegrini feared for his life when he saw a suspect wielding what appeared to be a deadly weapon. "People get nervous if they see a machete," Sell conceded. In a statement releasing the grand jury's findings, DA Morgenthau said the grand jury took into account that Cedeno failed to respond to Pellegrini's commands "to stop or to drop what he was carrying.... The appearance of Cedeno's weapon coupled with that behavior and Cedeno's subsequent movements—his turning, his dropping his shoulder, and his bringing the weapon around to point toward Pellegrini—led the officer to the conclusion that the gun Cedeno had was a shot-gun, and that he was about to fire."

Captain Gary McCarthy stood behind barricades outside the stationhouse where Pellegrini was assigned, fiddling with his gun belt. He was in charge at the time of the shooting and aware that his officers had voted Pellegrini "Cop of the Month" after killing Cedeno. As demonstrators shouted, "Hey, hey! Ho, ho! Pel-legrini's gotta go," McCarthy sought a meeting with Sharpton and Yvonne Sten-nett. Both activists appeared to shun McCarthy because officers had scuffled with protesters a week earlier in front of the stationhouse. Sharpton told an aide to tell McCarthy he was late for an appearance at the African Street Festival in Brook-lyn. McCarthy was eager to meet with anybody. "I will talk to Mrs. Cedeno," he said. "We just need to sit down."

A weary Leonard Cohen sat on a bench as the protesters dispersed. He sighed as if he were tired. But it wasn't tired from the marching. "It's the killings," he stuttered. "It's been going on since I was 17, when I saw my first police murder." That was more than 40 years earlier, in Detroit, when he witnessed a 13-year-old boy get shot dead while riding his bicycle. "There have been too many since then," said Cohen, then the editor of a medical journal. The boy's death spurred Cohen to join the burgeoning civil-rights movement and focus on documenting police brutality. "I wrote a li'l something," the retiree said modestly, reaching into a plastic bag he had wrapped around his right ankle. It was an homage to Kevin Cedeno that seemed at once to beatify the slain teenager and satirize

Giuliani's boast of a safe city: "No one can say/As they step delicately around/ The red rivers you have so inconsiderately left/On all the sidewalks of New York/ No one can tell/The always overburdened shoppers/That Rudy's angels/Shot you in self-defense/in the back/Sleep well my brother, sleep well/The city is clean and safe."

9

The Torture of Abner Louima

For those taken in rapid cars to the house and beaten
By the skillful boys, the boys with the rubber fists,
Held down and beaten, the table cutting their loins,
Or kicked in the groin and left, with the muscles jerking
Like a headless hen's on the floor of the slaughter-house ...
For those who spit out the bloody stumps of their teeth ...
For those who carry the scars, who walk lame ...

—*From Litany for Dictatorships* by Stephen Vincent Benet

IT IS 6 O'CLOCK ON THE HUMID morning of August 14, 1997. Rudy Giuliani, on the verge of re-election to a second term as mayor of New York City, is on a secure phone calling Una Clarke, the feisty Jamaican American councilwoman from Brooklyn. Clarke had been a critic of the mayor because of his unwavering support of police officers accused of wrongfully killing or beating and maiming suspects while in their custody.

Less than 24 hours earlier, the city woke up to the banner headline in the *Daily News*: TORTURED BY COPS. Abner Louima, a 30-year-old Haitian immigrant, had been arrested after he intervened in a fracas at Le Rendez-Vous, a popular Haitian nightclub he'd gone to hear The Phantoms, his favorite band, famous for *compas*, Haitian dancehall music. One of their songs laments the brutality of "Baby Doc" Duvalier's secret police in a poignant chant, "Sa fé mal (it hurts), sa fé mal, sa fé mal."

When Louima tried to break up a fight between two women screaming in Kréyôl, he got into a tussle with the cops. He told a horrific tale of being beaten by police officers and taken to the bathroom of Brooklyn's 70th Precinct stationhouse. Allegedly, Officer Justin Volpe had shoved the wooden handle of a toilet plunger up his rectum, then pulled it out, covered "with shit and blood," and jammed it into his mouth, shattering his teeth.

Louima, who suffered a punctured intestine and torn bladder, said at first that while beating him, the officers called him "nigger" and one of them told him, "Dinkins is not in power, it's Giuliani time," and blacks had to learn to respect police.

The *New York Post* reported that Volpe, who was indicted for wielding the toilet plunger, had bragged about the incident, saying he "had to bring the guy (Louima) down" because "he took a swing" at him. Later at the hospital, Volpe, who reportedly kept a collection of dreadlocks he snipped from Jamaican "collars," was overheard saying, "No one jumps me and gets away with it."

That a white cop allegedly invoked the mayor's name during the attack seemed to buttress claims by opponents that Giuliani had given New York police a license to brutalize blacks. After Officer Anthony Pellegrini fatally shot Kevin Cedeno, in the back, Giuliani said he would always give cops the benefit of the doubt when their actions are called into question, unless facts proved he should do otherwise. After the Louima beating, protesters marched over the Brooklyn Bridge to City Hall, burning Giuliani in effigy. In the Democratic primary for mayor in the fall, contenders Al Sharpton and City Councilmember Ruth Messinger from Manhattan would make reference to "Giuliani time."

From the beginning there were complexities. Volpe's girlfriend was black, and whether linking Giuliani and the torture of Louima ever made sense, the link would get murkier. It didn't help any that Louima would later say that he never heard the cops say "Giuliani time." The incident at once incited all the feelings that are likely to explode when white cops and black victims collide and also exposed the ambiguities of Haitian Americans' quest for respectability, the rising power of West Indians in New York, and their complex relationship not just with white police, but with African Americans and with America's color line. All these dimensions would take full form in a tug of war between Giuliani and Clarke. The gruesome details of what had happened to Louima finally moved a city that seemingly had taken in stride a string of highly questionable police killings of blacks and Latinos. Now, political pundits were predicting that the torture of Louima would greatly embarrass the Republican incumbent and become the catalyst for a change at City Hall. As an outraged city teetered on the brink of a multicultural riot, a wily Giuliani reached out to Clarke.

"Councilmember Clarke, this is Rudy," a raspy voice crackled over the phone.

"Rudy who?" inquired the usually unpretentious Clarke, whose 40th District encompassed the city's largest concentration of Caribbean immigrants—in Flatbush and East Flatbush, and in Crown Heights, where West Indians, ultra-Orthodox Lubavitch Jews and blacks live tenuously cheek by jowl.

Clarke's harsh interrogatory may have had to do with her simmering fury over a political maneuver by Giuliani the night before that forced her and about 30 West Indian community leaders, including a large contingent of Haitians, to meet with him on his terms.

Clarke said she'd demanded an emergency meeting between the leaders and Police Commissioner Howard Safir, and it was set for 5 p.m. on August 13 at Medgar Evers College in Crown Heights. But after Giuliani learned that an unidentified member of Clarke's contingent had leaked the location to the media, he canceled the meeting and instead summoned the group to NYPD headquarters at One Police Plaza in Manhattan.

There was the grim-faced Giuliani, flanked by Safir and other officials within his inner circle. Both the mayor and his police chief seemed anxious to placate the angry blacks who barely had settled into their seats when, according to Clarke and several of the leaders, Safir declared: "There is no justification, there is no excuse we could give. This was done by a criminal. It was a criminal act."

Giuliani interrupted, saying that the allegations were shocking and would be investigated quickly and thoroughly. He told the group that Volpe and Charles Schwarz, another officer implicated in the attack on Louima, had been arrested and that nine other officers who were in the stationhouse at the time of the incident were put on desk duty until officers came forward and talked.

Clarke frowned. She sensed Giuliani was revving up to commandeer the meeting—a move she pre-empted with a stentorian declaration: "*I* asked for this meeting, so *I* am conducting it."

The imperious mayor waved off his deputies and yielded the floor to Clarke, whose aggressive style often caused comparisons with that of her heroine, Winnie Mdikizela Mandela.

"We want to know what you are going to do to address the concerns of our [West Indian] community," Clarke said, presenting a list of demands, including the immediate removal of the commanding officers of the 70th Precinct, "or whoever had information" on how Abner Louima wound up "spit[ting] out the bloody stumps of his teeth" in the stationhouse bathroom.

Giuliani likely knew that Clarke and the other leaders left the meeting thinking nothing would come of their demands. His telephone call the following morning was meant to assure Clarke he was serious.

"It's Rudy Giuliani, Councilmember Clarke," the mayor said. "Did I reach you at a bad time?" Clarke cleared her throat.

"We listened to you and your community last night," Giuliani said. "Commissioner Safir and I have decided to take the advice of the community. We intend to transfer the entire command of that precinct."

Clarke thanked the mayor and urged that he and Safir canvass black neighborhoods, particularly West Indian enclaves, and assure residents that nothing like this would ever happen again.

After he hung up, Clarke paused. Why, she wondered, was the usually dismissive Giuliani suddenly listening to what black leaders like her had to say? Was this the same Rudy Giuliani from whom she had tried to exact an apology for cheerleading a racist police riot near City Hall, where a brazen cop called her "nigger" and blocked her way into the building?

The latter question troubled her the most. In 1992, about 15,000 mostly white, off-duty officers gathered near City Hall to protest then-Mayor David Dinkins' criticisms of police actions in dealing with black suspects. Dinkins had joined growing calls to reinstate a residency requirement for hiring cops, and was reorganizing the Civilian Complaint Review Board to be independent of NYPD control.

There were beer-drinking cops in the raucous crowd, many of whom stomped on the hoods of parked cars and shrieked racial insults. Some carried signs calling Dinkins a "nigger" and "washroom attendant," and telling him to "lead black people back to Africa." This was the climate in which Giuliani, who was seeking to oust Dinkins at the time, climbed onto a platform and denounced the mayor in an impassioned speech. Of the officer who'd called her "nigger" and blocked her path to City Hall, Clarke said, "Can you imagine if he found himself in an unfamiliar neighborhood?"

Sometimes the 5-foot-4 Clarke was all that stood between the police and a younger generation of Jamaicans, the dominant immigrant group in her district, who were quick to say, "Ruud bwai an' poliis a no fren," ("The street tough and police are no friends.") Caribbean New Yorkers tend to favor either the island politics of racial resentment, no matter how proud they are of their blackness. But the growing alienation of younger, poorer West Indians was made clear during the Crown Heights rebellion in 1991. A shadow group of third-generation Guyanese, Trinidadians, Barbadians, Grenadians, Vincentians and Dominicans joined in the street violence. They were openly contemptuous of African American activists like Sharpton, Alton Maddox and Sonny Carson. Who were these "bombaclaat foreign" pimping off their grief and telling them how to react to the death of the Guyanese boy, Gavin Cato, killed by the motorcade of the Lubavitch grand rebbe? (One Jamaican youth said, "We nah listen to dem bloodclaat, you know. We ah go bu'n dem devils, Rasta. We want justice. Night time ah de right time. We ah fe dead fe justice. Dead!") Before long, rude boys and cops were mixing it up in the streets.

In January 1997, Clarke raised the alarm about an internal police memo targeting Caribbean Americans. The memo directed borough commanders to fax arrest sheets to a street-crimes unit "in an effort to identify individuals arrested of West Indian or Jamaican descent." A high-level NYPD source said the department had been providing the Department of Immigration and Naturalization Service with a list of West Indian suspects so that immigration officials could initiate deportation proceedings against them. "Jamericans" (Jamaican Americans) are among the largest number of undocumented workers being rounded up and sent back to their economically depressed homeland.

In 1989, Clarke was a member the Jamaican Committee on Civil Rights that blasted the NYPD, Manhattan District Attorney Robert Morgenthau and the federal Bureau of Alcohol, Tobacco and Firearms for suggesting that most Jamaican immigrants belong to violent drug gangs known as posses.

Clarke's district had grown more culturally diverse in recent years with an influx of Haitian immigrants determined to shed their "boat people," "AIDS-carrying" and "voodoo-worshipping" image to join the ranks of the so-called "New Jacobins"—the name adopted by young, upwardly mobile Haitians digging for gold in "New Jack City."

The sojourn of the million or so Haitians in the New York City area is full of ambiguity. In the post-Aristide era, they are torn between looking backward to their homeland and becoming American. If at times they keep their distance from African Americans and cling to their cultural identity, once in New York they discover that they cannot escape American-style racism. The white mob in Howard Beach that chased Trinidad-born Michael Griffith to his death onto the Belt Parkway didn't stop to ask if he was native-born. And the Haitian community did not fail to note the contrast between the welcome given exiles from Castro's Cuba and the forcible detention of thousands of Haitians fleeing "Baby Doc" Duvalier's oppressive regime. As a high official in the Reagan Justice Department, Giuliani helped shape and implement that policy.

No ambivalence is more marked than the West Indians' relationship with the police. It's not always clear whether they fear crime or the NYPD more. On the one hand, crack and what goes with it have devastated Flatbush, East Flatbush and Crown Heights, which are less underclass ghettos than precincts of struggling working people. Giuliani's success at battling crime tangibly did improve everyday life and got rave reviews. At the same time, virtually every West Indian knew someone—often their own children—who'd had a bad experience with the police. For anti-Duvalier Haitians who grew up fearing the Tonton Macoutes, Duvalier's dreaded secret police (former members reportedly used to start trouble at Le Rendez-Vous), the torture of Louima seemed like a betrayal of their struggle in the United States. A relative of one of the club's owners told me Louima was for him "a symbol of the irony of coming from suffering in Haiti, thinking that we had escaped that kind of pain."

In Flatbush, tension between New Jacobins and police had been rising. Some cops at the 70th Precinct stationhouse who called themselves the "Laws of Flatbush" had been arresting unlicensed Haitian dollar-van drivers, demanding excessive documentation of their immigration status and even beating them.

Clarke talked to Inspector Jeremiah Quinlan, commanding officer of the precinct at the time, about the alleged harassment and beatings. Quinlan told her he would take care of it after he returned from vacation in Negril, a beach resort in Jamaica.

"I arranged for the police command in that area to receive him, to talk about policing and cultural sensitivity, and to take him out for an evening to show him the nicer side of what Jamaicans and other Caribbean Americans are all about," Clarke told me. A high-ranking police source told the *Daily News* that under Quinlan cops at the stationhouse "always had a cowboy attitude." With 64 civilian complaints in 1996, the year before the Louima incident, the precinct ranked 11th of 76. On July 31, "cowboys" and mourners at a church service clashed when they began giving tickets to double-parked cars, escalating tensions between the Caribbean community and police. "They don't like us, and we don't like them," a cop was quoted as saying.

Abner Louima was part of the wave of West Indians who were clawing their way up, reclaiming neighborhoods in Brooklyn and the suburbs through home ownership and gaining political recognition. Their influence is symbolized by the West Indian Day Carnival, a colorful celebration of steelband, calypso, and reggae, that draws two million people to Eastern Parkway. Carnival is a sign of a distinct Caribbean identity, but as the major politicians who flock to it from throughout the state attest, it also is a sign of a burgeoning Caribbean American influence.

At the time of the incident, Louima was a college graduate and naturalized U.S. citizen, and had been married for almost two years to Micheline, also an immigrant from Haiti. The couple had a one-year-old son, Abner Jr. Louima worked as a security guard patrolling a sewage plant in Brooklyn, and was licensed by the NYPD to carry a gun. He trained in Port-au-Prince as an electrical engineer; Jean-Bertrand Aristide was dean of his school.

"He wasn't a homeboy from Bed-Stuy with a long rap sheet," said Carl Thomas, Louima's Trinidad-born attorney. But Officer Justin Volpe wanted to humiliate the law-abiding Louima—to "break a man," as he allegedly put it. One officer reportedly told investigators that when he walked into the bathroom, he saw Volpe holding a large stick and standing behind Louima, who was bent over. When the officer asked what happened was going on, Volpe replied that Louima had become incontinent.

While Louima grunted and crawled around on his knees in a pool of his own blood and feces for about an hour and a half, the rogue cops allegedly raised the specter of deportation. Louima told his lawyer that a cop had searched his wallet and did not find his green (naturalization) card. It was one of the rare occasions during his ordeal that Louima broke his silence. "I am an American citizen!" Louima declared.

Sonya Miller was the Jamaican nurse in the X-ray room of Coney Island Hospital early on the morning of August 9. White cops from the 70th Precinct stationhouse had brought in a 30-year-old black man they claimed they found injured, and with his pants down, lying in the street in front of Le Rendez-Vous, which the cops initially described as a "homosexual club." The man was horrifically injured.

At least one cop tried to convince Miller and doctors that Louima was a victim of "abnormal homosexual activity." But Miller's hospital training taught her that the vicious injuries she saw could not have been from gay sex.

"He was nervous and in intense pain," Miller would later recall. "Every time he looked at the police has was terrified."

With Louima's bloodshot eyes staring vacantly, beads of sweat welling on his forehead as he tugged anxiously at the handcuffs that shackled him to a gurney, Miller ordered the cops out of the examination room and drew the curtains.

She loomed over the swollen, broken mouth of Louima and cocked her ear. He told her he'd been arrested, beaten and sodomized by the cops. Miller knew that violating the hospital's strict policy on patient privacy could get her fired. But Abner Louima was no ordinary patient. "Who should I call?" Miller whispered in his ear. Two days later, Miller called the Internal Affairs Bureau of the NYPD, as well as NY1, the local all-news cable-TV outfit. Next, Miller told another nurse, Magalie Laurent, a Haitian, to make a follow-up call to Internal Affairs and to contact Louima's family.

On August 14, the morning after the incident was front-page news and Louima had become, as *Daily News* columnist Mike McAlary put it, "America's most famous victim of police brutality since Rodney King," Miller reached out to Una Clarke, in whose district office her mother was a volunteer worker. "It was too much for any human being to have gone through," Miller told Clarke. "You have to do something about." That's when Clarke called Police Commissioner Safir, with whom she'd clashed over the infamous "West Indian memo."

THE BRUTALIZATION OF ABNER LOUIMA paved a path for the Haitian American elite, long searching for an inroad to city politics. It was the afternoon of August 12, four days after the police torture of Louima had come to light. Mayor Rudy Giuliani had come to the Croisade Evangelique church on East 31st Street, a section of Flatbush some call Little Haiti, to huddle privately with Louima's relatives. The meeting was fraught with tension.

Caught in a web of political machinations spun by Giuliani's administration, the more socially active side of Louima's family was locked in a bitter quarrel with the wealthier, more conservative half of the family, led by Abner's uncle, the Reverend Philius Nicolas. The white-bearded minister lived on Long Island, but was a member of Little Haiti's power elite and had a back-channel link to City Hall.

"The meeting was organized by the rich side," said a source who attended the meeting. "Abner's father, his brother, his sister, his mother, and wife have nothing to do with this. Essentially, Abner's family's survival is tied to Reverend Nicolas." Louima's parents were renting an apartment in a building owned by Nicolas and were members of his church.

According to an insider, the rift between the two sides that afternoon resulted in the "deliberate exclusion" from the meeting of Carl Thomas and Brian Figeroux, Louima's Trinidad-born lawyers. The Nicolas faction contended that the lawyers' militancy and strong ties to the New York chapter of Lavalas—the movement that backed Jean-Bernard Aristide and swept him to power in Haiti's first free elections in 1990—were annoying the Giuliani mayoral campaign. But friends of the Louima family said that Thomas and Figeroux weren't at all interested in Giuliani damage control; the lawyers' association with anti-Giuliani Haitian activists served as a reminder of Giuliani's legacy to Haitians, they told me.

As an associate U.S. attorney general in charge of the Immigration and Naturalization Service in the early 1980s, Giuliani was responsible for enforcing the policy that led to the detention of thousands of Haitians fleeing the brutal regime of Jean Claude "Baby Doc" Duvalier. Giuliani insisted that the Reagan administration quarantine Haitian refugees to save Miami from being overwhelmed by crime and disease. But now, the Republican-Liberal mayor was asking the immigrants he once feared not to organize against him in the fall elections.

A source who was at the meeting said Giuliani appeared remorseful. No longer was he demanding that New Yorkers reserve judgment about the white policemen accused of sodomizing Abner Louima with a toilet plunger while uttering racial slurs in a bathroom of Brooklyn's 70th Precinct stationhouse. As the meeting dragged on, a member of the Louima faction slipped away and alerted Abner's lawyers. "They were not invited," Reverend Nicolas intoned.

Once inside, Thomas and Figeroux took Giuliani to task for initially insisting that what happened to Louima was an isolated incident. The mayor hardened. "He said his hands were tied because of the police union," the insider recalled. "He said if he fired the officers, they would be back to work in a month."

Shortly after the lawyers had their say, the meeting broke up. Giuliani left, but his staffers, as well as Figeroux and his colleague Casilda Roper-Simpson, who practices criminal and personal-injury law, remained behind, working the crowd inside the church. Thomas was waiting outside when a black stretch limousine pulled up. Out stepped Sanford Rubenstein, a personal-injury lawyer who'd represented Haitians in a couple of high-profile, police-related cases, including that of a cab driver who was shot and critically wounded by a cop in Greenwich Village in 1992. Rubenstein was with Dr. Jean Claude Compas, Louima's personal physician who runs Family Medical Practice, a popular Haitian clinic in Crown Heights, and is closely aligned with Reverend Nicolas. The men were greeted by the preacher and his son Samuel, and quickly took their whispered meeting inside.

"I was getting ready to leave because I felt some kind of deal was being cut between the Nicolas family and Rubenstein," Thomas later complained to a colleague. But according to the insider, Roper-Simpson emerged from the church and told Thomas that Figeroux was "going off" on Rubenstein; he was raising questions about Rubenstein's motives, accusing Rubenstein of ambulance chasing. Figeroux was portraying Rubenstein as "a little vulture" feeding upon tragedy and wanting a piece of the $55-million lawsuit he and Thomas had filed against the city on behalf of Abner Louima.

Thomas, with the build of a linebacker, pulled Figeroux aside.

"Do you know who I am?" an angry Rubenstein demanded of Thomas.

"I think you're an obsequious piece of shit," replied Thomas, a former deputy director for community affairs in the Brooklyn district attorney's office. Rubenstein's presence in the case had fanned the flames of racial mistrust. "You're a bloodsucker! You only pimp off our community!" the insider quoted Thomas as saying.

"It was a bit rocky at the beginning," Rubenstein admitted understatedly.

Reverend Nicolas intervened and ushered the lawyers and Louima's family into a nearby room. There, according to a witness, he told Thomas and Figeroux that they had been hired to pursue the criminal aspect of the case, while Rubenstein had been invited to handle the multimillion-dollar lawsuit.

"Why would you do something like that?" Thomas shouted. "It makes no sense! We are getting screwed from the front and behind. White guys did this to Abner! Why would you bring in a white guy to make money off the case?" (Nicolas declined comment.) According to the witness, Thomas then suggested that if Nicolas wanted to add a heavyweight lawyer to the team, why not dump Rubenstein and hire O.J. Simpson's attorney, Johnnie Cochran?

"I represented Aristide," Rubenstein said in self-defense. "I have a good reputation in the Haitian community."

CARL THOMAS AND BRIAN FIGEROUX did not inject themselves into Abner Louima's life. Until the events of August 9, they were relatively unknown adjunct professors at Brooklyn College who also ran a law firm. Thomas, a specialist in criminal and civil litigation, taught two courses, "The Politics of Criminal Justice" and "Understanding the Supreme Court." Figeroux, a general-practice attorney with experience in divorce law, taught "Blacks and the Law." Current and former students, mostly black and of West Indian heritage, maintained close ties to them.

After Louima was arrested and hospitalized, one of Figeroux's former students (whose sister was dating Abner's brother) urged what he referred to as "the poor side of the Louima family" to contact Thomas and Figeroux. But "the rich side," arguing that the black lawyers had little trial experience and were considered by consultants to be "weak and ineffective," disagreed, and instead hired Sanford Rubenstein, though he was not interested in the political ramifications of the case. "He thought it was a regular police-brutality action," said the insider.

As Louima lay still handcuffed to his bed in Coney Island Hospital, Rubenstein dispatched an associate with a retainer agreement for him to sign. On learning of the move, Figeroux rushed to Louima's beside and dismissed Rubenstein's emissary. "We have this case!" he declared.

The rejection of Rubenstein reportedly angered Dr. Compas, a member of the Haitian American Alliance that had organized an August 29 justice-for-Louima protest march on City Hall. Compas, a prominent member of New York's Haitian American upper crust and a force in Haitian political circles, demanded that Rubenstein be put back on the case. That was when Rubenstein and Compas showed up at Nicolas' church. But not everyone in the Nicolas family marched to the dictates of its patriarch.

Enter Al Sharpton.

"It was Tuesday night when I got the call from Abner's first cousin, the nationalist in the Nicolas family," Sharpton told me. By Wednesday morning, the brutal beating and maiming were on front page pages. Sharpton, Thomas and Figeroux, and Abner's wife arrived at Coney Island Hospital, where they met Norman Siegel of the New York Civil Liberties Union.

"Oh God, it's Sharpton," a white reporter said contemptuously. "He's gonna make this Haitian the poster boy of his campaign."

Indeed, Sharpton was running for the Democratic mayoral nomination. He was lagging in the polls, which at the time showed Manhattan Borough President Ruth Messinger leading the Democratic pack. But long before Giuliani's belated denunciation of the toilet-plunger assault, the civil-rights activist had been drawing the line between the normal and the abnormal. For decades he'd campaigned to weed out brutal and racist cops. When a questioner at a Democratic mayoral debate implied that Sharpton was ambulance chasing in the Louima case to attract votes, the candidate replied matter-of-factly, "I am the ambulance."

Outside the hospital, in the glare of cameras, Sharpton could not have hoped for a better photo op. Abner's grieving wife collapsed in Sharpton's arms in stunning similarity to Roma Cedeno's fainting spell when she and the preacher-activist marched in Washington Heights the previous April to protest the "bullet-in-the-back" killing of her 16-year-old son Kevin by a white police officer.

After holding a news conference, Sharpton and his entourage attempted to enter the hospital, but were barred by an official who said Louima was still under arrest and could not have visitors.

"We're his attorneys, and Reverend Sharpton is visiting as a minister at the request of the family," Figeroux protested. When the official resisted, Sharpton dispatched an aide, Anthony Charles, to reason with the hospital administrator. Sharpton was befriended by the administrator during a stint at the hospital for treatment of a stab wound. A white man had plunged a five-inch stiletto into Sharpton's chest as he was preparing to lead a justice march through Bensonhurst in January 1991.

Just as Sharpton was about to take his battle to see Louima to the press corps, a police officer told him he was cleared to visit the prisoner on religious grounds. Sharpton, Abner's father and Thomas were escorted to the room where Abner lay handcuffed to the bed, flanked by a phalanx of cops. "You would have thought this kid was Tupac Shakur," recalled Sharpton, the first public figure to see Louima.

"Whatever you could do, please help. Get justice for my family," Louima begged Sharpton and Thomas. Sharpton prayed with the victim.

By the following day, Abner Louima was a household name in New York. His image was everywhere, and so was Al Sharpton's. But not everyone wanted Sharpton to trumpet Abner's rage. That evening, someone telephoned a death threat against Sharpton to the *Amsterdam News*. "The caller said, 'Reverend Sharpton's life is in danger,'" said Wilbert Tatum, publisher of the Harlem-based weekly. Tatum said those were the only words the caller said. "It was not a crank call," he insisted. Police were notified.

On Friday morning, former Mayor David Dinkins, whose administration tried, but failed, to excise brutal cops, appeared outside of the hospital with Sharpton and Thomas. Sharpton and Dinkins, who endorsed Messinger for mayor, embraced in a show of unity and raced upstairs to visit the brutally injured man. Louima recounted the horror of his torture. Dinkins asked if there was anything he wanted him to do.

"I was the only breadwinner for my family and I don't know how we're going to survive," said Louima.

"We'll look into something," Dinkins promised.

"No," Sharpton interrupted, "let me see what I can do right now, because I don't want that on his mind."

Other than genuinely wanting to alleviate Louima's financial burden, the candidate had a hidden motive, according to an aide: He didn't want to leave the door open to Rudy Giuliani.

"When Yusuf Hawkins was killed in Bensonhurst by whites in 1989, [former Mayor Ed] Koch offered Yusuf's father a job to try to win the family over to his campaign. Rev. was thinking that Giuliani would try to buy the Louima family off," Sharpton's aide, Anthony Charles told me.

While Sharpton and Dinkins were at the hospital, Police Commissioner Safir was meeting with Haitian community leaders, some of whom did not endorse Sharpton's involvement in an anti-police brutality protest planned for the next day in front of the 70th Precinct stationhouse. Marilyn Mode, Safir's spokesperson, told *The New York Times* Safir's intent was to explain the department's stand against police brutality and to encourage a peaceful protest. But Safir had underestimated Sharpton's relationship with the Haitian community. In 1992, while Giuliani still was defending the policy under which intercepted boats packed with Haitian refugees were forced to return to Haiti, Sharpton was visiting the country and watched the Haitians arrive on U.S. Coast Guard ships. He denounced the repatriations and accused the U.S. government of racism.

"Lemme hold your cell phone for a minute," Sharpton told Dinkins as Abner winced and stirred in his bed. The minister called boxing promoter Don King and Luther Gatling, president of 100 Black Men. He reached King, who promised to visit Louima. On Saturday, shortly before Sharpton led his own demonstration in front of the stationhouse, he took King to Louima's bedside. Louima's weary eyes lit up on seeing King. Sharpton introduced them and prodded Louima about the financial assistance he needed.

"How much do you make a week?" King asked.

"Four hundred," Louima replied.

"I'll give you $5,000 right now," said King in a raspy voice. He wrote a check and handed it to an astonished Louima.

"Does anybody have a camera?" the bewildered Louima asked. "I want to take a picture with Don King and Reverend Al." Sharpton's assistant took the photo, which the *Amsterdam News* published. Sharpton had pulled off a public relations coup, but the political battle for Abner Louima was far from over.

The day after Sharpton's visit, *New York Post* columnist and Giuliani backer Steve Dunleavy claimed that the quick-witted Sharpton had planted the infamous phrase "Giuliani time"—the words Louima swore police officers shouted at him as they shoved the wooden handle of the toilet plunger into his rectum. "There's no indication at all that he told police that the alleged perpetrators ever said anything to him about it being Giuliani time.... Then the Rev. Al Sharpton visited Louima on Wednesday. Suddenly, the lawyers were heard to say: 'This is Giuliani time, not Dinkins time,'" Dunleavy wrote.

However, by that time, Rudy Giuliani's reputation for gun-butt diplomacy was firmly planted in the consciousness of most fairminded New Yorkers.

The attempt to enlarge the cast of characters unintentionally landed the conflict in the domain of black American community activists anxious to make a show of force. This was not the first racially charged incident in which African Americans tried to get hold of a Caribbean-dominated issue. During the boycott of a Korean grocer in Flatbush who was accused of "disrespecting" a Haitian woman (Sister Jiselaine) American black militants wrested control of the street protest. And in the Crown Heights conflict of 1991, African American activists criticized West Indian leaders for proceeding with Carnival and their healing gesture of inviting some of the Lubavitch rabbis to march in the parade.

The West Indians struck back hard in *Carib News*. Where did African American activists get the nerve "to tell the Caribbean community ... how best to conduct struggles for justice?" And they rejected another American black leader's comment about "grinning and skinning on Eastern Parkway" as "disrespecting Caribbean people."

On August 16, Haitian American leaders supposedly were in control of thousands of demonstrators who converged at the 70th Precinct stationhouse. "As temperatures steamed into the mid-90s, the raucous crowd swelled to 4,000, with many pounding drums, dancing, and hoisting Haitian flags and plungers in the air in a racially charged, sometimes carnival-like scene," the *Daily News* reported. "Despite scattered skirmishes, no one was arrested in the tense standoff ... even as many in the crowd chanted, 'Pig,' 'Shame on you,' and 'Seven-0, KKK.' Someone from the crowd lobbed an empty water bottle, hitting a police officer in the eye."

Una Clarke was among the protesters that day, urging calm. "Rioting is not going to get us anything," she told a group of young marchers, who were not Haitians. "There is a legal process, and although we may not always get just justice in the court, we think that this is such an open- and-shut case, there is very little anybody could do to sweep it under the rug."

But some in the crowd said it was naïve to think that merely playing the role of establishment agitator could ensure justice.

"Mau mau the pigs!" an old Garveyite shouted.

Enter Sonny Carson, the gerontic militant known for his icy temperament. He and Clarke had had the same clash before. Again she warned the people not to succumb to the lure of Carson's explosive brand of racial politics. Carson countered that the sodomization of Louima "should remind our young people of the legacy of the '60s," referring once again to the prospect of taking up arms against cops. Clarke said Carson didn't have that kind of influence on anybody. "The mayor believes that I am a leader in my own right and that the community of Flatbush and Crown Heights responds to me and my request of them," she said. "I organized some 30 leaders who met with the mayor, so he already saw legitimate leadership."

In the weeks leading up to the Democratic primary, Giuliani was unusually cooperative with Clarke. "I called the mayor directly and the mayor called me directly," she recalled. "Most of the time [when] I talked to him he would say, 'Councilmember Clarke, I trust your judgment completely.'"

On August 19, 1997, the day before Giuliani announced he had allocated as much as $15 million for a new task force to investigate police misconduct, Deputy Mayor Randy Mastro called Clarke in Wilmington, Del., where she was on City Council business. "He said the mayor wanted me to serve on the task force," recalled Clarke. She grilled Mastro about the makeup of the group that included Norman Siegel of the NYCLU; Abraham Foxman of the Anti-Defamation League of B'nai B'rith; Michael Myers of the New York City Civil Rights Coalition; commentator Felipe Luciano; and *Daily News* columnist Stanley Crouch.

Clarke was running for re-election and was wary about being used. "I told Randy Mastro that I would think about it. I also reminded him that it was an election year and that I was a Democrat who was seen as a wild card because I spoke my mind and called things the way I saw them." she said. "I told him that I didn't want to waste my time on a task force that wouldn't make any difference." Clarke said Mastro told her that the mayor was serious about improving relations between blacks and the police. She said she accepted the appointment only after thinking that the militants would view her absence as a sign that she really couldn't achieve justice working along with the system.

Maybe pre-election jitters moved Giuliani to reach out to Clarke; maybe Giuliani truly wanted to reach the "other New York" that felt left out of his New York. Ironically, West Indians, who prize civic order and property values, were potential recruits to his constituency, and Clarke's principled pragmatism had far more support than the alienated fury of the Carson types. Neither possibility would unfold if law and order meant beating up Caribbean kids. Rudy Giuliani could only make his tentative efforts at reaching out more than ceremonial by showing that he would be as tough on police brutality, racist disrespect and the blue wall of silence as he would be in fighting crime.

PART IV
All Politics Is Local: Black Democrats Switch Allegiance to Giuliani and the Republicans (1997–1998)

for Hugh Hamilton, Andy Johnson, and Amy Virshup

and in memory of Ron Plotkin

10

The Great Betrayal

Negroes are human, not superhuman. Like all people, they have differing personalities, diverse financial interests, and varied aspirations. There are Negroes who will never fight for freedom. There are Negroes who will seek profit for themselves alone from the struggle. There are even some Negroes who will cooperate with their oppressors. These facts should distress no one. Every minority and every people has its share of opportunists, profiteers, free-loaders and escapists.

—From *The Sword That Heals* by Martin Luther King Jr.

ONE MONTH BEFORE THE 1997 MAYORAL ELECTION, as many as 40 black leaders switched their allegiance from Democratic nominee Ruth Messinger to Republican Mayor Rudy Giuliani. In a city reeling with racial tensions heightened by rampant police brutality—and presided over by a controversial mayor on the verge of being re-elected to a second term—only 13 of them were brazen enough to want to be seen venturing into Giuliani Land.

At least 30 of the defectors were civil-rights advocates, community activists, business people, and religious leaders who pledged their troth to Giuliani after Al Sharpton finished a close second in the primary and then lost a court battle to force a runoff with Messinger. Though Sharpton praised Messinger in a speech at a Queens church, even he doubted whether it was enough to stem a new tide of black power-broker support for Giuliani. (Sharpton told me he chose Queens to announce his support for Messinger because he wanted to "declare war on the turf of the silent Giuliani supporters." He said he went there "to smoke them out and step on them like the roaches that they are.")

Political operatives said some of the leaders were swayed partly by Giuliani's much-vaunted record on crime and his support for illegal West Indian commuter-van drivers who had been trying to get city licenses. According to Haitian political activists, the Reverend Philius Nicolas, uncle of police-torture victim

Abner Louima, quietly was urging members of his conservative Croisade Evangelique church to throw their support behind Giuliani. There was no hard evidence that the black leaders had sold out to curry favor with the Giuliani administration, but clandestine wheeling and dealing to split the leadership in black strongholds hostile to Giuliani was a tactic of the mayor's campaign strategists.

The prominent blacks lured to Giuliani included Brooklyn Congressman Edolphus Towns; Brooklyn-Queens State Senator Ada L. Smith; Queens Congressman Floyd Flake; Queens Assemblyman Thomas White; City Councilmembers Lawrence Warden of the Bronx, Adam Clayton Powell IV of Harlem, and Priscilla Wooten of Brooklyn; and DeCosta Headley and Diane Gordon, Democratic state committee leaders in Brooklyn's 40th Assembly District. On September 27, when Towns and Flake endorsed Giuliani, Flake didn't mind tarnishing Dinkins' tenure as mayor. "It would be unfortunate if New York City returned to the era of drive-by shootings, children unable to play in playgrounds because of rampant crime, and young men and women involved in illegal drug dealing found dead in alleys," he told reporters.

The mayor also received endorsements from Stanley Hill, the powerful leader of District Council 37, and Charles Hughes, president of the School Cafeteria Workers Union; the Reverend Arlee Griffin of Brooklyn's Berean Missionary Baptist Church; and Deborah Wright, president of the Upper Manhattan Empowerment Zone Development Corporation.

The high-profile black support for Giuliani provoked strong reaction from Dinkins. "I believe that those Democrats who have endorsed Giuliani in the face of police brutality and all the things that are going on now—that I say are bad for black folks in this city—should be seen not as allies but as the opposition," he said. In an extraordinary move to punish the defectors, the usually stolid Dinkins encouraged Sharpton to challenge the incumbent Towns. On October 8, at a celebration of Jesse Jackson's 56th birthday at a Manhattan restaurant, Dinkins, fashionably late, walked in, congratulated Jackson, pointed to Sharpton, and proclaimed, "This is the first meeting of the Sharpton for Congress Committee!"

The crowd erupted in laughter.

"I'm serious!" Dinkins declared. "Al ought to run against Ed Towns, and I'll be the first to back him."

Sharpton, his political appetite whetted, seemed to relish the idea of going after Towns. He shoved aside a plate of roast chicken and linguini and listened intently.

"Jesse, you could get him to do it," Dinkins implored "You need to lean on him!"

Soon Jackson was caught up in plotting Towns' political demise, recalling how, in a 1992 contest with then City Councilmember Susan Alter, he helped pull Towns from the brink of almost certain defeat.

Sharpton, though pledging to work to ensure Towns' ouster, wouldn't commit to running against him. "Dave's request is under careful consideration," he said diplomatically.

Dinkins and Giuliani had loathed each other since Giuliani's triumph over the city's first black mayor in 1993. Dinkins relentlessly criticized Giuliani's abysmal record on police brutality. Referencing the iconic police torture of Abner Louima, City Council hearings on police misconduct, and Giuliani's courtship of black political powerbrokers to bolster his campaign, Dinkins was exhibiting renewed zeal for political retribution. Yet, exhorting Sharpton to run against Towns came as more than a surprise; it was the first time Dinkins was backing the civil-rights activist for elective office. In the mayoral primary, Dinkins endorsed Messinger over Sharpton who, without consultants, pollsters or TV ads, garnered 32 percent of the vote.

Now Dinkins was actively wooing a would-be insurgent, and he didn't care who knew it. "I did tell him to run," Dinkins confirmed. Towns' attempt to interest Sharpton in backing Councilmember Priscilla Wooten—one of Giuliani's most outspoken black supporters—should have triggered alarms about the congressman's ultimate motive. But it didn't.

Wooten and Charles Barron, a former Black Panther, were in a heated battle for Brooklyn's 42nd Councilmanic District. According to Sharpton, Towns set up a breakfast meeting that included himself, Sharpton and Headley at Sharpton's Flatbush home. Towns told Sharpton that he and Headley were ready to support him, but had one problem: Sharpton was backing Barron against Wooten, Headley's candidate. Sharpton told them he wouldn't withdraw his support for Barron, who had gone to jail with him after a 1987 "Day of Outrage" civil-disobedience protest. Besides, Wooten had hosted a town hall meeting to introduce Giuliani to her supporters. (Towns denies this account.)

"This woman is despicable!" Sharpton declared, upsetting Headley.

Wooten, Headley insisted, was the more experienced candidate and deserved to be re-elected.

"Priscilla Wooten is a sellout to Giuliani!" insisted Sharpton, "and even if I didn't like Barron, I would do anything to defeat Priscilla."

("That's not the Al Sharpton I know," Wooten would later tell me. "He has supported me in the past.")

Towns intervened. He said he was locked in a bitter fight with then-County Leader Clarence Norman over judicial delegates. Norman was supporting a mostly white slate. Towns said he would support Sharpton and Wooten if Sharpton backed his black judicial candidate.

Unlike the black elected officials who visibly stood with Sharpton, Towns chose to express his support indirectly, through the media. During Sharpton's court fight to force a runoff with Messinger, Towns' aide, Jennifer Joseph, notified Sharpton that the congressman desperately wanted to see him. By then, as Sharpton remembered, he was hearing "unbelievable rumors" that Towns was going to endorse Giuliani. Sharpton said that Towns had even assured Harlem's Congressman Charles Rangel that he would not cross over. But when Sharpton and Towns finally spoke by phone, Towns told Sharpton "out of respect" that he was going with Giuliani.

How could Towns do this?

Sharpton had helped elect Towns' son Darryl to the state Assembly and had been associated with Towns since 1972, when Sharpton was youth director for Shirley Chisholm during her run for president. Towns was running for district leader then, and Chisholm asked the young activist to support him. "This man has killed our people, Ed," said Sharpton, referring to Giuliani's unequivocal support for white cops who shoot black suspects under questionable circumstances. Sharpton told Towns, "There is no way I'm gonna sit by and let Giuliani gain inroads in the black community."

Bill Lynch, Dinkins' former deputy who was vice chair of the Democratic National Committee, said Towns' defection made no sense. He said he hadn't seen "any evidence of campaign largesse" being funneled to Towns' district. "Usually, in return for an endorsement, a politician would get some kind of project or program for the community—a movie theater," Lynch said. "But what did Towns get? Oh, man, you ain't seen cheap."

Was black power for sale?

"Absolutely!" said Lynch.

11

The Battle Over Al Sharpton's Next Move

Remember that sometimes the threat of action is more effective than the real thing.

—Martin Luther King Jr., on leadership

ELEVEN DAYS AFTER THE MAYORAL RACE, Al Sharpton—mopey, his massive torso deflated—is slouched behind a desk in a fourth-floor office overlooking Eighth Avenue in midtown Manhattan. Dressed in a white V-neck T-shirt, the trousers of a pinstriped business suit, and occasionally stroking his unruly pompadour, he looked more like a man in pain than the always-taunting New Jack activist with the pit bull simper.

Certainly the former mayoral candidate had pressing problems on his mind: mounting campaign debts, income tax headaches, and trial in a $165-million defamation lawsuit brought against him by former Dutchess County prosecutor Steven Pagones, whom Sharpton had accused of raping Tawana Brawley. But on this morning, he seemed not nearly as rankled as he ought to be by all this. "There is infighting in my camp," he said wearily—confirming the rumor that had spread like a wildfire: David Dinkins wanted him to run for Congress, for Edolphus Towns' seat, as political payback.

One group of advisers was goading Sharpton to parlay his new-found popularity into a reform-oriented campaign for Congress. Another faction, composed of some of his most trusted allies, rejected the idea of a congressional bid and instead wanted to groom him for the mayoral election in 2001. "The arguments are so heated, it borders on hostility," Sharpton confided. "They are at each others' throats."

Dinkins headed the Sharpton for Congress forces, who included Jacques A. DeGraff, Sharpton's campaign manager; Assemblyman Clarence Norman Jr.,

133

leader of the Democratic Party in Brooklyn; the Reverend DeVes Toon, Sharpton's Brooklyn campaign coordinator; Frank Mercado-Valdez, a Giuliani backer
and president of the African Heritage Network who contributed $7,700 to
Sharpton's campaign; and Sharpton's longtime confidant, Anthony Charles.

The other group was led by the Reverend Wyatt Tee Walker, who raised the
initial $15,000 in startup money to launch Sharpton's mayoral campaign; Byron
Lewis, CEO of UniWorld Group Inc., a black-owned advertising agency, who
contributed $6,700 to Sharpton's campaign; and Carl Redding, Sharpton's body-
guard and chief of staff.

The feud opened up a floodgate of conspiracy theories, with Walker's team
warning that the push for Congress might have been a Machiavellian strategy by
longtime enemies to derail Sharpton's mayoral ambitions. "They feel it is a plot
to get me off the citywide scene for 2001," Sharpton said.

According to Sharpton, Walker and others suspected that top Democrats
already were cutting deals with mayoral hopefuls like City Comptroller Alan
Hevesi, a staunch critic of Sharpton's ties to Nation of Islam leader Louis Farrakhan and Africentric historian Leonard Jeffries. During the week when it looked
like there might be a runoff, Hevesi attacked Sharpton for saying that Farrakhan
was not anti-Semitic and for refusing to denounce Jeffries. Some political analysts
saw the broadside as a calculated move by Hevesi to remind Jewish voters that
such alliances should be hard to forgive.

The row set Sharpton and Hevesi on a collision course. On November 2, at a
Democratic fundraiser for Messinger attended by President Bill Clinton, Hevesi
walked over to Sharpton, who was in the company of Bronx Borough President
Fernando Ferrer and Carl Redding. The comptroller shook hands with both
men, and extended the gesture to Sharpton, who pouted and left Hevesi hanging.
"My problem with Hevesi was not that he attacked me," Sharpton told me. "I felt
that he was disingenuous and was race baiting. He reminded many of us of Ed
Koch, who said Jews would be crazy to vote for Jesse Jackson. Alan Hevesi is an
Ed Koch Democrat, and we defeated them in 1989."

It was the same Hevesi, according to Sharpton, who endorsed Roger Green,
the black Democratic assemblyman from Brooklyn, for public advocate over the
white incumbent, Mark Green, "so he could get cover" to back Deborah Glick
for Manhattan borough president over C. Virginia Fields, the popular councilwoman from Harlem, "and not look racist." Sharpton said that if he wound up in
the race for mayor against Hevesi, he would remind black voters that Hevesi
joined controversial Brooklyn Assemblyman Dov Hikind in leading "racist demonstrations" against Mayor Dinkins during the Crown Heights upheaval. "Any

man who can stand on a flatbed truck with Dov Hikind has got some nerve telling anybody to denounce anybody," Sharpton fumed. "Dov Hikind is perceived by many of us in the black community the same way many in the Jewish community perceive Leonard Jeffries."

Would he support Hevesi if Hevesi were the Democratic nominee? "I supported Ruth Messinger in '97 as the best alternative to Giuliani, but under no circumstances would I support Alan Hevesi," Sharpton vowed. "We do not intend to go back to that kind of racially polarizing Democrat in 2001." Sharpton said Walker theorized that "the one person who could upset Hevesi in 2001 is me. But if political strategists get me into a local race, they'll take me off the citywide push."

Dinkins maintained he wasn't part of any conspiracy to deny Sharpton the mayoralty and had no ulterior motive. He conceded, though, that if Sharpton were to go after Towns, it would protect his old friend, Congressman Major Owens, a bitter, 20-year rival of Sharpton. "Friendship goes by the board on this one, but I assume Owens would be very pleased I did that," Dinkins said. *The Village Voice* reported that Sharpton's real aim was not the mayoralty but to build a political movement for an all-out battle against Owens.

"Owens and I have never had any great love for each other," Sharpton admitted. "He is aligned with the white-liberal establishment, which has always been critical of me."

The competition for Sharpton's attention was unrelenting. On October 31, amid the clinking of champagne glasses at a 17th wedding anniversary party for Sharpton and his wife Kathy at their home in Flatbush, Dinkins, Norman and Toon raised the issue once again. "Reverend, get on board. Get this thing going," Dinkins cajoled. Norman, according to Sharpton, backed the idea of going after Towns, with whom he had been feuding over a judicial candidate for Surrogate Court in Brooklyn. He said Norman told him he wasn't opposed and that he knew "a lot of people who were excited" about his possible run against Towns.

Toon approached Brooklyn Assemblyman Albert Vann, seeking his backing for a Sharpton fundraiser in a possible race against Towns. On November 10, the day *The New York Times* finally got around to acknowledging the Sharpton-for-Congress story, Walker demanded a meeting with the very reluctant candidate. Walker, who also chairs Sharpton's Harlem-headquartered National Action Network, rebuked Sharpton for giving "serious consideration" to the Dinkins power play.

"We did not build a citywide movement to run for a congressional seat," Sharpton said Walker told him. Walker reminded his friend that in 1988, political opponents masquerading as friends concerned about Jesse Jackson's future almost convinced Jackson to shelve his presidential ambitions and instead mount a challenge against Washington, D.C., Mayor Marion Barry. "Now they're trying the same thing with you," Walker asserted. "Do not forsake the movement you've built up by going for a congressional seat," he pleaded.

Two days after the meeting, a confused Sharpton called Dinkins and told him what Walker was demanding of him. "They're crazy!" Dinkins retorted. "We must punish defectors. Al, you won Ed Towns' district three times." Dinkins, Sharpton recalled, argued that snatching Towns' seat would help build momentum for a mayoral bid. "One does not cancel out the other," Dinkins reasoned.

In 1996, when Sharpton announced he would run for mayor, many considered it a joke and he was written off as a publicity-seeking charlatan. Today, with speculation that he may be one of the Democratic Party's rising stars, many of those same critics treat him with grudging respect. "I am a political reality," he boasted to me. "I came within an inch of forcing the first runoff in two decades in the City of New York."

Sharpton pointed out that some of his most persuasive advisers, like Dinkins and Norman, did not believe in his candidacy for mayor and endorsed Messinger over him. "Now everybody's jockeying to ride me," he said. "You have a former mayor of New York and a county leader aligned with members of my own staff fighting other members of my staff over what I should do politically."

The infighting over Ed Towns might have been a reason that Carl Thomas, the outspoken lead attorney for Abner Louima, was mulling over Sharpton's invitation to join his NAN board. Thomas, an admirer and political ally of both Sharpton and Towns, reluctantly was drawn into the fray. Like Sharpton, Thomas was a crossroads politically. "He was torn between working with us and the fact that he got Towns to do a favor for Louima," Sharpton said.

The affable Thomas had a far more solid relationship with Towns. It was Towns who introduced him to the cutthroat world of Brooklyn politics by engineering his candidacy for chair of the judicial convention, which meets during the Democratic primary to nominate state Supreme Court judges. Towns reinforced his ties to Thomas by cutting through Justice Department red tape to secure a visa for Louima's 6-year-old daughter to leave Haiti and visit him in the hospital. Feeling indebted to Towns and Sharpton, Thomas skirted the question of loyalty.

"Carl Thomas is a good friend of mine," said Sharpton. "But does Carl's support of me mean that he is working to defeat Ed Towns? I don't know, but we sure would like to have him on our side."

The decision about which office, if any, he would seek ultimately rested with Sharpton. Lately he'd been remonstrating with the ghost of Adam Clayton Powell Jr., the legendary Harlem congressman and Baptist minister who defied the political establishment, vigorously advocated black power, and became mired in a series of legal and financial fiascos that eventually resulted in his expulsion from Congress. "I've always felt that somebody should have continued to fight for the many social programs that Adam put through for the underclass but are now being abandoned," said Sharpton. "If there's anything that bothers me in the wee hours of the morning, when I think about these efforts to draft me, it is Adam saying, 'You can go there!'"

Almost every morning since that internal struggle began, Sharpton said he'd awake with "a growing compulsion" to declare his candidacy for Congress, where he could practice what Powell preached. Sometimes, he confided, "the ultimate kick in the pants"—the one factor that compels him to run—is the irony of Powell's son, Councilman Adam Clayton Powell IV from Harlem, endorsing Giuliani for re-election. "Giuliani's hero is Fiorello LaGuardia. My hero is Adam Clayton Powell, and Powell used to kick LaGuardia in the behind about his racism," Sharpton said. "It's almost as if Powell's son, who gave up his Council seat in an unsuccessful bid to become Manhattan borough president, endorsed LaGuardia's legacy over that of his father."

Caught up in a debate over a decision that would affect him for years to come, Sharpton's understandable reluctance to dash the hopes of backers in both camps who believed he could win an important election in New York City also could doom his chances of victory. Suddenly, saying, as he often did, "I will do what is best for the movement," simply wasn't enough.

12

The Battle for Harlem

IN MAY 1998, ON *NYI'S* "Inside City Hall," Reverend Butts, a quasipolitical adviser to Governor Pataki, accused Mayor Giuliani of cultivating an atmosphere among the police that had led to an increase in brutality toward young blacks and merchants along 125th Street. Butts also criticized the Giuliani administration's decision to fire 600 employees at Harlem Hospital.

"Are you calling him (Giuliani) a racist?" asked host Dominic Carter.

"Yeah. Yeah," Butts responded. "I don't believe he likes black people."

Carl Redding, a top aide to Sharpton, denounced Butts' attack on Giuliani as a "desperate attempt" by Butts to pull ahead of other black mayoral hopefuls. Moreover, Redding charged, it was a desperate move by the firebrand preacher to smother community outrage over his support for Governor Pataki, whose administration reportedly was trying to wrest control of Harlem's historic Apollo Theater from one of Butts' longtime political foes.

Redding told me that some of Sharpton's campaign advisers—who felt Sharpton would be the black mayoral frontrunner—were shocked by Butts' "racial sound bite." They predicted it would come back to haunt him. "He hit the Freddie (Fernando) Ferrer self-destruct button," scoffed Redding, referring to the Bronx borough president who, in an alleged bid to win black votes during the 1997 Democratic mayoral campaign, called the police killing of 16-year-old Kevin Cedeno "an execution."

"Freddie Ferrer tried to out-Sharpton Al Sharpton and wound up having to drop out of the race for making a controversial remark that annoyed white voters," Redding said.

Butts panicked, Redding said, because "he was seeing establishment blacks" and powerful Latino allies rallying around Sharpton's crusades. "Everyone—from Congressman José Serrano to Jesse Jackson and a whole new generation of black elected officials like Congressman Gregory Meeks—supported Sharpton for mayor. We're not seeing that type of coalition around Reverend Butts."

Redding noted that, with the exception of disgraced former Tawana Brawley attorney C. Vernon Mason and Nation of Islam minister Benjamin Muhammad (the former Ben Chavis, who was fired as executive director of the NAACP after a sex scandal), no prominent blacks were standing with Butts at his news conference at his church with several Harlem residents who said they had been harassed by police. "Butts couldn't get one prominent black to come out," Redding declared. "They're upset with this Pataki Tom for trying to bring Republicans into Harlem to meddle in our affairs."

Many uptown political observers believed the Sharpton camp was on to something. Allegations of financial mismanagement at the Apollo might have created a phony invitation for upstate Republicans to intervene in one of the community's most divisive power struggles, they said. At the heart of the dispute—and, apparently, the Republicans' prime interest—were blacks jockeying for a congressional seat, a stake in nominating the next black mayoral hopeful, and, some said, a six-year-old vendetta that pitted a black frontman for Pataki against four of the inner city's most powerful leaders.

The Apollo controversy widened a schism that, political insiders said, provoked open hostility from some Republicans for former Manhattan Borough President Percy Sutton, Congressman Charles Rangel, former Mayor David Dinkins, and former Deputy Mayor Basil Paterson. The main negative focus, however, was on Sutton and Rangel's stewardship of the Apollo Theater Foundation, the nonprofit group formed in 1992 to guide the theater into profitability. In early May, the *Daily News* reported allegations that the Inner City Theater Group, Sutton's television company that produces "It's Showtime at the Apollo" on NBC, had failed to live up to its licensing agreement with the Apollo and owed the landmark theater more than $4 million. Rangel, chairman of the foundation, balked at the inference that he and Sutton bankrupted, cheated or stole money from their beloved enterprise.

As Rangel put it, "Is it that difficult to believe that two guys from Harlem could be straight and not have this crooked relationship?" In the cutthroat arena of New York politics, where, Rangel pointed out, "it's popular to pile on," there seemed to be no simple answers to the congressman's rhetorical question.

Uptown Democrats claimed that a Republican conspiratorial maneuver triggered state and city officials to hold up $750,000 in loans and grants for the financially troubled Apollo, as well as an investigation by state Attorney General Dennis Vacco. These developments were supposed to signal the political demise of Rangel and Sutton, Harlem's political godfathers. Local black Republicans, smelling blood, showed up at Sharpton's House of Justice in Harlem, where Rangel and Sutton had been summoned to a community hearing to debunk gossip about a financial scandal.

The black Republicans denounced the makeup of the panel that was convened, charging it was stacked with Democrats and political cronies of Rangel and Sutton. The awkward showdown led an infuriated Sutton to suggest that he was being attacked because he was black; he vowed to file a lawsuit. In the aftermath, however, some of Pataki's operatives beat a hasty retreat.

Insiders told me that Randy Daniels, the black senior vice president of the Empire State Development Corporation, the Apollo's landlord, pleaded with Pataki not to abandon him as Republicans headed for cover when community reaction to the investigation began to rumble against them. It was Charles Gargano, Empire's chairman and a top Pataki aide, who authorized Daniels to pull the plug on the Apollo's funding.

"Gargano asked Randy Daniels to withhold additional funding for the Apollo until questions regarding its finances could be resolved," Caroline Quartararo, a spokeswoman for the Department of Economic Development, told the *New York Post*.

Daniels was truly alone as his bosses sought to deflect blame. An Albany insider said Daniels asked Butts to "please tell the governor don't leave me hanging out there." Butts initially had advised Daniels against "doing the Republicans' dirty work" in Harlem, the insider said, but Daniels was adamant.

Butts distanced himself from this account, saying he wouldn't discuss the controversy with Daniels or Pataki. And Quartararo said that Daniels was advised not to comment while Vacco was conducting his investigation. But Daniels allegedly was on a mission to destroy the "Gang of Four," the disparaging moniker opponents used to describe Rangel, Sutton, Dinkins and Paterson. Rangel told the *Post* that Daniels had an ax to grind because Dinkins had fired him.

In October 1992, Daniels was forced to resign from the Dinkins Administration—days after his appointment as a deputy mayor—amid unproven charges of sexual harassment. His accuser, former *NY1* reporter Barbara Wood backed down from her initial charges in a pretrial deposition two years later. "In a highly charged political atmosphere, my patron betrayed me," Daniels told free-lance reporter Philip Nobile in a 1995 interview. "Bush stood behind Clarence Thomas to the end, but Dinkins gave me three days. I was told to find three white feminists to take my side, or else my appointment was dead. A year after Anita Hill, no Black man could do that."

A former Dinkins aide, who asked not to be named, claimed Daniels "had said privately after he started working with Pataki that he was going after the uptown establishment, which is Charlie, Percy, David and Basil. He said at a minimum they should have provided him with a golden parachute, a good-paying job outside of government," the ex-aide said.

"I had nothing to do with it," Rangel insisted.

"We had nothing to do with David not appointing him," reiterated Sutton.

"Why did they take us on? I guess it's because Percy Sutton is on one side and Charlie Rangel's on the other, and we're part of the Dinkins team," Rangel said. "That's the only thing I can speculate on."

If indeed the Republicans had a master plan to exploit the power struggles, some blacks warned that the battle eventually would be not just over the Apollo Theater, but for Harlem itself.

"It's about George Pataki and Charles Gargano wanting to turn that prime real estate called Harlem over to their developer friends," said the former Dinkins official. "To accomplish that, they must erode some of the community's icons and diminish their power. They hope to get a free ride under the guise that they are going to develop this community. Who are they going to develop it for? Who is going to own and take control of Harlem?"

If the power struggle around the Apollo was predictable, the outcome was not. As rumors of Butts' involvement in a Republican dirty-tricks campaign to discredit Rangel, Sutton, Dinkins and Paterson continued to resonate within Harlem, Butts was forced to redefine his relationship with Daniels and Pataki. "The perception is that Randy Daniels is Butts' man, but Butts is sincere in telling me that he is not," one of the targeted Harlem Democrats told me.

But in an interview with me, that wasn't how the minister characterized his relationship with Daniels, whom he described as a "walking deacon" in his church and his neighbor. "Our families are friends, so I would consider him a friend," Butts said. When Daniels was informed by Dinkins in 1992 that he would not be appointed deputy mayor, he immediately turned to Butts and sought refuge at the Abyssinian.

Despite such close ties, Butts declared: "I knew absolutely nothing about the origin or the plan of attack regarding the Apollo Theater situation," adding that though he might have engaged in "some political jousting" with Sutton in the past, trying to embarrass a dean of Harlem politics simply was not his style. "I have too much regard for Percy to do that to him," Butts said.

As for his relationship with Pataki, Butts bragged: "I am close to the governor. There are things that the Pataki Administration is doing, and will do, to benefit the African American community, particularly Harlem. I don't intend to end a positive relationship with the governor." Because of the relative ease with which he accomplished projects that often required more than pledges of commitment from federal, state and city officials, Butts was labeled "the Republicans' poverty pimp in Harlem" by envious community leaders. "I'm not a poverty pimp," he retorted. "I'm out here struggling, working on behalf of the community. Everything I do is above board. People have gotten used to dealing with me because they know where I work. Anybody can come and look at the books, look at the deals we've made with people who don't think we are trying to shake 'em down."

Butts renovated several units of low-income housing, won contracts to restore landmark Harlem businesses like Small's Paradise and the Renaissance Ballroom, and also was credited with muting community opposition to the construction of a Pathmark supermarket on 125th Street. Some speculated that Butts, who has said he wrestles with "the idea of whether or not to go into politics," was reinforcing his political connections all along. "It's a genuine quest," he said of a possible political life, "and it looks more and more like I would do it."

On April 12, demonstrators with placards touting "Butts for Congress" and "It's Time for a Change" showed up outside the Sharpton-led community hearing in Harlem. "Whoever did it made Butts look foolish," said a longtime admirer of the minister. "It didn't help him at all." A perennially rumored candidate for public office, Butts emphatically denied that he had organized the demonstration or was planning to challenge Rangel, who has been in Congress since 1970. "Those signs were not mine; whoever did it was trying to sabotage me," Butts insisted. "Charles Rangel himself knows that I've said when I'm ready to run, before I make a public announcement, I would sit down and tell him first. I'm not going to go out there and plant little bombs near him or try to implicate him in something."

The fact that Butts has not yet formally announced that he wouldn't challenge Rangel might explain why the issue remains so sensitive to C. Virginia Fields and David Paterson (Basil Paterson's son), who will not challenge Rangel because of their reverence for the elder statesman—although they're both waiting in the wings to succeed him when he retires. Said one old-guard politician: "I told someone that what Butts ought to do is prepare himself, because Charlie will not be running all his life. The people he will be up against are Virginia Fields and David Paterson. Charlie is not his enemy, they are. They are the new generation when Charlie is gone."

"I'm not going to run against Charlie now, but it does look like there is a strong possibility that I would go for the mayor's seat," Butts revealed to me.

That prospect was seen as a far more serious danger by his opponents. "It's making some folk upset because they think they got some kind of magic hold on who runs for mayor," the minister asserted. "I don't think it's Percy or Charlie. Some people have mentioned some [names] to me, but I'm not interested in dignifying those people by mentioning [their names]."

Some of Butts' allies were not so evasive. They pointed to the usual suspect—Al Sharpton, whose sights were already locked on the 2001 mayoral race. It's no secret that the frosty relations between the two civil-rights leaders grew colder in January after *New York* magazine juxtaposed their pictures on its cover, posing the question, "Which Would You Choose, Dr. King?" while asserting, "Calvin Butts Challenges the Old Model of Black Leadership in the City."

PART V
Getting Used to Dying
(1998)

for
Piggy, Chicken, Snail, Rickie, Howell, Boney, Val, Evrol, Farmer, Ishmael, Din-din, Smacker, Boy, Live, Ralphie, Ken, Watson, Sonny, Arthur, Lickshot, South, Kent, Toppin, Glen, Winston, Alan, Fraser, Toto Man, Kiwi, and Poungcin'

13

If We Must Die

✦

Khallid Abdul Muhammad and the Making of the Million Youth March

If we must die, let it not be like hogs
Hunted and penned in an inglorious spot,
While round us bark the mad and hungry dogs,
Making their mock at our accursed lot.
If we must die, O let us nobly die,
So that our precious blood may not be shed
In vain; then even the monsters we defy
Shall be constrained to honor us though dead!
O kinsmen we must meet the common foe!
Though far outnumbered let us show us brave,
And for their thousand blows deal one deathblow!
What though before us lies the open grave?
Like men we'll face the murderous, cowardly pack,
Pressed to the wall, dying, but fighting back!

—Claude McKay: *If We Must Die*, (1919)

ON A STEAMY MORNING IN JULY 1998, Khallid Abdul Muhammad knelt on the pavement outside Sylvia's Restaurant on Malcolm X Boulevard in Harlem and began frantically rifling through the contents of a bulging black leather bag—dumping out a ream of private correspondences with city lawyers, maps, confidential memos, surveys, and other strategic plans regarding his controversial Million Youth March.

For months, Khallid's National Black Power Organizing Committee had been working on a day of outrage meant to draw a million young blacks to Harlem to protest police brutality, black-on-black crime, and joblessness. The march had provoked heated opposition from the Giuliani administration, but that morning, Khallid was preoccupied with resistance from a very different quarter: The day before, he had been informed that Nation of Islam leader Louis Farrakhan—his onetime mentor and sometime antagonist—had sent him an "urgent correspondence" by Federal Express, and at the moment, Khallid was ripping through the city's considerable correspondence in a frustrated attempt to locate the FedEx tracking number for Farrakhan's letter.

As a small group gathered on the sidewalk to watch him, Khallid finally pulled out the missing number. But while we rode the A train to 42nd Street to pick up the letter, his anxiety mounted; beads of sweat broke out on his forehead. By the time we pulled into the 42nd Street station, he was shaking and tears were welling in his eyes. "All that time on the train, I was trying to fight back tears," he confessed later. "I didn't want you to see the softness and tenderness that came out of me over my anticipation of what the minister would say in his letter. I wanted to hide its emotional impact on me. I wanted to hide that."

At the FedEx terminal near Eleventh Avenue, a clerk handed over the letter. Farrakhan began by praising Khallid as a first-rate "warrior," then proceeded to scold him for his rush to destroy the enemy. "'You can only kill just a few of them,'" Khallid read. "'But your God can kill more than that. Haven't you noticed the irregular rains, snow, hail and earthquakes, the fires that are raging around the country? I know you are angry at this enemy who has oppressed our people. But if you will be patient, our God can offer much more punishment than you.'"

The letter lectured Khallid about the dangers of his impatience, not only to himself but also to the black youth Farrakhan feared Khallid was pitting against Giuliani's "racist" police force. Farrakhan ended by reiterating his stern warning about the violence that could be incited by the march.

Khallid read and reread the letter. But if it was intended to persuade him to call off the march, at no time did he consider doing so. He couldn't do that even if he wanted to, he confided. Black pride was at stake. His own reputation hung in the balance. With all due respect to the minister, said Khallid, no one was going to stop his march.

Khallid had kept his word. His brinkmanship had pushed the city toward its most serious racial conflict in years, pitting blacks against Giuliani, black leaders against one another, and Khallid Muhammad against everybody else. On September 5, if Khallid's plan is realized, upwards of 100,000 black youth will gather on Malcolm X Boulevard. Arrangements had been made to bus in Crips and Bloods from Los Angeles and Vice Lords from Chicago as well as other gang members from around the country. Gangsta rappers and other entertainers also were expected, and the numbers would be swelled by children and teenagers from the five boroughs.

To Rudy Giuliani, who had been crisscrossing the country touting his accomplishments in bringing order to New York City (and who was trying to persuade the GOP to choose New York as the site for its millennial convention), a huge, angry march by young blacks in the heart of the city was something to be avoided by any means necessary.

Giuliani quickly vetoed Khallid's initial request to hold the march in Harlem on September 5, claiming that the event would stretch an already taxed police force and shutter area businesses on one of the busiest shopping days of the year. Khallid firmly rejected the city's counteroffer of Van Cortlandt Park or Randalls Island. With negotiations at a standstill, both sides agreed to meet personally on May 20 to discuss the issue. Two days before the meeting, Malik Zulu Shabazz, the then 31-year-old Washington attorney who was the national youth director of the march, wrote a strongly worded letter to Gabriel Taussig, chief of the city's administrative-law division. Shabazz insisted that the only acceptable site for staging the Million Youth March was Harlem's Malcolm X Boulevard, calling the neighborhood "sacred ground from which our greatest ancestors have loved us [and] labored to uplift us."

Khallid's proposed rallying ground stretched from 118th Street to 147th Street. In an attempt to appease the city on the issue of public safety, he suggested that an emergency lane could be kept open along the entire route to Harlem Hospital. Other major thoroughfares, such as 125th, 135th, and 145th Streets, would remain open to emergency vehicles and other traffic. Despite their public pronouncements, as early as May, organizers had privately reduced estimates of the anticipated crowd to "more than 100,000."

If Harlem was unacceptable, Khallid said, organizers would accept only two other venues: the plaza outside the United Nations or Brooklyn's Eastern Parkway. The last choice—a neighborhood that is home to 10,000 Orthodox Jews—was Khallid's trump card. "We wanted to scare all the yarmulkes and rabbis to death" he said.

Given the lingering bitterness, Khallid's venomous diatribes were the equivalent of throwing acid on a burn. "We wanted to take this right to the area that had slapped us in the face by killing our little baby, Gavin Cato," he told me.

"We would love to have had this march on Malcolm X Boulevard. But we would equally love to take a million black people to Eastern Parkway and just kick it to these crackers."

At a news conference in Harlem on July 30, an unrepentant Khallid repeated his threat to move the march to Brooklyn for "a direct confrontation with the Jews who have misused and abused our people in Crown Heights for so long." His threat prompted an equally combative response from Mordechai Levy, leader of the militant Jewish Defense Organization, who warned that if "one Jew is touched by the Farrakhan-led Black Nazi of the Nation of Islam there will be serious reprisals. No Jew must allow the black-skinned storm troopers to make a pogrom."

On August 5, Giuliani fought back in kind, branding the event a "hate march" and Khallid a "hatemonger." With both sides holding firm, the issue ended up in the courtroom of Judge Lewis Kaplan, who ruled that the city's refusal to grant a permit was unconstitutional. With Khallid by his side, Shabazz crowed that the city's blacks had won a crucial victory over "Adolph Giuliani."

A grandstanding ex-con who survived an attempt on his life by a fallen black Muslim and death threats from white extremists, Khallid Muhammad styled himself a "truth terrorist." His violently racist, anti-Semitic, anti-Catholic, and anti-gay vitriol played to an inner-city audience of disaffected, jobless youth, gang members, and Africentrists.

At a time when there appeared to be a black-leadership vacuum, Khallid's rise put mainstream blacks in a vexing position: Privately, they disdained much of his message, but publicly they often held their tongues for fear of alienating his growing constituency. Khallid learned his political tactics from Louis Farrakhan, whom he served as national spokesman from 1991 to 1994. But Farrakhan eventually expelled Khallid because his "vile" rhetoric proved too much for even the minister to tolerate. By co-opting the radical wing of the Nation of Islam, Khallid became a threat to the minister's power. His supporters view him as a reincarnation of Malcolm X, expressing their rage in ways that traditional black leaders could not.

The details of his private life belied his carefully crafted image as a pious roughneck. A six-foot-tall former high-school quarterback, he was a fastidious dresser, given to curious moments of vanity. He refused, for example, to divulge his exact age, saying only that he was "somewhere in my forties." His head was a cue ball perpetually brilliantined with baby oil and buffed to a shoe-shine gloss. On the day we met, the Ray Ban sunglasses, black swat-team uniform, and combat boots he'd recently donned for his televised showdown with the Ku Klux

Klan in Jasper, Texas, were gone—replaced by gold crocodile-skin shoes and a matching $2,000 single-breasted, custom-tailored suit that made him look more Edwardian than Mac Daddy.

But Khallid insisted he was "no GQ revolutionary." It's just that "brothers and sisters around the country got tired of seeing me wearing the same old shoes and jackets and suits." Khallid said the gifts poured in at a time when "I kept on trying to survive. I was down. Bookings for my lectures were down, plans for a CD of my speeches and raps fell through. Allies stopped working with me for one reason or another. So people who love me began sending things. Alligator shoes, Rolex watches, and suits and stuff. No money, just nice things."

Khallid had no office. Instead, he had been conducting business out of the trunk of his $140,000 ocean-blue Rolls-Royce. An unabashed materialist ("The Honorable Elijah Muhammad said that the black man should have the best of everything"), he used a second Rolls, a 1954 Classic, to cruise the city. He said he derived the lion's share of his income from speaking engagements at campuses like Brown University and Spelman College, where he reportedly commanded up to $10,000 a speech. For the past three years, workers had been painstakingly refurbishing the landmark nineteenth-century brownstone he purchased on Harlem's historic Strivers' Row. The house, which he estimated would be worth $1 million when it was completed, had five bedrooms, six bathrooms, and a private master-bedroom suite that overlooked a rear yard where horse carriages once parked. Khallid selected Kente cloth and other African fabrics for the curtains, drapes, and upholstery; sculptures and paintings by black artists would adorn each room.

C. Virginia Fields, then Manhattan's borough president, bought a house across the street. In recent years, a procession of whites had moved in as well. "They need to remember," Khallid growls, "we got there first."

KHALLID ABDUL MUHAMMAD WAS BORN HAROLD MOORE JR. in Houston sometime in the late forties. When he was two years old, his teenage mother, Lottie, moved to Livingston, Texas, and left young Harold in the care of an aunt, Carey Vann, who eventually legally adopted him. He grew up with Vann in a tiny house in downtown Houston that abutted the interstate, and while he maintained contact with his biological parents, Khallid grew emotional when he talked about his "second mother."

"My mama Carey took in sewing, sacrificed for me, nurtured me, and nourished me," he said. "I never saw her with another man but my uncle." Both his father and his uncle were alcoholics, he said, "but they were very good people."

Harold grew up in a segregated society that mandated separate drinking fountains and rest rooms for blacks and whites. His devoutly religious aunt taught him that God created all the races and didn't favor one over the other. Early on, Harold wanted to become a preacher. "I used to stand on the porch on a box and use the banister as my pulpit and preach to the cars passing by," he recalled.

A gifted student, he attended a segregated high school, where he was quarterback on the football team, a champion debater, and an active member of the school's drama organization. In the late sixties, he spent four years at New Orleans's Dillard University, though he never graduated, and also spent a summer at Harvard, where he studied urban politics and urban sociology. "In a week's time, I developed a Bostonian accent," he would later tell an interviewer about his Ivy League experience. "I felt that we were the cream of the crop." But he was increasingly affected by the growing black-power movement then taking root in the nation's urban centers. "I was really impressed with the brothers and sisters with their dashikis and their big, big Afros on their heads and their little babies."

Those images had a profound impact on Harold. Around the same time, he read *The Autobiography of Malcolm X* and became obsessed with the activist. "I went to the barber shop where Malcolm used to get his hair cut. I talked with men and women who knew him, and went to their homes. I wanted to trace the footsteps of Malcolm and understand his upbringing as much as I could. It was in that lily-white environment at Harvard that I really turned black."

Around this time, Harold became enamored of a radical campus group called *The Ten Blacks*, which espoused black separatism and further calcified his own increasingly extreme views. "I had never seen black people so tough in my life," he said. "The Ten Blacks would have these weekly meetings and white folks would come in from different corporations, and the black folks would beat the heck out of them. But the white folks kept writing them big checks and left all kinds of donations." Khallid admitted that throughout his life, white people and even Jews offered to help him achieve his goals or finance his movement, but he could not bring himself to associate with "the devil," adding, "I believe with all my heart that the government killed my heroes, and the government is representative of white folks and Jews. I have to hate all of them."

In 1967 he was introduced to Louis Farrakhan, whom he considered the most profound influence on his life. When they met, Khallid was attending Dillard, while Farrakhan had recently become national spokesman for Elijah Muhammad. "I was a student leader on the campus, so I picked him up at the airport," Khallid recalled. "I got to ride with him and talk with him. I had on my long

Nigerian dashiki and a big Malcolm X medallion around my neck that must have weighed a pound or two, with Malcolm's picture etched into one side and by any means necessary on the other.

"My Afro was touching the roof of the car. And I didn't really do too much bathing at that time, because I was rebelling against everything. I didn't want to use the honkie's soap. I didn't want to use the honkie's deodorant. I didn't want to use nothing from the honkie. So my dashiki, you could lay it down in one corner and it would walk to the other side of the room by itself. And this is the kind of savage that Minister Louis Farrakhan came into contact with."

Farrakhan's lecture was one Khallid would never forget: "He was so gentle, so kind and full of wisdom. And he told me, 'Brother, one day you're going to help resurrect our people." But while Khallid was impressed with Farrakhan, he remained distrustful of the Nation, whom he blamed for the murder of Malcolm X.

Curious, Khallid started attending Nation of Islam meetings in New Orleans. "There was always a question-and-answer period in those days, and I would go to the meetings and argue with the ministers," he remembered. "I'd go with my posse, and we would challenge the minister.

"At that point, I was very close to the Black Panther Party and always wore my black beret and leather jacket. So I insisted on wearing my beret into the mosque and the lieutenants weren't going for that, so they escorted me firmly to the door. I was banned from the mosque for a short while. Ultimately, the minister there said, 'Aw, let him come back.' But I came back fighting harder than before."

After a while, Khallid began to be impressed by the doctrine of self-control and self-reliance preached by the black Muslims. During one meeting at the mosque, he even found himself applauding. "I was almost frightened by that," he said. "I knew that they had me. That night, I stood up and accepted Allah." The next time Farrakhan saw Harold Moore Vann, he had adopted the name Malik Rashadeen and had traded in his beret and leather jacket for the starched suit and bow tie of the Fruit of Islam.

By 1985, Khallid had become Farrakhan's most trusted adviser. The name the minister gave his new deputy, Khallid, means "warrior." When he had ascended to the top position in the Nation of Islam, Farrakhan had faced a series of death threats. Khallid, who carried a .38 in a hollowed-out Bible, soon became Farrakhan's personal bodyguard and the Nation's minister of defense. He accompanied Farrakhan on fund-raising trips to Libya, where he became well acquainted with Muammar el-Qaddafi. Farrakhan also appointed him to deliver a speech on his behalf at the United Nations (which Khallid would later derisively refer to as the "Jew-nited" Nations).

DURING HIS OFF-HOURS, KHALLID CUT a wide swath through upper Manhattan, clad head-to-toe in Versace and doused in African oils, Polo Sport, and Calvin Klein's Obsession. He was seen escorting a procession of beautiful black women, "sisterfriends," including models and actresses. Though he refused to talk about his personal life, friends said that during this time, Khallid, who was twice married and divorced, fathered two sons by two different women. His older son, Khalfani, was 19 then, and in college. The younger, a 13-year-old named Farrakhan, frequently accompanied his father on his trips around the nation.

In February 1988, Khallid's standing in the Nation suffered a devastating blow when he was sentenced to three years in federal prison for using a false Social Security number to secure a $175,000 home-mortgage loan in Atlanta. Evidence also showed he submitted doctored tax returns to the mortgage broker.

At his sentencing, U.S. District Judge J. Owen Forrester admonished Khallid for betraying the trust he had earned among followers of the Nation of Islam. Incensed over the incident, Farrakhan sent a letter to the judge saying Khallid would not be allowed to continue teaching within the ministry. But three years later, Khallid was back, heading up a mosque in Los Angeles. Not everyone was happy to see him return.

From his first day back, recalled Khallid, "there was murmuring around the Nation that I would be the next "hypocrite" after Malcolm X. Those murmurings were fanned by Jabril Muhammad, a Nation elder and spiritual adviser to Farrakhan.

"Whatever Jabril said was gospel," said Khallid. "He started saying that he saw me as the next Malcolm—but not in a positive sense. He felt that I would defect and turn on Minister Farrakhan the way Malcolm had turned on the Honorable Elijah Muhammad. Maybe he really believed that; I'm not sure. But Jabril considered himself a prophet, and when he made his prophecy, it stuck to me like glue. No matter what I did, it was whispered that I was going to turn on the minister." As Farrakhan tried to move the Nation more mainstream, Khallid's vitriol began to seem anachronistic. His comments about hook-nosed Jewish bloodsuckers and white devils started to embarrass Farrakhan, who repeatedly warned his disciple against going too far. Khallid's notorious 1993 speech at Kean College proved the last straw.

Then, on May 29, 1994, four months after Khallid's demotion, and moments after he'd delivered a speech at the University of California, Riverside, James Edward Bess, a former minister in the Nation of Islam, shot Khallid and three others. Bess was beaten by a crowd before police dragged him away. Khallid's son Farrakhan saw the shooting and began screaming, "They shot my daddy! Kill that bastard!" Khallid, who suffered a serious wound to his leg, spent three months in an L.A. hospital. When he got out, he took refuge in a luxury co-op in Cliffside, New Jersey, called Briarcliff, which featured tennis courts, a health club, and an Olympic-size swimming pool. His neighbors in the building were virtually all upper-middle-class white professionals, and 50 percent were Jewish. "We don't have any trouble out of him," a Briarcliff doorman told the *Daily News* that year. "He's quiet, and he doesn't bother anyone."

In public, however, Khallid was far from quiet; in fact, when he emerged from seclusion in 1995, he had become even more incendiary. He found a natural constituency among gangsta rappers whom he had courted while in the Nation of Islam. Khallid was invited to perform at concerts with NOI-associated groups like Kool-Aid and Rapp Operaman, and even rapped on albums by Public Enemy and Ice Cube, developing a following among their hard-core fans. He also became a familiar presence in South Central L.A., where he was called upon to mediate between warring gangs, urging them to organize themselves into a united army against white oppression.

"My greatest appeal is among the grassroots, the hard-core, the roughnecks, the gangsta-rap culture," said Khallid at the time. "It's my automatic weapon; it satisfies my soul. I don't just say things like 'Kill the enemy'; I honestly wanna kill the enemy. I want us to wage war against this bastard and I'm frustrated. I cried many times, hurt."

Khallid said he understood Long Island Rail Road mass murderer Colin Ferguson. "I mean, goddamn it, we're supposed to have at least one Colin Ferguson," he said. "I would be embarrassed if we couldn't point to one Colin Ferguson that decided one day to catch some train or walk in some place and just kill every goddamn cracker that he saw."

A year after he was expelled from the Nation, Khallid enlisted in the New Black Panther Party, a Dallas-based faction of the original Black Panthers that advocated armed resistance against the police and other self-defense tactics against racism. As a former minister of defense in the Nation of Islam—whose duties involved training the elite military guard known as the Fruit of Islam—Khallid soon had wrangled his way to a leadership role in the group. He renamed his ragtag, shotgun-toting militia the New Black Panther Party and New Black Muslim Movement. The cadre claimed about 500 members.

He functioned as a kind of mercenary, cropping up at the center of racial tempests nationwide. He led the Panthers on "show-of-force missions" throughout the South to protest the firebombings of black churches. Five months before his Million Youth March, Khallid and his New Black Panthers went to Jasper, the East Texas town where a black man had been shackled to the bumper of a pickup truck and dragged by his ankles until an arm and his head were torn off. His 75 armed troops tensely faced off against a phalanx of local cops, FBI agents, and Texas Rangers, and eventually chased a dozen Ku Klux Klansmen out of town.

Not surprisingly, the Giuliani administration jumped on Khallid's demagoguery to justify its opposition to the march, questioning whether a person who "has engaged in the worst kind of rhetoric about Jews, about whites, about Catholics, about the pope … should be allowed to carry a banner leading a lot of children."

But Giuliani wasn't the only opponent Khallid faced. Sources within the Nation told me Farrakhan feared that the march would erupt in violence that would tar him as well as Khallid. Instead, the minister had been backing a group of Atlanta-based youth activists who planned a counter-rally in Atlanta around the same time as Khallid's march.

In the June 2 issue of *The Final Call*, the Nation of Islam's newspaper, Farrakhan warned Khallid that Allah would punish him severely if he channeled black youth discontent into violence. "While the mayor and city officials in Atlanta seem to be acceptable to the Million Youth Movement, this more than likely is not the case in New York," Farrakhan wrote.

"Therefore, I would advise the organizers of the march in New York to make sure that you have dotted all the legal I's and crossed all the legal T's for you do not wish to give Mayor Giuliani and some of the racist New York City police an opportunity to exercise their hatred against our youth."

Nationwide, black leaders seized on Farrakhan's Atlanta rally as a less militant alternative to Khallid's. In New York, leading business, civic, and political leaders were so upset by Khallid's leadership of the march that they began calling people like State Senator David Paterson, urging him to mount a challenge to the so-called race rally. Paterson rejected the idea. That task was taken up by the organizers of the competing Million Youth Movement in Atlanta, who turned down several requests by Khallid to unite the marches.

Organized predominantly by civil-rights activists with strong ties to the Nation of Islam, the Atlanta rally was the prelude to a racially mixed youth conference planned by the NOI for 1999. Khallid's group shunned the integrationist direction of the NOI and its allies and wanted to keep the focus on young blacks. The Atlanta rally was scheduled four days, September 4 to 7, and won the endorsement of groups such as the National Association for the Advancement of

Colored People, the AFL-CIO, and the Rainbow/Push Coalition, headed by Jesse Jackson.

NAACP board chairman Julian Bond said he would await the outcome of "a test of wills" that would determine who drew the biggest crowd. "It may not reflect who is really reaching the young people, but we will all be looking if 10,000 show up at one march and 1 million show up at the other," he told *The Associated Press.*

FROM THE START, KHALLID HAD PUT PROMINENT BLACK leaders in a peculiar dilemma, torn between their constituents on one side and their white supporters on the other. Congressman Charles Rangel, the community's most powerful Democrat, was the first black leader to attack Khallid, predicting that the activist would spark a violent showdown with police and disappear. C. Virginia Fields condemned Khallid's "deplorable rhetoric." State comptroller H. Carl McCall railed against "the negative leadership of the hurtful and hate-filled Khallid." Freshman city councilman Bill Perkins, a staunch Rangel ally, warned that Khallid's "use of anti-Semitic statements [was] irresponsible, inflammatory, and dangerous." Perkins's main complaint was that "the organizers were based in Brooklyn and were not working directly with community leaders and residents of Harlem."

March organizers fought back, warning politicians like Perkins in a letter that their voiced fears of violence would be an "invitation to Giuliani and the police to move on us.... The whole Black nation will hold you responsible." But the attacks on Khallid backfired. Suddenly parents and relatives of young blacks began bombarding the offices of black politicians with phone calls, charging that the virulent remarks had created an unsafe atmosphere for their children. Since the march was going to proceed anyway, the politicians should have been thinking about ways to avert bloodshed. Black leaders reluctantly lined up behind the march, simultaneously trying to separate themselves from Khallid's rhetorical excess.

As controversy raged over his leadership of the march, Khallid jetted off to West Africa, where he had been promoting the march for three weeks. In New York, there was infighting over Khallid's role, with some on the organizing committee complaining that his rhetoric and reputation had overshadowed the march. Some prominent blacks complained that his confrontational style was threatening the safety of the marchers. "It is time to move the focus [of the march] beyond Khallid Muhammad," declared Fields. "We need the other organizers to come forward and take control of the message and the logistics of this event to find a [way that] a rally of this magnitude can be managed effectively, successfully, and peacefully."

While the Giuliani administration was appealing the federal ruling in support of the march, the police shooting of a black teenager who allegedly brandished a toy gun gave its organizers a new imperative. "If this case doesn't energize young people to march," said Sharpton, a cautious Khallid ally and the "religious coordinator" of the event, "what will?"

The NYPD had gone into "full mobilization" in preparation for the march, and organizers braced for the worst. Erica Ford, the New York coordinator of the march, called on the black community to drop off medical supplies at churches and other designated points in Harlem. Organizers also formed a private security force to supplement the 3,000 cops expected to ring the crowd.

IT WAS THREE HOURS AFTER THE MAN KHALLID would later call "a Jew judge," inadvertently increased the black Muslim's power in the city by giving him the green light to protest. As the Giuliani administration prepared to appeal, a jubilant Khallid raced to Harlem to attend a rally by the United African Movement. His audience of black ultranationalists gave him a hero's welcome.

"The youth chose me by a mandate," he shouted from the stage. "Why? Because this is not a generation of Uncle Toms.... This is a rebellious generation! ... Some silly Negroes say, 'We don't want it to be a Tiananmen Square.' When you don't know what to say, goddamit, just shut up! ... When are we ever gonna fight? You're not gon' vote your way outta this one! You're not gonna boycott your way outta this one! Somewhere down the line, there must be direct confrontation with the enemy!"

But Khallid was preaching to the converted. What he planned to say to the youth who would mass along Malcolm X Boulevard worried both critics and supporters alike. Some feared Khallid would blow it: that his combustible rhetoric would get their sons and daughters killed—if not on that day, some other day when an angry young blood with the words thug life tattooed across his chest feels inspired to take a stand against the oppressor.

Ultimately it was up to Khallid to determine whether his "Million Truth March" will be remembered as New York's version of Tiananmen Square. What will he do? As I watched Khallid prowl across the stage, I remembered something he told me after he and Farrakhan bumped into each other at Chicago's O'Hare Airport shortly after Farrakhan had sent him the chiding letter. "He had a big smile when he saw me," Khallid remembered. "We hugged for a long time. He had tears in his eyes. Tears ran down my face. He kept saying to me, 'Brother

Khallid, it's all right.' I didn't know what he meant. What was all right? He told me, 'You know what to do out there. If anybody knows what to do, it's you.'"

14

The Hunt for Khallid Abdul Muhammad

As we prepare to close out this rally, we want you to be steadfast. Look these bastards in the eyes, and if anyone attacks you, already decide who will be the one to disconnect the railing where you are, and beat the hell out of them.... The no-good bastards! And if you don't have a gun, every one of them has one gun, two guns, maybe three guns. In self-defense, if they attack you, take their goddamn guns from them and use their guns on them! In self-defense. Giuliani is known for taking his police and sending them off in riots. If any one of these bastards riots here today, you take their nightstick the way they did brother Abner Louima and ram it up their behind and jam it down their damn throats!

THE NOTION THAT KHALLID ABDUL MUHAMMAD TRIED TO INCITE a riot with those words at the Million Youth March, then ran like a bandoliered coward as cops stormed the stage, jibed well with the Giuliani administration's version of the tumultuous events of September 5. More than a month after Police Commissioner Safir conveyed the impression that every cop on the beat was hunting an aggressive adversary armed with ideology as well as guns Khallid had not been heard from or sighted.

Until I tracked him down.

Speaking from a safe house "somewhere in the hells of North AmeriKKKa," Khallid told me that he considered life as America's most wanted fugitive, as well as surrendering if a Manhattan grand jury, which was investigating "the persons responsible" for the "disorder and acts of violence," formally charged him.

"I am a freedom fighter," declared Khallid, whose unified New Black Panther Party and New Black Muslim Movement, I'd reported exclusively, was under investigation by the Joint Terrorist Task Force. "I have to be prepared every day that I open my eyes to fight the enemy in any way that the enemy presents itself," added the activist, who was often shadowed by members of his heavily armed militia.

Khallid—whom attorney Malik Z. Shabazz introduced at the Harlem march as "that bad, baldheaded black man" who "makes the enemy quiver at night"—remained "underground" because he felt that Giuliani and Safir had "created an unsafe environment" for him. Khallid insisted that he was not in hiding. "I never fear for my life!" he snapped. "My God has removed the fear from me!"

Nevertheless, fear of "white law" apparently was what Manhattan District Attorney Robert Morgenthau wanted to instill in Khallid. Judging by published remarks attributed to the aging criminal justice czar, his investigation was leaning toward absolving the cops of any wrongdoing, and throwing the book at the prime suspects. "Morgenthaus said that the inquiry would extend to any criminal activity, whether by demonstrators, speakers or police," David Habfinger of *The New York Times* reported. "He added, however, that he had yet to hear of any crime committed by an officer at the scene."

Khallid argued that an indictment would work in his favor, and he would call Safir and Giuliani as witnesses at his trial to account for their high crimes and misdemeanors. Ultimately, he asserted, jurors would focus on their reckless attempt to enforce a court order minutes after the march permit had expired at 4 p.m. "I have used white law before to beat them," said Khallid, referring to the federal appeals court ruling that blocked the city's attempt to deny a permit for the march, "and I'll use white law to beat them again." Although there was no warrant for Khallid's arrest, nothing prohibited edgy cops from stopping and interrogating him. He noted that he would not be able to achieve his goal (putting Safir and Giuliani on trial) if he was "laying up in some hospital" because "brute-beast Gestapo police" had preempted his day in court with one of their "classic beatdowns, frame-ups, or assassination attempts."

If Khallid was indicted and decided to remain underground, the NYPD would have no qualms about bringing him in dead or alive. Chief of Patrol John Scanlon told *The New York Times* that about two hours before the rally, Khallid vowed that "he was willing to kill or be killed that day to accomplish his agenda." Advisers feared that psychological profile of the Black Panther and Muslim leader already had been disseminated throughout the 40,000-member force by department brass. Indeed, wildly irrational comments by Safir in the aftermath of the disturbance had both the former Nation of Islam minister of defense and cops looking over their shoulders. Within hours of the incident, Safir told reporters that Khallid should be arrested for trying to incite a riot. "He invoked a crowd to kill police officers," Safir said. "He then had people throw chairs and barriers at his request at police officers."

Two days later, Safir reinforced the image of Khallid as a dangerous demagogue. At the West Indian carnival on Labor Day, a black man with dreadlocks allegedly pulled a cop's gun from his holster and shot the officer in the leg. Police claimed that the suspect fled but left the weapon. Safir said the attack may have been inspired by Khallid's gun talk toward the end of the march. "I think this is the kind of preaching that Khallid Muhammad is saying, 'Take guns from cops and shoot them!'" Safir told reporters. Khallid said the suspect "probably doesn't even know me," and may not have attended the march. "They could have set this up to make me appear to be a cop killer so they could hunt me down and shoot me on sight. The no-good bastards!"

On September 8, the day prosecutors confirmed that there would be a grand jury probe of the violence, Safir said of Khallid, "This man is like a black Hitler." But as the phalanx of menacing cops descended on the crowd, Khallid viewed himself as a black Moses. "I know what I did was right," he argued. "I wanted to warn my people, to prepare them, to calm them. I believe I kept them from stampeding. I believe it was my divine duty not to incite a riot, not to turn my people against the police because I had told them all along, at every press conference we had before the march, to be courteous and respectful to each other, and even to the police. I said no drugs, no alcohol, be slow to anger. I said it over and over, and that was our posture. I believe I saved their lives."

IT MAY COME AS A SHOCK TO HIS CRITICS, but Khallid had decided not to address the crowd at the Million Youth March. For nine months he had worked on his speech titled *The Role and Responsibility of Black Youth in Preparing for the 21st Century*. "I put the finishing touches on it during the time I spent in West Africa," he recalled. "I thought I would shock everybody and just leave them with their mouths open, with nothing to attack me. I could hear them in their disappointment saying, 'After all of his anti-Semitic and racist attacks and worry over what he would say at the rally, Khallid Muhammad didn't even speak. He did not deliver the major address of hate that we were all waiting to hear, that some didn't want to hear.'"

But around 3:30 P.M., Malik Shabazz noticed that his mentor had been "flippin' the script" by ushering activists to the microphone who were not scheduled to speak. "I'm just gonna take over the program and call you on up," Malik threatened. "Don't keep bringing speakers up here. The people might revolt if you don't give the keynote."

"Trust me," Khallid said with a nervous grin. "It will turn out fine."

But Khallid relented when some of the women who were onstage "came to me with a look of fear in their eyes" and pointed at an advancing throng of police officers. "I looked back and saw riot-gear clad cops in a marching formation," Khallid remembered. "They kinda had a rhythm."

Then he heard the brutal staccato of a police chopper, which reminded him of gunshots in a South Central gang driveby. This was the urban warfare Khallid had predicted and feared. This was the aggression he wanted to protect the people from. According to his Rolex watch, it was about 3:40 p.m. "I saw that the police presence had increased everywhere, down in the trenches, through the center of the people," he said. "It looked like they had snipers and sharpshooters on the rooftops."

Khallid ordered the women and children off the stage. Only a few burly brothers who had been standing security with him remained. He decided there was no time for a speech; it looked like the cops were about to attack and he had to give the people what he considered a warning.

Convulsed by the chaos, he summoned his warrior African ancestors. Among those he believed answered his plea were Jamaican-born poet and novelist Claude McKay, a voice of the Harlem Renaissance. McKay's battle cry came to mind: "If we must die, let it not be like hogs/Hunted and penned in an inglorious spot."

The police chopper swooped over the astonished crowd. In a moment of paranoia, Khallid and his frontline resistance thought that the people were being mowed down. "I knew that potential was there because the police were trying to fill the atmosphere with terror and fear," he charged. As rage built within him, Khallid continued to draw inspiration from McKay, muttering, "Like men we'll face the murderous, cowardly pack/Pressed to the wall, dying, but fighting back!" Then, as cops bumrushed the stage, he launched into his "shout out" to the people to seize the time. He said while he spoke, Malik Shabazz and black activist attorney Michael Warren constantly reminded him of the approaching deadline.

"When we knew it was four o'clock, I stopped right on the dot," Khallid claimed. "I stepped away from the mike and we cleared the stage completely. We were down the steps, feet just hitting the ground, and that's when we saw them attack the back of the stage." Khallid said that as cops and participants battled, he snatched a black man from members of the riot squad who were pummeling him. "The strength was there, and I pulled him back into the ranks," he added. "For some reason, the cops just stopped. It looked like they froze. We were close enough to reach out and touch each other." As the liberators departed with the man, the cops charged into the crowd again. "But the people met their charge for the second time, and in that moment security and people from the crowd came and grabbed me."

Members of Khallid's unarmed militia guard had come back to rescue him, but he wanted to stay and try to resolve the conflict. "No, Khallid!" one Black Panther shouted as he and others tried to reason with their incensed leader. "I can't let them hurt our people!" Khallid cried. "We gotta stop them from hurtin' our people!"

"We gotta get you outta here!" insisted Harlem fitness guru Herman Smalls, who was guarding Khallid that day.

"We can't lose you, Khallid!" declared Quannel X, his minister of information.

No one could restrain the buck-wild Khallid, whom Louis Farrakhan once compared to an untamed black stallion. As the disturbance heightened around them, the men wrestled Khallid to the ground. "They were all over my back, my arms," Khallid remembered. "I was thinking, 'How can I get away from them?' I got on my knees and with all of my strength I threw my arms, my entire body, upward and broke loose."

Khallid jumped back into the melee. But his equally determined bodyguards collared him again and dragged him away. "We see everything flying over our heads, people fighting the police," he recalled. "I didn't see nobody back up or run from them. The people stood their ground and fought them." Khallid was passed from hand to hand. They got him as far as 119th Street where the frustrated revolutionary argued bitterly with his security. "There, I continued to fight and wrestle with them, and they were just muscling me and telling me, 'You gotta get outta here!' and 'We can't let you go back!'" Khallid broke loose again and leaped on top of a car. Someone pressed a bullhorn in his hand, and he began to call on the police to open up the side streets to allow the crowd to disperse peacefully.

The disturbance had not spread beyond the staging area, but Khallid felt that the cops were bottling in those who wished to leave. He kept his eyes on the cops who manned the barricades. "You're gonna create an incident!" he warned. "Don't keep them penned in!" He claimed that "with the force of the people" behind him the cops were compelled to remove the barricades. Khallid and his band walked toward 125th Street, urging the crowd to stay calm. "They were angry and pained over what was happening, and I didn't want anyone to do anything that would harm Harlem," he said. "But it didn't look like anybody even had rioting on their mind."

Khallid now had a new following, one that pleaded with him to stick around and fire them up. "They kept telling me they wasn't gon' leave," he said. His security escorted him to 128th Street where they commandeered a van and shoved Khallid inside.

"The people wouldn't let the van move," he recalled. "They kept beating on the van and hollering, 'We love you, Khallid!' It was like they were going to break the windows. Then I had to get back out and tell them, 'Please, don't break the brother's window. Let him get me outta here so that everybody can go home.' Finally, they opened up a little, and the brother was able to ease out of the crowd." As the van sped uptown, two NYPD helicopters appeared to give chase. The choppers followed the van for about 12 blocks, then turned back.

It was the last anyone saw of Khallid.

It seemed as if Congressman Rangel's prediction, "When it's over, no one would know where to find Khallid Muhammad," would come true. Reporters combed the city for the firebrand orator, who *New York Times* writer Dan Barry quipped had "vanished in a puff of anti-Semitic exhaust." On September 8, the *Daily News* reported that Khallid had turned up in Atlanta at the rival Million Youth Movement rally, backed by Farrakhan, Jesse Jackson, and the NAACP. "Smiling and raising both fists, Muhammad left quickly without speaking," according to writers Barbara Ross, Greg Smith, and Maureen Fan. "His lieutenant, Malik Shabazz, then led the crowd of 4,000 in a raucous chant, 'The hell with Giuliani!'" their story added. But the *Daily News* article was inaccurate. At the time the tabloid placed Khallid in Atlanta, he was meeting with me in New York. And Malik Shabazz was in Washington. Khallid bristled, "It just shows you how the devil can lie!"

While he was underground, Khallid had little or no time to reflect on the people who crossed his path, or as he put it, "changed his-story." But as we talked some, like Norman Siegel of the NYCLU, had left an indelible impression on the accused anti-Semite. Siegel had intervened in the permit impasse as a "friend of the court," and argued that the Giuliani administration's attempt to scuttle the rally flew in the face of constitutional guarantees. "I saw him as a true libertarian, actually putting himself in a position where many of his own people were going to attack him," said Khallid. "They were dealing with a vendetta and he was dealing with matters of the constitution, which I believe is not worth the paper it's written on." After a divided three-judge panel issued its ruling, Khallid combed the courthouse in search of Siegel. "I looked for him because I was anxious to hear what he would say to me," Khallid recalled. "I approached him and I shook his hand," Khallid recalled. "I don't want to make it seem like he was kissing up to Khallid. He seemed a little taken aback, but I told him how much I appreciated what he did and we talked. I believe in giving credit where credit is due."

Some might think that because Khallid endeared himself to Siegel Khallid wasn't as tough as he portrayed himself to be. But it would take more than a conciliatory gesture from Siegel to sensitize the man Farrakhan once dubbed "the Sword of Allah." Some of Khallid's critics began to question his claim that he embodied the life and philosophy of Malcolm X. Once an outspoken separatist who referred to white people as "blue-eyed devils," Malcolm made a pilgrimage to Mecca, the Islamic holy city in Saudi Arabia, and returned transformed, denouncing racism.

When I suggested that he, too, might undergo a similar conversion, Khallid retorted, "I've been to Mecca—*three times!*"

SENSING DISCONTENT ABOUT HIS ILL-TIMED call for the arrest of Khallid for allegedly inciting teenagers to riot and kill cops at the Million Youth March, State Senator Paterson ambled into a jam-packed auditorium at the National Black Theatre in Harlem appearing more contrite than combative. If Paterson felt he had found a middle ground to brood over his embarrassing blunder, and shelter from an outbreak of political vengeance that raged uptown one week after the controversial march, his calculations were way off.

He had wandered into New Jack power-broker Conrad Muhammad's debut summit of raptivists, black nationalists, gangbangers, and Africentrists eager to work for CHHANGE (Conscious Hip Hop Activism Necessary for Global Empowerment), a political and cultural movement Conrad founded for black youth. (Conrad had resigned from the Nation of Islam to lead CHHANGE).

Jeers, boos, and catcalls greeted the senator, who had become the favorite whipping boy of the Marxist-influenced New York Black Power Organizing Committee. To some, like Erica Ford, the committee's coordinator and acid-tongued agitator, who were among the hecklers at the CHHANGE rally, Paterson, Charles Rangel, Bill Perkins, and C. Virginia Fields, had contributed to the tense atmosphere that led to the violence. They then, critics like Ford charged, "buckdanced" (equivocated) on their support for the event.

Shortly after protesters scuffled with cops, Paterson told reporters that Khallid's words "were like yelling fire at a movie theater; it was dangerous and it showed no respect for life." But after the dust settled and criticism turned on the Giuliani administration's alleged mishandling of the affair, Paterson retracted his demand for Khallid's arrest. That political screwup, as well as the attacks on

Khallid by Rangel, Perkins, and Fields, was hot a topic in Harlem as the Bill Clinton's sex scandal.

As Conrad gauged his audience's reaction to Paterson, his speech focused on "mostly negro politicians" and the fact that "a strong one" like Paterson had the courage to show his face. Conrad's announcement that Paterson would be accorded an opportunity to speak provoked applause as well as a chantdown.

"No!" someone shouted.

"He's a good brother!" said Conrad.

"Don't do that, Conrad!" Ford pleaded, her voice thundering above the angry colloquy. She repeated her charge that Paterson had sicced the cops on protesters.

"He's a racist!" a man shouted.

Now it was Conrad searching for middle ground between the far right and extreme left of black angst. "Wherever you see a black politician that's weak [and] you need to call him [an] 'Uncle Tom,' a 'handkerchief head,' [or] a 'negro,' stay on his case," he said. "But he is ours. They belong to us. And we gotta stop, brothers and sisters, being ideologues. Yes, brother Khallid is ours, and that's why I was with him at the Million Youth March [and] will stand for his right to say what he said. But it's not an either-or proposition. I'm gon' stand with Charlie Rangel, and where I don't agree with him I'm gon' wear him out. But he's mine. He's ours."

When his audience seemed to miss or ignore the point about embracing political pariahs, Conrad dropped "this bomb on Sister Erica" that she and other blacks refused to acknowledge. "We don't talk about it much in the black community, but we really benefited from ole Uncle Tom," he offered. "See," he added, "a lot of negroes don't talk about the good that Uncle Tom did: Uncle Tom didn't always sell us out. Sometime he would let the field negro know what was about to come down from the house."

Paterson was no Uncle Tom—not by anyone's definition. Despite his post-march faux pas, he remained a counterbalance to the argument that outspoken black politicians were easily intimidated by uptown militants or downtown neo-fascists. Again, Conrad praised Paterson for wading into unfriendly fire, declaring that his presence was "a good sign; because at least you can talk" to politicians like him.

But after the rally, the anti-Paterson sentiments filtered onto the sidewalk outside the theater. Paterson, wanting to talk, walked over to Ford, who was with a group of about ten members of her committee and key supporters. "Erica Ford started yelling and screaming at me about something," Paterson recalled. "So I started to explain to her about my misstating about Khallid. And she said, 'It's not about that motherfuckin' Khallid Muhammad!' She referred to him twice as a 'motherfucker,' which I thought was interesting. We just looked at each other when she said that. Now, I don't know if that was just her way of being mad, because every three words out of her mouth was a cuss word, or whether she actually [had] a problem with Khallid.

"I said, 'Then what is it about?' She said, 'You got the brother arrested and you got people hurt.'" Ford was referring to Shaheed Muhammad, a member of the organizing committee who was arrested for allegedly punching a police officer in the face. Shaheed, also known as James Washington, surrendered to police a few days later following a manhunt. (Prosecutors admitted later that Shaheed was not on the police videos that were released to the media, but said a camera caught the activist in the area where the injured officer was moments after the alleged attack.)

Paterson said he was puzzled by Ford's accusation that he was responsible for Shaheed's arrest and injuries suffered cops and civilians. "I really couldn't get that," he added. "And she said [I was] working with Giuliani and the police! I said, 'Well, neither Giuliani nor the police have been willing to talk to me through this whole thing. But while we're on that subject neither have you.' She says, 'I reached out to you.' And I said, 'Erica, I've never met you before in my life until today.'"

Ford then pointed to Paterson's aide, Joe Haslip, insisting that she had reached out to him but got no response. Haslip recalled that he had been contacted by Ford, but added that he told her to make an appointment to see Paterson. "You never came in, but we can talk now," Haslip told Ford.

Haslip, Paterson, and other witnesses said they heard Ford shout, "Fuck you! I don't wanna talk now!"

Ford's enraged supporters yelled obscenities at Paterson, calling him a "sell-out," and threatened to run him out of office. Viola Plummer, a senior member of the December 12th Movement, whose leadership dominated the New York Black Power Organizing Committee (NYBPOC), finally intervened. "She came over and told me she could explain because Erica was, like, insane," Paterson said. "They had to, like, take her away." According to Paterson, Plummer said organizers had been upset with him for "contradicting" Ford when she appeared on *Open Line*, a black talk show on KISS-FM, prior to the march. "I said, 'When I was on KISS, Erica came on and said most of our youth are on drugs and in prison.' I said, 'I would expect Rudolph Giuliani to say that. But I'm not gonna allow that to be said about young people in my district by Giuliani or Erica or you or anyone else.'"

The sidewalk squabble shifted to City Hall's alleged control of black politicians in Harlem. Roger Wareham, an attorney and member of the NYBPOC, had charged that Giuliani checked the pulses of elected officials before making statements they all seemed to back. "Giuliani doesn't check anyone's pulse before he does what he's gonna do," Paterson opined. "That's what part of this whole fight is about. The city never cooperates with anybody. You could be a radical or a Tom, or whatever. As long as you're black and live in Harlem, Giuliani doesn't talk to anybody. They seem to have it in their minds that there was some kind of tacit approval [between black politicians and Giuliani] before Harlem got turned into an armed camp. But that's not the Rudy Giuliani I know."

Plummer concluded that although they espoused opposite political views, both she and Paterson showed respect for others who disagreed with them. "She said, 'When I open my mouth in public I don't insult people and use profanity and try to get a whole lotta people killed.'" Paterson believed that remark was a tongue-in-cheek reference to Khallid's choleric temper and racist taunts.

15

A Pattern and Practice of Police Brutality

Brute Force

RACISM ALLEGEDLY TURNED THE AMERICAN DREAM of Jean Charles—who was only trying to obey the law—into a nightmare on a recent fall morning in 1998. When his story was first brought to my attention, Charles, then a 53-year-old father of three, who had emigrated from Haiti 18 years ago, had been languishing in a coma in Brooklyn Hospital. His family and lawyers were appalled by the circumstances surrounding his arrest and what subsequently happened to him.

Around 9 a.m. on September 24, police said in a statement, Charles went to the headquarters of the Brooklyn South Task Force on Coney Island Avenue to turn himself in on a very unusual warrant. Forty minutes later, he was taken to Criminal Court in downtown Brooklyn. "While at court," according to the police statement, "Mr. Charles suffered a seizure and was transported to Brooklyn Hospital by EMS." Four days later, Internal Affairs investigators who went to the hospital to interview Charles were told by a doctor that he was in "critical condition following surgery to relieve pressure which caused a blood clot [on] his brain. As a result of the blood clot, Mr. Charles had suffered a stroke." Police said that when the investigators "specifically asked … if there were any signs of force," the doctor replied that "there were no signs of trauma to his head." Charles' condition "was related directly to his hypertension," the NYPD quoted the physician as saying.

Veteran civil rights attorney Eric G. Poulos, who was representing the family, said a doctor at the hospital told Charles' son, Jean Charles Jr., a different story. "When he arrived at the hospital, he was told by the doctor that the police said they had to use force on his father," Poulos said. "When Jean Charles Jr. began to

170

question the doctor, a police officer who was in the room reading a newspaper confirmed that officers had to use force."

Whatever happened to Jean Charles, the questionable circumstances surrounding his arrest infuriated Poulos and his colleagues, Michael Smith and Michael Ratner of the Center for Constitutional Rights. Jean Charles Jr. told the lawyers that in late May two white cops pulled up outside of his father's autobody shop in East Flatbush, saying they had come to issue a summons because he had improperly displayed a certificate to operate an air compressor. Poulos said the cops noted that Charles had affixed a copy instead of the original to a wall in the shop.

When the younger Charles said they lived nearby and he could get the original, one of the cops replied that it was too late and wrote out a summons. Poulos said Charles "went to court on the date he was supposed to, but the police weren't there and it was put over. He returned the next day; the police still weren't there. So he went home. Apparently, it was when he didn't show on the third day that a warrant was issued for his arrest."

Poulos said that Jean Charles Jr. had accompanied his father to respond to the summons. "Two hours later, the son got a call from Brooklyn Hospital saying that his father was in a coma and needed brain surgery," the attorney recalled. "As best as we can determine, something happened in the police van while they were transporting him to Criminal Court."

An ambulance report obtained by me stated that Charles was "unresponsive" when taken from the back of a police van. The report indicated that his blood pressure was normal.

"He has never been arrested in his life, has no history of stroke, high blood pressure, or heart disease," Poulos noted. "It's clear that something happened in the van. Even if they didn't beat him into a coma, his head was struck against something in the back seat, and they didn't even look around while driving to court. Nobody looked in the rearview mirror to see the condition of their prisoner?"

Poulos said "the worst irony" was that Charles got into trouble even though he repeatedly tried to obey the law. "He went to court twice, and then to the warrant squad," Poulos lamented. "He did whatever was asked of him, and [he still ended up] in a coma. Whoever heard of a warrant being issued for not answering a summons for having a photostat of a compressor certificate? It defies the imagination."

THE STOIC ATTENDANT AT BROOKLYN'S Kings County Hospital morgue did not have all the answers to the questions Carmen Torres lobbed at him as she gazed in disbelief at a coroner's mug shots of her dead cousin.

"What happened to her?" Torres, 48, tearfully demanded.

Two grim photographs she'd carefully inspected on the afternoon of October 1, 1998 seemed to prove that the body of Yvette Marin Kessler—a 36-year-old heroin addict who was the mother of a month-old baby and five other children—bore marks from a beating.

"I don't know," the attendant said, shrugging his shoulders. "She was brought in that way."

Torres reluctantly signed one of the pictures, a routine rite of identification that the relative of a deceased person goes through at a city morgue. She tugged at them slightly as the attendant tightened his grasp. He said that the only way she could have the photos was by showing him a subpoena.

"Those pictures better not disappear!" Torres warned.

Later that day, after making funeral arrangements, Torres contacted the office of Dr. Beverly Leffers, the medical examiner who performed the autopsy on Kessler. According to Torres, Leffers said the family would have to wait another two or three months to learn how Kessler died.

Write a letter, she was told.

Ellen Borakove, a spokeswoman for the medical examiner's office, said Torres misunderstood Leffers. "We always let the family know what the cause of death is," Borakove said. "She was apparently referring to her receiving the written autopsy report."

"By the way, what hospital did she die in?" Torres remembered asking Leffers.

"She died at Central Booking," the pathologist reportedly replied.

Given the runaround Carmen Torres had gotten since her cousin died, she no longer had any doubts: Someone was trying to cover up the circumstances surrounding Kessler's death. Borakove said that the medical examiner's office would issue its preliminary findings in one week.

The family hired a lawyer.

"Based on information we have, we are alleging that the police beat Yvette Kessler," said attorney Casilda Roper-Simpson, who, with her partner, Carl W. Thomas, represented the family.

A source in the 75th Precinct told the attorneys that two officers and a detective beat Kessler. "Apparently, she kept asking to go to the bathroom, and I guess they got annoyed," Roper-Simpson said. "Citing the source and two other alleged witnesses, she added, "They removed two other inmates from the cell and beat her."

When I inquired, police said the case was under investigation, but maintained there was no evidence that Kessler was abused by jailers. Cops claimed that on September 28, she was arrested in the East New York section of Brooklyn on unspecified drug charges. Those charges eventually were dropped, but she was held on an outstanding warrant from Norfolk, Virginia. The reason for the warrant was not disclosed. (Torres told me that the cops were mistaken or were deliberately misleading about the warrant. She said there was a warrant for Kessler's arrest in New York because she failed to complete a court-ordered sentence of community service for a drug offense in Virginia. "She was pregnant and couldn't finish it," Torres explained.)

Kessler was transported at midnight to Central Booking at 120 Schermerhorn Street in downtown Brooklyn, police said. Two hours later, she complained of abdominal pains, and was taken to Long Island College Hospital, where she was treated and released. At about 5:30, she was returned to a cell at Central Booking. At 8 a.m., one of the women in the cell notified officers that Kessler was unconscious. EMS technicians pronounced her dead at the scene.

Roper-Simpson said that another of Kessler's cellmates saw cops come into the cell and beat her. And a man arrested on drug charges with Kessler, who was in a cell nearby, claimed he heard a female screaming. Both were afraid to go public with their allegations, Roper-Simpson said. The attorneys allowed me to examine independent photos of the body, which showed facial bruises and a broken nose.

Carmen Torres recalled that before leaving her home in the Cypress Hills section of Brooklyn at about 4 P.M. on September 28, Kessler complained of stomach cramps and a tingling sensation in her arm, but speculated that she was perhaps feeling ill due to postpartum pain. She argued that Kessler's symptoms could not have resulted in death. "It was not right for the family to bury her and not know what she died of," said Roper-Simpson.

As allegations of police brutality in Kessler's death came to light, civil rights advocates proclaimed that, on the heels of the Giuliani administration's violent disruption of the Million Youth March in Harlem, the incident capped a particularly brutal September—one of the most notorious periods in the administration's so-called "quality-of-life" crackdown. And that was before it was revealed that six days prior to Kessler's death, Jean Charles, a Haitian immigrant with no known history of medical problems and no history of criminal wrongdoing, had been discovered comatose in the back seat of a police van.

Both Giuliani and Police Commissioner Safir insisted that in each incident police did not use excessive force. The outcry from the activist community might have been muffled by City Hall's dismissive spin had it not been for the coincidental release of an Amnesty International report, which concluded that New York City under Mayor Giuliani was plagued with killer cops and abusive prison guards. The report singled out the NYPD for the horrific attack against Abner Louima and the 1994 choking death of Anthony Baez. It also criticized the department for excessive use of deadly force. Giuliani responded with his usual inflated rhetoric, claiming that the NYPD had one of the lowest per capita shooting rates in the country. He also said that the report looked at only a few incidents, and to call his cops among the worst in the nation was an "outrage."

Three days after the report was released, federal judge Shira Scheindlin sentenced former Bronx Police Officer Francis Livoti for using an illegal choke hold, which resulted in Baez's death. In sentencing Livoti to seven and a half years in prison, Scheindlin berated the officer for showing little remorse over the killing, and added that the NYPD "knew [Livoti] was dangerous" and did nothing about it.

Under fire, Safir—clearly acting on orders from Giuliani—pulled off what many activists viewed as a cosmetic racial hustle. The commissioner axed Officer Joseph Locurto, a white cop who had donned blackface and rode on the racist float in Queens. In a statement, Safir, who downplayed the charges in the Amnesty International report, said Locurto did not deserve to wear the shield of a New York police officer and should be dismissed. He added that Locurto's behavior at the parade set a poor example, which brought shame to the NYPD.

Norman Siegel countered that if the dismissal of Locurto was intended to cover up Giuliani's embarrassing record of combating racism within the NYPD, that act of "self-righteous hypocrisy" would backfire. "This is the same NYPD that does not fire cops who beat people up while on duty, call them racial names, have disciplinary records, and lie," charged Siegel, who represented Locurto at his departmental hearing. "The decision is utterly baffling and irrational. Moreover, it demonstrates that both the mayor and the NYPD leadership still do not get it when it comes to realistically ameliorating racism within the NYPD."

"Radio As Club"

MADISON AVENUE BETWEEN 124TH AND 126TH STREETS is part of "the new, new Harlem Renaissance." The avenue cuts a wide swath across 125th Street, where Elvy Simon's *Flavored With One Love*, a West Indian restaurant, and *A Taste of Seafood*, a mom-and-pop fish-and-chips joint run by Rickey Thomas's family, symbolized the cultural and economic rebirth of the fabled community.

But some things had not changed, including the events that led to the alleged police murder of Kenneth Banks.

For years the two blocks had been home to the ubiquitous hard knocks—down-on-their-luck black men who earned a living dealing marijuana and crack. Some said that the 36-year-old Banks, a reputed drug dealer who was convicted of criminal trespass in 1997 and petty larceny in 1984, was a hard knock who "did what he had to do" to survive. As Rickey Thomas intimated to an assistant district attorney, for all he knew, Banks, who was "sometimes homeless," sold bootleg videotapes. He had no proof that one of the desperate moves of his childhood friend involved dealing in drugs.

"Kenny wasn't doing too good," recalled the then 38-year-old Thomas, a devout Christian who attended Julia Richmond High School with Banks and his brother Benny in the early '70s. "I sensed when Kenny was slipping," he added. "Was it drugs? Being that I used to live that life before, I can tell who was using and who was not. But like I told [the prosecutor], I don't know that he was using or selling drugs."

Police said that on October 29, 1998 cops observed Banks in a drug transaction and when officers tried to arrest him he fled. Witnesses said that Officer Craig Yokemick came within a few feet of Banks as he tried to get away on a bicycle and threw his two-pound walkie-talkie at the suspect.

Banks fell from the bike. He died at Metropolitan Hospital Center on November 10. Twelve days later, the medical examiner ruled that the thrown radio had killed Banks.

With a toxicology report pending, Yokemick's attorney, Bruce Smirti, alleged that Banks swallowed vials of crack to destroy evidence as he was fleeing. "I still believe that a contributing factor to his death—or the most important factor—was the voluntary ingestion of cocaine," Smirti said.

Thomas never wavered in *his* belief that Yokemick alone was responsible for killing Banks. Unlike Yokemick's attorney, Thomas said he saw what happened on that sunny day as he sat in his Ford Explorer, double-parked outside of his family's restaurant, impatiently looking for a parking spot. He recalled that around 3:30 p.m. (others put the time at 2:30), he heard sirens, then saw a police van, lights flashing, speeding up Madison. It seemed like routine police business; cops are always "jackin'" suspects on the avenue. "Around here a lot of guys sell reefer," said Thomas. "I don't know if they sell anything hard, but you have a lot of Jamaican brothers who are into the weed. Ain't nobody stoopid. The police are doing they job. You out there standing too long, they're gonna make you move, search you."

About 15 minutes later, Thomas saw "Kenny shooting around the corner and this cop on his tail." Banks was pushing hard on a tiny dirt bike and Yokemick, who Thomas described as about six foot three and heavyset, seemed breathless. "As Kenny gets to the corner, he starts pulling away from the cop," said Thomas. "The cop sees he is not gonna catch him."

Thomas said that without missing a step, Yokemick grasped his two-way radio like a football and threw it at Banks as he rode into the crosswalk. The radio struck Banks in the back of the head; the blunt force of the impact sent him sprawling. "I saw in Kenny's eyes that he was knocked out," Thomas remembered. "Once he was out he proceeded to fall." Banks fell off the bike in front of the restaurant. "The first thing he hit was his head," added Thomas, reiterating that he believes his friend was out cold from Yokemick's brutal pass. "If you're falling and you're conscious you gonna put your hands out," he reasoned. "He was unconscious and when he fell he hit his head."

Yokemick picked up his radio, straddled the suspect, and radioed for backup. According to Thomas, the officer searched Banks' pockets, then turned him over and handcuffed him behind his back. "The cops didn't remove nothin' from Kenny's pocket," he insisted. "They didn't find no drugs on him. If they had found it they woulda held it up to the people and yelled, 'Look what we found!'" An angry crowd of about 70 people gathered around Yokemick and his partner, who had responded to his call for assistance.

"You muthafuckaz!" Thomas heard an eyewitness shout.

"Fuck you! You fuckin' whiteys!" declared another. "That's why y'all be gittin' kilt now 'cause y'all always be doin' stuff like that."

Thomas remembered the beleaguered cops responding, "Get back! Get back!" Banks, he swore, was unconscious. "Kenny was laying flat on his face," he said. "I saw blood coming out of his mouth, and where he had scraped his nose, his head, and his eyes from falling flat on his face."

Moses Stewart was manning the crisis center at Sharpton's National Action Network when a man rapped on the door of the second-floor office overlooking Madison Avenue. He told Stewart that a white cop had "knocked a brother out" with his police radio; a crowd was surrounding two officers "and he was afraid there might be an ugly situation." Stewart raced to the scene. "When I got there, the officer that had hit brother Banks was standing over him in a gesture of humiliation, as though he had captured an animal," said Stewart, whose son, Yusuf Hawkins, was shot and killed by a gang of white thugs in 1989.

Then Yokemick allegedly did something that confirmed Stewart's worst stereotype of police officers. "The police began dragging brother Banks, unconscious, to the van," claimed Stewart, who said he told the same story to Detective Stanley Mahabeer and Sergeant Nicholas Rivera, the two cops who investigated the alleged attack on Abner Louima in the 70th Precinct stationhouse. "They literally dragged the brother to the van and threw him in as though he was a dead deer who had been hit crossing the street," adds Stewart, who provided the investigators with names of other witnesses. "They just dropped him in there. I don't know whether they really knew that he was never going to regain consciousness."

As the crowd shouted racial epithets at the officers, Stewart said he confronted Yokemick. "I asked him why he had knocked brother Banks out in the manner that he did, and why was he being so rude to the people." He said Yokemick told him to stay out of police business. Stewart responded that he was an aide to Sharpton and that it was his job to monitor allegations of police brutality. "Immediately after identifying myself as working for Reverend Sharpton he took on a very arrogant attitude," Stewart charged. "He didn't like my presence there."

The officers cautiously backed away from Stewart and the crowd, got into the van, and sped off. Neither Stewart nor Thomas heard them radio for medical assistance. Police said Banks was conscious when they took him into custody, but that he suffered three seizures at the 25th Precinct before slipping into a coma on October 30.

Allegations of police brutality once again were dividing Rudy Giuliani' great city. The day Banks died, Sharpton appeared on *NYI*'s Inside City Hall expressing outrage over yet another example of the NYPD's senseless approach to apprehending black suspects. Although there had been complaints about police using radios as weapons, there was no specific policy about the practice. The Civilian Complaint Review Board had a separate category for such incidents it called "Radio as Club."

One irate viewer dispatched this angry e-mail to the station the next day: "I understand Reverend Sharpton's motives when he questions how some officers overstep their bounds. So, I am not against Reverend Sharpton questioning the manner in which the officer chose to apprehend an alleged drug offender. However, Mr. Sharpton needs to ask himself how many black and Hispanic people truly care that this drug dealer was hit in the back of the head and suffered a seizure because he swallowed his own poison? Reverend Sharpton must also recognize black and Hispanic people are tired of seeing these people in our community selling their drugs, endangering the well-being of our children, and making life more uneasy. He should talk more about how we can take back our community from people who don't pay taxes and roam around the neighborhood as if they own it."

Sharpton said his critic was ignorant about his history as an anti-drug crusader, pointing out that in the 1980s he recruited celebrities and politicians who roamed drug-infested neighborhoods painting red crucifixes on suspected crack houses. His message had been heard in hundreds of public schools, including the one Banks attended. He conceded that black communities should have zero tolerance for drug dealers, but argued that such an attitude could not change what happened to Banks. "We cannot allow the police department to use an alleged drug dealer to set a precedent—the use of police radios as lethal weapons," said the activist. Sharpton said after Abner Louima was sodomized with the toilet plunger, he began speaking out against "the new weapons of choice," adding, blacks had evidence of "how brutal [cops] can be with anything they put their hands on. If we don't cry out, they will be throwing radios with the intention to kill."

Sharpton said he felt close to Banks because he had a half brother also named Kenny, who was an addict jailed for a drug-related offense. "You put drug dealers like Kenny banks in rehab; you don't kill them," he suggested. "If one of the Kennedy boys was caught buying drugs uptown and a cop threw his radio at him, there certainly would have been a different reaction." Sharpton declared that cops like Yokemick should have been kicked off the force a long time ago.

In 1993, Yokemick was accused of excessive force and discourtesy, and lost ten vacation days. A year later, he was reprimanded for using a police scooter without permission. In 1995, he was docked 15 vacation days for assaulting a Department of Transportation employee.

Sharpton contended that Yokemick might have been identified as an officer prone to commit acts of misconduct had the NYPD not blocked the CCRB's request for the files of hundreds of officers suspected of misconduct or brutality. (Then Public Advocate Mark Green had requested the files after learning that police officials in the first half of 1996 took no action on 53 of 96 police brutality and misconduct cases that were substantiated or recommended for discipline by the independent review board. An appeals court would later rule that Green was entitled to the files.)

Months after Banks' death the debate over whether Yokemick intended to kill him raged at the corner where he was struck down. "Being that Kenny was sitting down on the bike, it was easy for [Yokemick] to connect to his head," Rickey Thomas explained to reporters after the medical examiner's ruling. "You figure you hit somebody in their back with a police radio it will hurt, but it's not gonna stop them. His intention, to me, was to stop him. If you're riding a bike and not maneuvering and I throw a radio at you, intending to hit your head, it's gonna hit your head."

"Homicide By Cop"

LIKE MOST BLACKS IN NEW YORK CITY, A.B. Bannerman had accepted the argument that his sons were more likely to be brutalized or killed by white police officers. He'd never challenged the notion that black cops were capable of committing vicious crimes against their own people. "My son was killed by seven black-ass niggers!" said Bannerman, adding that Mayor Giuliani and the NYPD "figured the family was of [the] gullible type who [would not] push the issue" of murder because all of the officers involved in the alleged killing of his son were black.

Nearly two hours after seven black undercover narcotics cops allegedly stomped, kicked, and then shot at him as he fled, stumbling, into the darkness in December 1997, Reginald Bannerman wound up battered and bloody on the Manhattan-bound side of an IRT subway station in Brooklyn. At the time, a source close to the investigation told me that the last two witnesses to see Reginald alive at the Sterling Street station provided NYPD Internal Affairs officials with key information, which fit the family's contention that one of Reginald's alleged assailants caught up with him and pushed him in front of a train.

But other law enforcement sources maintained that the 36-year-old Reginald dived into the path of the Number 2 train that killed him.

A female subway clerk at the station told investigators that sometime after 1 a.m. on December 19 she sold a token to a man who then paid his fare and went through the turnstile. Shortly afterward, according to my source, another passenger claimed he saw two men scuffling on the platform. "His reaction was, 'Oh shit!' And he ran upstairs," the source said.

Law enforcement sources denied there was a scuffle. "The lone independent witness on the platform said he saw Bannerman pacing up and down, and both he and the motorman said they saw him leap in front of the train," a source said. (The Bannerman family filed a notice of claim with the city, arguing in part that the motorman was negligent because he failed to stop the train when he spotted Reginald. "Our position was that he did have time," said attorney Ron Kuby who was representing the family with Michael Mossberg.)

In December 1998, after four detectives were indicted in connection with Reginald's death, some of the accused officers' colleagues began trumpeting the theory that the case was probably another example of "suicide by cop." Within days of scraping Reginald's mangled body off the subway tracks, the medical examiner ruled his death a suicide. Yet everyone who saw Reginald that night remembered him begging for his life—not acting like someone trying to get cops to kill him.

Officers Lloyd Barnaby and Mark Cooper faced assault charges for allegedly stomping and kicking Reginald with their boots, beating him with a glass bottle, and firing over his head as he ran away. Along with Officer Edward Howard, Barnaby and Cooper were accused of tampering with evidence by recovering shell casings to conceal what they did. And according to the Brooklyn District Attorney, who unsealed the indictment on November 23, Cooper, Barnaby, and Officer Orice Connor were charged with official misconduct for failing to report the use of physical force. Barnaby also allegedly intimidated Karen Ramsey, a 35-year-old witness. (Marvyn Kornberg, the attorney for Connor and Howard, denied that his clients were present when Reginald was allegedly beaten.)

A veteran detective, upset over the indictment, argued that when Reginald "picked a fight" with the off-duty cops inside the BBB Soul and Seafood House restaurant in Crown Heights, he fit the pattern of a distraught person seeking death by police gunfire. "That's just absurd," responded Kuby. "If he wanted to commit suicide that night all he had to do was stand still because the cops were trying to kill him." Although "suicide by cop" was a controversial topic gaining serious attention from law enforcement agencies nationwide, that theory was not adopted by lawyers for the alleged killer cops or by Police Commissioner Safir, who said that "the NYPD took immediate disciplinary action against officers believed to be involved in the Bannerman case."

The Bannerman family had no doubts.

"My brother's street name was 'Life,'" said George Bannerman, who tried to save Reginald as the cops allegedly pummeled him. "He had everything to live for. He was the opposite of me."

"He was working two jobs," added the dead man's father. "He was a happy man. He loved his seven-year-old daughter, NaeNae. If you gon' kill yourself, why bother to pay your fare at the subway?"

Mr. Bannerman's theory was that his son's death was instead a case of "homicide by cops." He speculated that "after beating him like they did they knew they was gon' lose their jobs so they killed him to cover up, so he won't talk," he said. "I think they tried to make it look like he jumped in front of the train." While Mr. Bannerman clung to his belief, Kuby said there was no evidence that Reginald was pushed. "Common sense dictates that he was chased, common sense dictates that he was followed, that the police officers played a direct role in his death," he told *The Associated Press*. Kuby told me later: "The most likely scenario is that he was beaten so badly—one of his eyes was hanging out of its socket—that he became dazed, confused, and fell."

None of the alleged killer cops were charged with murder.

IT WAS SIX DAYS BEFORE CHRISTMAS 1997. Lefferts High School, where Reginald Bannerman worked as a phys-ed instructor for 18 years, was closed. Reginald usually worked two jobs, but that Christmas he devoted all of his time to helping out at the "Three Bs," the restaurant at Bedford Avenue and Crown Street co-owned by his brother-in-law, Michael Knight. Reginald, the restaurant's maintenance man, liked to rub shoulders with the prominent clientele, who included Mike Tyson, Erykah Badu, and Chico DeBarge. Protective of the restaurant's image as one of the trendiest in Brooklyn, Reginald doubled as security when patrons got rowdy. According to George Bannerman, who was working at the restaurant the night his brother was attacked, Reginald walked over to a raucous group of black men, who were celebrating a birthday, and asked them to tone down their revelry.

"One dude asked my brother, 'Do you own this?'" George recalled. "My brother said, 'No, I know the owner.'" George said that both he and Reginald continued with their chores. Around 12:30 a.m., as the restaurant was getting ready to close, he heard a commotion and stepped outside. George remembered that he saw about seven men—some dressed in urban-awareness wear—one with oversized construction boots kicking and stomping someone on the ground.

It was Reginald.

"This dude is jumping in his face, stomping!" he recalled. George said he wedged himself between his brother and the man, who he described as bald-headed, stocky, and light-skinned. He clasped his hands and thwarted another attempt to stomp Reginald, who appeared to be unconscious. "Man, you can't stomp him in his face, that's my brother!" he protested.

George said one of the men took a beer bottle and beat Reginald in the face with it. Michael Knight reportedly rushed to his brother-in-law's aid, shouting, "Man, what the fuck you doin'?" Meanwhile, George, hovering over his brother, tried to protect him from the mob. Twice he blocked blows. Then, as one assailant attempted to deliver what George feared would be the coup de grâce, he said he took off his shirt and threw it at him, signaling by the prizefighter's code that the opponent had had enough. Suddenly, George felt the cold muzzle of a 9mm pistol pressed against his temple. The gunman said nothing and George did not hear as much as a whimper from his brother. (A prosecutor's statement announcing the indictment identified Detective Cooper as the officer "accused of menacing George Bannerman … by intentionally placing him in fear of serious physical injury or death by displaying a handgun.")

"I thought they done stomped him out," George recalled. But suddenly, Reginald sprang from the ground.

"Somehow, my brother got up," George said. "They were all kind of shocked that he got up, the way they were stomping him." As Reginald broke free and started running down Bedford Avenue toward Empire Boulevard, several of the men allegedly whipped out guns and fired in rapid succession at him.

"They was tryin' to hit my brother," George insisted. He said he attempted to follow Reginald but was held back by Knight, who urged him to go back to the restaurant. Meanwhile, the gunfire had alerted uniformed cops in squad cars nearby. "'It's under control!'" George remembered hearing some of the men shout as they flashed badges at the arriving officers. "It was then I knew that they were cops," he said.

After the squad cars departed, the plainclothes cops scattered. Two of them darted in the direction Reginald had fled. According to George, his brother—terrified that the cops were chasing him—ran past his own apartment building nearby. George said one of his brother's friends told him that Reginald appeared at his Lefferts Avenue apartment early that morning "all busted up, eyes bleeding, face swollen up." When the friend sat Reginald down and went to grab a coat to take him to the hospital, Reginald said he was going to his mother's apartment. He ran off, and it was the last the friend saw of him.

George assumed that his brother had escaped and was hiding somewhere until it was safe to surface. "My brother was the type who would call his wife or our mother if he wasn't coming home," explained. "If I hadn't showed up, they woulda thought nothing of it."

"When he didn't call, I knew something was wrong," said the brothers' father, who lived in South Carolina, but was in New York for the holiday. "I never come into town and he doesn't call me. Never!" Sensing that something tragic had happened, Mr. Bannerman repeatedly called Reginald's wife, Joanna, looking for him. "I said this thing is very ugly. I didn't sleep all night. I just looked at television and cried."

Later that morning, after none of Reginald's relatives had heard from him, Mr. Bannerman drove his wife, Phemia, to Lutheran Hospital where she worked as a medical technician. Before leaving the hospital he told her, "I'ma find him today, but I believe he is dead. It's not like him not to call." Mr. Bannerman's agonizing search eventually led him to the Kings County Hospital morgue. As the attendant was about to show him a photo of a "John Doe" that had recently arrived, Mr. Bannerman remembered instinctively remarking, "Oh God, that's him!"

But he couldn't help looking.

"When I seen my son laying up there like that with his face all bust up, mister, something took my whole chest and tore it out," he told me as tears welled in his eyes. "I was so messed up I couldn't sign papers. As I walked back downstairs my daughter, Regina, and her husband, Michael, was coming in. Both got hysterical and fainted."

It was left to A.B. Bannerman to notify his wife about Reginald's death. "We went up to the room where she was working," he said, wiping away the tears. "Her back was turned, and as she looked around and seen us crying, she said, 'Not my boy. Oh, no! Not my boy!'"

PART VI

The Art of Racial Profiling (1999)

for
Sharome Roberts

16

Clothes Make the Suspect

For the boys and girls who grew in spite of these things to be
Man and Woman, to laugh and dance and sing and play
and drink their wine and religion and success, to marry
their playmates and bear children and then die of consumption and anemia and
lynching ...

—Margaret Walker, *For My People*

A RASH OF STOPS AND FRISKS bolstered charges by blacks and Latino leaders that the NYPD with the firm backing of the Giuliani administration had been engaged in a long-standing "pattern and practice" of racial profiling, a widespread, law enforcement policy of targeting blacks and Latinos they suspected were likely to commit certain crimes. An investigation into the NYPD's crime-fighting tactics revealed that in 1997 and 1998 the mostly white Street Crime Unit—whose members boasted "We Own the Night"—stopped and searched 45,000 men, mostly African Americans and Latinos, while making a little more than 9000 arrests. Even though the rogue squad was disbanded in the face of public outcry, racial profiling by cops continued. For every 16 blacks stopped and frisked, only one was arrested.

Was racism the motivating factor in all of the stops? In March 2000, I put that question to 50 white and black uniformed and undercover officers I knew and asked them to participate in an unscientific survey I was conducting for the *Voice*.

The cops told me that "the felon look"—that "Tupac-thug-for-life" image—account for a majority of the stops and frisks. Using a composite sketch, the cops assigned high and low percentages to every piece of brand-name clothing, headgear, and footwear that they said contributed to the makeup of a racial profile and caused them to confront a person. Whites donning similar clothing were rarely stopped. In the cops' opinion:

187

- A baseball cap, worn at any angle, accounts for ten percent of their stops.

- A bandanna, particularly red or blue, hints at gang involvement and accounts for 20 percent of stops.

- An XXL hooded sweattop, or "hoodie," accounts for 20 percent of stops.

- Sagging, baggy trousers, especially dungarees, account for 30 percent of stops.

- Exposed plaid boxer shorts account for 10 percent of stops.

- Expensive high-top sneakers—unlaced, suggesting that the person may have done prison time—account for 10 percent of stops.

When blacks and Latinos aren't looking like "hoodies" they might resemble the four Ivy League minority graduates who accused three white undercover cops of subjecting them to a night of terror as they drove through Manhattan. Their attorney, civil rights advocate Richard Emery, called the incident a classic case of racial profiling that should be filed the category "Driving While Black." In announcing a federal civil rights lawsuit against the NYPD, the two men and two women alleged that the officers used excessive force and unlawfully detained them. The lawsuit charged that none of the plainclothes officers identified themselves as police or showed badges.

According to the four—Jason Rowley, Sheldon Gilbert, Lauren Sudeall, and Marie Claire Lim, all of whom were in their twenties—their run-in with police began shortly after they left work in Brooklyn late on January 10, 2000. (Rowley was a Brown graduate; the other three graduated from Yale.) All four were in Rowley's car when another vehicle screeched to a halt in front of Rowley. A man jumped out and pointed a gun at Rowley. "Fearing for his life and the lives of his passengers, Rowley ducked behind the steering wheel, put the car in reverse, and drove backwards to escape," the lawsuit claimed. But Rowley could not go anywhere because he was blocked in by another unmarked police car.

When he stopped, Detective Robert Williamson allegedly smashed the driver's side window and pulled Rowley through it. Rowley said that after he was handcuffed, he was punched, kicked, and then struck with a hard object. Gilbert also allegedly was punched by two officers. Sergeant Andrew McInnis, a police spokesperson, said officers used "minimum force" in making the arrests, adding that they ran a check on Rowley's license plate after seeing him run a red light. The car was listed as stolen, and police began to follow it. (Rowley's car was stolen in November 1999 and he reported it to the police, who found and returned it to him.) All four were taken to a police stationhouse for questioning. Rowley was charged with reckless endangerment and reckless driving. The charges were later dismissed.

The Ivy Leaguers' story infuriated William Acosta, a former Internal Affairs investigator whose whistleblower Equalizer Foundation investigated brutality and corruption charges against members of the NYPD. Acosta blamed what happened to Rowley and his friends on Operation Condor, successor to the moribund Street Crime Unit, which was mandated to increase the number of daily drug arrests. Highly secret SNU (Street Narcotics Unit) teams focused on low-level street sales and buy-and-bust operations.

"When you run a department only to drive up arrest stats, there have to be victims," argued Acosta, who sued the department for firing him after he tried to expose corruption. "Let's say a group of young people are hanging around in the park or on the street corner and one guy is smoking reefer. These cops will profile the entire group, and then jump out and grab everybody, who is then taken to a precinct. They fingerprint them, take pictures of them, and put them through the system to see if there are any warrants. It's called a holy fishing expedition: 'Let's see if there is a miracle when we fish. We throw the net and whatever we don't want we just throw back.'"

Acosta disclosed that Operation Condor specifically targeted predominantly black and Latino neighborhoods such as Harlem, Washington Heights, the South Bronx, Bedford-Stuyvesant, Jackson Heights, and Corona. "They are not going into Howard Beach, Bay Ridge, and other white areas of the city," pointed out Acosta, who was born in Colombia and constantly was harassed about his race and national origin while on the force. "Show me the Operation Condor for white neighborhoods!" he added. "They don't have crime in white neighborhoods? Oh, kids do not stand on the corner in white neighborhoods! Kids don't smoke reefer in white neighborhoods! Kids don't smoke crack in white neighborhoods!" Acosta's work as a private investigator sometimes land him in courtrooms overflowing with black and Latino youths he said had been ensnared in Operation Condor's "racist profiling" and arrested on trumped-up misdemeanor drug charges.

He criticized the city's district attorneys and judges for participating in "sham arraignments" designed to make the Giuliani administration look good. Said Acosta: "To avoid a lawsuit against the city, the assistant district attorneys plea-bargained with the kids. They tell them, 'We have this charge of possession of marijuana we can put on you and keep you in the system. But if you sign here, we'll boil it down to a loitering arrest and you walk out of here right now.' They sign and they can't sue the city anymore because they've admitted they were doing something illegal."

Acosta's advice to "the profiled" is to clam up. "Do not plea-bargain," he reiterated. "If you didn't have any illegal stuff in your possession, if you're not the one holding the bag, why should you admit guilt?" Once back on the street, the youngsters were routinely checked by undercover cops who forced them to do their dirty work. "Any teenager caught 'Standing While Black' or 'Standing While Latino' on a corner in this police state could become an unwilling informant," Acosta charged. "The cops tell them, 'We've got you now. Give us some information. Who is selling drugs? Who has guns?'"

Even the late eccentric Manhattan millionaire Abe Hirschfeld was concerned about the treatment of blacks and Latinos by police. In a statement, Hirschfeld charged that "Giuliani [was] responsible for the killing of Amadou Diallo because he ... failed to implement the type of plan I proposed to end police brutality while I was Miami Beach City Commissioner. The Miami Beach Police adopted the plan and the city has been free of Diallo-type incidents for the past ten years." Hirschfeld proposed that cops reflect the ethnic makeup of the neighborhoods they patrolled. "For example, when two white officers get out of a car in Harlem, it is immediately clear to the residents that they do not come from the neighborhood," he stated. "They don't sleep there. They don't send their kids to school there. In the minds of the residents, 'Those officers don't know our problems.'"

A black undercover cop who participated in my survey said his commanders often asked him and his colleagues "to dress the part," or, in his words, "look ghetto fabulous," when going out on sting operations. "We blend in nicely, but our white partners always seem to mistake us for the criminals," the insider said. "We've been shot at, injured, and killed by our own partners because of what we were wearing. Isn't that racial profiling?" The officer said that the "friendly fire" killing of black Rhode Island police sergeant Cornel Young Jr. on January 28, 2000 was a sobering reminder that it didn't matter whether a cop was wearing hip hop clothes or was casually dressed.

The then 29-year-old Young was off duty and in street clothes when he was shot by two white Providence policemen. He was coming to the aid of the officers who had been confronted by a gunman. They mistook him for a suspect and shot him three times. Police said Young did respond when officers Michael Solitro III and Carlos Saraiva ordered him to drop his weapon. Solitro had only been on the force for a short time and Saraiva was in Young's academy class. Young was the son of Major Cornel Young Sr., the highest-ranking black officer on the Providence police force.

Then Lieutenant Eric Adams, the activist cop who headed *100 Blacks in Law Enforcement Who Care*, said members of his group were frequently cautioned not to consider a person's clothes as the primary reason for a stop. "I'm not saying that there aren't black cops involved in profiling; it's just that we make sure that our people don't look at clothes," explained Adams. "You will find that black and Latino cops in our organization don't fall into that trap of profiling people, because many of them dress in the same manner while off duty." Adams said that prior to the Diallo shooting, members bombarded him with complaints about being stopped by white cops because they were either sporting dreadlocks, "wearing hip hop clothes," or driving around in a Lincoln Navigator, a Lexus, or Mercedes-Benz. "We started looking into this and came to the conclusion that if this was happening to us, imagine what our civilian African American brothers were going through."

Adams's group authored a survival guide he said his members and black and Latino civilians could follow to avoid being victims of racial profiling. "When you purchase hip hop clothes or a Navigator you do so with the understanding that you are going to be profiled," he declared. Adams urged young hip hop aficionados to be "conscious of the clothes you wear" and what part of their attire they chose to stash items such as a wallet or ID. "If they are carrying the ID in areas where it's believed by some officers that weapons are concealed, they risk the possibility of being assaulted or fatally shot," he warned.

Black and Latino community activists in the city began eyeing with apprehension a Chicago ordinance that called for the city's police superintendent to designate specific "hot spots" of gang and drug activity after consulting with community leaders, residents, and others. Once an area was designated a hot spot, people on the street could be ordered to disperse for three hours or risk arrest. Alderman Dorothy Tillman warned other black members of the city council that it was not whites who would be targeted by the ordinance, but "your son, my son," adding, "They stand on the corner in hip hop clothes. They're going to jail."

17

A Bullet for Big Baby Jesus

If I go to jail, you know I'm blowin' on the sergeants.

—Ol' Dirty Bastard, *Caught Up*

IT WAS ALMOST A QUARTER PAST EIGHT on the evening of Dr. Martin Luther King's birthday on January 15, 1999 when a police siren from an unmarked black car with a flashing red light clamped to the roof on the driver's side buzzed a 1999 Chevy Tahoe cruising along Dean Street in the Brownsville section of Brooklyn. Such stops by undercover cops were routine in "the Ville," a mostly poor black community that was a flashpoint in Mayor Giuliani's vaunted war on crime. Such stops by warring drug dons who posed as fake undercover cops to rob rivals, or by "MC Jackers" who specialized in ripping off rappers, often erupted in gunfire.

That evening, then 29-year-old rapper Russell Jones, who was known as Big Baby Jesus, or less benignly as Ol' Dirty Bastard of the Wu-Tang Clan, felt he had reasons to be paranoid after two white men with guns drawn and wearing bulletproof vests approached his moss-colored jeep.

Frederick Cuffie, Dirty's 37-year-old cousin, who was also known as Sixty-Second Assassin from the rap group Sons of Man, said Dirty feared the men might be "legit Five-Os" harassing him, or hit men sent by the same gangstas who'd shot him during an invasion of his Brownsville apartment in the summer of 1998, or the vindictive "player hater" who shot him in the stomach in 1996 after an "ill" argument over rap music.

"He's been telling friends that somebody is trying to kill him," Sixty told me in an exclusive interview. After gangsta rapper Tupac Shakur died from wounds inflicted during a drive-by shooting in Las Vegas in 1996, Dirty changed his name to Osirus and began warning friends and relatives that he was next on an FBI hit list of un-American raptivists. "He's been telling me that the CIA and the

FBI wants to get him for some reason," Sixty said. The *New York Post* reported that Wu-Tang Clan was the target of a federal gunrunning probe. The newspaper quoted sources as saying that at least two members of the chart-topping rap group were involved in a gun ring linking the small town of Steubenville, Ohio, to Staten Island. The probe was sparked by two killings involving friends of the rappers. Both of the guns used were traced to Steubenville, where one of the band members, Robert Diggs, has family. Federal authorities refused to confirm the report. (A lawyer for Wu-Tang denied its members were involved in gun trafficking.)

Sixty also was concerned about his own criminal background and history with the NYPD. In 1996, he said he was wrongfully accused of shooting at cops after a performance at a nightclub in Bedford Stuyvesant. He plea-bargained to assault. In 1998, he was caught driving without a license. "Lately, I have been getting a lot of charges from police who are picking me up for no reason," Sixty complained.

Now two white men, who appeared to be cops, were tailing Sixty and his infamous cousin. Sixty had two bags of marijuana on him and there was an outstanding warrant for his arrest on unspecified charges. "I was scared they was gon' get me for that." Sixty's and Dirty's fears, as well as aggressive community policing, may have contributed to the explosive events that unfolded like the gut-crunching madness in a Master P. gangsta flick.

A Criminal Court complaint against Dirty identified Street Crime Unit Police Officer Christopher Roche as one of the cops who sidled up to the sports-utility vehicle. Sixty said one officer "had his gun pointed dead at my head" while another menaced Dirty.

"I'll never forget that white-boy face," Sixty said. "He has white hair and he looks like a cracker. He look prejudice. He looks like a redneck. He look like he was hungry to shoot somebody."

"Get outta the car!" he said the cop demanded.

But Dirty rolled down his window, opened the door, and shouted, "Yo, man, it's me, man. It's me! It's Ol' Dirty!"

"If you don't get out of the car, we're gonna blow your damn head off!" one of the cops allegedly shouted. Dirty, Sixty recalled, felt that the cop "was gonna hit him with the gun" and he wanted to drive off.

"Dirty, don't do it!" Sixty pleaded. "They gon' really think we up to something!"

"He comin'!" an antsy Dirty yelled. "I'm getting ready to go! I'm goin', man!" Dirty slammed the door and rolled up his window.

"Wait! Wait!" the cop shouted. "Where are you going? Stop!" Dirty sped off. Sixty said he tried to persuade Dirty to pull over when the cops opened fire on them.

"Man, put your feet on the pedal and push down!" he urged Dirty. "Go!" he commanded. "I believe you now, nigga!"

"Now you believe me, nigga?" Dirty said irately. "I told you they is tryin' to kill me!"

As the Tahoe skidded and swerved along Atlantic Avenue, Sixty began to reflect on Dirty's troubles with cops. NYPD officers arrested Jones seven times since 1987, and he had been arrested four times in less than a year around the country. In November 1998, he was arrested for allegedly threatening to kill his girlfriend. He was also accused of trying to steal sneakers from a shop in Virginia and threatening people in a West Hollywood, California, bar.

Maybe Dirty's allegation of an FBI and CIA murder plot wasn't real after all.

"I'm saying, 'What the hell Dirty did?'" Sixty recalled. "I'm still not wholly convinced. Now I'm thinking that he did something somewhere else. Maybe they was looking for him. Why would cops shoot at us?"

He demanded that Dirty fess up. "What the fuck you done get me into, man?"

"I told you these cops are tryin' to kill me, man!" Dirty insisted. "They're trying to kill me!"

But as the Tahoe drove down on the wrong side of the street, mounting sidewalks in an attempt to dodge the pursuing cops, Sixty gave his cousin the benefit of the doubt. "The boy was tremblin' so hard the shit jumped over to me an' cause me to start tremblin'," Sixty said. We ain't know where we was going or nuthin'. He's just ridin', tryin' to get away."

The chase ended at 1341 East New York Avenue, outside a boarding home for women owned by the rappers' aunt, Cheryl Dixon. Initial news accounts of the incident toed the police line: Dirty fired on the cops after they stopped him for driving his Tahoe with no headlights on; the cops fired back, hitting the vehicle with as many as five rounds. Police charged Dirty with first-degree attempted murder, assault, and criminal possession of a weapon. But they found no weapon, and Dirty denied shooting at the cops. He was later freed on $150,000 bail and faced up to life in prison if convicted.

"If Dirty hadn't pulled off I woulda got shot in my head," said Sixty, who was not charged. "They figured we had a gun or somethin'. But it wasn't no gun. It was nothing but a cellular phone."

OL' DIRTY BASTARD'S PARANOIA showed earlier that evening when he arrived at Brooklyn Sounds United Kingdom, a recording studio in the basement of the Bedford Stuyvesant Restoration Plaza founded by Papa Wu and Sonny Carson to tap into the raw talent of young blacks who wanted to rap out their frustration. Sixty recalled Dirty was anxious to find the right beat for a single on his new album. Although he would settle for the background music from an old Biz Markie hit, Dirty seemed to have a lot more on his mind.

"He's walkin' around like he's paranoid but everybody knows that Dirty's been paranoid," said Sixty. "It's been going on for four years now. We kept saying, 'What's wrong with Dirty? Why is he acting like this?' He'd say things like, 'All of us gotta watch out because we into this music. These crackers don't like us, man.'"

At the studio, Sixty finally confronted Dirty about his nervous pacing and banter with the other rappers. "Dirty, what's wrong? Talk to me, man." Dirty, he recalled, laughed, walked toward the door, then turned around and beckoned, "Yo, Sixty! Come upstairs with me." Sixty realized that Dirty wanted company because he feared driving alone. "Everytime I see him he got one of our cousins in the car with him." But that evening, Dirty was alone. Sixty recalled telling his cousin he was expected at his aunt's home on Dean Street and urged the rapper to go with him.

Before departing, Sixty told Dirty, "Do not drive crazy"—and warned him not to believe that someone was coming after them if they seem to be tailgaiting him. They turned on Brooklyn Avenue, then Sixty directed him to make a left on Atlantic Avenue and head straight for Saratoga Avenue. But Dirty missed the turn. He thought somebody was following them.

"Dirty, I thought I told you to make a left, man," Sixty snapped.

"I've got it man, don't worry about it," Dirty shot back. Shortly after Dirty assured him he was in control, they heard the police siren. "Now I think they was following us for a while because Dirty kept acting paranoid."

Shortly after the cops allegedly threatened to blow Dirty's head off, the cousins fled the scene and wound up at their aunt's home. As Sixty raced inside the building, Dirty pleaded, "Man, please don't go nowhere. Please!"

"Man, come in here with me!" Sixty said.

Suddenly, another unmarked car pulled up. Dirty jumped back in his Tahoe and attempted to drive off. The cops rammed the jeep and it spun around.

"I ran into the place, acting like I didn't do nothing and told my aunt Cheryl to go out there and make sure Dirty's all right 'cause the police got him," Sixty remembered.

A cop put a gun to Dixon's head. "Get back or we're gonna shoot your ass!" the cop allegedly barked.

"Stay right here, sugar!" Dirty told his aunt. "You ain't got to go nowhere!"

Dixon, Sixty recalled, remained on the scene. Apparently buying into Dirty's paranoia, he became convinced that the cops wanted to get her out of the way so they could kill Dirty. "I guess the other cops put the hit out on him," Sixty charged. "They wanted to kill him right there."

While the cops ransacked the home looking for Sixty and a gun, Sixty hid in one of the women's rooms. "They in my aunt's room lookin' for a gun. They told my aunt that Dirty was just drivin' reckless but that I had the gun shooting at the police." Outside the cops were pressuring Dirty to tell them where Sixty was hiding. Sixty said Dirty eventually told them that he was on the third floor. But Sixty got tired of running from room to room; the residents were terrified and Dirty was in trouble. He surrendered and was taken to the 77th Precinct stationhouse.

At the precinct, the cops whisked Sixty-Second Assassin to an interrogation room. "Now I really think they gon' kill me," he said. "They put me in this dark room with nothing but one chair in it. I thought they was ready to beat me down." Sixty said about five detectives later surrounded him. "This is what's going down," one of the cops said. "I don't want no bullshit from you. All I want you to do is tell the truth." But Sixty said he lied at first.

"I was so nervous, I was not trying to tell them I was in that car." Sixty swore he had arrived at his aunt's house by taxi.

"You're full of shit!" he claimed the cop declared. "I'm about to break your fucking neck. If it's one thing I don't like is a person breaking my balls! You're breaking my fucking balls and I'm gonna beat your fucking head into this wall!"

Sixty put up a front: "You gotta let them crackers know that you ain't scared, that you will go down with them." The cops tried another approach. Dirty, one of them said, had ratted on him.

"Your boy Dirty told us so you might as well spit it out," the cops said. "Dirty already told me you shot at the police." The cops tried to play Sixty: Ol' Dirty Bastard had turned on him to save his own skin.

"Man, that's a goddamn lie!" Sixty snarled. "The police shot the whole damn van up! These cops was trying to kill us in that car!"

It was not what the cops wanted to hear. All but one left the room. "We're about to kick your ass!" he said. Sixty stalled. A beat down was not necessary, he told the detective. "I teach righteousness. I got no hatred against white people; they like brothers unto me, too." The player was trying to play the players: "Y'all ain't gotta do all this."

"Did Dirty have a gun?" the cop asked.

"Nah, man," the puzzled rapper retorted. "I thought y'all said I'm the one that shot."

The cop painted a scenario of Sixty going to prison if he didn't finger Dirty. "You gonna fuck around and get 25 years to life for lying!" the cop said.

"Look, man, it was your peoples," Sixty said. "They shot at us, man. Dirty never had a gun. I'm telling y'all the truth."

Sixty stuck to his story: The police had shot at them for no reason. He told the story over and over again to a phalanx of detectives and to an assistant district attorney, in writing and on tape. Dirty's paranoia began to rub off on Sixty when the cops offered him a drink of water.

"I start thinking, 'Maybe these niggaz tryin' to poison me.' I took three sips and didn't drink no more. They gave me coffee after that." He thought it was drugged, "but I was so damn thirsty, I just needed something to drink."

Despite all that he had written and said on the videotape about the incident, a fresh batch of detectives kept hammering him about the gun Dirty allegedly used to shoot at the officers. The story was the same: Dirty did not have a gun.

Sixty fell asleep. He woke up. He smoked. They badgered.

"Tell us the truth, Dirty had a gun, right?" a detective inquired.

"I thought y'all said I was the one whom had the gun? I done told you a thousand times, Dirty did not have no gun."

"Did he have a bulletproof vest on?" another cop asked.

"I'm not sure."

"Does Dirty get high?"

"He didn't do nothing with me."

18

41 Bullets

✦

The Killing of Amadou Diallo

And the evidence will show that Mr. Diallo attracted the suspicion, not only of the officers, but, we believe, several other people on the block because he was alternately standing out on one of the platforms and peering down the street towards Westchester Avenue and then ducking back into the building, standing on the platform peering down towards Westchester and ducking back into the building. And as the officers passed, he peeked out and looked back again. And Sean Carroll spotted this. And so began the chain reaction.

—Defense attorney Bennett M. Epstein

In the 1990s in Bronx County, in Albany County, or anywhere else, a human being should have been able to stand in the vestibule of his own home and not be shot to death—especially when those doing the shooting are police officers sworn to protect innocent people.

—Bronx Assistant District Attorney Eric Warner

I neither started the protest nor suggested it. I simply responded to the call of the people for a spokesman.

—Martin Luther King, Jr., 1958

THE UNMARKED CAR THAT CRUISED 174TH STREET in the Soundview section of the Bronx, swerved suddenly at the corner of Croes and Fteley avenues on the night of February 4, 1999. Denise Marks, who was driving by on her way home, remembered slowing down at about 11:20 p.m. after she saw four white men "jump out of the burnt-red, ugly, beat-up Taurus in a frenzy—like they were on drugs, on something really hyped." The men, who the 37-year-old woman suspected were cops in plainclothes, stopped and frisked a young black man, rummaged through his knapsack, and then let him go. Denise, who drove slowly past the cops, was about to turn into the parking lot of her nearby building when she saw her husband, Brian, approaching.

"I got scared because I feared he was next," Denise said. She pleaded with her husband to get in the car. Brian, then 36, worked for the city, but that night he was dressed down, wearing baggy camouflage army pants and an oversized, black-hooded sweattop. Denise's fear that her husband's "ghetto awareness wear" would trigger the white cops to stereotype him was not unfounded. She felt that it was only a matter of time before the four antsy cops would be attracted by her husband's "perp colors"—as Brian would later describe his attire—and come after him.

Brian got in the car and the couple drove off. Minutes later, Denise pulled into her building's parking lot. While her husband was locking the gate, she said she noticed the same cop car reversing on Croes Avenue, as if to come after him. "I guess they noticed we were together when my husband started walking toward me," she said. "By the time we got to the front entrance of my building, they were again stopping people."

The couple watched the cops stop and frisk a number of residents and then get back into their car and drive away without making any arrests. The next morning, the Markses turned on their TV and there they were. Officers Sean Carroll, Edward McMellon, Kenneth Boss, and Richard Murphy—the same four cops Denise had feared might mistake her husband for a common criminal—were being accused of gunning down West African immigrant Amadou Diallo. The cops fired 41 bullets at Diallo, hitting him 19 times, in the vestibule of his Bronx apartment building at 1157 Wheeler Avenue, just blocks from where Denise and Brian Marks lived. A witness said all four undercover cops fired after one of them shouted, "Gun!" No gun was found. Prosecutor Eric Warner would later tell a jury what the Bronx district attorney believed happened:

> Let me just give you the sense of how this shooting took place. The evidence will show that on Wheeler Avenue at that time Richard Murphy pulled the trigger of his nine millimeter pistol four times. Kenneth Boss pulled the trigger of his nine millimeter pistol five times. Sean Carroll and Edward McMellon pulled the triggers of their nine millimeter pistols 16 times each. The shots were fired at very close range from in front of the vestibule. And let us be absolutely clear. Each shot required a separate pull of the trigger.

Warner would also describe in gruesome detail what each of the cops' bullets did as they tore into the 150-pound, five-foot-six-inch tall sidewalk peddler:

> One bullet went through Amadou Diallo's chest, his aorta, his left lung, his spine, and his spinal cord. Another bullet went through his spleen, his left kidney and his intestines. Three more bullets went through his left hip, causing perforations of his pelvis and his intestines. Another bullet went through the left side of his back, his spine, his spinal cord, his liver, and his right lung. Another bullet broke the bone in his right arm above the elbow. Another bullet fractured both bones in his left shin. Another bullet went through his thigh, exited his groin and grazed the scrotum. Another bullet went into his right leg, traveled upward and lodged behind his knee. Nine more bullets struck him from the torso to toe.

AL SHARPTON'S ROLE IN TURNING THE TIDE of public opinion against Mayor Giuliani and the rogue cops seemed clearly defined from the outset of the political fallout in the aftermath of the brutal slaying of Diallo. Since the reverend no longer injected himself into every potentially high-profile case that reached his headquarters daily, he was wary of the February 5 phone call an aide received from Mohamed S. Jalloh, the head of the Harlem-based Guinean Community Association. Jalloh, according to Sharpton, told Moses Stewart, the head of the Network's crisis-intervention center, that police were trying to cover up the circumstances surrounding the shooting of Diallo, and that this was a perfect case for Sharpton.

In the course of Stewart's inquiry, a detective from the NYPD's Internal Affairs Bureau allegedly called Sharpton to assure him that the department would leave no stone unturned in its investigation, and that the reverend should convey that message to the black community.

"They never call me," Sharpton sneered. "That got me suspicious." Sharpton felt himself being sucked into the maelstrom that was swirling around the incident. The activist organized a vigil at the site where Diallo was killed and, after a minor uproar within the Guinean Community Association over his role, he got the green light to act as an adviser to the family.

On Monday, February 8, when it was reported that Giuliani had contacted Amadou's father in Vietnam, and that he was on a plane to New York, Sharpton feared that City Hall would try to upstage him.

"I said to myself, 'Oh my God, the father may be persuaded by the mayor.'"

He subsequently learned that Amadou's mother also was headed to America.

"Oh God, what are they trying to do here?" Sharpton asked an aide.

Sharpton devised a plan to wrest control of the distraught mother from Giuliani.

"You and other members of the Association need to go to the airport and explain to the mother the politics of what's happening because the city is gonna try to separate us," he told Jalloh during a rally at Foley Square in downtown Manhattan. That was the plan, Sharpton insisted. If Giuliani got hold of Mrs. Diallo, it would be a public-relations victory for him. Jalloh delivered his remarks and left promptly for the airport.

About an hour later, he called Sharpton on his cell phone. "They took the mother off the plane," Sharpton recalled Jalloh saying nervously. "We can't talk to her! The police have her!"

"My heart sunk in my shoes," Sharpton said. "I went back to my office and waited for the other shoe to drop. I turned on the TV and there she was. Amadou's mother had been taken to Wheeler Avenue by the police. TV captured her collapsing. I'm sitting there saying, 'Well, they got them now.' I don't think the Diallo family is going to understand this picture; the city will feed them its version of the killing of their son."

Around 5:30 P.M., Jalloh and Dr. Delois Blakely, the black community's "ambassador to Africa," walked into Sharpton's office. They said that Mrs. Diallo wanted to meet Sharpton. Miffed by what he viewed as Giuliani's attempt to control Mrs. Diallo, the reverend snapped, "About what?"

"We don't know," Jalloh responded. Sharpton paused. Either Mrs. Diallo was summoning him to tell him to butt out of the investigation or to ask him to help her seek justice for Amadou. Sharpton accompanied the emissaries to the Stanhope Hotel on Fifth Avenue, where the city had put Mrs. Diallo. He was greeted by a phalanx of cops and Karl Waters, an attorney who had represented Amadou. "The ranking officer looked at his men and said, 'That's Al Sharpton, should we let him in?'" Waters vouched for Sharpton and he was allowed past the cops. On seeing Sharpton, Mrs. Diallo reportedly pleaded, "Reverend Sharpton, I know who you are and what you do; would you please get these police away from me? They killed my son!"

"My heart came back to my chest and that's when I knew she was with us," Sharpton recalled. For the next three hours, Sharpton consoled Mrs. Diallo, offering to move her out of the hotel, take care of her financial needs, and defray the cost of flying Amadou's remains back to Guinea. Sharpton reached out to Reverend Wyatt Tee Walker and Frank Mercado-Valdez, two members of his board, asking them to raise money. At about 11:30 that night, Mrs. Diallo called

Sharpton at home. "Reverend Sharpton? Madame Diallo," he remembered her saying. "I changed my mind."

Sharpton's heart sank again.

"I thought the city got to her," he said.

But Mrs. Diallo wanted no part of Rudy Giuliani. "I don't want to move tomorrow," she cried. "I want to move tonight! Get me out of here! Now!"

Sharpton pleaded with Mrs. Diallo to spend the night at the Stanhope at Giuliani's expense; he still had not raised the money. "She was determined to leave then," he remembered. The next morning, the reverend escorted Mrs. Diallo out of the hotel in the full glare of the cameras, denying Giuliani the photo op he was hoping for to diffuse mounting anger in the black community, and the chance to send a message that Amadou's mother had accepted his explanation of how her son was killed.

After Sharpton had checked Mrs. Diallo and her relatives into the Rihga Royal Hotel on West 54th Street, she reminded the reverend that her estranged husband was arriving that night. "You must meet him and warn him so that they don't trick him," she reportedly said.

The battle for the Diallo family began all over again.

"Me and Mohamed Jalloh go out to the airport that night," Sharpton recalled. "The father lands. The city is there. They are inside Customs. We can't go in. We're unauthorized." Suddenly, an attaché at the Guinean counsel general's office emerged from Customs and spied Sharpton and Jalloh, whom he ushered into the restricted area. Jalloh greeted Saikou Diallo and conversed with him in Fulani (the language of the Fulani tribe). Sharpton, not understanding one bit of what was said, kept nodding.

"The father looks at me and the cops and keeps on talking," Sharpton recalled. "Finally, the father tells the police, 'Thank you very much. I go with them'—and he walked out with us. The press went crazy. Now both the mother and the father was with Al Sharpton."

ON MARCH 3, 199, SHARPTON LAUNCHED a civil disobedience campaign during a lunchtime rally on Wall Street that drew thousands of angry blacks. He and ten others, including the Reverend Walker—who helped Dr. Martin Luther King plan sit-ins and marches during the civil rights movement—were arrested for blocking traffic after they sat down at the intersection of Broadway and Wall Street. Nineteen others were charged with disorderly conduct for staging a sit-in outside the offices of Merrill Lynch at the World Financial Center.

For members of Enemy Squad, a Detroit-based funk-rock-hip hop group, DWB was a frightening reality. It was shortly before noon on March 3 in a city on edge following the killing of Diallo. While hundreds of blacks were descending on Wall Street demanding the arrest of the four cocky white undercover cops, two weary members of Enemy Squad dozed in a van parked outside of an apartment building in lower Manhattan.

It had been a longstanding practice of the band to assign at least two of its members to sleep in the vehicle while on road trips to guard their expensive musical instruments. That day, the responsibility fell to Dunimie DePoirres, Dan Harris, and Chuck Haber, their then road manager, who is white. Haber left DePoirres and Harris—who had driven all night from Northampton, Massachusetts, to New York for a scheduled gig later that evening—to run an errand.

According to the band members, at about 10:45 a.m., two NYPD squad cars, accompanied by four unmarked vehicles, swooped down on the van. The raiding party included 11 white undercover cops from the notorious Street Crime Unit. "Get your hands up!" both DePoirres and Harris remember one of the officers demanding as the cops brandished an arsenal of weapons. The musicians dropped two slices of pizza they had been eating and threw up their hands.

"Don't move or I'll break your fucking nose!" another officer shouted.

"Where is it?" one officer asked.

The cops allegedly dragged DePoirres and Harris from the van, slammed them against a wall of the apartment building, and rummaged through the vehicle, tossing equipment out onto the street. The suspects promptly explained that they were musicians, not criminals, and that other members of the band were staying at an apartment in the building. Haber returned to the scene as six officers were about to escort DePoirres into the building.

The cops, according to Haber, said that they had received reports that people were dealing drugs from the van and a nearby apartment building. Haber denied the band members dealt drugs, adding that some of them had been holed up in an apartment owned by their manager, Jason Braunstein. Haber offered proof that he and band member Gabe Gonzalez had rented the van and that the club where they were scheduled to play had taken out an ad in *The Village Voice* touting the New York City leg of their tour.

After reviewing the documents, the cops, "forcibly, at gunpoint," demanded that DePoirres lead them to the apartment where Gonzalez, Kerry Clarke, and Ron Smith were staying, Braunstein charged in a statement he would later file with the Civilian Complaint Review Board. "Mr. Clarke, believing that it was one of his bandmates, opened the door and had a gun pointed in his face,"

Braunstein wrote. "He was pulled out of the apartment and the plainclothes officers entered my home with their guns drawn, never producing a warrant or identifying themselves as police. One of the officers then went to my closed bedroom door, where Mr. Gonzalez was sleeping, banged it open and yelled, 'Are you Gabe Gonzalez? Put your hands up and get out of bed!'"

Gonzalez complied with the cops' demands, explaining once again with other band members that they were just a group of musicians. "At this point, the police admitted that they had made a mistake and one of the officers inappropriately joked to Mr. Gonzalez that perhaps this would bring the band good luck," Braunstein wrote. It was upon leaving the apartment—"still reeling and shaking from the experience of having guns [pointed] in their faces"—that the cop allegedly brought up the Diallo incident. The officer reportedly asked DePoirres what was going through his mind when the cops confronted him.

"What do I have to do to not to get shot?" DePoirres responded.

"Come on, you were thinking about 41 shots, weren't you?" the officer allegedly countered, an obvious reference to the Diallo tragedy.

DePoirres protested, telling the cop that by invoking the Diallo case he was making a mockery of a tragic event. The members of the Street Crime Unit left without offering an apology.

Following the incident, "the band performed that night, and wanted to get on the road directly after the show as they were frightened to stay in the city," Braunstein recalled in his complaint. "I convinced them to return to my apartment to sleep. Mr. Haber spent the night in the van."

The next morning, at about 9:30, two of the officers allegedly involved in the raid accosted Haber, who was listening to the Howard Stern show on the radio. "The head officer," according to Braunstein, "asked Mr. Haber what was going on [because] he had heard there was going to be an investigation and demanded to know why we were looking into it. Mr. Haber took this as an overt act of intimidation and explained that their manager and the band members felt that their rights had been deeply violated, that they had no cause to harass them, [or to] enter and search the apartment without a warrant or identification. The officer then identified himself [I withheld his name] and suggested that Mr. Haber have his manager call him directly."

IN A MOVE AIMED AT ENCOURAGING WHITE CELEBRITIES to voice outrage over the police killing of her son, the mother of Amadou Diallo sought to arrange a meeting between her family and then U.S. Senate hopeful Hillary Rodham Clinton. That disclosure came as black leaders, led by Sharpton, positioned themselves behind Mrs. Clinton, urging her to run for the U.S. Senate, possibly against Giuliani. Black political leaders charged that the mayor had inflamed tensions between cops and blacks in the wake of the shooting.

At the time, Sharpton told me he had planned to consult with Mrs. Clinton's top black Democratic supporters with an eye toward launching negotiations with Senator Chuck Schumer, who was among the First Lady's closest political advisers and a Sharpton ally. If such a meeting were to occur, according to Sharpton, Kadiadou Diallo would implore Mrs. Clinton to issue a statement condemning the four white undercover cops who gunned down her son.

Mrs. Diallo reportedly also would ask Mrs. Clinton to volunteer to be arrested in a nonviolent civil disobedience protest outside One Police Plaza. The reasoning was that Mrs. Clinton's arrest would draw widespread attention to daily acts of civil disobedience, which Sharpton had organized to demand that the police officers who fired on Diallo be brought to justice. Sharpton said that Mrs. Diallo's objective was to stir the consciences of white celebrities, hoping they would in turn drum up support for allegations that the Giuliani administration and its city's predominantly white police force was insensitive to blacks and Latinos.

In addition to Mrs. Clinton, other white celebrities being wooed were former President Jimmy Carter, his daughter Amy, Paul Simon, Steven Spielberg, Barbra Streisand, Alec Baldwin, Gloria Steinem, and Pete Seeger. Sharpton said he planned to seek the involvement of prominent black celebrities as well, including Jesse Jackson, Kweisi Mfume, Stevie Wonder, Spike Lee, Harry Belafonte, Dick Gregory, Sean "Puffy" Combs, and Malik Yoba, as well as celebrity athletes.

He said that the whites he identified "show a sensitivity that I want to appeal to." For example, Streisand, he asserted, might consider reading a letter from him about rampant police brutality in New York City. The civil disobedience protests were seen as a throwback to the antiapartheid rallies of the 1980s, which attracted white celebrities. Members of Congress, top labor and Jewish leaders, and children of the late Robert F. Kennedy were among those arrested during the nonviolent, 1960s-style protests against the South African system, which denied political rights to the black majority.

Sharpton drew parallels between the former South African regime's attempts to destabilize major African governments that tried to counter sanctions and an alleged campaign by the Giuliani administration to vilify leaders of the civil disobedience movement. "This is what the New York Police Department is trying to do," he charged. "They're trying to destabilize the movement by meeting with little groups that don't represent anybody and carrying out personal attacks on me. We need blacks, whites."

The civil rights leader said that peaceful demonstrations would encourage whites in cities like New York, Seattle, Boston, Houston, Chicago, and Los Angeles to jump on the arrest bandwagon and demand justice. "I predict that within two weeks people will be protesting in front of their police departments in other cities," he said. "They need to come out, not just talking, but putting their bodies on the line. We must make the New York Police Department persona non grata until they prosecute these officers."

Richard Kahn, the influential former head of the New York State Urban Development Corporation, who was white, vowed during a rally at Sharpton's House of Justice that he would go to jail over the issue of police brutality.

Since the shooting of Diallo, his alleged killers, all members of the controversial "Street Crime Unit," refused to be questioned by NYPD internal affairs investigators, and remained on desk duty.

Sharpton's appeal to whites was bound to raise eyebrows in black ultranationalist circles, where much more militant responses to the Diallo killing had been urged by the 1999 Million Youth March Black Power Organizing Committee, the New Black Panther Party, December 12th Movement, and the Code Youth Organization.

"This is the time when Black men [with their] backs straight, eyes steely, no fear, legs strong, standing tall, God out front, guns in hand [should be saying], 'You shoot one of ours 41 times, we shoot 41 of yours one time. One shot, one kill,'" the group, which called itself the Black Power Coalition, declared in a statement that was read by its leader Khallid Abdul Muhammad at the February 12 homegoing service for Diallo. "This is no time to forgive!" added Khallid, who was flanked by followers disguised with black ski masks. "This is no time to beg for fairness! This is no time for the murderers of our brother to come and sit in our midst, mocking us."

Grandstanding or not, the coalition's inflammatory rhetoric typified the frustration many blacks felt about the police. "The New York Police Department's 'Street Crime Unit' is in fact organized death squads roaming the community under the motto 'We own the night,'" Khallid charged. The man who urged thousands of participants at his Million Youth March to grab the guns and nightsticks from cops if they were attacked argued that nonviolent civil obedience was not the answer at a time when, as he put it:

"Black men are being shot, six, seven, eight times, some 24, some 11, some 39 and 41 times, nine millimeter clips emptied.

"Black men are being doused in gasoline, set on fire, and burned alive.

"There are known cop codes for killing 'a nigger.'"

Khallid contended that blacks who preferred a nonviolent approach to civil rights should remember other past victims of police brutality as well as former L.A. cop Mark Fuhrman's declaration that the policeman was God.

"We remember Clifford Glover, Randy Evans, Eleanor Bumpurs, Phillip Parnell, Aswon Keshawn Watson, Kevin Cedeno, and Anthony Baez," he said. "We remember [racial profiling on] the New Jersey Turnpike, the sodomy, the shame, the mop stick, the cops, Brother Abner Louima." Khallid insisted that the time had come for blacks in New York to "rise up in self-defense! "This is the time for the Black Liberation Army!" he argued. "This is the time to speak the language of those whose language is killing, bombing, maiming, lynching, and genocide. This is the time for insurrection."

Khallid's message to brutal cops was even more direct.

"This is the time for you to come to realize that your violence will bring even more violence on you!" he said. "[This] is the time for you to know that black people are saying that you'll be burying caskets in your white communities. You'll be having funeral processions in your white communities. When black fathers [and] black mothers cry out for the fruit of their womb, their children, this is the time for you to know that your white mothers will shed tears—will cry, too."

At Sharpton's rally, the minister alluded to "other tactics" being advocated by various groups that had sprung up around the Diallo case. "I'm doing our tactics," he maintained. "I'm not arguing with nobody who says, 'Well, I don't believe in marching.' Whatever you believe in do that. You don't see me running outside stopping people; so don't get in my way. You don't have to announce it, you don't have to argue about it."

Sharpton's veiled message threatened to strike a discordant tone in Khallid's camp. Some of Khallid's allies, who had chided him for his close ties to Sharpton, were critical of Sharpton's pacifist approach to racial injustice. "Do what you believe in," Sharpton urged his detractors. "But if you only talking you must not believe in it; you're trying to convince yourself," he added. "You're foaming up your mouth and frowning and looking mean and ain't scaring nobody."

Sharpton addressed the potential for violence during the civil disobedience protests, but said he was worried about retaliation from rogue cops—not Khallid and his followers. "The New York Police Department is on the verge of buckling under in terms of this latest fight around Amadou Diallo—and this is the time when rogue cops would be desperate like never before," Sharpton said. "I abso-

lutely fear that some rogue cops who feel that this is it for them may try something dangerous. There is no way they could get around a movement this big
without trying to make an example out of someone. My feeling is that a rogue
cop would feel that the one to make an example of is me."

At his rally, parts of Sharpton's speech sounded like his mentor, Dr. King, the
night before he was gunned down by a sniper's bullet. He said that after he was
booked at Manhattan's 7th Precinct and released, a woman walked up to him
and pledged her support for what he was doing, but in the same breath she urged
him to be careful "because we are fighting people that will do dangerous things."

Sharpton paused. He told the crowd that he lived in a neighborhood that was
patrolled by cops from the 70th Precinct—the same precinct in which cops allegedly took Abner Louima to their station house and jammed a toilet plunger up
his rectum. He said he often wondered whether he would have the courage to call
on officers from that precinct if his family were in danger.

"This is no joke to me," he said. "This is no publicity to me. I know that we
can be harmed or even killed."

IT HAS BEEN SIX HOURS since Sharpton orchestrated the largest multi-eth-
nic sit-in of his 15-day campaign of civil disobedience in front of One Police
Plaza. On this evening of March 26, 1999, Sharpton's mentor, the Reverend
Jesse Jackson, and 215 other people had been arrested protesting the police killing of Diallo, and booked and released. The throng of New Yorkers—choked
with rage built up from the antiapartheid movement of the 1980s—pushed the
number of demonstrators who already had been charged with blocking the building's entrance over the 1000 mark.

Sharpton, wide-eyed and restless, was on an emotional high, pacing the second-floor office of his Harlem-based National Action Network, flipping channels
and pumping his fists at reports highlighting the NYPD's double standard for
blacks and whites. The news was all good; it was beyond anything the man who
was being propelled to the leadership of a growing civil disobedience movement
had imagined could be possible.

There, on NY1, was the somber-faced Police Commissioner Safir, grudgingly
conceding that his predominantly white Street Crime Unit—four of whose
members were expected to be arraigned that week on charges that they murdered
Diallo in a hail of gunfire—perhaps had become a law unto itself and had to be
dismantled.

Sharpton's phone rang consistently during an interview with me. He took
some calls and dismissed others. But when an aide announced that union leader

Dennis Rivera was on the line, Sharpton grabbed the phone. Rivera and former Deputy Mayor Bill Lynch were on a conference call, congratulating Sharpton for bringing the hard-hearted Safir and Mayor Giuliani to their knees. Consider what you have accomplished, Sharpton said they urged him: How was this pesky political pariah able to convince an ex-mayor, an Oscar-winning actress, scores of council members, congressional representatives, lawyers, students, academicians, blacks, whites, Jews, gays, lesbians, and antiwar activists to join his crusade?

Hadn't Sharpton realized by now that his movement had a lot to do with Giuliani's approval rating plummeting to an all-time low? Who could have forced the imperial mayor to rescind his racist policy of not meeting with black leaders he had not handpicked? Should Lynch and Rivera sponsor a resolution at a leadership meeting, calling on Giuliani to meet with his arch-nemesis?

"I don't want a resolution," Sharpton shot back in my presence. While he appreciated the proposed gesture, the last thing he wanted was for them to appear to be rallying around Al Sharpton, the personality.

"Giuliani is on the run," Sharpton asserted. "If he can make this a personality fight between me and him, he gets away. I don't want him to get away with this."

Sharpton's rejection of the resolution was a testament to how far he had matured in New York City politics. At 44, he seemed to have finally attained what was denied him throughout a career as one of the nation's most controversial civil rights activists: RESPECT. Gone were the tight-fitting jogging suits, dangling bronze medallion, incendiary sound bites, and alleged publicity stunts that sometimes landed him in jail for tying up traffic and disrupting subway service. Al Sharpton, in the opinion of a growing number of people, had evolved from "racial arsonist" to statesman.

After he got off the phone with Lynch and Rivera, Sharpton called Bobo Diallo, one of Amadou's uncles, who had been waiting patiently among the throng of camera crews and reporters, into his office. He told Bobo that all the adulation meant nothing to him if Bobo did not get to Brussels by the weekend to finalize arrangements for Amadou's mother to return to the United States.

A Bronx grand jury reportedly had indicted the four officers on second-degree murder charges, and Sharpton had learned that Bronx District Attorney Robert Johnson would unseal the indictments that week. A week earlier Sharpton and Mrs. Diallo had talked about plans for her to return. Sharpton suggested that this time Amadou's teenage sister and two brothers should accompany their mother. The last time he had seen the Diallo family was at Amadou's burial in Guinea, when they were traumatized, not fully aware of what had happened. Sharpton told Mrs. Diallo that he would take them to the Wheeler Avenue apartment building where the cops had gunned down Amadou. "I can't explain it," he said. "They have to see for themselves, feel it. People need to hug and embrace them. They must understand the impact of their brother's death and what it started."

That, Sharpton said, was his "secret agreement" with Mrs. Diallo. In addition, Sharpton made her a promise. "I promised her that these cops would be arrested," he recalled. "I promised to take her and her family to the courtroom on that day. All I want is when those four cops walk out there and are indicted for second-degree murder, they are looking into the faces of African parents who believed in America and allowed their son to come here to chase the American dream that turned into a nightmare. I want them to go to sleep at night seeing Mrs. Diallo's face. I want them to be haunted by the faces of his brothers and sister. I want them to come face-to-face with the reality of what they did to a human family."

NINE MONTHS BEFORE THE DEATH OF AMADOU DIALLO spawned the city's most successful anti-police-brutality movement, Sharpton realized he could not exploit popular outrage over alleged police abuses all by himself. With prominent activists like attorney Alton Maddox, the Reverend Herbert Daughtry, and Charles Barron firmly behind him, Sharpton tried to reach out to whites. "Some would go so far, but none wanted to be seen with me in public," he lamented. "Privately, they said, 'Al is cool.'"

Norman Siegel, the vociferous civil libertarian, noticed a change in Sharpton's tactics and rallied to his side. "We had some conversations, and it seemed to me that he was evolving," recalled Siegel. Before they embarked on joint projects, however, Siegel said he felt compelled to clear his conscience. "I told him I think Tawana Brawley was a hoax," Siegel said. "I think he made a mistake with Freddie's. I think he made a mistake in Crown Heights."

Putting their troubling disagreements aside, Siegel and Sharpton forged a formidable alliance. On Christmas Day, for the past two years, Siegel traveled uptown to the headquarters of the National Action Network to assist Sharpton in feeding the homeless. "I watched how he reacted and interacted with the homeless people when there were cameras around, but also when there weren't cameras," Siegel pointed out. "I mean, when you see that [people like Sharpton] empathize with people who are powerless, that's important to me."

Sharpton began to pick his battles more carefully. He surprised everyone when he testified on behalf of Joseph Locurto, the white cop who was fired from the NYPD after participating in a skit that mocked the white supremacist dragging death of a black man in Jasper, Texas. "I thought he fully understood the issue of an off-duty police officer's right to engage in First Amendment expression," Siegel said. Sharpton continued to jump on the issues that generated headlines. When Governor George Pataki and Safir advocated DNA testing of felons for a criminal-justice database, Sharpton and Siegel screamed. "We decided we would work together on that," recalled Siegel, adding that he "took a lot of hell from people in my community."

After Diallo was killed and Sharpton began to call for the arrest of the police officers involved in the shooting, Siegel publicly differed with his activist comrade, explaining that it was "a mistake for him to call for the arrest of the officers [without due process]."

As the movement grew around the Diallo killing, Siegel's newfound faith in Sharpton seemed to be justified. At a rally, Siegel listened intently as Sharpton told supporters that the movement should not be built around one person or group. "One of the conversations I had with Sharpton was over the concept of sharing," Siegel remembered. "If you're gonna build a movement, it can't be one person riding on the horse; we learned that when they killed Dr. King. Sharpton told me over and over again he is into sharing."

Sigel added: "What I like about Sharpton is that he has not allowed the attention that has been focused on him to go to his head. He has his feet on the ground." Even Siegel confessed to "flying high" after the protests attracted international attention and shook the political foundations of the Giuliani administration. "The scenes I have always dreamed of have become reality in New York City," said the advocate, who had flashbacks of himself as a young lawyer defending civil rights demonstrators in the South.

"Back then, I kept hoping that some day in my hometown of New York we would show that kind of strength," he said. "I was buoyed by the participation of Jewish and Asian students, everyone coming together and singing 'We Shall Overcome.'" Sharpton warmed to the idea of recruiting civil rights activists from the South to buttress the front lines of the fledgling civil disobedience movement. "We have been joking about it," Siegel said in a moment of levity. "We said, 'If they think Al Sharpton is a rogue, wait till they see Josea Williams and James Bevel.'"

Siegel praised Sharpton for helping to assure white New Yorkers that the daily protests outside of One Police Plaza would be nonviolent. "There is a lack of real civil disobedience tension here because everything is orchestrated," he noted. "This is 1999, and you have to recognize that you can't repeat what happened 40 years ago."

He said that as a result of Sharpton's novel approach in the Diallo case, a whole new generation of activists were being better educated about the power of civil disobedience based on the nonviolent tactics of Gandhi and King. "If you create a climate like we have been able to create in the last few days," he declared, "everybody will want to play a role."

Sharpton harbored no illusions that he'd finally won the approval of his critics. It was clear that he had become a threat to powerful lobbies, such as the Patrolmen's Benevolent Association, which took out full-page ads in the city's dailies, declaring that his crusade for justice was meant "to destroy the mayor politically and to railroad into jail unfortunate New York City police officers whose only motivation was to fight crime, protect the public and get home safely."

Wasn't the bottom line of Sharpton's argument that it was those very police officers who never gave Diallo the chance to return home safely? Sharpton, like many blacks, believed that the PBA protected killer cops. The cop union's media campaign, they insisted, was a waste of money. It was because of Sharpton, supporters maintained, that the police siege of New York City appeared to be finally lifting. "Clearly, the demonization of Al Sharpton isn't over," said the father of the new movement, "but I am proud that I was able to achieve a level of acceptance without selling my soul. We united New Yorkers on our own terms."

Rudy Kisses Butts

LONG SHUNNED BY CIVIL RIGHTS ACTIVISTS for his close ties to right-wing Republicans, Reverend Calvin Butts, was one of the few black leaders who did not join the civil disobedience protests led by Sharpton. Butts' decision to remain on the outside came as no surprise to some. Even the pro-Giuliani *New York Post* noticed the Abyssinian minister's absence and asked, "Is Butts jealous of fellow clergyman-activist Al Sharpton's hogging of the media spotlight?"

While the Sharpton coalition recruited celebrities, politicians, and other ministers to engage in daily acts of civil disobedience, Butts tried for a second time to start a citywide black consumer boycott of the Fulton Mall in Brooklyn and the 34th Street shopping corridor in Manhattan. Both attempts ended in failure. "Of the many publicity stunts staged in the wake of the Amadou Diallo shooting, surely the most bizarre was Rev. Calvin Butts' call for blacks to boycott shopping centers in Manhattan and Brooklyn last weekend," the *Post* declared in an editorial. "There's little indication anyone listened to Butts' proposal. Even those New Yorkers who feel the need 'to do something' in response to the Diallo incident seem to have understood that Butts' boycott was an exercise in self-aggrandize-ment that could accomplish absolutely nothing."

In 1998, Butts, who was considered one of the city's most influential black leaders, created a stir by calling Giuliani a racist. Relations between Butts and the city's frontline black activists worsened after activists refused to back Butts' asser-tion that Giuliani was a racist. "There were a lot of questions about Reverend Butts when he called the mayor a racist," said Sharpton. The activists had been upset with the minister's earlier support for the mayor, Governor George Pataki, and perennial presidential candidate Ross Perot. "[Butts'] partner, George Pataki, [was] building jails all over the state," Sharpton said at a rally. "[And if] that's not bad enough [Giuliani was] taking people on welfare and putting them in slavery, making them clean up parks with no rights as workers. The closest thing to sla-very in modern times was his workfare program. On top of that, this police bru-tality, telling us we ought to be happy we're alive."

One day, during a meeting at St. Patrick's Cathedral with the Diallo family, Cardinal O'Connor asked Sharpton if the family would attend a reconciliation service designed to ease racial tension and heal the city. Cardinal O'Connor said the cream of the city's leadership would be attending. Suspecting that the service was designed to exclude him and other leaders of the civil disobedience move-ment, Sharpton said that two weeks before the event he asked the cardinal for a list of names of those he would be rubbing shoulders with. "I ain't going to no meeting that I don't know what I'm going to," he declared during the rally, "because they [would have had] us sitting in an audience like we agree with what's going on, on the stage, just because we're sitting there. [They'll] have everybody on the program on one side, and then flash us in the audience and say that everybody was healed."

The cardinal faxed the program to Sharpton. "Nobody on the program had anything to do with the movement against police brutality," he complained. "Forget about Al Sharpton. How do you not have [Reverend Wyatt Tee Walker]? How do you not have Reverend Gary Simpson? He went to jail. How do you not have Reverend James Forbes? How are you gonna have healing when the people leading the movement are not brought into the room?"

Sharpton said organizers of the service then reached out to Reverend Calvin Marshall, who was scheduled to deliver the opening prayer: Marshall canceled his appearance after he realized the list of speakers included no other protest leaders. "Reverend Marshall said, 'I'll pray at home' and refused to go," Sharpton remem-bered. "The reason that they invited him to do the prayer is so he can't say noth-ing."

The so-called reconciliation service exposed one of the most humiliating episodes in the ongoing drama between Giuliani and his black critics. In what seemed to be a prearranged gesture, Butts called Giuliani to the altar. The two met halfway, Butts coming from the pulpit and Giuliani from the front pew. They hugged warmly and spoke quietly for several seconds. "Now I'm all for unity, but enough is enough!" said Sharpton.

At a rally in Brooklyn following the service at St. Patrick's, Sharpton told a cheering crowd: "Everybody that want to come to town and take a shot at me takes a shot at me [but] you got these Uncle Remuses running around, selling out the movement, and nobody will say nothing. I'll be damned if I'll sit here and allow them to turn around the work that we've done in New York City." Giuliani, Sharpton said, was entitled to hug whomever he wants, but "we're gonna fight until these four cops is hugging a pillow in jail for the rest of their [lives]."

Sharpton hammered Butts relentlessly over his sudden embrace of the mayor. "This is absolutely ridiculous!" he said. "One minute you call a man racist, then all of a sudden he ain't a racist? Explain to me what he did, that all of a sudden he ain't no racist no more. They [the Giuliani administration] just admitted yesterday that only 3 percent of the Street Crime Unit is black. That was worse than the percentage of blacks in the armed forces in South Africa under apartheid. And 24 hours later, you gonna hug them for that?"

Butts did not return my calls for comment.

As condemnation rained down on the maverick minister in the wake of his audacious alliance with Giuliani, organizers of the nonviolent civil disobedience protests moved swiftly to assure concerned black leaders that political pressure on City Hall would not subside.

Some, like Charles Barron, viewed the so-called reconciliation as "a clear attempt by Giuliani and Butts to undermine the black liberation struggle," which had been reinvigorated by the public outcry following the Diallo shooting. "They are trying to create alternatives to the progressive black leadership that is involved with this movement," charged Barron. With the mayor's approval rating plummeting to new lows, Barron asserted that Giuliani would "do anything to divert attention from the real issue, which is our demand that he advocate the severest punishment for police officers who murder or brutalize our people."

Barron claimed that before Giuliani hugged Butts the mayor had been scrambling to find a political strategy that would embarrass leaders of the movement and black politicians who supported them. He said that the mayor's tactics seemed to change after advisers warned that his isolation of almost all of New

York's black leaders would shore up the perception of him as a racist, and thus harm his almost certain bid for the U.S. Senate.

Eventually, Giuliani was forced to meet with C. Virginia Fields, whom he had shunned since her 1997 election, despite her persistent requests for a sit-down. Giuliani also finally met with Carl McCall, whom he had avoided since 1994, and followed up by meeting with several black and Latino members of the City Council.

The call for an end to the angry exchange of words between Butts and the mayor came five days after Giuliani tried to discredit thousands of protesters who had marched across the Brooklyn Bridge in one of the largest anti-police brutality demonstrations of the mayor's tenure. Giuliani suggested that signs carried by some protesters, depicting him as Hitler or Satan and comparing the NYPD to Nazis, alienated potential demonstrators, causing a low turnout.

Allies of the movement, like Eric Adams, joined Giuliani in denouncing the signs. Barron lashed out at Adams. "I think it's foolish to allow Giuliani to back you into talking about signs when people are dying," the activist declared. "He fell for an old trick—diversion. If Eric Adams wants to come to demonstrations to monitor signs, let him go ahead and do that. This movement is not about signs." Adams told me that his criticism of the protesters should not be construed as support for Giuliani or the mayor's alleged plan to sow dissension among the movement's leadership.

At the rally, Sharpton said that Mrs. Diallo, lamented that Butts had hugged the man she held partly responsible for the killing of her son. "She says, 'I don't know who this preacher is. I've never heard of him. But how can he heal for me, when I'm here? I'm the mother that lost her child. He hugged the mayor and never hugged me.' Can you imagine if I called a healing session for Yugoslavia, and the [Kosovo] Albanians wasn't invited? Have you and I lost so much self-respect that they can take any negro they want, and just throw them out there like they represent us, and think we ain't gonna say nothing about it?"

Referring directly to Butts, Sharpton said, "If you are not going to stand for nothing, you should sit down and shut up. If you are afraid, stay home! But I'm not afraid of Giuliani; I don't care what he comes with. It's ridiculous!" he added. "It's an insult to our ancestors. And for me to sit in that room today and look at the pain while Mrs. Diallo watched [the reconciliation] is an insult to our people all over the world. How do we look in Guinea tonight? How do we look all over this country tonight? A bunch of shameless, back-biting people!"

Giuliani refused to meet with Sharpton, who responded to the snub by saying he would meet with Giuliani "only if he called me and told me he is going to resign." By defiantly embracing Giuliani in the throes of a popular movement, Butts joined the ranks of black accommodationists, or "Uncle Toms," who were accused of bartering the lives of those they professed to protect for their own political gain.

19

Revelations

✦

Amadou Diallo Wakes the Dead

Raising Patrick Bailey

AMADOU DIALLO WAS NOT THE FIRST YOUNG BLACK MAN gunned down by Police Officer Kenneth Boss. On February 5, the day after Boss and his anti-crime-crusading buddies shot Diallo, Brooklyn Assistant D.A. Adam S. Charnoff contacted Attorney Casilda Roper-Simpson. Charnoff told Simpson that Boss was the same cop who had shot Patrick Bailey, whose family Roper-Simpson was representing in a law suit against the Giuliani administration.

On Halloween night 1997, a special squad of cops was patrolling black neighborhoods in Brooklyn, and police had stepped up surveillance in the subway stations because of rumors that members of the Bloods gang planned violence to create a citywide scare. Among the plainclothes anti-crime officers who fanned out in "Operation Red Bandana" that night under a directive from Mayor Giuliani were Boss and two other cops, including a sergeant.

Witnesses interviewed by Roper-Simpson and Charles Barron said that about 11:25 p.m., an alleged drug dealer, who had been warned earlier that day by Bailey not to sell drugs in front of his mother's house, stopped an unmarked police car. He reportedly told the officers—later identified as Boss and his partners—that Bailey had menaced him with a shotgun. Roper-Simpson and Barron claimed that when the drug dealer spotted Bailey and two friends, Deborah Chuck and Horace Campbell, as they walked to a grocery, he accosted them as the cops looked on. "The witnesses, who were with Patrick at the time, said that the drug dealer had his hand in his waistband like he had a gun," Barron recalled. "It's strange for someone who is being accompanied by the police to act like that."

"One of the many theories we have is that the drug dealer was used as an informant by police," added Roper-Simpson. "It was a setup," she added. The drug dealer, according to the Bailey family advisers, "cornered" Campbell. Bailey and Chuck, Campbell's girlfriend, bolted and ran back to 731 Sheffield Avenue.

"The police, who were with the drug dealer, gave chase," said Barron. Witnesses told the activist that the pursuing cops kicked open the front door and an inner door and barged in. "They had to come in right behind him because Patrick was running down the stairs to the basement," Barron theorizes. That's when shots rang out and Patrick stumbled down the stairs. "Kenneth Boss fired," Barron claims. "His two bullets hit Patrick."

A bullet grazed Deborah Chuck. "She had to be in front of Patrick because she got hit in the back of her knee," Barron pointed out. Chuck told the advisers that as Bailey lay gasping for breath, bleeding profusely, one officer ground his knee in Bailey's chest and handcuffed him. "I'm going to kill you, motherfucker!" Chuck remembered the officer shouting.

Barron said that Chuck and at least two other witnesses feared they were being attacked by a gang. "She didn't know they were police because of the way the drug dealer had led the chase."

During his phone call to Roper-Simpson, Charnoff, the assistant prosecutor in charge of the Bailey investigation told the attorney that his boss, Brooklyn D.A. Charles Hynes was "on my back to close this case out." Charnoff requested to meet with "all the witnesses you have." Buoyed by the D.A.'s apparently renewed interest, Roper-Simpson rounded up some of the witnesses. But her exuberance was short-lived.

Three days later, as condemnation of the Diallo shooting engulfed Giuliani and the NYPD, Charnoff told Roper-Simpson that the witnesses she had provided already had been interviewed by his office, and that unless she came up with new ones, Hynes would terminate his investigation. As Roper-Simpson put it, "I used a few expletives. I was upset. I told him, 'This is not fair. Mr. Hynes is playing with the family's emotions.'" Then, in a follow-up letter to Roper-Simpson, Charnoff blamed the Bailey family for the confusion, claiming that they had promised to provide additional witnesses who would "contradict the police officers' recollection of the events leading up to the shooting."

Roper-Simpson denied that the Bailey family made such a promise, adding that it was "Hynes's excuse for sitting on the case for the past 16 months." On February 18, Charnoff met with the Bailey family and their advisers, but Roper-Simpson and Barron also perceived that meeting as an attempt by Hynes at damage control. Barry Schreiber, chief of Hynes's homicide bureau, angered the

Bailey group when he allegedly declared that Hynes—and Hynes alone—would decide whether the evidence in the Bailey shooting was strong enough to be presented to a grand jury.

THE INVESTIGATION HAD BEEN DEADLOCKED over a dispute with Patrick Bailey's family concerning prosecutors' alleged refusal to interview some witnesses to the shooting of the 22-year-old aspiring stockbroker, who doubled as a super at his mother's two-story brick house at 731 Sheffield Avenue in the East New York section of Brooklyn. But in an apparent about-face, Hynes, speaking through his top aide, Dennis Hawkins, told me that "recent publicity [had] generated some interest" in the Bailey case. Hawkins said the D.A.'s office was interviewing "potential extra witnesses."

One of those witnesses, sources told me, was a black youth who identified himself as "Chucky McDaniels." In 1997, Daniels told Christopher O'Donoghue, a reporter for Channel 9, that Boss and three other unidentified members of the NYPD's controversial Anti-Crime Unit did not identify themselves before opening fire on Bailey. "They didn't say, 'Freeze!' or nothin'," said McDaniels of the elite team, which had been condemned in black neighborhoods as a "snuff squad" empowered by Giuliani to take back the night. "They just kicked the door in an' started shootin'."

Based on Hynes's dismal record of prosecuting allegedly brutal cops, Roper-Simpson and Barron were wary. (Since Hynes took office in 1990 there have been 76 fatal police shootings in Brooklyn, but only 23 cases were presented to grand juries.) Roper-Simpson and Barron viewed Hynes's eleventh-hour maneuver as a public-relations gimmick. The D.A., they charged was a selective prosecutor, and they predicted he would let Boss walk.

"He's pathetic!" scoffed Barron, a former Black Panther Party member. "We've brought him all kinds of evidence in the past. We've brought bullet-riddled bodies, eyewitnesses. He does not indict police officers!"

Hawkins shrugged off charges that Hynes botched the investigation into Bailey's death, allowing a racist killer cop to remain on the force and allegedly kill again. "The blood of Patrick Bailey and Amadou Diallo is on the hands of Charles Hynes," Barron declared.

Shortly before telling me that Hynes would extend his investigation, the D.A.'s spokesman maintained the Bailey family's contention that the shooting was unjustified did not match the evidence. "There are police and civilian witnesses who place [a] shotgun in Patrick Bailey's hands before he was shot," Hawkins said.

Although an unloaded and inoperable shotgun allegedly was recovered at the scene, witnesses interviewed by the family insisted that Bailey was unarmed. Police said that Bailey—a Wall Street clerk and amateur DJ, who was known in his neighborhood as "Teacher," was wielding a sawed-off shotgun when Boss and his partners chased him into his home. They said that upon entering, the officers encountered Bailey sitting on the steps pointing the gun at them.

According to handwritten notes of an autopsy conducted by the city medical examiner, Bailey "is said to have ... fired on police who returned fire." Boss reportedly squeezed off two rounds from his 9mm Glock. One bullet struck Bailey in the right thigh, the other pierced his right hip and right buttock and passed through his penis, severing a main artery. Bailey died at Brookdale Hospital. As the investigation unfolded, police, after first conceding that the shotgun was empty and could not be fired, then claimed that the officers had opened fire because they believed that Bailey was holding a woman hostage.

IN OCTOBER 1998, BAILEY'S PARENTS, LLOYD AND EVADINE, filed a $155 million civil rights complaint in U.S. District Court in Brooklyn, claiming that the cops responsible for their son's death were enforcing "a policy and custom of overly aggressive policing created and established by" Mayor Giuliani and Police Commissioner Safir.

The accusations appeared to rattle the tough-talking Giuliani administration, which tried to portray Bailey as a petty criminal and gang member whose actions caused his own death, according to documents related to a separate wrongful death claim filed with the city corporation counsel shortly after the shooting. In April of that year, Assistant Corporation Counsel Grant Cornehls met with the parents to evaluate their claim of emotional distress. But a routine hearing, intended as a forum to elicit evidence about the impact of the tragedy on the victim's family, degenerated into a barrage of hostile questioning that left the then 52-year-old Mrs. Bailey sobbing and pleading, "[W]hat does that have to do with my son's death?"

The Giuliani administration, it seemed, had put Patrick Bailey and his parents on trial.

The Baileys were interrogated separately in the presence of Roper-Simpson, who repeatedly challenged Cornehls about the legality of his tactics. Despite her objections, Cornehls pried into Bailey's background.

"Was Patrick ever arrested?" the city lawyer demanded of the victim's father, a then 52-year-old health-care worker.

"I heard that he had some former incident with some guy that was living in the apartment," replied Mr. Bailey, who seemed thrown off by the question but struggled to muster an explanation. "What happened is, the guy was moving out without paying the rent and [Patrick held] onto a television, but I think that case was thrown out ..."

When Cornehls asked for the former tenant's name, Roper-Simpson objected, reminding her adversary that the purpose of the hearing was to allow the city to gather information about the shooting, not the victim's past.

But Cornehls persisted.

"Do you know whether Patrick was arrested for robbery in 1992?"

"He's not answering that!" Roper-Simpson intervened.

"Do you know whether he was arrested for robbery in 1996?"

"He's not answering that question either!"

"Do you know whether Patrick belonged to a gang?"

"He's not answering that question either!"

"Do you know whether Patrick owned any weapons?" Cornehls shot back.

Roper-Simpson became enraged. "Now, I'm not sure why you're asking him these questions," she snapped.

After an off-the-record exchange Cornehls continued grilling the father.

"Did Patrick own a Remington shotgun?"

"Don't answer," Roper-Simpson advised.

In their multi-million-dollar federal complaint, the Bailey family alleged that "negligent, careless [and] reckless" cops left Patrick to die. Roper-Simpson claimed that an independent autopsy performed by Dr. Barbara Wolf determined that Bailey's "wounds were survivable." She said Wolf concluded that Bailey "bled to death." Barron said that prosecutors in the Brooklyn D.A.'s office told him that Bailey was shot at 11:37 p.m., and that police called for paramedics two minutes later. EMS allegedly failed to respond, and the cops placed another call at 11:46 p.m. The medical examiner's autopsy notes stated that paramedics brought Bailey to Brookdale Hospital at 12:17 a.m. on November 1.

"What were the cops doing with Patrick Bailey after 11:39 p.m.?" Barron asked. "He gets to the hospital at 12:17—that's 40 minutes."

Barron said that after the shooting, several top cops hypothesized that officers at the scene felt it was too dangerous for the paramedics to enter the house because other "suspects" may have been hiding inside. That explanation may account for Cornehls's otherwise bizarre insinuations that Bailey's behavior that night was in some way gang-related, or perhaps the result of a lover's quarrel that culminated in Bailey assaulting Deborah Chuck.

Consider Cornehls's line of questioning of Lloyd Bailey at the April 1998 hearing:

"Do you know whether [Deborah Chuck] was dating Patrick?"

"I don't know," the bemused father replied. "I don't think so, because Deborah Chuck [has] a boyfriend that was, I think, Patrick's friend."

"Do you know whether Patrick and Deborah ever argued or fought?"

"No," Mr. Bailey said.

"Do you know whether Patrick had ever hit Deborah Chuck?"

Roper-Simpson interrupted, demanding, "What does that have to do with what happened on the night of this incident?"

"On the night of October 31, 1997," Cornehls explained, "apparently Patrick was involved in an altercation with a woman who we believe may be Deborah Chuck. I think what their prior relationship is relevant to that."

In the ensuing months, Barron reluctantly reached out to Hynes. Barron had been critical of Hynes' handling of a number of controversial shootings of blacks, including Aswon Watson. Hynes backed the grand jury's decision not to indict the officers, angering many in the black community.

Evadine Bailey cried throughout her harsh interrogation by Grant Cornehls, a tightfisted guardian of the city's coffers. The tears were for her Patrick, not a gangsta named "Popa," a thief, or the woman-beater Cornehls made him out to be. Her Patrick mowed the lawn, helped his mother with her vegetable garden, took the garbage out, mopped the hallways, cleaned the yard, and contributed $400 each month toward the mortgage. "He cooked," she told Cornehls. "Anything I asked him to do he would just say, 'Yes mommy.'"

The last time Mrs. Bailey spoke to her son was two days before he died. Patrick, she recalled, had planned to spend Halloween night with his cousins working on his DJ equipment. Shortly after midnight—after the ghouls in blue had snuffed out Patrick's life—Mrs. Bailey's eldest daughter, Angela, roused her. "Mommy!" she bawled, "Patrick is shot!"

In his final affront to the grieving mother, Cornehls—implying that Bailey may not have suffered before he died—asked, "Do you know how long Patrick was alive after he was shot?"

"I don't know," she sobbed. "I wish I knew."

Shot Execution-Style

IN THE MIDST OF THE UPROAR OVER FATAL confrontations involving police and blacks, a white Brooklyn patrolman claimed that he shot a black drug suspect in the head after the man tried to grab a sergeant's gun during a struggle, but as I would later discover, the shooting was not made public by the NYPD and the cop's story was overwhelmingly rejected by a Brooklyn grand jury. It also had become more apparent that black suspects who survived to claim that they were wrongfully arrested, beaten, or shot while in police custody—but later were acquitted—received no empathy from Mayor Giuliani, Police Commissioner Safir or D.A. Hynes. Neither cared about prosecuting the victimizers.

Hynes's office originally charged Allen McKnight, a popular East New York amateur boxer who survived the April 22, 1999 shooting, with first-degree attempted murder; aggravated assault upon a police officer; two counts of grand larceny; two counts of robbery; resisting arrest; two counts of criminal possession of a controlled substance; unlawful possession of marijuana; and three counts of criminal possession of a weapon. McKnight, then 35-year-old, would have faced life in prison if convicted of attempting to kill Sergeant Charles Tyrie.

Without hearing McKnight's version of what happened, a grand jury dismissed complaining officer Matthew Hutchinson's tale, throwing out 12 of the 13 charges. The boxer, who spoke to me exclusively, said that the two cops stopped and frisked him for no reason, and that one of them shot him in the head "execution-style" while his hands were cuffed behind his back.

According to a complaint filed by Detective John Grosse of the 75th Precinct, Officer Hutchinson claimed that about 7:15 a.m. on April 22, while on patrol on Barby Street in the East New York section of Brooklyn, he and Sergeant Tyrie observed McKnight "in possession of a quantity of marijuana." Tyrie and Hutchinson, who "had professional training as a police officer in the identification of marijuana," approached McKnight in uniform, identifying themselves as officers. As they attempted to arrest McKnight, they said, the suspect "refused to be handcuffed, flailed his arms and started walking backwards whereby a struggle ensued" in front of 605 Barby Street. As the men tussled on the ground, Hutchinson "felt something [tug at] his holster ... and observed that his gun was missing." Hutchinson alleged that McKnight had the gun, that his "finger was on the trigger," and that the gun "brushed up against Sergeant ... Tyrie's stomach."

The cops alleged that McKnight, then firmly in possession of the weapon, threatened to "shoot them" and "pointed the loaded gun at Sergeant Tyrie's chest." The complaint stated that Hutchinson, bruised from the struggle, "fear[ed] imminent physical injury"—but it did not explain how McKnight was shot. Hutchinson told Detective Grose that he also "recovered a black bag" with crack cocaine. (It was unclear whether Hutchinson discovered the drug before or after McKnight was shot.) Another officer, Dino Anselmo, reported that he found heroin on McKnight: McKnight was not indicted for possession of either smack or crack.

SEVEN WEEKS AFTER THE SHOOTING, McKnight, who was known in his East New York neighborhood as "Black the Boxer," or "Black the Barber," struggled with the pain inflicted by a cop's bullet, which, he maintained, was fired at point-blank range into his right temple. McKnight remembered that shortly after 7 a.m. on that near-tragic day, he left his fiancée's apartment on Stanley Avenue on his way to Queens. Although the three-time Golden Globe contestant was in training for an upcoming bout, McKnight feared walking through "Ghetnam," another street code for the East New York area, which was plagued by a rash of robberies and gang wars.

"I live in a neighborhood where people dress as police officers and do stick-ups," said the father of three.

As he walked along Schenck Avenue, a blue-and-white squad car pulled up and one of two cops inside shouted, "Hey, you, come here."

"You what?" McKnight recalled responding to the officer he would later identify as Hutchinson. "What you mean come here?"

He said Hutchinson stormed out of the car, accosted him, and began to dig into his pockets.

"What you doing all in my pockets?" McKnight protested.

"Shut up!" Hutchinson demanded.

"What you mean 'Shut up'?" McKnight retorted, pushing Hutchinson's hand away.

Hutchinson then grabbed McKnight's jacket and yelled, "Hey, Sarge, look at this guy; he's trying to take my gun!"

Sergeant Tyrie allegedly got out of the car, wrestled McKnight to the ground, and handcuffed him. "He just handcuffed me and pulled the gun out," the boxer recalled, adding that in an attempt to talk to Tyrie he turned his head and found himself staring up at the muzzle of the sergeant's 9mm Glock.

"As I turned the side of my face ... and looked right at him, I saw the gun right there," Mcknight said. "He handcuffed me, put me on the floor, and shot me in my head."

After the bullet ripped into McKnight's temple, Tyrie allegedly sat on the suspect. "I was like, 'I can't breathe! I can't breathe!' And he said, 'This is procedure! Shut up! Shut up! This is procedure!'" The bullet exited through McKnight's mouth. McKnight began to pray, reminiscent of the way in which the late novelist James Baldwin, questioning "Why God don't protect a man from police brutality," had visions "of being laid out cold and dead."

Says McKnight, "I was saying, 'Please don't take me out this way.'" McKnight blacked out and woke up inside a CAT scan machine at Brookdale Hospital Medical Center. "When I woke up I saw a light, the light that was from the CAT scan," he recalled. "I thought that's how God appears. I didn't see nobody in a white robe with long hair. I just saw the light up ahead."

What McKnight saw caused him to think back about the journey of a sensitive boy discovering manhood in a pressure point called East New York. The youngest of six children, McKnight began stealing cars at age 12. "Just joyriding," he recalled. "I was a short guy driving, barely could see the dashboard." But many people watched as young Allen McKnight turned from a life of petty crime to hardcore criminal. "I have felonies," he volunteered. "I've been involved with weapons and shit." McKnight shied away from discussing how many times he had been to prison, preferring to focus instead on the times he had beaten the system.

"There wasn't no gun ever found on me, but they always said the gun was near me," he said. When cops retrieved a gun in a taxi in which McKnight was a passenger, he denied the weapon belonged to him. "I took it to trial and won," he bragged.

At the time, McKnight was writing a novel, *From Ghetto Life to Prison Life*, which he revealed was autobiographical in a way. It was about a character named T, "a walking time-bomb," who eventually turned his life around.

"In order to be accepted by his peers, he feels he has to smoke cigarettes, smoke marijuana, commit robberies, and steal," said McKnight. "When he gets arrested, he finds that prison is no different than living in the ghetto because there's rules and things that's abided by in the ghetto—it's like a bigger jail, but [one] with a sunroof. So he relives the same struggle inside the jail; now he gotta fight for his sneakers, fight for the phone, then family separation comes between that."

The strong-willed T truly was a reflection of Allen McKnight. He was adamant about making a citizen's arrest of the cops who almost killed him. But McKnight and his attorney, Casilda Roper-Simpson, would later discover that Hynes did not feel like "getting his hands dirty." The prosecution of Sergeant Tyrie and Officer Hutchinson by local authorities was out of the question. McKnight's attackers were cleared of any wrongdoing by Hynes. "We did not find anything wrong with the shooting," said Kevin G. Davitt, a spokesperson for the

D.A. "Shootings are always unfortunate, but sometimes they are found to be within guidelines."

The $65,000 Question

HIS FIVE KNOWN VICTIMS WERE BLACK AND JEWISH. Three of them, neighborhood dirt bike thrill-seekers, were barely teenagers. One was a frightened 12-year-old who urinated in his pants at the 78th Precinct station-house in Brooklyn. The others were an interracial couple on a night out—she, a Columbia University lecturer, he, a black man in the company of a white woman. All crossed paths with undercover Police Officer Fred Napoleoni and suffered from his brutal fists or humiliating rhetoric. Despite this alarming dossier on Napoleoni, he remained on the force, a cop—a white cop who could depend on the Giuliani administration to compensate the victims of his rage.

Napoleoni's first known involvement in an allegedly racial encounter occurred on the night of January 20, 1997, after he and three other cops pulled up behind Daniella Liebling's car, which had stopped at a traffic light at the intersection of Fourth Avenue and Union Street in the Park Slope section of Brooklyn. The officers trained their patrol van's high beams on the rear window of the car in which David Rackley was a front-seat passenger.

According to court documents, when the traffic light changed to green and Liebling drove off, the turret lights on the van activated, indicating to Liebling that she should pull over. The woman complied. Four officers approached Liebling's car, two on each side. One of the officers allegedly told Liebling that he "had seen Rackley hitting her and believed that she was being abused." Liebling emphatically denied that, but the officer persisted, claiming that he also had observed Rackley reaching for something, which might have been a gun. The officer told her he and his partners were only doing their job and had intervened for her "own good." Liebling rejected the explanation.

When Liebling did not go along with the setup, the officer demanded to see her driver license. The cops also ordered Rackley out of the car. "He was taken several feet away from the car and questioned by officers with their hands on their guns," the couple's lawsuit charged. "He was never questioned about striking Ms. Liebling, or possessing a gun, or even asked his name."

The officers did ask Rackley where he was coming from. "Manhattan," came the terse response, infuriating the officers, who pressed for specific details about the couple's evening together. After responding that he and Liebling had been at a restaurant, the officers demanded to know precisely where the couple were headed. "As he began to answer that question the officers finally demanded in a hostile and angry way to know what he was doing with her," the court papers stated. Meanwhile, Liebling was being peppered with racially tinged questions by one of the officers.

"How do I know who this guy is?" he asked her. "I don't know if he is your husband, your boyfriend, or what." Unable to intrude on the couple's privacy, the officers hopped back in their van and prepared to drive away. That's when Rackley approached the van and asked for their badge numbers. "The officers at first refused to provide such numbers, saying that they were doing [the couple] a favor by letting them go," the court papers noted. "Mr. Rackley persisted, telling the officers that he believed that the stop was a form of harassment."

"If you think this is harassment, you haven't seen anything," one of the officers shouted. Alighting from the van, another officer demanded that Liebling hand over her license and registration for the second time. He ordered Rackley and Liebling to return to their vehicle. The couple sat there for about 20 minutes. Then, one of the officers approached the car and handed Liebling her documents along with two summonses for driving without seat belts and one for a defective side-view mirror.

At a hearing in which Napoleoni testified, a judge threw out the summons for the defective mirror but found Liebling guilty of failing to wear a seat belt (she would later appeal the conviction). The couple filed a multimillion-dollar suit, naming Napoleoni as the chief defendant, and charging that the traffic tickets were just a sham by the officers to "justify their improper and illegal conduct" in stopping and interrogating them. Liebling and Rackley contend they were ridiculed, shamed, and put through "emotional distress, anguish, and mental suffering."

ALMOST SIX MONTHS LATER, ON JULY 1, 1997, Napoleoni ran into 14-year-old Stephen Griffith and two of his friends, Ronald, then 15, and his brother, Kendall, then 12. In a videotaped interview with his attorney, which I obtained for an investigative story, Griffith charged that around 4:30 p.m., while bicycling around Prospect Park, Napoleoni and three other undercover officers on bike patrol began to follow them.

Ronald was riding atop the handlebar of Griffith's new Pacific Black Diamond mountain bike. The boys, diehard enthusiasts of bicycle motocross, had been cruising, looping, doing wheelies, and other freestyle acrobatics, and ogling the dirt bikes of other cyclists. They kept on riding, looking over their shoulders at a white man on a bike who was trailing them. The man then rode off in a different direction. The boys thought nothing of it until they came upon a second white man, who appeared to be fixing his busted bike. A short distance away, a third man with a bike kept staring at Ronald. Then the man who initially had been following them suddenly reappeared. Kendall eyeballed him.

"Do I know you?" the second man shouted, startling the boys, who got back on their bikes and began to pedal like crazy. The man who was fixing his bike, and the other strangers, pursued. Kendall fell behind. The man caught up with him on St. John's Place between Eighth Avenue and Plaza Street in Park Slope. "He grabbed Kendall off his bike and Kendall had fell," Griffith told his attorney. "Ronald told me to stop and turn around. So I stopped and he got off and went back to see what had happened to his brother."

Griffith said he and Ronald saw Kendall on the ground being handcuffed. It was then they feared that the white men might be cops. Griffith thought the manhandling of Kendall "was kind of wrong" and remained at the scene in silent protest. Suddenly, the boy maintained, one of the men "dragged me off of my bike and threw me on the floor and handcuffed me." By then a crowd had gathered, staring at the boys. According to Griffith, some seemed to be thinking, "Yeah, they did something wrong." But one of the onlookers was suspicious of the police action.

"What did they do?" the onlooker inquired.

"Stay back!" Griffith remembered one of the men shouting at the crowd as he flashed a police officer's shield. "Stay the fuck back!" Backup officers arrived, and the undercover cops put the boys and their bikes in separate vehicles. The undercover cop, whom Griffith and his friends later identified as Napoleoni, sat next to Kendall as they drove to the precinct and told him he would never see his bike again. "Stop looking at me or I'll snuff you!" Napoleoni reportedly told Griffith. Griffith said he kept on looking at Napoleoni "because I was scared, I didn't know what else to do."

"Look at me one more fucking time and I'm going to snuff you," Napoleoni said.

When the terrified teenager told Napoleoni he wasn't looking at him, the officer "punched me, three times under my right eye." Griffith said the driver and other officers ridiculed him and laughed. "Kendall was really scared, and Ronald kept asking, 'What did we do?'" Griffith said. Napoleoni's constant refrain was, "One more time and we'll beat you with this nightstick." As the cops debated among themselves what charges to bring against the boys, the suspects kept pestering them for an explanation. Then one of the cops accused Griffith of lying about his age. He said Griffith first told him that he was 13. "I should kick your ass!" the cop bellowed.

"I gave my right age," Griffith insisted. "It was you who put the wrong age down." But at 14, even Griffith could see through the cop's attempt to confuse him.

"It seemed kind of humorous because all that was happening, constantly telling him my age, [he was] putting down the wrong thing and blaming me."

When Griffith's mother, Leontine, arrived at the station house, Napoleoni, who stood five feet nine inches tall and at the time weighed about 185 pounds, claimed that Griffith and his friends had tried to wrestle a bicycle from him. A judge later dismissed charges against Griffith that included second-degree robbery and criminal possession of stolen property.

Before his run-in with Napoleoni, little Stephen Griffith never had been arrested or scolded by an officer. In fact he liked cops and hung around them often at a Police Athletic League center in Flatbush. At the PAL center, Griffith played basketball with the cops, but the motocross whiz always heckled his cool and hip friends about their city-issued patrol bikes, which supposedly were better and faster. "My bike is probably better than yours," Griffith remembered bragging to one officer. "It would be a good idea if one of y'all raced," the officer replied, challenging the boy. Griffith boasted that, during one competition, he left two of the department's best bicyclists churning in a storm of dust as he sprinted toward the finish.

He recalled that after the race, the officers took him to McDonald's and "I had a lot of food that day." Griffith knew that there were "certain police I shouldn't trust because as much as you think that police are nice they have some of them that's bad." The experience with Napoleoni, the cop who sucker-punched a kid, left Griffith embittered. "Now I'm kind of upset and angry about it, because I always trust police and I thought that police would never do anything like this to somebody, especially little kids," he said. "The one thing that I don't know is why they did this at all."

TWICE IN 1997, THE GIULIANI ADMINISTRATION settled police-brutality lawsuits against Napoleoni. Following a hearing in U.S. District Court in Brooklyn, the city agreed to pay the family of Stephen Griffith, $50,000 for violating his civil rights (The CCRB substantiated allegations that Napoleoni repeatedly punched one of the young blacks, falsely accusing him of attempting to steal the officer's bicycle). It also coughed up $15,000 to Daniella Liebling and David Rackley for violating their constitutional rights (The CCRB substantiated allegations that Napoelon had issued trumped-up summonses to the interracial couple who complained that pulling them over was "a form of harassment"). In settling the cases, the city did not admit any wrongdoing by Napoleoni. But as part of the settlement in the couple's case, Napoleoni agreed to enroll (at his expense) in a course entitled "Police and Community Relations" at John Jay College. The CCRB recommended that the NYPD take disciplinary action against Napoleoni. Six other officers who did nothing to stop this misconduct were not charged.

That Napoleoni was still on the force angered Matthew Flamm, a former assistant city corporation counsel. Said Flamm: "The suits illustrate the police department's flawed disciplinary system—a system that has imposed no penalty despite substantiated CCRB complaints, and a judgment of $65,000 in civil rights settlements for claims against Officer Napoleoni." How much more the Giuliani administration doled out as a result of Napoleoni's overly aggressive law enforcement tactics was unknown. Citing an internal investigation of the CCRB's charges, the NYPD refused to release background information on Napoeloni or to comment on the settlements.

"My Uncle Vinny"

IN JULY 1998, TWO MONTHS BEFORE Thomas Curto officially learned what really happened in the moments his uncle, Vincent "Vinny" Curto, lay dying on the floor of an East Village bodega, the CCRB had given police internal investigators the heads-up on its findings. In a stunning ruling, the board substantiated charges by Thomas that police brutally beat Vinny before and after he had been mortally wounded in a hail of gunfire by cops responding to a report of a robbery.

But one year after the board assured Thomas in writing that the case had been turned over to Police Commissioner Safir "with the recommendation that charges be preferred against the officer(s)," Thomas said he heard nothing from Safir about the progress of the investigation. The board did not specify in the letter what the charges were, and its final report remained confidential.

NYPD spokesperson Marilyn Mode told me that "the whole matter was reviewed" by the deputy commissioner for trials, who had recommended in May 1999 that "no disciplinary action" be taken. While vowing to look into Thomas's claim the department had not reached out to him about the final determination, Mode argued that the CCRB had rendered its decision too late—a year after the statute of limitation expired on April 10, 1997. "There was an exception the department could make if a penal law crime had been committed, but none was committed," she said.

The NYPD's ruling confirmed what critics such as Thomas had long contended: cops accused of brutality often go unpunished. Others said that more complaints, like the one filed by Thomas on behalf of his uncle, would continue to fall into the NYPD's black hole. At the time, Safir had been pushing a controversial proposal, which the *Daily News* reported would allow the department to send substantiated complaints back to the board on the ground that they do not constitute misconduct or require discipline.

Cries of justice for "Vinny" seemed to echo louder in the wake of a "blue streak" of homicides. On September 1, an undercover cop fatally shot 32-year-old Richard Watson in Harlem after Watson allegedly cheated a cab driver out of the fare he owed for a ride from jail. The NYPD claimed that the officer's gun went off while he was trying to pull Watson out of a second cab. About 100 people gathered at the scene, chanting, "Killers! Killers!" at the cops. It was the second time in three days police had shot and killed a New Yorker. On August 30, four officers in the Orthodox Jewish neighborhood of Borough Park fired a barrage of shots at Gary Busch, an emotionally disturbed man who allegedly was beating a police sergeant with a claw hammer and refused orders to put it down. The shooting prompted hundreds of Hasidim to demonstrate into the early morning hours as community leaders questioned whether deadly force was necessary. Safir and Giuliani declared that a preliminary investigation had concluded the officers acted appropriately. Other police officials said that the shooting of Richard Watson appeared to be accidental.

Pressure had been mounting on Safir to revamp the department's disciplinary practices after a federal investigation confirmed that it did not properly police its 40,000 officers, some of whom routinely violated the civil rights of New Yorkers. Zachary Carter, then U.S. attorney for Brooklyn's Eastern District, was believed to be focusing on a plan to create an independent panel to review brutality complaints and oversee the department's response to them. The CCRB, which was controlled by Giuliani, was viewed by some as ineffective. Police critics repeatedly cited statistics showing that of the roughly 5000 reports of misconduct received by the CCRB in 1998, only 300 were found to be substantiated and forwarded to Safir. Less than half of those cases resulted in disciplinary action.

IN JANUARY 1997, Benjamin Lugo, Sigfredo Mendez, and Edwin Rivera pleaded guilty to first-degree robbery and assault in a botched holdup that ended in the friendly-fire shooting of Officer Keith Prunty and the killing of Vincent Curto inside the Lopez Deli Grocery Store, on East 3rd Street near Avenue C. None of the defendants, according to Rivera's attorney, Lynne F. Stewart, who was interviewed by *The New York Times*, had prior criminal records and there was no evidence that they had fired on officers investigating the robbery. "I want to make it very clear that my uncle did not shoot at these officers," said Thomas Curto, then a 27-year-old dentist's assistant. "My uncle never owned a gun and the police never presented one."

But that's not how the case originally was reported, resulting in, Thomas contended, a plea bargain for the robbers that was built on "lies and distortions" blaming his uncle for the tragic events.

The October 10, 1995, incident was described in initial reporting by the *Daily News* as a "wild shootout." Officer Prunty and his partner, Gerald Derby, were on patrol about 11:20 p.m. when a man told them that a robbery was taking place at the bodega, which was known as a drug spot. The cops, both assigned to the 9th Precinct, called for backup.

According to the police version, as reported by the *News*, Prunty, then 29, was cuffing a suspect inside the deli when Vinnny, wielding a gun, burst from the back room. Four cops rushing in spotted the gunman, and Prunty was caught in the crossfire. Prunty was hit by two of 30 shots fired from both cops' guns. But he managed to empty his gun of all 15 shots. When the shooting stopped, Prunty lay badly wounded. (He was paralyzed from the waist down.) Nearby, 33-year-old Vinny lay dead.

From that point, the story got murkier. Thomas said that upon seeing photos of his uncle's body, he became suspicious of bruises on his forehead, nose, and cheekbones. He said he also tried to determine whether the robbers had fired on officers and which cops had killed his uncle. "There are two sides to the story," asserted Thomas, playing detective, "the police version, which was concocted with lies, and the version I got from someone a short time after the incident." During his investigation, Thomas learned that his uncle supposedly had brandished an old-style Colt .45 at the cops. Not so, he insisted. According to Thomas' findings, this is what happened: About two months after the shooting, he, his father, and his aunt received a call from a source who laid out a different scenario than the one police had painted.

An autopsy report concluded that Vinny was shot in the right arm and chest and that the bullets had perforated his lungs, heart, aorta, liver, and spleen. "He literally bled to death from the wounds and the beating he sustained after he was shot," Thomas maintained. As to the allegation that his uncle was shot at close range, the autopsy report stated that "the exact sequence of these wounds could not be determined."

Thomas charged that after the shooting, his grandmother, Rose Curto, went to the 9th Precinct to determine how her son had died. Ms. Curto, who was suffering from breast cancer, allegedly encountered an officer who told her, "Vincent

Curto is dead and he deserved it." Thomas said that his grandmother collapsed, and none of the officers in the precinct summoned an ambulance. "I am not aware of any discourtesy by detectives towards your family," Lieutenant Arthur Monahan of the 9th Precinct Detective Squad would later declare in a letter to Thomas, which Monahan said he was directed by Mayor Giuliani to write. "The day of the incident we made every effort to provide information to Vincent Curto's mother and a woman who said she was his sister, informing each of his death."

In November 1996, Thomas took his findings and suspicions to investigators at the CCRB. Thomas said he presented them with a videotaped TV news account of the shooting and photos taken of the body by a relative that showed the abrasions. Thomas also asked the board to investigate allegations that police knew that drugs were being sold at the bodega and did nothing to stop it. It was initially reported that 50 bags of heroin bearing the street name "Knockout" were taken from the store and four other men were taken into custody on drug charges. "They charged three kids, my uncle is dead, and no one was ever prosecuted for selling drugs, which is very fishy," Thomas pointed out. "They've stopped talking about the drug money and the 50 bags of heroin they claimed to have found."

But the board was not authorized to conduct investigations into allegations of corruption. That was handled by Internal Affairs. The board's letter to Thomas substantiating the charges against the cops made no reference to corruption. Thomas' disappointment with that aspect of the probe came as state Supreme Court Justice Richard F. Braun ordered the Giuliani administration to immediately establish an independent board to investigate police corruption. The order, issued on August 31, was hailed by then City Council Speaker Peter Vallone as an important step. Vallone had been pushing since 1995 for an independent board, which would focus on corruption.

"This is an important victory for the public and for cops," Vallone said. "The board will strengthen public confidence in the Police Department and it will give officers a place to look outside the blue wall of silence when they want to expose corruption within their ranks." The Civilian Complaint Review Board would continue to investigate police brutality complaints. The Giuliani administration—which, along with Manhattan District Attorney Robert Morgenthau fought the formation of the new board—said it would appeal the judge's decision. The Giuliani administration had argued in a lawsuit that the new board would restrict efforts by police and prosecutors to battle corruption.

The City Council passed a law creating the board in 1995, heeding recommendations made a year earlier by the Mollen Commission, which investigated police corruption. But the Giuliani administration successfully argued in court that it was unconstitutional. The Council came back in 1997 with a modified version of the board, which Giuliani promptly vetoed. The Council overrode the veto, and the mayor once again sued to stop the creation of the independent corruption board. Under the revised plan, the board would make recommendations to the NYPD about its handling of corruption, but not get involved in the investigations.

Thomas said that had the defendants not pleaded guilty, a trial would have aired allegations of corruption and exonerated "my Uncle Vinny."

20

The Louima Trial

Two summers ago a man named Abner Louima was brutally beaten right here in Brooklyn. The attacks on Mr. Louima began about shortly after 4 o'clock in the morning. Mr. Louima was beaten on the streets of Brooklyn by four men who punched and kicked him all over his body. And Mr. Louima was also beaten by two of those same men at a different location. And less than an hour later, Abner Louima was taken into a back room and beaten a third time. That third beating was far more vicious than the first two beatings. And that's because inside that bathroom, Abner Louima suffered more than just a beating. Ladies and gentlemen, Abner Louima was tortured in that bathroom, and his torture was cruel and it was simply inhumane.

—Opening statement of prosecutor Kenneth P. Thompson,
U.S. District Court in Brooklyn

I want to start with what [the] government said, that Abner Louima used the phrase ['Giuliani time'] to call attention to the case. Giuliani time. That he used that to get attention to it. That worked. Absolutely worked. Because you know what? It was Giuliani time. It was the time of the election of the mayor. What you are going to see in this case is that the speed at which this investigation moved forward, because Mayor Giuliani was running for election, was the speed of lighting.

—Opening statement of defense attorney Stephen Worth,
U.S. District Court in Brooklyn

As soon as I get inside the bathroom, Officer Volpe close the door and I saw him pick up something by the garbage can ...
Officer Volpe put an object in my rectum and pull it out and he put it in my mouth ...
He pushes me to the ground ...
Then he kick me on my groin ...

—Abner Louima testifying, U.S. District Court in Brooklyn

235

ABNER LOUIMA'S FATHER, JEAN, winced and buried his face in his hands as a defense lawyer played back a videotape of his son's first news conference on August 14, 1997. It was the bedside TV interview civil rights attorneys had organized five days after police officer Justin Volpe rammed a stick into Louima's rectum in the bathroom of Brooklyn's 70th Precinct stationhouse. Until Abner had gotten to the point where he described "the blood and shit" he threw up following the infamous assault, Jean had been staring at his son—the Haitian immigrant and former used-car salesman whom no one in the U.S. Attorney's office had fully prepared for the role of professional victim.

It was the afternoon of May 10, 1999, Day Two of Abner Louima's testimony in U.S. District Court in Brooklyn at the trial of four white officers accused of beating and sodomizing him. Louima, dressed in a dark suit, stuttered and mumbled, barely mustering dramatic details in the searing narrative he'd rehearsed for federal prosecutors a month earlier. More than a year after I'd exclusively reported Louima's confession that he never heard his attackers declare "This is Giuliani time! It is not Dinkins time," as they pummeled him, Louima shifted in the witness chair and fessed up to the lie under cross-examination from attorney Stephen Worth, who represented Officer Charles Schwarz.

"Tell the truth," a black spectator whispered from her back seat in Judge Eugene H. Nickerson's hushed courtroom. Louima testified it was Jean-Claude Laurent, the brother-in-law of Magalie Laurent (the Coney Island Hospital nurse to whom Louima first told his horrifying tale), who planted the notorious phrase in his ear. But Worth wanted Louima to spill it all, to reveal more about the dirty politics he hinted were behind the words that portrayed his client as one of Mayor Giuliani's sadistic enforcers.

Louima straightened up. No, he swore. His attorney—Carl W. Thomas, the one Worth described as "the heavyset man in the suit," was not part of any conspiracy to drum up outrage over the alleged attack. Then it must be the other fat one, the soundbite king who lately had been articulating black rage all over the country.

"Did you call the Reverend Al Sharpton before you gave this news conference?" asked Worth.

"No," Louima replied coolly.

"Isn't it true you saw the Reverend Al Sharpton the day before the bedside press conference?" Worth hammered.

No, reiterated Louima, who never wavered. Louima insisted that it was Jean-Claude Laurent who had coached him, adding that he had met the man for the first time just minutes before the news conference, when Laurent told him that he was an auxiliary police officer.

"And the stranger tells you [that] you should say something about 'Giuliani time'?" asked Worth.

"Yes," Louima answered.

Worth glanced at the jury of eight whites, one black, and three Latinos. No one stirred. Perhaps they had already gotten the point. (Attorney Marvyn M. Kornberg, who represented Volpe, had beaten the issue to death a week earlier during testimony.) And what if Louima lied about a slogan? What did that have to do with what really happened in the early morning hours of August 9, 1997?

Worth persisted: "Did you tell your lawyers you were going to tell this lie? Did you discuss with your attorney what you were going to say?"

"No," Louima insisted for the umpteenth time. "No, sir."

Worth, growing impatient with Louima's terse answers, asked again: Didn't Carl Thomas and his former law partners Brian Figeroux and Casilda Roper-Simpson consult with Sharpton?

"No, sir," Louima said.

After Louima's testimony that afternoon, I contacted Sharpton in Riverside, California, where he had been arrested earlier at a civil disobedience protest surrounding the 1998 fatal police shooting of Tyisha Miller. Sharpton denied that he had consulted with Louima's lawyers about what Louima should say at the August 14 news conference. He said he met Louima for the first time that day and prayed with him in the presence of police officers, who were guarding their handcuffed prisoner. "Stephen Worth knows this and is purposely trying to politicize this trial," charged Sharpton, who was held at the Riverside County Jail for three hours, along with comedian Dick Gregory and Martin Luther King III. "He is acting like we used Abner Louima for our own political reasons," Sharpton added. "We showed Louima to be the victim that he is."

The angry reverend challenged Worth to subpoena him to testify at the trial. "If Worth thinks that I helped plant this story, why doesn't he subpoena me and put me under oath?" Fourteen days after Worth and other defense lawyers tried unsuccessfully to discredit Louima, the case against Volpe took a shocking turn.

"WE WOULD LIKE TO ENTER A PLEA TOMORROW," was how Volpe's lawyer, Marvyn Kornberg, appealed to Judge Nickerson. My colleagues, Robert D. McFadden and Joseph P. Fried, of *The New York Times*, were in the courtroom following "a quiet conference of defense lawyers and prosecutors at the bench at 3:45 p.m., on May 24.

"Confronted with devastating testimony by fellow officers and a crumbling defense," Fried and McFadden reported, Volpe decided to "plead guilty to all charges ... and throw himself on the mercy of the court.... With chances of an acquittal all but gone and prosecutors rejecting any plea bargain in a case that stunned the city and the nation ... Volpe appeared to have no choice but to admit that he rammed a broom handle into the rectum and then into the mouth of the handcuffed Haitian immigrant in a fit of rage."

A confidant of Volpe's father ultimately may have been the one who prevailed on the former detective to persuade his son to plead guilty. "Bob and I discussed this," James Ridgway De Szigethy, a self-styled investigative reporter for the online zine AmericanMafia.com and a member of the controversial national police defense foundation, told me. "I said, 'Bob, there is a very good chance that your son is going to be convicted and spend the rest of his life in jail. Now, how do we get around that?'"

De Szigethy, who sat next to Robert Volpe during his son's explosive trial, said he advocated a temporary-insanity defense.

"When this whole thing started, everybody [asked], 'Why would some young man do such a strange and insane thing?'" De Szigethy said. "I looked into his background and although one source had called him a psycho I could find no evidence of mental illness on his part. [But] what would happen if Justin Volpe changed his plea from not guilty to guilty by reason of insanity?" he said he asked the father.

De Szigethy chided the NYPD for not considering the theory that Volpe's rumored use of steroids may have triggered violent outbreaks known as "'Roid Rage."

"Unfortunately, the NYPD don't test for steroids," he said. "The theory never took off." (The late *Daily News* columnist Mike McAlary, the only reporter to interview Volpe, observed, "It was easy to see him as some version of Mark Fuhrman on steroids.")

The family friend pointed to the testimony of another Haitian immigrant, Patrick Antoine, who claimed Volpe punched him for no reason while police searched for suspects in the nightclub melee. Antoine testified that he too was taken into the bathroom by Volpe, where Volpe apologized for acting like a madman. "He told me he was sorry," said Antoine, who, like Louima, was arrested on an allegedly false charge of assaulting a cop. "He told me he was like somebody who was going crazy."

Before testimony resumed on May 24, De Szigethy had told me he planned to raise the insanity defense again with Volpe's father. He said he was going to tell the father, "Look, Bob, I know you believe your son is innocent, but is it possible he is a little psychotic?" De Szigethy suggested that Kornberg might argue that "the blow to [Volpe's] brain [the sucker punch] threw him into a psychotic state." He added, "You can find a psychiatrist [with] the credentials who will say, 'Yes, this man was insane.'"

After prosecutors turned down a plea-bargain request, the embattled cop considered taking the witness stand. Volpe might have been motivated to plead guilty after a parade of law enforcement witnesses gave devastating accounts of his activities the morning of the alleged assault. The defense suddenly went silent after a burly sergeant named Kenneth Wernick appeared as a surprise witness. In a never-before-made-public account, he testified that Volpe bragged, "I took a man down tonight." Wernick said Volpe also confessed he "took a stick and put it five or six inches up [Louima's rectum], took it out, and put it up to his mouth and teeth area, kind of like showing it to him." He said Volpe then took him into the bathroom to see the two-to three-foot stick, which was stashed by a sink. Kornberg declined to question Wernick and a second surprise witness, Officer Michael Schoer, who said Volpe had taunted him by brandishing the end of an excrement-soiled stick in his face. His first thought, he told the jury, was about a black dog Volpe kept around the station.

"Off the cuff, I asked him, 'What is that, dog shit?' ... And he replied, 'Human shit,'" testified Schoer, who at the time faced disciplinary charges for initially lying to internal affairs. "That was the end of it."

Despite De Szigethy's effort to get Volpe to set the record straight, he was not a supporter of Abner Louima. In fact, it was De Szigethy who helped reporters track down information challenging Louima's honesty. He said he dug up a lawsuit in which two men contended they were fired by an insurance company to keep them from disclosing information about "fraudulent insurance claims" allegedly filed by Louima. Lawyers for Louima told *The New York Times* that the allegation about bogus claims were false, and a lawyer for the company, Country-Wide Insurance, said that "there was nothing to cover up" and that the men were fired for other reasons.

De Szigethy said his feelings about Louima would not change. "Maybe [the accused officers] did this to this man, but this man is a liar and a fraud [because] he is involved with Johnnie Cochran and all these other things," he contended. He claimed that Louima lied on the witness stand to protect Sharpton, who many in De Szigethy's inner-circle believed had urged Louima to use the phrase "This is Giuliani time!"

"[Louima] said on the witness stand that it was this total stranger who convinced him to make the 'Giuliani time' remark and not Sharpton, with whom he had met," De Szigethy argued. "This conveniently protects Sharpton from being sued like he was by Steven Pagones [the Dutchess County prosecutor whom the black activist had falsely accused of raping Tawana Brawley]." Sharpton, who repeatedly denied the charge, counterargued that Volpe's decision to admit guilt vindicated Louima and himself. "The judge should remember that not only did Volpe torture and sodomize Abner—he also raped his character by falsely accusing him of engaging in a homosexual act," Sharpton said.

Sharpton added that Volpe's change of heart could not have come at a worse time for Mayor Giuliani, who was considering a run for the U.S. Senate. "It is ironic that on the day before the U.S. Civil Rights Commission was to question Giuliani under subpoena, Volpe's plea comes down and the mayor is thrust in the public spotlight," he said. "After Abner Louima and Amadou Diallo, does Giuliani still want to be quoted as saying that what happened to them were isolated incidents?"

Ultimately, it may have been Jesus Christ pounding on Justin Volpe's guilty conscience that caused him to abandon the incredible defense strategy that Louima was injured during consensual gay sex before he got involved with police. Patrick Antoine said Volpe noticed he was wearing a cross and asked if he believed in Jesus. "I said, 'Yes,'" Antoine recalled at the trial. "He told me he believed in Jesus, too."

21

A Lesson Before Dying

He may be a very nice man. But I haven't got the time to figure that out. All I know is, he's got a uniform and a gun and I have to relate to him that way. That's the only way to relate to him because one of us may have to die.

—James A. Baldwin

MY HEART RACED AND MY PALMS SWEATED as I gripped the rubberized butt of a modified 9mm Glock 19 pistol. That, warned a poker-faced firearms instructor, is the eerie sensation you get when you're entrusted with one of the most powerful handguns in the NYPD'S Arsenal. Accorded this rare privilege, I was supposed to throw out all of my prejudices about the cop on the beat (even the one who chants, "no justice, no police," at PBA rallies to defend fellow officers accused of brutality), and get into his freaking mind. But no matter how hard I tried—eyes wide shut, my sixth sense kicking in—I could not think, act, or react like a police officer in Giuliani time. That cop has a brutal streak; he's the one civil rights activists like Sharpton say shoots to kill. His victims—Amadou Diallo, Kevin Cedeno, Aswan Watson, Nathaniel Gaines Jr., Patrick Bailey, and William James Whitfield—did not have to die.

For a while, I seemed to forget why I'd come, on that humid afternoon on July 28, 1999, to the department's Firearms and Tactics Training Outdoor Range in the Rodman's Neck section of the Bronx. I was one of about 30 reporters who had volunteered for, as our host, Police Commissioner Safir, put it, "a behind-the-scenes look at what it is like to be faced with real-life situations where split decisions need to be made."

I thought the idea of a reporter playing cop for a day was another one of "Hollywood Howard's" stunts to shore up departmental arrogance in the wake of a series of controversial slayings of blacks by white cops. During a Q&A session held prior to the "war games," Safir appeared to scold the media. He chastised reporters for harboring "preconceived ideas" about cops accused of firing their weapons unjustifiably at suspects. Safir implied it should not be difficult for anyone to understand why officers use deadly force, "an area of police work," he emphasized in his invitation letter to reporters, that is "often misperceived by the public and the media."

"All of you have seen TV shows in which the police or the sheriff shoot the gun out of somebody's hands," Safir said. "I think you'll find out that even an Olympic marksman don't have the capability to do that."

The commissioner's comment would have been laughable if he hadn't metaphorically put his gun in his mouth and pulled the trigger. Though Safir had invited us to "gain a greater understanding into the complexities of policing," that objective seemed lost when he used the event to side with the cops who killed Amadou Diallo. "I believe when the Diallo case finally comes to trial we'll know all the facts," he said. "One of the key facts will be what the police officers believed. If you believe that you're in danger, if you believe that your partners are in danger, then you react the way you're trained. And again, without commenting specifically on the Diallo case, in every tactical situation that's the driving force."

The top brass on the force were all around us. Some followed my group into the "F.A.T.S. [Firearms Training Simulator] Room," chortling, insinuating in careless whispers that our views on police brutality—especially in situations involving fatal shootings—would change after a rigorous three hours of training.

Indeed, my opinions on the phenomenon of deadly force were enhanced by the crash course. The F.A.T.S. room conjured up the image of a crime scene as my instructor deployed me behind a steel drum that he said would be my cover in the event an encounter with a suspect turned ugly. "This is my lesson before dying," I muttered, crouching behind the drum like I'd seen "ma niggaz" do in those gangsta rap videos depicting surrealistic shootouts with "tha muthafuckin' police."

As I practiced loading and aiming my Glock to fire center-mass at the perp, I looked over at my partner, *NY1* news director Peter Landis, who seemed to make all the right moves, eager to take a bite out of crime. In addition to the Glocks, "Officer" Landis and I were given Mace and told how to use it to disable the suspect.

In the simulation, developed by the Sacramento Police Department, two cops pull over a minivan for a traffic violation. They emerge from their patrol car, shout commands to the driver—"Get outta the car!" and "Put your hands in the air!"—and walk toward the van. Suddenly the van backs up, knocking one of the officers down. A burly white motorist storms out of the van and charges the officer's partner with a knife.

"Stop!" Landis commands. "Put the weapon down!"

I freeze.

I remember, from viewing an earlier simulation involving two other cop-for-a-day volunteers, not to shout, "I will kill you!" I can't decide whether to blow this apparent example of road rage away or kneecap him with a full metal jacket and then attempt to subdue him with the Mace.

Pop!

Silence.

Landis guns down the man with a single shot. I'm shaking, because in one chaotic moment, my partner may have killed John Doe. I try not to look at Landis, but I cannot turn away from what I perceive to be a poignant pallor on his face. It looks like he is going into shock. "If I'm feeling fucked up about the whole thing, imagine what Landis is going through," I think.

Our instructors reviewed the sequence, pointing out the mistakes in policing that might have proved deadly for the knife-wielding motorist. Apparently, Landis and I had stayed too close to the suspect who swung at us with the knife. "If you're gonna shoot the person, you should really get outta the way—if you feel you're gonna shoot him at close distance," the instructor suggested. He asked how we felt during the role-play. "I didn't shoot because I was thinking about how best to control the situation," I responded.

"Did you know it was a knife when he pulled it out near the vehicle?" he asked.

"Yes," I replied. It was the wrong answer to a setup question. I should have warned Landis instantly upon seeing the knife, the instructor pointed out. "You gotta let your partner know," he stressed. Then Landis offered an insight into the mind of a good cop caught in a shoot-don't-shoot dilemma. "I wasn't sure," he explained. "The issue to me was I wasn't sure what it was. But he got close enough so that I could see it."

Landis wasn't as trigger-happy as I thought. He'd deliberated carefully before firing. Like me, he never wanted to kill anybody. "I was concerned that if I'd shot him before, it [the knife] might have been something else," he said. "I waited [to shoot] till I actually saw the blade."

According to the instructor, an experienced officer would have yelled at the suspect, "Don't come near me! Stop! Stop! Stop!"

The instructor's words echoed loudly in my ear as we broke up and headed toward a firing range. "We don't teach people how to kill; we teach people how to stop a threat," he said. But in Giuliani Land things didn't turn out that way. Like most blacks, I'd long suspected that white cops, especially, didn't shoot black suspects by the rules. Before injuring or killing suspects, some allegedly have been overheard shouting racist commands such as, "Freeze, nigger! You're dead!" or "Nigger, don't make me have to shoot you!"

I also began to reconstruct possible scenarios that might have led to the shooting of Amadou Diallo and other victims we had lost to "split decisions." They died because cops allegedly mistook an object (a steering-wheel lock, a *Three Musketeers* bar, keys, a beeper, a cell phone) for a gun or some other deadly weapon.

Along a dusty roadway to the firing range, I suggested to the affable Inspector Michael Collins that the department expand its "sensitivity training" to include people from Harlem, Bedford-Stuyvesant, Brownsville, and other mostly black neighborhoods. It was in these areas that residents often were viewed by white cops as permanent suspects.

An NYPD ad campaign, in which cops were portrayed as gentle, caring role models and big brothers, just wasn't cutting it in the 'hood, I told Collins. At least, these white cops must be sensitized to black street culture in a way that teaches them how to distinguish between a 40-ounce bottle of beer and a gun. Assign rookie cops, I suggested, to the real training grounds—the housing developments, street corners, school-yard hangouts, barber shops, and pool halls. Remind the officers that not every souped-up black SUV with tinted windows was a dope don's chariot. Not every unusual gait by a teenager should be interpreted as a prison-yard swagger, making him a suspect for any unsolved crime.

A working knowledge of neighborhood argot also was important. Consider this: If an officer approaches a group of teenagers, then singles out one of them for questioning, and the teen's response, for example, is, "Why you all in ma grill [face]?" that officer should not perceive this natural reaction as a terroristic threat, resisting arrest, or obstructing governmental administration—three likely charges the teen faces for advocating his civil rights. His refusal to be handcuffed should not be regarded as an invitation to body slam him and crack his head open with a nightstick. In addition, the officer should be able to distinguish between genuine concern on the part of the teen's friends for his safety and a mob wanting to incite a riot.

Inspector Collins listened intently. He passed the word on to Marilyn Mode, the deputy commissioner of public information. The department, she said, already had outreach programs in some neighborhoods where cops bond with kids and role-play certain "choose-to-defuse" scenarios. Mode mentioned the stellar working relationship Richard Green's Crown Heights Youth Collective had with officers in several precincts.

I suggested that Commissioner Safir consider busing a group of adults and teens to the NYPD's training academy. The idea would be for them to understand what goes on in a cop's mind when he is confronted with situations in which the suspect looks like them—not like the burly white motorist in the Sacramento Police Department's scenario. It was the least Safir could do, I argued. And if critics like Al Sharpon said that's not good enough, the commissioner might respond, in his typically dismissive manner, "These got a lesson before dying."

22

The Return of Khallid Abdul Muhammad

THE BLACK RAGE KHALLID ABDUL MUHAMMAD had so carefully finessed with super-rationality to cover up his extremist agenda degenerated into a kind of obscene entertainment when he suddenly reappeared in New York City in August 1999, vowing that "no devil, racist, cantankerous, constipated cracker like Mayor Giuliani can stop" his controversial Million Youth March. Within hours of his arrival, the antsy ultranationalist began roaming Harlem with a gang of wannabe revolutionaries trying to force-feed a fast-food militancy to residents, allegedly in preparation for all-out war with the NYPD. One black leader who got in the way was sidelined by unnecessary roughness.

Giuliani and Police Commissioner Safir, governing by tantrum and vendetta, declared that, barring a court order, Khallid had been denied a permit to stage the second Million Youth March on September 4. Giuliani and Safir had repeatedly denounced the event, which organizers maintained was dedicated to black and Latino youth, as a "hate march." Since that September day at the inaugural Million Youth March, when Khallid was hustled off the stage by his personal bodyguards, Harlemites said he rarely had been seen in the community and had done little to build grassroots support.

Backing for Khallid dwindled to such a low ebb that black politicians who had been reluctant to criticize him for fear of alienating segments of the black community began to publicly shout him down. "This march shouldn't take place in Harlem or anywhere but hell, and Khallid can go down there with it," said Councilmember Bill Perkins, who surfaced as Khallid's most outspoken critic. "There is no support for it. Period."

Frustrated and isolated—an alienation some say was loosely related to his estrangement from Farrakhan—Khallid unleashed his ramshackle "people's militia," reportedly to push the Giuliani toward a showdown. As Perkins left a forum at which Democratic presidential candidate Bill Bradley had fielded questions from Harlemites, he was menaced by members of the group and derided as an "Uncle Tom" for not supporting the march. Someone told him: "We should kill people like you."

The bitter feud with Perkins stemmed partly from Khallid's disappointment with the councilmember's background investigation of him after a war of words erupted between the Giuliani administration and organizers around the issue of public safety for the 1998 Million Youth March. According to Perkins, during a meeting with organizers at the Emmanuel A.M.E Church in Harlem, Khallid told him not to needlessly worry himself about public safety because he had been "head of security" for the historic Million Man March. Perkins contacted Minister Benjamin F. Muhammad, the former Benjamin Chavis, who was Farrakhan's chief representative in New York, about Khallid's alleged boast. (At the time, Khallid's march was competing for attention with the Million Youth Movement in Atlanta, which was staging a march that same weekend, backed by Farrakhan.)

Minister Benjamin asked Perkins to put his queries about Khallid in writing. Farrakhan himself responded to four questions raised by Perkins: No, Khallid had not been security chief for the Million Man March. That task was left to D.C. police, Capitol police, federal marshals, and the Fruit of Islam, the NOI's paramilitary force. Another Perkins question: Is Khallid a member in good standing of the Nation of Islam? Farrakhan replied that Khallid was still a member although the Minister had distanced himself from his former disciple, saying, "At present ... he is not under the jurisdiction nor the spiritual direction of the leadership of the Nation of Islam." Farrakhan added that Khallid was "free to do that which he feels is in his best interest and in the best interest of those who follow him."

Khallid told me that Perkins either had misunderstood him or deliberately was trying to embarrass him. "I told him that I had trained most of the men who worked out the logistics of the security arrangement for the Million Man March," explained the former captain of the FOI. "How could I claim to be head of security for the Million Man March when everybody knew that I was no longer in Minister Farrakhan's inner circle of leadership?"

Perkins' appearance at a forum in Harlem, which was organized by Al Sharpton, became a rallying point for Khallid, but the selective harassment was disturbing to some who said there were many more apt political enemies on whom Khallid might have focused. Since the militia embarked on its campaign to confront opponents of the march, none of the symbols of black oppression—Giuliani, Safir—had been accosted.

Bypassed on the militia's list of possible targets was Imam Ezekiel Pasha, leader of Masjid Malcolm Shabazz on 116th Street, who Giuliani appointed to a controversial 15-member commission to change the City Charter. Imam Pasha, a member of the racially mixed American Muslim Mission led by Wallace Moham-med, had criticized Khallid on the explosive issue of anti-Semitism. But the two Muslims have clashed before. In 1992, Khallid berated Wallace for being the first Islamic leader to pray in the "racist United Snakes Senate," which approves "the guns and bombs that blow up … people throughout the world."

In 1997, aware that Khallid had been ostracized by Wallace's faction, the top leadership of the Senegalese Muslim community, who follow the teachings of Cheik Amadou Bamba from a black liberation theology perspective, tried to make peace and invited Khallid to Imam Pasha's mosque to "make salaat" (wor-ship) and address them.

"When they came to get me, they had me wait up the street from the masjid in an apartment with some of their leadership," Khallid recalled. "They let the offi-cials at the masjid know that I was coming, and they said, 'No, he can't come in here.' They tried to negotiate," he added. "These Muslims were outraged—never heard of a Muslim who can't come into a mosque to make salaat when Giuliani had been there twice."

Khallid softened his rhetoric at the second Million Youth March, urging about 2000 people to commit their lives to the black liberation struggle. A third March in September 2000, drew only a handful of participants. Khallid insisted that was because he had heeded calls from some of his advisers to further tone down his attacks on Giuliani and black politicians who did not support the march.

Reporter's Note: *On February 10, 2001, Khallid suffered a brain aneurysm and died. Lying helpless and hooked up to a machine in the white man's hospital in Geor-gia was not how Khallid envisioned he would die. Every time I interviewed him for* THE GODDAMNED WHITE MAN, *a book we were planning to co-author, he would begin the session by reciting Claude McKay's epic poem* "If We Must Die."

At times, Khallid changed some of the words to reflect the alienation he also sensed from his followers. "If I must die," Khallid would declare, "though far outnumbered let me show me brave/And for their thousand blows deal one death blow/What though before me lies the open grave?/Like a man I'll face the murderous, cowardly pack/ Pressed to the wall, dying, but fighting back!"

I would like to think that was how Khallid faced down death. Khallid, who had been renovating a brownstone on Harlem's historic Strivers Row, was in New York

City on February 10. He had met with a group of vendors at the Harriet Tubman School in Harlem. After the meeting, Khallid returned to Atlanta, where he had a home. His wife told supporters that Khallid complained about "feeling tired and achy," went to lie down, and began vomiting profusely. He was taken by ambulance to a hospital at which the family was told that they did not have the facilities to handle neurological emergencies. He was then driven to WellStar Kennestone Hospital in Marietta, a suburb of Atlanta. Akbar Muhammad, a top Farrakhan aide, rushed to Khallid's bedside and prayed with the family.

Sharpton was the first prominent civil rights figure to go to the hospital. "His family seemed stunned," recalled Sharpton, adding that he did not question them about Khallid's medical condition. After praying with Khallid's wife and top aide Malik Zulu Shabazz, the Baptist minister was led into a room where the once fiery activist lay motionless. Sharpton again prayed and after about one minute he was escorted from the room.

"Khallid was just lying there," said Sharpton, who struck up a friendship with Khallid after being stabbed in Bensonhurst by a white man in 1991. "He sent me a note after the incident," Sharpton remembered. After Khallid was gunned down in 1994, Sharpton wrote Khallid a letter of support. "Imagine that! When I saw him, I couldn't physically do anything for him," the activist said.

When Khallid got into trouble and was sentenced to community service, he appealed to Sharpton, who arranged for Khallid to serve out his term delivering a series of lectures to street gangs Sharpton had been trying to mentor. "Reverend Sharpton and Khallid developed a strong relationship over the years," said Timothy Ford, who ran the program at Sharpton's headquarters. "One of the reasons Reverend Sharpton is so touched by this tragedy is that he and Minister Khallid had both vowed never to duplicate the mistakes of their respective heroes, Jesse Jackson and Farrakhan," Ford explained.

"Minister Khallid wanted to lead black nationalists and Reverend Sharpton wanted to lead people in the civil rights movement," Ford added. "Minister Khallid saw Reverend Sharpton as a true believer in Dr. Martin Luther King, and Reverend Sharpton viewed Minister Khallid as a true follower of the Honorable Elijah Muhammad. Although Minister Khallid sometimes referred to Reverend Sharpton as 'a glorious fool' for believing in Dr. King, they never got in each other's way. They found a way not to hurt each other."

Khallid often vowed to me he'd die fighting, "either the cracker or the no good nigga." A source told me that five days before Khallid fell gravely ill, members of a disgruntled faction of the Panthers in Atlanta were planning a violent showdown in New York to settle once and for all their challenge to the legitimacy of Khallid's group.

PART VII

Blacks and Jews Under Giuliani (1999)

for Elizabeth Warner

23

Rage of a Jewish Mob

"If I'm an anti-Semite, what am I doing here?"

—Al Sharpton to followers of the late Meir Kahane

IT WAS AN INDIAN SUMMER AFTERNOON on September 7, 1999—eight days after Gideon Busch, wearing a prayer shawl and tefillin, was gunned down by cops in the orthodox Jewish community of Borough Park in Brooklyn. At 46th Street and Sixteenth Avenue, an angry crowd of Hasidim, men and boys, had swooped down on a burgundy Windstar minivan carrying Al Sharpton, Ron Daniels, executive director of the Center for Constitutional Rights, and me. What followed was 45 minutes of high tension that would have ignited a racial powder keg had Detective William J. Jackson Jr. not put his life on the line to save ours.

In December 2001, Jackson, a troubleshooter for the NYPD, retired at the age of 62 after nearly 35 years of peacemaking among what David Dinkins called "the gorgeous mosaic." During the late '80s and '90s, he was a key behind-the-scenes figure, cooling tempers at several "Day of Outrage" protests against racial violence. This unrivaled mediator left the department at a time when it was in dire need of cops with people skills—as opposed to those who resorted to the "continuum of force," which allowed police to increase the level of their response as circumstances escalated.

"Terrible! Terrible! Never should have happened!" was a typical Jackson response to accusations of excessive force, abuse of authority, discourtesy, and offensive language by cops, which tarnished the image of his beloved NYPD. "Respect is a two-way street, though," he also would remind hotheaded militants who harassed the police. "Bill had proven to the department that he was unsurpassed in his ability to mediate and bring about peace and understanding between the community he loved and served and the police department he believed in," said Sergeant Vanessa Ferro.

Jackson, who joined the department in 1966 at the height of America's racial tumult, thwarted more classic confrontations between "the blacks and the blues" than he cared to acknowledge. In 1989, while assigned to the chief of department's Liaison Unit, Jackson helped quell a violent outburst after police closed off the Brooklyn Bridge to 15,000 demonstrators who had marched through Brooklyn in protest of the racially motivated killing of Yusef Hawkins in predominantly white Bensonhurst. More than 50 cops and an undetermined number of protesters were injured during the melee, which could have been far worse had it not been for Jackson's backdoor negotiations with the top echelon of the city's black activist movement.

"It's a pressure cooker!" the detective would announce over his walkie-talkie or declare to his superiors as he assessed large protest marches. Invariably, he then would seek out the firebrand activists and gung ho cops who were bringing tensions to a boil, and squeeze the peace out of them.

ON THAT AFTERNOON IN SEPTEMBER 1999, the pressure cooker was Borough Park. The tightly knit Hasidic community, which had exploded in rage over the fatal shooting of Gideon Busch by police officers, was on the verge of erupting again because Sharpton, many Jews charged, had come to exploit simmering tensions. Several young men wearing the traditional black suits and hats of the Orthodox faith, brushed up against the Windstar, peering into its darkly tinted windows. I switched on my tape recorder as Sharpton grabbed the car phone on the first ring. On the other end was his top aide, Anthony Charles. He and Andrew Stetner of Jews for Economic and Racial Justice had been sent ahead to conduct surveillance. Borough Park was a neighborhood openly sympathetic to Kahane Chai, followers of slain extremist rabbi Meir Kahane. The group had been declared a terrorist organization in the United States.

"What does Andrew think?" asked Sharpton. "I'll do whatever he says."

Seven months earlier, 125 members of Stetner's group had been arrested in front of One Police Plaza with Sharpton, protesting the killing of Amadou Diallo. Now Sharpton was returning the favor by making this bold foray into unfriendly territory to "unify black/Jewish outrage" over the Busch slaying. Charles told Sharpton that Stetner had identified "Meir Kahane guys" who were part of a cabal chanting anti-Sharpton slogans. They were madly asserting that Sharpton had no business in Borough Park. I was thinking, maybe we should turn back.

"I've been screamed at before!" snapped Sharpton as he leveled the volume on a CD deck playing James Brown's "I Feel Good." He shot down suggestions by Charles and Stetner that perhaps he ought to rethink this one.

"Anti-Semite! Go to hell!" shouted a small boy, who then spat at the van. But when the boy tried to break through, a hand reached out of the mob and pulled him back.

"No! No! No!" warned a powerful voice. "Don't go there, young man!" It was the voice of "the peacemaker," Detective First Grade William Jackson. An elder whisked the boy away.

"I don't like the flavor of this," Jackson told Sharpton as the van, inching slowly to the spot where the NYPD alleged Busch attacked officers with a hammer, was ringed by more demonstrators. "They don't have a detail," he added, sounding skeptical about whether the clearly outnumbered cops would be able to control the surging crowd. "They're supposed to have a detail out here, Ok? They don't have a detail out here." Jackson stared at Sharpton, half expecting an answer, half praying that the Baptist minister would agree to cut and run.

"Al! Get out of here!" one protester shouted.

"Let me out!" demanded Ron Daniels, sliding back the door, and jumping head-on into the fray. I'm feared we would be trapped—that the "Meir Kahane guys" would firebomb the vehicle.

At that point, Jackson told Sharpton that he had spoken to an inspector who did not feel comfortable with the situation.

"Why not?" responded the activist.

"Do you feel comfortable with this?" Jackson fired back, staring at Sharpton in disbelief.

"Hey, I'm just gonna stand there and do a prayer and get back in the car," the crusty preacher said nervously.

"Even some of the Jewish cops don't feel comfortable with some of these people out here," Jackson intimated. "They don't feel comfortable. So I want to give it to you straight up, let you know what's going down. They don't feel comfortable. Unless you want us to surround you with cops."

"Yes," said Sharpton.

The demonstrators were still chanting, "Anti-Semite! Go home!" Some were declaring, "Kahane lives!"

"I don't feel comfortable with this. It's your call," Jackson emphasized. "I don't feel comfortable, and they don't [pointing to some uniformed cops]."

"Let's just sit here a minute," Sharpton suggested.

"OK, you wanna pull up a bit, or you just wanna sit here?"

"Sit right here," Sharpton said.

"'Cause once you get out, you're in it," Jackson cautioned. "You're in it once you get outta the car." As Jackson was pushed against the vehicle by Kahane Chai protesters, he flashed his badge. They backed up.

"Are you going to shoot anybody?" a young Kahane militant taunted. Jackson ignored the remark. Reporters pounded their fists against Sharpton's closed window, signaling to him that they wanted to talk.

"Step back!" Jackson barked at one overzealous scribe.

"Reverend, are you gonna be able to come out?" the reporter asked.

"I didn't come to come out," Sharpton said, backpedaling strategically. "We're having the vigil on Sunday. As I said, we knew we'd get a rocky reception. I think it's important to make the statement that we would risk getting heckled to show unity [with] people [who] stood with us when a lot of people didn't want them to. So they called, we came. We know that there would be many that don't want us to come, but there would be many who would appreciate that some of us would put our differences aside to stand [against] what is wrong. What happened to this man is wrong. I could take a few catcalls to help put the spotlight on the fact that police brutality must stop wherever it is."

"What do you say to the folks who call you an anti-Semite?" asked another reporter.

"If I'm an anti-Semite, what am I doing here?" Sharpton pointed out. "The majority of the crowd is not saying anything. It's a few of them who want to agitate, and I think their agitation shows they're really not concerned about getting to the bottom of this."

"Has the mayor done enough so far?" asked a reporter, referring to Giuliani's efforts to reach out to the Hasidim after Busch was gunned down.

"The mayor didn't do what I did," asserted the reverend. "He didn't even come out here and face the hecklers."

"How could he be here?" asked one of the "Meir Kahane guys," who was blocked by a steely-eyed Jackson as he tried to move nearer to Sharpton.

"I appreciate that," Sharpton told Jackson. "Thank you."

"What happened in Crown Heights?" shouted another critic, referring to the 1991 racial upheaval. Although Sharpton was not at the scene when the rioting flared, some Jews blamed him for inciting tensions that led to the fatal stabbing of Yankel Rosenbaum. Sharpton sidestepped the question and beckoned to Jackson to allow one Hasidic Jew, who had yelled, "Thanks for coming!" to get through.

"Let him up! Let him up!" Sharpton shouted. "Can you let him through? Can that guy come?"

"Rev, don't get out!" Jackson pleaded.

"Just let me talk to one guy," insisted Sharpton.

"I appreciate you coming down to show solidarity," said the man, who identified himself as a journalist for an Israeli newspaper. A heckler from Kahane Chai, peeved by the reporter's gesture, interrupted, screaming, "What happened in Crown Heights, Al? What happened in Crown Heights, Big Al?"

Sharpton leaned out of the window and talked to the Israeli journalist. "Just like many Jews who stood with us for Abner Louima and Amadou Diallo, I felt it was no more than right for me to come and show solidarity here," he commented. But Jackson signaled to Sharpton to wrap up the interview because many more Jews were pouring out of their homes to join the protest. Sharpton grinned.

"Do you think that there is a similarity between Diallo and Busch?" the reporter asked.

"I think there is a similarity between the fact that a man did not have to be killed," Sharpton contended. "I think it's much more similar to Eleanor Bumpurs [the 66-year-old 300-pound grandmother who was shot to death in her Bronx apartment when she allegedly lunged at a white cop with a knife], and I think when all of us start dealing with the same standards, then we can deal with the city that has a set of rules for everybody."

Jackson eyed his watch: It was now 3:54 p.m.

"What kind of standards are you looking for?" the reporter asked.

"One standard is that you don't shoot a man when there is a life-extenuating circumstance."

Suddenly a Kahane Chai protester confronted Jackson, shouting, "I wanna talk to him. How can he come over here? Why is he here?" Jackson shrugged.

"Al, lemme ask you a question," the heckler persisted, edging over Jackson's shoulder. "Answer me, please. How can you come here in the Jewish community and the next word you say by the next demonstration is 'kikes'?"

Sharpton vehemently denied ever using the slur.

"You did say that!" the heckler charged, pointing a finger at Sharpton.

"That's not true!" Sharpton reiterated.

Then someone demanded to know what role Sharpton played in the massacre of seven people at Freddy's Fashion Mart, a Jewish-owned clothing store in Harlem that was being picketed by black activists when it was firebombed in 1995. Summarily, several members of the mob accused Sharpton of causing the deaths.

"Go on!" a man who said he was a Talmudic scholar bellowed at Sharpton. "Get outta here! We don't need you! You preach hate against Jews!" Finally, Jackson told Sharpton in no uncertain terms that this was a good time to get out of the pressure cooker.

"Don't shout!" Sharpton replied to the man mischievously. "Behave yourself. I'll be back Sunday."

"Go make some riot somewhere else!" shouted a little boy.

"Give him some room!" Jackson ordered. "Give the reverend some room!"

"Anti-Semite!" howled a young Kahane Chai protester running alongside the departing vehicle. "You'll pay!" he added. "We're gonna get rid of all youse. We're gonna put in Chinese. We're gonna move the Chinese into our neighborhood. We don't need your kind!"

As the van pulled away, Sharpton raised the volume on the James Brown CD, and *The Big Payback* resounded throughout the vehicle. I looked back at Jackson through the driver's side-view mirror. He saluted. No sweat. Just another meltdown in the pressure cooker.

24

The Redemption of Mayor Edward I. Koch

I remained very popular with the electorate even after having lost the Democratic primary to David Dinkins in 1989 ... [A]s I walked around the streets of the city, I would be importuned—sometimes ten to fifteen times a day—by passerby with, 'Mayor, you must run again, you must run again.' My respose was always the same: 'No, the people threw me out and now the people must be punished.' Often their retort was, 'Oh, Mayor, we have been punished enough!'

—Edward I. Koch, Giuliani: Nasty Man

"DO YOU MISS ME?" the gangly figure chimed, his nutcracker face, once pudgy and jowly like a self-described overweight "Jewish god," beaming in response to a standing ovation from a jam-packed, predominantly black audience at Sharpton's 45th birthday celebration in Harlem on October 9, 1999.

"Rudy Giuliani has made their memory of me affectionate," asserted former mayor Ed Koch as he reminisced about the "generous reception" he got at the historic Canaan Baptist Church after David Dinkins introduced him. In many ways, Koch's appearance at Canaan was a stunning achievement for the former top politician and Sharpton. Their joint advocacy of a Second Chance initiative—which would wipe clean the criminal records of mostly black non-violent offenders—became the turning point in ending years of feuding, testing the depth of racial reconciliation in their beloved city.

"I got calls from people saying, 'What are you doing? You're making him kosher!'" the then 74-year-old Koch remembered. "I said, 'Look, if we can find people who are leaders, he is a leader. When he asks 500 people to get out in the streets to demonstrate they come. Most people can't do that. That's a leader. If I

259

can change him so that he recognizes that he has a responsibility to quit being a demagogue, isn't that helpful to New York?' The people say, 'Yeah, it is.'"

But Ed Koch soon discovered that black people could be wary of putative pariahs like him, even though he and Sharpton had been united in declaring that black men and women were facing a social crisis and needed the Second Chance project as a way out. Some of the strongest opposition came from members of the nearly all-Democrat black caucuses.

"I am discouraged by the lack of interest displayed by a number of advocacy organizations, all of which like the concept, but, for whatever reasons, will not add the proposal to their agendas," Koch complained. "We have attempted to interest the NAACP, the Black Caucus in Washington, and the Black Caucus in Albany, but we have not been successful."

The trip to Canaan could have been disastrous for the bad-ass "Citizen Koch" turned racial conciliator. Despite his call for healing, Koch contended in his book, *Giuliani, Nasty Man*, that Dinkins "egregiously mishandled the response to the pogrom in Crown Heights," and that's why he threw his support behind Giuliani in 1993. In fact, Koch did not know what to expect as he traveled late uptown to Sharpton's birthday party in a shiny, black Lincoln with tinted windows.

He'd long sensed that his controversial tenure still might ignite strong feelings among some blacks, particularly over the issue of, in the words of one critic, "Koch-era police brutality." But as he strode boldly to the podium, warmly embracing Dinkins, Koch did not look like a fearful man.

"The last time I felt this brotherhood was in 1964 in Jackson, Mississippi, when I went there to defend blacks and whites who were fighting for the right to vote," Koch recalled. "I felt very secure in that church."

At Canaan, Koch felt safe in the company of an eclectic black and Latino leadership that included activist attorney Alton Maddox and the Reverend Herbert Daughtry, two of his fiercest political rivals. Neither Maddox nor Daughtry showed any evidence of the hostility that sparked years of warfare in which Daughtry often referred to Koch's policies as "anti-black," and Maddox depicted the ex-mayor as "a racist." As Koch reflected on his greeting of Maddox and Daughtry, he remembered "mulling over" their racially charged battles. "I used to fight with these guys," he said. Koch intimated that he felt sorry for Maddox, the ultranationalist who chaired the United African Movement, which barred whites from its weekly rallies. "I kept thinking about him and how awful it must be for him," said Koch, referring to Maddox's then nine-year suspension from practicing law for refusing to cooperate with a lawyers' disciplinary committee, and for controversial comments he made during and after the Tawana Brawley investigation.

"When I saw him, all kinds of emotions ran through me," Daughtry said. "Obviously, my mind went back to the battles we've had." Daughtry led a group that disrupted Koch's mayoral inauguration in Brooklyn in 1978. "I snatched the mike and said, 'You can't speak in Brooklyn until you address the police killing of 15-year-old Randy Evans.'" Although the alleged police brutality had occurred under the administration of outgoing mayor Abe Beame, Daughtry felt that Koch—"with whom we had been friendly"—should have taken up the cause for justice. Koch recalled the incident in a 1994 *Daily News* column: "I turned to Daughtry and asked, 'Why are you doing this? I just got elected. I didn't have anything to do with that police matter.' Then I offered to meet with him at City Hall to discuss it. He agreed and left with his entourage."

Koch's relationship with the black community began its downward slide in 1978 with the death in police custody of popular black businessman Arthur Miller. Two years later, Koch and Daughtry would clash over the closing of the city-run Sydenham Hospital in Harlem. Declaring that the hospital was losing money and did not deliver effective medical services, Koch shut down the facility, calling protesters "rabble-rousers." To Daughtry and other community leaders, the closing symbolized the mayor's indifference to the needs of the black community.

Then there were the congressional hearings on police brutality in 1983, which became a bitter symbol of racial animosity. Black leaders had called for the hearings to probe what the Reverend Butts called "an alarming rise in racial violence and racially motivated police misconduct." Koch dubbed the hearings a "circus." He recalled in an interview with *NY1*'s Dominic Carter that subcommittee chair John Conyers, who presided at the sessions, "had to apologize for his earlier statements" that brutality and corruption in the NYPD under Koch was "systemic and pervasive."

Embracing Ed Koch at Canaan was intended to reinforce calls by Sharpton for black leaders and their supporters to forget past disputes. Koch's popularity, Sharpton said, had a lot to do with the way blacks now viewed him. He was gaining viability as an anti-Giuliani firebrand and winning back their hearts. If they had forgiven him, how did this happen?

SHORTLY AFTER ED KOCH was elected mayor for the first time, many blacks felt that the man who'd had a distinguished career as a trailblazing First Amendment attorney, Democratic district leader, councilman, and congressman had turned his back on decades of civil rights struggle. In assessing "the Koch years," some black leaders, who spoke to me on condition of anonymity, argued that Koch was one of the first politicians in New York to figure out that if you moved to the right on race and you were loudmouth about it, you benefited, particularly if you were Jewish or Italian ("I'm for capital punishment, are you?" he asked a white woman in an oft-quoted 1977 campaign appearance in Brooklyn). He was one of the first to openly declare that not all Jews were liberals.

These unyielding critics of the former mayor contended that his Machiavellian politics helped to create a robust Jewish-Italian constituency of closet racists that Rudy Giuliani eventually was able to tap into when he ran against David Dinkins. "Koch laid the groundwork for someone like Giuliani," one Harlem leader claimed. "Some people compare him to former Alabama governor George Wallace, who tied together racism and populism and transformed the result into a national movement."

But other blacks resented the characterization of Ed Koch as a stiff-necked Southern cracker. "Indeed Rudy Giuliani is Ed Koch's Golem," said a former Koch insider, but Giuliani exploited his populism and did "things that Koch never would have done" to the black community. Koch unleashed criticism of Giuliani's stewardship with a vengeance. "You know he turns down demonstration permits," Koch told one interviewer, "he doesn't let people come to the steps of City Hall to petition their representatives. He's running the city like a petty tyrant, which may be appreciated in some Third World countries, but not here."

But why now? Koch's black critics asked. Was he making amends for creating the monster? What had changed him? The answers may be found in what Koch himself attributed to "my Lazarus heart" in his book titled, *I'm Not Done Yet!* "I've had a stroke," Koch wrote in the book, which was to be published in 2000, coinciding with his 75th birthday. "I have a pacemaker to correct an erratic heartbeat. I take seven different prescription medications every day: one to keep my blood thin, another for my benign prostate condition, several beta-based drugs for my arrhythmia … you get the idea."

It was possible that in his waning years, Ed Koch was trying to reconnect with his roots. (At the time, he was supporting Councilmember Una Clarke for Congress.) Maybe, some argued, he felt guilty about breaking the covenant that liberal Jews were supposed to observe regarding social justice. By forging an alliance with Sharpton and other black activists and speaking out against the repressive policies of the Giuliani administration, Koch had performed what religious Jews call *T'shuva*. He had repented. He had atoned for his political sins.

Blacks had come to understand the concept of atonement as laid down by Minister Louis Farrakhan, and now some were beginning to view Koch's sudden shift toward them as an act of atonement. You can come back as a new person and black people will accept you. It worked for Washington, D.C., mayor Marion Barry, who was caught in an FBI sting smoking crack with a woman in a hotel room. Political pundits said Barry was finished, but he begged for forgiveness and was swept back into office by his core constituency.

"I come out of a people who at times go too far in forgiveness," said Daughtry. "However, I must confess that when people express a sincere desire to want to move on from the past—who recognize that they might have made mistakes—I'm prepared to say, 'Fine, let's move on from here,' provided that the person has exhibited sincere behavior patterns that support that they truly want reconciliation."

Sharpton convinced Daughtry that Koch was sincere about working with blacks once again. "Based on what Reverend Sharpton has said to me, I'm prepared to extend my hand to Mayor Ed Koch and to say in a biblical phrase, 'If your heart is as my heart, give me your hand.'" It was a hand that Koch said he extended to make a pact with God in 1987 when he had his stroke. "God has kept his word with me," Koch declared in *I'm Not Done Yet!* "He has not taken me one slice at a time. I intend to keep my bond with Him, and use my alloted time in a positive way. The untimely and truly tragic death of John F. Kennedy, Jr., at age thirty-eight brought home for me with even more emphasis how fragile we all are, and posed for me the question I now ask myself every day: Why was I saved? The simple response is that God is not yet finished with me, and I remain relevant."

ED KOCH WAS HAVING the time of his life with his newfound ally Al Sharpton, a political up-and-comer who routinely faced questions from Koch about his more bombastic past.

"Over the years, we've had discussions and I've always said to him, 'You're a black leader; you apologize for Tawana Brawley and for your statements that were anti-Semitic and anti-white. I don't happen to believe you're anti-Semitic. I believe you're a demagogue.' And he said to me on a number of occasions, 'I'm thinking about it. I'm thinking about it.'"

The mayor and the reverend had a rocky relationship from the start, and Koch liked to remind people that he was "the first American" to send Sharpton to jail after Sharpton staged a sit-in at City Hall in 1978. Koch could not remember whether Sharpton had an appointment that day he showed up at City Hall with about 25 black members of the clergy. The deputation demanded to meet with Koch. The mayor obliged and ushered Sharpton and the ministers into the Blue Room.

"I don't think I had met him before," he said of Sharpton, adding that the medallion-wearing activist was "in full regalia, big this, big that." After introducing all of the ministers, Sharpton declared, "I have a petition here."

"Well, let me read it," said Koch, who perused the document and asked Sharpton to elaborate on its demands. As Koch remembered, it called for $50 billion in reparations. "It required me to have 200,000 summer jobs and a whole host of things. I think we had about 65,000 summer jobs. So I'm thinking to myself, I don't wanna start a big riot here by just saying, 'Please leave.'" Koch tried to disarm Sharpton.

"Look, you just presented this to me, why don't you leave it with me and let me study it?" he told the minister. "I'll get back to you."

"No, you're gonna sign it now!" Sharpton demanded.

"The meeting is over!" declared Koch, who stood up and stormed back to his office. Sharpton and three ministers followed him.

"We're gonna sit down here in your office so that nobody can get in or out!" Sharpton said.

"Please don't do that," Koch pleaded. "You have an absolute right to picket me. Go out on the steps and do whatever you want, but you cannot stop people from entering my office."

"We're sitting down here until you sign it!" came the rebuff from Sharpton.

Aghast, Koch turned to a police officer.

"Cop!" he shouted, "Remove them!"

As far as Koch could remember, no police officer had ever ejected anyone from City Hall for engaging in a civil disobedience protest.

"Mayor, what if they resist?" the cop whispered.

"Have you never heard the word arrest?" Koch bellowed. "Arrest them!" Koch swore that that historic confrontation "in a way bonded" him and Sharpton.

Several years later, as Sharpton was raiding crack houses and painting red crucifixes on the doors to exorcise drug dealers, Koch was privately declaring war on the criminal-justice system. Koch was appalled that the mandatory minimum sentences and stepped-up enforcement that began with Nelson Rockefeller's so-called "war on drugs" had fallen disproportionately on blacks. Nearly one in every three young black men was serving a criminal sentence in prison, on probation, or on parole. Blacks, Koch realized, were more likely to be prosecuted under federal drug laws than whites guilty of the same offense. "Many of these kids—a lot of them white—who use powder cocaine, get probation," Koch emphasized. "Blacks using a cheaper drug, crack cocaine, in less quantity, get a minimum of five years and more. And it's just wrong."

In 1994, Koch launched an ill-fated campaign to enlist New York's prominent politicians and major black-advocacy groups in his fight. They blew him off. Maybe it was a racial thing, he thought. He recruited Charles Ogletree, the noted Harvard law professor, who was black. That didn't help. Koch was discouraged. Then one day in 1998 he was invited to participate in a panel discussion on Black Entertainment Television. The moderator said Sharpton would be there.

"I'm really frustrated, and maybe you can help me," Koch told Sharpton after the show. He then revealed the details of his Second Chance project. Its main purpose, he pointed out, was to afford those with non-violent felony records, who have served their jail sentences, an opportunity to earn a pardon, have their criminal record expunged, and turn their lives around.

"The Second Chance proposal is not a retreat from being tough on crime," he told Sharpton. "In fact, we believe that individuals who complete the program—because they will be able to obtain jobs and be more likely to marry—will less likely become repeat offenders. The program would be available only to those who have not engaged in violent crime. We believe that most of those who would be eligible have been convicted of drug possession or sale." While the program will be available to all without regard to race or gender, the group most affected is young black males, Koch argued. "Those with felony records are often unable to get a decent job and find it difficult to marry, since young women prefer spouses who can support a family," he explained. "They also lose their right to vote, and they become pariahs and crime recidivists. We want to break that cycle."

Under the program, executive pardons and expungement of criminal records would be authorized by Congress and participating state legislatures. "Then, when asked if they have ever been convicted of a crime by a prospective employer, the former felons could honestly answer, 'No,'" Koch said. "In addition, their civil rights would be restored."

After Koch defined the project, he asked Sharpton if he had any ideas, since he and Ogletree were at an impasse with the advocacy organizations. "I'm gonna see Jesse Jackson this week, and if Jesse likes it I'm with you," the minister told Koch. Two days later, Sharpton contacted Koch. "Jesse loves it," he said. "I am with you." Sharpton, Koch recalled, also brought up the subject of making a public apology for his role in the alleged Tawana Brawley hoax.

Sharpton told Jackson about Koch's appeal to him to apologize.

"'You listen to that man,'" Sharpton quoted Jackson as saying, giving the impression that Jackson had urged Sharpton him to come clean. "He is giving you good advice."

Ed Koch wanted the world to know that he and Al Sharpton, former political enemies, were working together now. He invited his new friend to dine at the upscale Four Seasons restaurant.

"Could I bring the press?" Sharpton joked.

"Why do you think I called you?" Koch replied.

As he left the Canaan Baptist Church, Koch may have reflected on what some blacks were calling his Day of Atonement. Finally, Koch had bridged the racial divide, resolving the painful debate over his turbulent relations with the city's blacks. He left Harlem not as a recidivist liberal Jew but as a *mensch* whose "Lazarus heart" had grown bigger—and blacker.

25

Blacks vs. Jews at the KKK Rally

The oppression of Negroes by whites has left an understandable residue of suspicion. Some of this suspicion is a healthy and appropriate safeguard. An excess of skepticism, however, becomes a fetter. It denies that there can be reliable white allies, even though some whites have died heroically at the side of Negroes in our struggle and others have risked economic and political peril to support our cause.

—Martin Luther King, Jr.
(Quoted in *There Is A Balm In Gilead*, by Lewis V. Baldwin)

A JITTERY POLICE CAPTAIN checked his watch and straightened his sagging gun belt. It was 4:20 P.M. on October 23, 1999, and the commander's repeated radio calls for cops in riot gear had been muffled by the uproar of a surging crowd. Although 16 unmasked members of the American Knights of the Ku Klux Klan had been hounded from Foley Square in downtown Manhattan, thousands of angry protesters—feeling cheated out of a showdown with the white supremacists—lingered to agitate in the streets.

Some turned on grouchy, steely-eyed officers—taunting the "Blu Klux Klan" who, they contended, were all that stood between a multi cultural posse and "death" to "the lynch-mob murderers." But in an uncanny twist of events, others, blacks and Jews—who hours earlier had locked arms in outrage at the Klan's presence—suddenly broke into separate fight clubs, opposing pockets of anti-Klan resistance that began to menace each other with racist and anti-Semitic chantdowns, which almost escalated into fisticuffs.

Tension between the groups erupted after Jewish protesters tried to confront black participants about placards they were carrying, blaming Jews for "the black holocaust" and decrying "revolutionary alliances" with whites. These blacks said they felt that Jewish civil rights activists especially were trying to co-opt "a black-led struggle" against the KKK. "Tell me the last time a bed-sheet cracker hung a muthafuckin' Jew from a tree?" asked a black protester who held up a sign proclaiming: "Niggers, beware of white interlopers. Fight your own battles."

At the intersection of Chambers and Centre streets, where a crowd gathered shouting anti-Klan insults, Maya Paz, an 18-year-old Israeli conscript, broke through police lines and stormed after a tall black man in a gray gabardine suit. Hoisted above the man's head was a huge placard with a picture of a white Jesus, asserting: "The White Man Is The Devil." (Paz told me later she heard the man make an anti-Semitic remark and felt compelled to challenge him about it.)

"Get outta my face!" he sneered, turning his back on Paz as he walked away. Paz hounded him. "This is wrong!" shouted the teenager with Chelsea Clinton hair, who was wearing a trendy Southpark fall coat, green cargo pants, and dusty army boots. "I have a lot of black and Latino friends," she added. "All my life I have been fighting for racial equality, for these people. What about that? Isn't that something?"

"You're still white!" the man shot back.

"You don't know me," declared the tempestuous idealist, who had been scheduled to report to the Israeli army by January of 2000. "I don't even consider myself Jewish." The man turned his back again.

"I had so much to say to him," Paz told me as she propped herself against a lamp post and began to cry. She felt humiliated by a man she thought was united with her in the fight against bigotry, intolerance, and outright hatred in New York City. Now all of her volunteer work surrounding the interracial mobilization against the Klan seemed to be for nought. "I came out at 11 A.M.," Paz recalled. "I had been on my feet all day yesterday trying to bring people here." Maya Paz's appalling encounter with the black protester typified the white response to raw black rage. Some astonished Jews and whites who helped to organize the largely successful anti-Klan rally walked away teary-eyed and confused. What had they done to blacks to deserve this? Would blacks ever stop blaming them—the other victims?

SHORTLY AFTER THE KKK departed, Yigal Yavin, a then 31-year-old Israeli citizen, surveyed the volatile scene and picked his battles. Yavin wandered into a session of the Hebrew Israelites, a black religious group known for its often profane anti-white and anti-Jewish tirades.

The Israelites had preached in the tourist-packed Times Square area for much of the last two decades, and were regularly seen on public-access TV. But in 1998 the group was denied sound permits and police began to harass its members, forcing them to proselytize elsewhere in the city. Eventually, the Giuliani administration agreed to pay the Israelites $59,000 to settle a lawsuit, charging that police had infringed on their First Amendment rights.

On the day the KKK came to town, the Hebrew Israelites, with bullhorns blaring, rallied in front of the Court Square Building at 2 Lafayette Street. In defiance of the KKK, they hung a stuffed, hooded, and masked white-clothed doll from one of the points of the Star of David.

Yavin approached one of the Black Israelites, as they were also known, and raised questions about the group's anti-Semitic sermons. The Israelite argued that the group taught what was in the Bible and spoke out against white people only because the Bible identified them as wicked.

"Forget about *your* teachings; it's what the Bible teaches. You're a hoax!" the Israelite told Yavin. "The same God that took Moses outta Egypt, he said that you're not a Jew."

"What in your mind is a Jew?" Yavin asked.

"You're all white people," the Israelite replied. "You use God's word outta your mouth, OK? [Jews] don't know anything about God."

"Keep your eyes on God!" shouted a young white woman who had been listening to the Israelites consign whitey to an everlasting hell. Yavin gave up and left. But another anti-Klan protester, who described himself as a Moroccan-born Jew, picked up the challenge and waded into the group. His debate with one of the leaders about the Nazi Holocaust wound up in a shouting match. The fiercely proud Jew almost had his yarmulke handed to him.

The Hebrew Israelite denied there was a Holocaust. "My granddaddy died. He was killed in the Holocaust," the man said.

"Fuck that!" the Israelite responded. "I'm honest. I don't give a damn if he was killed in the Holocaust." Blacks, he added, suffered worse atrocities than "the so-called Jews" but Jews never talk about that.

"Y'all didn't go through no Holocaust!" the Israelite snapped. "And 6 million Jews didn't even get kilt in that Holocaust!"

"There was a holocaust before that," the man retorted.

"Name 'em!"

"Pogroms?"

"What about them? Pilgrims?" The Israelite seemed lost. How much of the Jew's tragic history had he nullified? When the Jewish protester disclosed that one of his parents was Puerto Rican, the Israelite lectured him on the Spanish conquest of the island and the evils of race mixing.

"That's why we got a lot of Puerto Ricans [who] look like you," the Israelite said, adding, with the same blasphemous tongue, that the late reggae king, Bob

Marley, was not a pure black man. "If you look at Bob Marley, he's the so-called white man," the Israelite said. "His grandmother was white. His father [was] a white man."

"There are no winners here," a Jewish protester conceded.

Farther down the street, six young Jewish women were surrounded by a group of blacks and Latinos, who included Harlem activist Delois Blakey. "There has been a lotta dialogue going on," said Blakey, alluding to a heated quarrel that had broken out among black militants and white members of the "October 23 labor/ black mobilization to stop the KKK." Of course, the beef was about race.

"Now," said Blakey, updating a reporter, "they're talking about the differences between the Jews and the blacks—the white skin privilege." Blakey recalled that a black spokeswoman for her group had lambasted one of the Jewish women who tried to argue that the black struggle for racial justice was similar to some Jewish causes. "So the question was raised, is she [the Jewish woman] willing to go back and bring others that think like her because she [the disbelieving black spokes-woman] is not gonna accept her as one," Blakey explained.

Blakey said the entire group also had debated the contentious issue of repara-tions, "payback [for blacks], since the Jews [Holocaust victims who are getting back millions in deposits stolen by the Nazis] get paid every year." The argument reached its most volatile pitch when the Jewish activist said she was only trying to help blacks overcome white racism.

"We got one Jewish girl over here," announced the spokeswoman for the blacks. "Ok? Let's get it going. We got five nice Jewish people over here and a nigger lover that saying they wanna help us. So let's see if we can git this party started. We got a Jewish girl over here claiming to help."

"You know what," the Jewish activist interrupted, "the second I talk, you shut me down! I'm simply saying all white people are racist and I'm here to show you I'm me."

"Because you're the white nigga?" her opponent scoffed.

"Fine! So we are," the Jewish activist said. "But you know what I'm telling you, that I'm here. I'm here!"

One of the Jewish women intervened: "We really need to scrutinize ourselves and maybe we'd work a little harder."

"See you at the club tonight," a black man heckled. "See you at the dancehall." But the woman ignored him, pointing out that she understood how blacks react when they are stereotyped because she's sometimes tailed in department stores by people who think she looks Jewish and is there to steal.

"I'm sitting here saying, I have white privilege, and because I have white privilege that would make me white, right?" She said she had been reaching out to other "people who are white," telling them it was time that they admit that "all white people are racists. The KKK are not the only racists. There's racists everywhere!"

Nothing the woman said convinced her black accusers that she felt their pain, that she knew what it was like to be black in America. "You have to cleanse yourself, become natural," a black man suggested.

"The white man made you," another protester declared.

"Why do you want me to become natural?" the woman asked. "What should I do to become natural?" When the reference to ethnic cleansing seemed too painfully obvious to ignore, the woman, tired and sobbing, blurted out, "Six million people got fucking killed." That fight club broke up as police moved in, ordering protesters to clear the streets.

Back at Foley Square, three black men tried to remind a phalanx of battle-ready cops why protesters were reluctant to disperse. A black officer said he was only doing his job and would arrest anti-Klan demonstrators who behaved violently.

"We're here fighting for you, too, brother," one of the black men said. "We're fighting for all of y'all. Y'all should never have them [the Klan] standing on that ground. We shoulda never let them off the bus. We're all together now: blacks and whites, Chinese, Jewish. We're all together now."

INDEED, ORGANIZERS OF THE anti-Klan rally had hoped that New Yorkers would be united against race hate. That was the objective. But when frustrated black protesters began to vent their rage against Jews and whites, veteran conciliators began to wonder who blacks believed their real enemies were. Just when bewildered observers were concluding that the skirmishes signaled a setback for the fragile black-Jewish political alliance, a daring Klan sympathizer yelled "Fire!" in the crowded street theater. A multiracial mob—some of whom had been arguing bitterly—jumped on the woman and began to kick and punch her. Some spat on her.

"She said she was the KKK," recalled Yigal Yavin, the Israeli who'd squared off with the Hebrew Israelites. "She hated Puerto Ricans and the 'black animals.'" Another witness said he heard the woman shout, "Heil Hitler!" and curse at Jews. For a moment, people noticed, blacks and Jews were allies again, countering the KKK hate rhetoric with a righteous beatdown.

PART VIII

Giuliani vs. Clinton:
The U.S. Senate Campaign
of 2000
(1999–2000)

for
Rose Samuel and the boys,
Deron and Fareed

26

The First Lady and the Street Fighter

I remind Mrs. Clinton that this is not a professional boxing match, this is a street fight. There's no referee, there's no bell, there's no gloves. Rudy Giuliani fights with a broken glass in one hand, the cover of a trash can in the other, and a knife in his back pocket. So you've got to come in with street fighters to fight this ultimate bully. If you come in with some professional fighters, you're in the wrong match.

—Al Sharpton

IN THE SUMMER OF 1999, after months of stumbling toward a showdown with key advisers to Hillary Rodham Clinton, Al Sharpton seemed more determined than ever to inject himself into her likely U.S. Senate campaign, despite concerns among the first lady's innercircle that he would be a liability. Sharpton embarked on a "hotter than July" offensive on Mrs. Clinton's behalf to help her grab the Senate seat being vacated by Daniel Patrick Moynihan. Actually, it was more like a contingency plan to rescue the campaign in the event it appeared to be on a collision course with black activist politics.

He boasted that he could deliver crucial black votes that would deny Rudy Giuliani victory. He sketched out a series of 30-second campaign commercials highlighting an alliance between himself and Mrs. Clinton, all designed to intensify black voter interest in the race. He even stoked a behind-the-scenes feud with two key figures in the Clinton camp, former deputy White House chief of staff Harold Ickes and ex-deputy mayor Bill Lynch. (My repeat efforts to talk to Ickes and Lynch proved futile.) Suddenly, Al Sharpton was popping up on right-wing TV, in the tabloids, and in conservative magazines, creating an uproar in political circles. His essential message to the Clinton campaign strategists was this: If anyone in Mrs. Clinton's cabal believed blacks did not need New York's most influential civil rights leader to help them decide how to vote, take the low road and risk losing core black voters who would not be motivated to go to the polls.

Sharpton spent an entire week huddling with top black Democrats, get-out-the-vote strategists, black ultra-nationalists, and civil rights leaders in Harlem about his unauthorized offensive. Despite Sharpton's nagging fears about the outcome of the election, said one aide, Mrs. Clinton would not be allowed to enter by the back door at the eleventh hour and then arrogantly make demands on Sharpton. What happened to former Governor Mario Cuomo, he said, should serve as a warning. In 1994, Cuomo, locked in a bruising gubernatorial battle with the relatively unknown George Pataki, allegedly asked Jesse Jackson to persuade Sharpton to endorse him. The governor and the reverend had been estranged over the Tawana Brawley rape scandal.

"He refused to call me himself," recalled Sharpton, who had two impressive runs for the Senate and forced a runoff in the last mayoral race. "I told Jesse, 'I'm not supporting anybody who won't call me, far less don't come before my community.' Word came back that he would accept a call from me. My answer was, 'If you want my support, you call me. I'm gonna call you to offer my support?' He never called, I never supported him." In 1998, Chuck Schumer's at first moribund senatorial campaign received a jolt of credibility among black voters after the candidate raced Uptown to enlist in Sharpton's battle for racial justice. After beating Al D'Amato—a former Sharpton crony turned nemesis—Schumer returned to the reverend's National Action Network headquarters, conceding he couldn't have won without the activist's help.

With key federal and state prosecutorial agencies conducting investigations of recent cases in which white police officers killed or brutalized blacks and Latinos, Mayor Giuliani was in the political fight of his life. But Mrs. Clinton, Sharpton warned, should not underestimate the desperate, ill-favored Republican whom Ed Koch once described as a "nasty man" with "behavioral problems."

"I remind Mrs. Clinton that this is not a professional boxing match, this is a street fight," said Sharpton, pointing to independent polls, which showed Mrs. Clinton either slightly trailing or locked in a tight race with Giuliani, her likely GOP challenger. "There's no referee, there's no bell, there's no gloves. Rudy Giuliani fights with a broken glass in one hand, the cover of a trash can in the other, and a knife in his back pocket. So you've got to come in with street fighters to fight this ultimate bully. If you come in with some professional fighters, you're in the wrong match."

By "professional fighters," Sharpton was referring bitterly to political heavyweights Harold Ickes and Bill Lynch, with whom he had been wrangling for four months over what *The New Republic* called "Hillary's Sharpton Problem." Ickes, Mrs. Clinton's top adviser for her possible Senate run, was a New York political veteran who played major roles in Bill Clinton's 1992 and 1996 presidential campaigns before serving as deputy White House chief of staff. Previously, he was a key adviser to David Dinkins.

Aides to Sharpton told me that the activist preacher flew into a rage in April after *The New York Observer* reported that Giuliani allies were spreading "rumors that Ickes is the secret puppetmaster" behind Sharpton's two-month-long civil disobedience campaign. Sharpton, said one aide who spoke on condition of anonymity, suspected that the rumors, if not planted by Ickes, were fueled by the adviser to assure Democrats wary of Sharpton that Ickes could assert control over him. "Reverend Sharpton rarely talks to Harold Ickes, and certainly the reverend's history demonstrates that he does not need anybody to tell him how to conduct civil disobedience protests," the aide said.

If Ickes had contacted Sharpton during his "fit of black rage," according to the aide, Sharpton would have told him off and hung up on him. That was how the miffed activist allegedly treated Bill Lynch when the veteran Democratic operative tried to get Sharpton to stop bad-mouthing Mrs. Clinton on national TV and in the press.

Quarreling broke out after Sharpton had intensified his public sniping at Mrs. Clinton. When he expressed his indignation at her in an interview with *The New Republic* (saying that "at some point [Mrs. Clinton] is gonna have to deal with people like me"), the White House allegedly dispatched Sharpton's old mentor, Reverend W. Franklin Richardson of the powerful National Baptist Convention, on a mission to muzzle the sound-bite king.

Although Sharpton confirmed that Richardson contacted him about his comments in the article, he directed me to an aide to discuss the details of their conversation. "Buddy, I got a call from Washington, and people said to me, 'Just tell Al to be cool,'" the aide quoted Richardson as telling Sharpton.

The aide said that Richardson advised Sharpton "not to make a public issue" out of the fact that Mrs. Clinton, as the magazine put it, had not yet kissed Sharpton's ring. Mrs. Clinton's people need time "to work this thing out, just like the president has to work things out when Jesse Jackson gets involved" in the Democratic Party's business, Richardson added. The aide claimed that Sharpton was tempted to explain to his old friend that Bill Clinton's criticism of Jackson during the 1992 presidential race for associating with the then controversial raptivist Sister Souljah partly explained why he was so tough on Mrs. Clinton. (In 1992, while addressing Jesse Jackson's Rainbow Coalition, Bill Clinton rebuked rapper Sister Souljah, who had been quoted in a *Washington Post* interview as saying, "[I]f black people kill black people every day, why not have a week and kill white people?" Clinton said that if the words black and white had been reversed, "you might think David Duke was giving that speech." One news analysis at the time concluded that Clinton's attack "served to portray him as opposed to both racial prejudice and the harsh brand of militant rhetoric that chills middle-class suburbanites." Clinton apologized after Jackson told reporters the former Arkansas governor used "very bad judgment" in attacking Souljah before his group.)

But Sharpton never brought up the issue. The Clinton attack, the aide said was an "embarrassing moment [that] left a lump in the throat of many people in the activist community." Sharpton, the aide claimed, feared that Mrs. Clinton would pull a similar stunt and criticize his alliance with controversial black leaders such as Minister Louis Farrakhan and Farrakhan's former spokesman, Khallid Abdul Muhammad. "The question that many people are asking is, 'Is Hillary going to play off the black community on Al Sharpton like her husband did Jesse?' The only way for her to make the black community understand she's not going to play that polarizing act is by coming clean with Reverend Sharpton."

According to the aide, shortly after Richardson importuned Sharpton, Lynch followed up with a phone call, reiterating Mrs. Clinton's advisers' stance on his irritating analysis of her "nonrelationship" with New York's black community. The aide said he was in Sharpton's office when the call came in. "Reverend Sharpton told me Lynch said that he was talking to people in the campaign about Reverend Sharpton's importance and that Reverend Sharpton should wait till Hillary finishes deciding whether or not she's running," he remembered. The conversation allegedly got heated when Sharpton asked Lynch why Mrs. Clinton seemed to be listening to other, less influential political players and wasn't reaching out to him. "Reverend Sharpton was upset," the aide said. "He was shouting, telling Lynch if Hillary is talking to Tom, Dick, and Harry, she's gotta talk to us." Sharpton refused to curtail his criticism of the first lady, vowing, "I'm gonna be very public about it."

Sharpton continued to harangue Mrs. Clinton for not including predominantly black communities like Harlem in her so-called "listening tour" of New York. After a local TV station carried Sharpton's comment at an NAACP convention in Manhattan, that Mrs. Clinton was taking black voter support for granted, Lynch allegedly contacted Sharpton a second time. Lynch told Sharpton, "Man, it's all over TV," said a Sharpton operative, who had acted as an intermediary between both figures and was present when Lynch called.

The operative said the intensity of the conversation suggested that Lynch was under tremendous pressure to put a stop to the pillorying. "You guys will never give me orders!" he recalled Sharpton yelling. "You're probably telling her y'all got me under control, and you don't have me under control. No one calls my shots but the people that work with me. Let us be clear, you all didn't run me for Senate or mayor or get the votes I got. I respect you guys, but I'm going to publicly call on Hillary Clinton to be accountable, just like I've done with every other Democrat that I supported or haven't supported."

When Lynch argued that the Clintons' invitation to Sharpton to attend the White House ceremony for the Yankees was a sign that Mrs. Clinton was reaching out to him, the aide said Sharpton retorted, "My idea of reaching out is to discuss issues. I don't need to see the Yankees and I've been going to the White House for the past 20 years with James Brown. I'm concerned with whether Hillary will be coming to my house."

The conversation ended when Sharpton declared, "We have nothing else to talk about."

ONE SWELTERING JULY MORNING, after he had cooled off, the "street fighter" rocked back in a lazy boy in his second-floor office overlooking Madison Avenue in Harlem, looming bigger and blacker in a brash $800 three-button suit custom-designed and modeled for GQ magazine. He grabbed his Palm Pilot, a tiny handheld computer, and called up a file slugged "Healing Hillary," a series of hypothetical 30-second campaign ads aimed at exploiting heightened black voter interest in a possible Clinton-Giuliani Senate contest. Sharpton never meant for its details to be made public, but in light of his divisive spat with Mrs. Clinton and her advisers, he was "airing" the spots so that her strategists could benefit from his political acumen.

This would show, after all, that he had the temperament and the personality to agitate on behalf of the would-be candidate. All of the ads featured Mrs. Clinton.

Here were some of the talking points, as directed by Sharpton:

- Commercial No. 1 presented Mrs. Clinton as a racial healer who finally had included Harlem in her listening tour and wound up at Sharpton's House of Justice answering provocative questions on issues such as police brutality and racial profiling before receiving Sharpton's endorsement.

- Commercial No. 2 expanded on the racial healer theme, dredging up the 1988 presidential primary in which then mayor Ed Koch declared that

Jews would be crazy to vote for Jesse Jackson. But an announcer chimes in, saying, "We should never return to that ugly and polarizing era." The camera pans to a news conference in which Koch, Mrs. Clinton, and Sharpton are on the steps of City Hall talking unity and taking the high road.

SHARPTON: "Hillary Clinton can heal the city by bringing together those who were involved in the racial polarization of 10 years ago."

MRS. CLINTON: "I can bring Ed Koch and Al Sharpton in the same room. I can bring Daniel Patrick Moynihan and Al Sharpton in the same room. I'm not going to be like Rudy Giuliani, who says I'm not talking to certain people." Koch then portrays Giuliani as a racial polarizer and plugs his book *Giuliani, Nasty Man*.

- Commercial No. 3 exploited the mayor's troubled relationship with the city's blacks and Latinos. Then a voice declares that tensions have been running especially high since the fatal police shooting of Amadou Diallo. The ad features Mrs. Clinton outside the Bronx apartment building where Diallo was gunned down. She is surrounded by Sharpton and a bevy of black and Latino mothers who have lost their sons, allegedly to police brutality. The camera zooms in as Mrs. Clinton, tears streaming down her face, embraces Margarita Rosario, whose son, Anthony, 18, and his cousin Hilton Vega, 21, were shot to death in 1995 by police investigating a robbery.

SHARPTON: "I present to you our Healing Hillary."

MRS. CLINTON: "Rather than sympathize with a grieving mother, whether or not he agrees with her version of the events, Rudy Giuliani gets on his radio call-in show and suggests to Mrs. Rosario that maybe she raised her son to be a criminal, maybe its her fault that her son is dead. Where is the compassion, Rudy? There is a perception, Mr. Mayor, that some police Officers are out of control."

- Commercial No. 4 attacked Giuliani's policy of isolating those he disagrees with. Mrs. Clinton and Sharpton are gathered on the steps of City Hall flanked by Democratic members of the City Council, including its rising star Bill Perkins; Manhattan Borough President C. Virginia Fields; and Carl McCall, the state comptroller and New York's highest elected black official.

MRS. CLINTON: "It took Rudy Giuliani four long years before he could sit down in a meeting with Comptroller McCall. He didn't meet with Borough President Fields until hundreds of people—blacks, whites, Jews—started going to jail to protest his policies. How do you send a man like this to Washington, who won't see people, won't talk to people. Say no to the Prince of Polarization and give a resounding yes to the healer."

Since foreign policy often compelled a U.S. senator to deal with foreign leaders he or she may not like, the ad also depicts Giuliani as xenophobic and rude. It shows a clip of the mayor gloating in an interview with reporters after confirming that he has thrown Palestinian leader Yasir Arafat out of Lincoln Center. The ad captures Giuliani implying that during the 1995 visit of Fidel Castro the Cuban president was not welcome in New York City.

SHARPTON: "Do we need a senator who brings people of differing nations together? Or do we need a senator who kicks a head of state out of Lincoln Center by the seat of his pants?"

In addition to the spots, Sharpton said he would fan out to the city's predominantly black housing developments, conducting teach-ins to drive home the devastating impact a Giuliani Senate victory would have on their lives. "People must understand that a U.S. senator has the power to hurt us," he told me. "I would tell them that a U.S. senator nominates federal prosecutors and judges; do we want Rudy Giuliani to have a say in who will replace [then retiring U.S. Attorney] Zachary Carter, who successfully prosecuted police officers involved in the beating and sodomy of Abner Louima? If Rudy is elected it would take us another 30 years to get out from under the havoc he wreaked."

Any fears Mrs. Clinton may have had of the controversial Al Sharpton joining her dream team probably were magnified by a scathing editorial in the pro-Giuliani *New York Post*. The city's medical examiner had ruled that a drug suspect—who Sharpton quoted witnesses as saying was "savagely beaten" by cops—actually died of "acute cocaine intoxication," and was not a victim of police brutality.

"Which leads to an interesting question," the editorial writers contended. "Will Hillary Rodham Clinton welcome the Rev. Al among her cadre of campaign supporters? Or will she shut him out? A lot of New York voters would like to know the answer. There's good reason to suspect that the first lady would like to have Al Sharpton aboard, despite his unceasingly reckless charges."

If that was the case, Mrs. Clinton should have put an end to the speculation and infighting about Sharpton's role: A lot of black New York voters had a score to settle with Giuliani and would like to see Mrs. Clinton and Sharpton together on the front line of their struggle.

AS MRS. CLINTON INCHED closer to running for the Senate, she inflamed—or defused, depending on your political perspective—a potentially explosive confrontation over the issue of David Dinkins's role in her campaign.

One thing was certain, I would later learn: The First Lady personally had assured the man who supported her throughout Whitewater and the presidential sex scandals that she would not shun him.

The timing of their rekindled alliance prompted charges from some Jewish backers of Giuliani that it was politically motivated—coming just days before the eighth anniversary of the slaying of Yankel Rosenbaum in Crown Heights. These Giuliani operatives continued to blame Dinkins for prolonging the 1991 racial upheaval in a neighborhood where two of the city's most influential voting blocs—blacks and Orthodox Jews—remained poised in a standoff.

The fear among some of Mrs. Clinton's supporters was that Giuliani, who had aided and abetted the dispute by shelling out more than $1 million to Jews who claimed in a lawsuit they were not protected during the riots, ultimately would use this race card to incite outrage against Dinkins and the candidate.

A week after Dinkins told *Newsday* no one from Mrs. Clinton's camp had contacted him since winter—a disclosure spurred by accusations from Sharpton in the August 10 *Voice* that she was taking the black vote for granted—Dinkins confirmed that he had met with key campaign advisers and that negotiations with them led to a phone call from Mrs. Clinton the next day.

Dinkins and Mrs. Clinton spoke for about 20 minutes. "I am very pleased with the conversation we had, and I expect that whoever is going to be running the campaign will be seeking closer ties with me," Dinkins said cautiously. Mrs. Clinton, he added, "recognizes that I can be helpful to the campaign." Dinkins left no doubt, however, that it was important to him that Mrs. Clinton and her advisers continue to view him as an asset and not the political untouchable some in the Jewish community had made him out to be.

"The people who seek public office have consistently sought my endorsement and support," Dinkins pointed out. "When I am introduced before audiences or my presence is acknowledged, the reaction is always very positive—and I don't mean just black audiences."

Sharpton, who was not told about the meeting with Mrs. Clinton's advisers and the phone call, rallied to Dinkins' defense. "He is the most moderate, most balanced of the black leaders on Jewish issues," said Sharpton. "If they can demonize him, make a pariah out of him, they have absolutely eliminated blacks from the political process in this state. We can't stand by and allow this to happen."

The apparent thaw in the icy relations between the First Lady and the city's first black mayor came on the heels of Sharpton's warning that Mrs. Clinton would lose the Senate race if she failed to align herself with powerful leaders like him and Dinkins, who could influence a massive black voter turnout. "I would imagine that in time she would be meeting with all kinds of people, including Sharpton," predicted Dinkins, who declined to say whether he had raised the civil rights leader's concerns with Mrs. Clinton. "I can't see why she wouldn't [meet with Sharpton]," Dinkins elaborated. "She certainly has reached out to me."

Dinkins remained tight-lipped as to whether he and Mrs. Clinton talked about a backlash from Giuliani's more militant Jewish supporters as a result of her embracing him. It was the decency in the Democratic statesman, not naïveté, that won't allow him to think of Giuliani as a political cutthroat.

"I don't think the mayor wants to try to attempt to make a racial issue of this; I certainly hope not," said Dinkins of his successor, who apologized to the Hasidic community, saying it was Dinkins' fault the city had to pay the $1.1 million. "It really isn't good for the city," Dinkins argued. "It's not good for him." But can Dinkins envision Giuliani standing on the steps of City Hall, with the brother of Yankel Rosenbaum and a cadre of Jewish leaders, discrediting his stewardship in Crown Heights? "I can't say he won't do that," replied Dinkins, who had pleaded with Sharpton in the toilet of a funeral parlor to help put an end to the Crown Heights rebellion.

Giuliani, he emphasized, would be ill-advised to make Crown Heights a campaign issue. "The world knows by now," Dinkins asserted. "I don't care how many times they try to spin it with respect to the Jewish community. Not everybody in the Jewish community buys that. Gavin Cato died. I don't think [Giuliani] wants to do that."

In the event Giuliani signaled he intended to fight nasty, Dinkins would rely on the media to expose the mayor as a hypocrite who condoned racism. In fairness, he argued, reporters should question Giuliani's coddling of former deputy mayor John Dyson after Dyson authored a racist memo on welfare reform. In the 1994 memo to Peter Powers, another Giuliani senior aide, Dyson referred to a *Daily News* article that questioned whether Powers and Giuliani were capable of running a diverse city like New York. "Do not worry," Dyson wrote. "Two white guys have been running this city of immigrants for over 200 years."

There were no persistent front-page stories or editorials calling on Giuliani to fire, in columnist Bob Herbert's words, the "arrogant and obnoxious" Dyson. That, Dinkins complained, smacked of a racist double standard. "The media reported it but if they thought I had said something anti-Semitic or had a relationship with someone who they suspected of being anti-Semitic, they would have been all over me," he charged. "He said some crap like that—in writing, mind you—and got away with it."

Dyson, incredibly, also got away with a "watermelon" insult during a dispute over whether the city should retain a company owned by a black woman. "The City Comptroller ought to know the difference between a bid and a watermelon," Dyson remarked.

"So you tell me about Rudy playing the race card," Dinkins said. "I don't think it's in his interest to attempt to play it," he reiterated, "because if you're going to play the race card as far as Crown Heights goes, it's not an appropriate issue."

Raising Crown Heights raised the temper of Bill Lynch. In fact, Crown Heights evoked a poignant response from the Democratic operative who underwent open heart surgery and a kidney transplant, which some friends charged were hastened by racist media criticism of his role in the handling of the tragic events. While insisting "we did the right thing there," Lynch snapped, "I don't want to talk about it! This is traumatic enough for my family and me. I'm sitting here with a scar above my heart and a scar on my stomach with a kidney from my kid. Leave it the fuck alone! If you go back and look over the records, during that period I went temporarily blind."

27

Kiss My Ring

✦

Showdown in Harlem

How Hillary treated Reverend Sharpton is a lot better than how Bill treated Jesse.

—Unidentified aide to Al Sharpton

FOR SEVERAL MONTHS FOLLOWING HIS CONDEMNATION of Mrs. Clinton for bypassing key black neighborhoods during her so-called listening tour, Sharpton had been anticipating a political victory. On a wintry, Martin Luther King Day on January 17, 2000, the long-awaited meeting between the likely Senate candidate and the reverend was only minutes away: The First Lady had bowed to months of political pressure and finally agreed to meet with him. "They said it wouldn't happen," he told the parents of Amadou Diallo, the Reverend Calvin Marshall, and me, who had joined him in his office at his House of Justice to await Mrs. Clinton's arrival.

Sharpton appeared to be nervous. He sprang to his feet when the phone rang, screened calls, and consulted with Michael Hardy, his attorney and confidant, who acted as a buffer that day between Sharpton and scores of dignitaries coming out of the cold, clamoring for a seat to this political showdown. At the podium, Sharpton moderated as usual. Things moved along smoothly until the Secret Service signaled to Hardy that Mrs. Clinton was in front of the building and Sharpton should come out to greet her. "We were all thinking, 'What could possibly go wrong?'" Hardy said. Before departing, Sharpton told Hardy to ask Reverend Charles Norris, who was on the dais, to take over. He also instructed Hardy to caution Norris "to keep it spiritual. Stay away from politics. Keep it on King."

Hardy whispered the directives in Norris's ear. Norris seemed to be doing okay until he had to stretch his remarks because of a delay in getting Mrs. Clin-

285

ton into the building. In impromptu remarks Norris implied that he had missed King's historic March on Washington because he was working for Jews. Referring to his former employers, the pastor of the Bethesda Missionary Baptist Church in Queens declared: "Miller No. 1 was a Jew. Miller No. 2 was a Jew. I was then employed by yet another Jew by the name of Jesus and will not be fired until he thinks it's necessary."

Hardy recalled, "I was clearing the area because the Secret Service were saying, 'Until she takes the stage, nobody can be sitting behind her.' In my other ear, I heard Norris talking. I heard him say, 'Jew.' Then I heard Jesus. I didn't hear the context. So I didn't know if it was positive or negative, but then I kind of saw people looking kind of weird."

Hardy seized the microphone and introduced another speaker. But it was clear to some astonished visitors that Norris'remarks threatened to mar the historic moment. With all of Sharpton's enemies poised for battle, Hardy noted, "if you're looking to start trouble, you can take what Norris said and then make it into something." The first to make something of it was one of Sharpton's body-guards, who was Muslim. "Norris did something very insensitive," he complained.

"What did Norris do?" Sharpton inquired.

"He had everybody yelling 'Jesus!' and as a Muslim I was offended."

"Why would he have people yelling 'Jesus' at a rally like that?"

"I don't know," shrugged the bodyguard (who did not mention the offensive reference to Jews).

Shortly after Mrs. Clinton and her entourage, which included Ed Koch and David Dinkins, were ushered into Sharpton's office, Bill Lynch told Sharpton that someone had complained to him about Norris's speech. Sharpton summoned Hardy, who confirmed that Norris had gone off the deep end.

"I'm not going to tolerate Jews or Muslims being offended. I will make a statement," Sharpton declared.

"As soon as [Mrs. Clinton] walked in, Representative Eliot L. Engel of the Bronx raced over to inform her press secretary, Howard Wolfson, of what had taken place," according to *New York Times* reporter Adam Nagourney. "Mr. Wolfson sent a note up to Mrs. Clinton on the podium, who inserted a line in her prepared speech specifically criticizing anti-Semitism."

After Mrs. Clinton's speech, one of Norris's former colleagues at the New York City Commission on Human Rights confronted him in the presence of onlookers.

"You made a mistake!" the friend shouted. "You offended a lot of people and you must apologize!"

But the tremendous pain Norris's statement had caused had not hit home to Norris. He could not figure out what all the fuss was about. "I was surprised at his approach because I thought he was my friend; he is Jewish," Norris recalled. "My feeling was if I had offended him I would think that my friend would have approached me individually and not in a crowd. I didn't know what offended him." Norris then asked another friend what was so bad about what he'd said. The friend retorted: "Rev, your statement was somewhat risqué, and maybe it should not have been made at this time."

"GET NORRIS ON THE PHONE!" Sharpton barked as he stormed into his office. It was the morning after Norris—"an insensitive knucklehead" with a "forked tongue," as one editorial would later describe him—had stabbed his old friend Sharpton in the back at the King Day celebration.

With every minute it took to contact Norris, Sharpton's foul mood worsened. He'd been up all night, replaying on his VCR the minister's controversial comments about being fired by two Jews. Of all the days Norris might have spewed his anti-Semitic rage, why, mused Sharpton, as he fiddled with the VCR, did he pick the day Mrs. Clinton had come to coronate him? To Sharpton, it seemed like a sick ploy spliced into the videotape to discredit one of the greatest triumphs of his burgeoning political career. Norris had some explaining to do.

"Norris on line three!" an aide heard a secretary announce. According to the insider, Sharpton grabbed the phone and lit into Norris before the politically connected preacher could utter a word. "Norris!" he shouted. "Either the Republicans told you to set up Hillary Clinton or you're one of the dumbest Negro preachers I ever met! Either way, I'm denouncing the statement. It's insensitive to Jews and I resent that you would use our platform to do that."

After the telephone confrontation, the aide recalled Sharpton saying that every time Norris tried to tell him he'd been apologizing for his mistake, he cut Norris off. "Apology or not," Sharpton fumed, "I don't tolerate people misusing our platform and misusing our people!"

Sharpton hung up, and paced angrily in his lawn-green carpeted office. A political firestorm had erupted over Norris's remarks, and although Sharpton repudiated Norris emphatically, critics demanded that he remove Norris from the board of his National Action Network. The next day, Norris again attempted to reach out to Sharpton, who was attending a black economic-empowerment conference at a downtown hotel. In a conference call with Sharpton and Network chair Dr. Wyatt Tee Walker, Norris, one Sharpton aide confirmed, offered to resign. "He said if they want to put him off the board he'd accept the punishment," the source recalled. Walker reportedly told Norris the entire board would decide his fate at its next meeting, on January 29.

The political fire directed at Sharpton in the aftermath of Norris's remarks touched off a vicious debate on the politics of guilt by association. On King Day, Mayor Giuliani held a prayer breakfast at Gracie Mansion. Sharpton's supporters loudly criticized Giuliani's tribute, claiming that those who attended were hand-picked lackeys who would have broken with Dr. King for denouncing the mayor's alleged mistreatment of blacks.

Among Giuliani's guests were the Reverend Betty Neal, chief executive officer of Ministers of Harlem USA Inc., a conservative group that "works closely" with the NYPD and was one of Giuliani's biggest boosters in black neighborhoods overrun by brutal cops. During a prayer that she offered, Neal locked arms with Giuliani, and asked God to grant him "the Senatorship" if he desired it. For some blacks, Neal's "God Bless Mr. Devil" prayer blasphemed King's legacy. But even the devil felt that Neal's political entreaty went over the edge. Giuliani laughed throughout the prayer, a response other blacks contended was symbolic of his attitude toward them. "The only mayor of a big city who could not go into any African American community on Martin Luther King Day is the mayor of this city," Sharpton declared.

Giuliani seemed impervious to the criticism. After all, he had black friends, too. Later that evening, Giuliani joined about 2000 people, including Joerg Haider—the then right-wing extremist leader of Austria's anti-immigrant Freedom Party—at a dinner given by the Congress of Racial Equality, which was led by conservative black activist Roy Innis. Two days after the event, Ed Koch blasted Giuliani for sharing a dais with Haider, who had once openly praised the policies of Adolf Hitler. "Is that a place to celebrate Martin Luther King Day, to be on the same dais as the leader of the neo-Nazi party in Austria?" Koch asked at a City Hall news conference. "Why didn't he denounce Joerg Haider? Why didn't he order Joerg Haider out of the hall?" (The mayor's spin doctor, Sunny Mindel, said Giuliani—who was known to be obsessed with guest lists for security reasons—"didn't know" Haider was there.)

Innis and his son, Niger, fired back, with the elder Innis referring to Koch as "a political prostitute, palling around with a known political gigolo, [Congressman] Charlie Rangel [who was] pork-chopping for Al Sharpton!" Consider this exchange with conservative talk show host Sean Hannity on the *Hannity & Colmes* show on the *Fox News Channel*:

Roy Innis: Well, Sean, first of all, there is absolutely no moral equivalent between this person, Sharpton board member, making some obscene remark, with obscene implications, and Joerg Haider, the leader of the second largest party in Austria, coming to the CORE dinner, especially after ...

Hannity: Are those charges true about Mr. Haider?

Roy Innis: No, its not true. It's not true at all, and I can tell you why it's not true. First of all, I challenged Haider before a panel of blacks, Jews, whites, Christians, journalists, a broad cross-spectrum of people [at] the Marriott Hotel on November 4. He denounced all Nazi association or sentiments ...

Niger Innis: Look, the fact of the matter is, our dais is made up of over 80 people. We had the Israeli ambassador sitting there. We had the former New York regional director of the ADL. For the fact of that matter, I talked with a couple of friends over at the ADL a couple of days ago, who told me that Joerg Haider is not an anti-Semite. He's not a Nazi.

Hannity: It's a lie.

Roy Innis: He's an extremist. They believe he's extremist. They don't particularly like him, but they do not consider him to be a Nazi. And this guy, Charles Norris, sits on Al Sharpton's board right now!

Young Innis maintained that Koch had declined an invitation to confront Haider at the November 4 meeting. "Yeah, we invited Ed Koch," he said. "Ed Koch said, 'I'm sorry, I can't make it, but the next time you guys invite me to something, I'll be there.'"

But Koch never dines with alleged Nazi sympathizers.

At the National Action Network, some of Al Sharpton's lieutenants were relieved that Norris'comments had not evoked a stronger response from Mrs. Clinton. They had feared that Mrs. Clinton, in her quest for votes, would make the same mistake her husband made by rebuking Sister Souljah.

After praying over the matter and asking God to enlighten him, Norris said he began to realize Sharpton and others were justifiably upset. "There are times when people who are speakers say the wrong thing at the wrong time," he reflected. "This is something that should not have been said, and I regret it."

Norris denied he told the story to illustrate his former employers' alleged insensitivity to his desire to participate in King's March on Washington. "I regretted not having gone, but it had nothing to do with my employers," he emphasized. "My intent was to show that at a critical time in my life I had no animosity toward Jews."

When I asked him to respond to the allegation that he was a plant by Republicans to sabotage Sharpton, Norris laughed. "I had no political agenda," he swore. "I have always been a registered Democrat. I have never been tied to Republicans. That's so left-wing, so radical, it's unbelievable." He noted that he and Sharpton had been friends for 10 years. "I would do nothing to hurt, to camouflage, or to impede the progress that Reverend Sharpton has made in his years of leading African American people," he vowed. "Nothing!"

Mrs. Clinton, an insider pointed out, did not hold Sharpton responsible for Norris' comments and refused to pander to Sharpton's critics. "How Hillary treated Reverend Sharpton is a lot better than how Bill treated Jesse," the source argued. "What would have been devastating is if Hillary had attacked Sharpton: 'You know, Al, you shouldn't have had somebody like that there.' Some of us felt that Norris gave Reverend Sharpton an opportunity to look good in his finest hour—he denounced bigotry and anti-Semitism. So in the Sharpton camp we were thinking, 'Some tremendous victory!'"

PART IX
Black Blood is Cheap (2000)

for
Ahmaad and Junior Samuel, Jamal Thomas, Sashay Roberts, Seaver Warner Jr.,
Allison, Indy, Noel, Jojo, George, Kadisha Telemaque, Mitchell Samuel Jr., and
Nicole Laidlow

28

The Diallo Trial

Reverend Sharpton, are you accusing me of throwing the case? Do you know who you're talking to?

Wait a minute! Not only do I know who I'm talkin' to, I'll be all the way up your ass if somebody doesn't turn this around!

—Bronx District Attorney Robert Johnson and Al Sharpton

PREVIOUSLY GOOD RELATIONS between Al Sharpton and Bronx D.A. Robert Johnson began to sour on January 25, 2000 after Sharpton emerged from a meeting at the Justice Department with Eric Holder, Jr., Attorney General Janet Reno's top assistant and the most powerful African American in the Justice Department; Bill Lann Lee, head of the attorney general's Civil Rights Division; Amadou Diallo's parents; Congressman Rangel; and a group of clergy. At a news conference afterward, Sharpton announced that federal officials would monitor the trial of the four officers accused of recklessly gunning down Diallo. That did not sit well with Johnson, the state's first black district attorney, whose prosecutors, according to a Sharpton aide, "went ballistic" upon the delegation's return from Washington.

Why were Sharpton and Rangel asking for the feds to look over Johnson's shoulder, they asked. Sharpton insiders said the activist began to perceive Johnson as a "political patsy" from whom powerful white politicians and judges were snatching authority.

In 1996 Johnson emerged at the center of a controversy over the use of New York's reinstated death penalty law. Johnson, who once prosecuted a case in which an innocent man was convicted of murder and opposed capital punishment, refused to seek the death penalty in the case of Angel Diaz, who was accused of shooting Officer Kevin Gillespie to death during a wild police chase of suspected carjackers. Governor George Pataki removed Johnson from the case and appointed state attorney general Dennis Vacco as special prosecutor to pursue the death penalty. In the Diallo case, Sharpton, along with other black activists, were upset by Johnson's tepid response after state appellate judges, claiming that the wave of pretrial publicity would make it impossible to find an impartial jury in the Bronx, moved the trial to upstate Albany.

Sharpton, the aide said, intended to go over Johnson's head.

"What are you doing?" a befuddled Johnson aide reportedly asked one of the Diallo family lawyers. "You don't trust us? Why is Sharpton undermining us?"

"We don't know what Sharpton is doing, but we consider it wise to have this as an option," the lawyer responded. "Why are you taking it so personal?" Johnson allegedly banned the Diallo lawyers and Sharpton from future meetings between the parents and prosecutors who regularly briefed the family about the case.

The day before the trial started, prosecutors insisted on meeting only with Diallo's parents at the Marriott Hotel in Albany. "No other family members. No lawyers. No advisers," a Sharpton aide recalled. "It was interpreted in Diallo family circles that they were still pissed off about the Washington trip." Sharpton bristled at Johnson's alleged attempt to isolate the advisers. "The prosecution's briefing on how they planned to handle the case would be known only to Saikou and Kadiatou Diallo, who really didn't understand the American legal system," the aide noted.

But the Diallos stepped out of the fray, telling their advisers they wanted to hear what prosecutors had to say. "When they came back," according to the aide, "they said that the prosecution was confident they could win, and outlined how they were going to present the evidence." During jury selection, Sharpton and Deveraux Cannick, a lawyer for Saikou Diallo and a former Bronx assistant D.A., privately sharpened their criticism of the prosecution for not immediately pointing out to the judge that defense attorneys were trying to have jurors removed based on race. "Reverend Sharpton began to wonder whether prosecutors would go for the jugular or just put up a 'presentable case,'" the aide said. "Rev saw that the defense was trying to knock all the blacks off the jury and that prosecutors wasn't saying anything about it in open court. That's when he called a press conference and blasted the defense lawyers for being biased. By Reverend Sharpton raising a stink, four blacks got on the jury. The judge was forced to back up because Rev called the jury selection racist."

As testimony got under way, Sharpton and lawyers for the family felt that prosecutors should put Mrs. Diallo on the witness stand to explain what Amadou meant to her. "Everyone knows how magnetic she is," an aide asserted. "She would have won the hearts of the jury, but the prosecutors did nothing to humanize Amadou. This whole thing about him being an immigrant and a peddler played into the anti-immigrant feelings of people in Albany." Johnson rebuffed the suggestion to call Mrs. Diallo, and told the advisers to back off. "The prosecutors said that they did not want their case influenced by lawyers who had a monetary interest or by Al Sharpton who had a political interest," the Sharpton aide recalled.

After all of this, not calling Johnson was out of the question as far as Sharpton was concerned. The minister demanded to speak to the D.A. after the attorney for Officer Carroll—the cop who had broken into tears as he testified—argued that Diallo's body was not tampered with after he was shot. According to an aide, Sharpton suggested to Johnson that prosecutors trip up that defense argument this way: "The logical thing to have asked is, 'Didn't Sean Carroll's attorney in his opening statement say that Carroll had in fact intended to give CPR to Amadou? He had to move the body to try to give him CPR. So why wouldn't the prosecution in their redirect come back with that so the jury can be reminded of what was said?'"

Johnson reportedly thanked Sharpton for making a "good point," adding that he wanted to think about it. "He never said whether he would talk to them or not, which might have been strategic," the aide said.

Tensions escalated after Sharpton and Cannick concluded that prosecutors failed to properly cross-examine Schrrie Elliott, a key witness who had refused to meet with defense attorneys but was subpoenaed by them to testify about what she heard the night Diallo was shot. In television interviews, Elliott had said that one officer yelled "Gun!" And she also indicated Diallo appeared to be on his feet for most of the shooting—all proof, the defense contended, that the officers fired because they believed Diallo was an armed threat.

In court, Elliott reiterated that someone yelled "Gun!" before a volley of shots. But the defense gamble backfired when Elliott also claimed that the officers cornered Diallo and opened fire without warning. She further testified that the officers kept firing at the unarmed victim after he fell to the ground. Elliott, Sharpton said, should have been the prosecution's star witness. "She was a good witness that the prosecution never emphasized." Out of respect for the Diallo family, Sharpton held back from publicly blasting the prosecution team, but then erupted over what he considered the prosecution's biggest blunder. "They never really aggressively went after the cops," he charged.

ON THE MORNING OF FEBRUARY 17, Sharpton arrived sallow-faced in the lobby of the Justice Department. As the Diallo family's chief adviser, he had come—at the urging of black activists, politicians, as well as the family and their lawyers—to hand-deliver a complaint to Eric Holder. Sharpton, as he stated in a letter I later obtained for a story I was doing for the *Voice*, was "greatly concerned with the manner in which this case has been prosecuted."

The day before, Temple University criminologist and former NYPD cop James Fyfe, testifying for the defense, argued that the four white cops who killed a Diallo were right to charge the vestibule of his Bronx apartment building. Eric Warner, Johnson's lead prosecutor, had not tried a major case since the Happyland Social Club inferno trial nine years earlier. In some legal circles, Warner's opening argument was considered weak. Others felt he neglected to develop a clear theory of the case, and then made a grave omission when he failed to proffer expert witnesses on police training and procedures.

When the defense provided Fyfe as an expert on police practices, Warner and his team seemed surprised. The prosecution did not refute any information or cross-examine Fyfe. Fyfe was the only authority on police practices and procedures in the entire case: The jury had no choice but to accept Fyfe's testimony as an accurate representation of acceptable police procedures. Fyfe's convincing testimony dealt a severe blow to the already lackluster performance by prosecutors. Shortly after the defense rested, prosecutors asked Justice Joseph C. Teresi to direct the jury to consider lesser charges—manslaughter and criminally negligent homicide—in addition to the top counts of second-degree murder, depraved indifference, and reckless endangerment. Several observers, including Sharpton, interpreted the prosecution's move as an omen that it had lost the case.

As Sharpton handed the letter to the clerk, he remembered that "those of us with a sincere interest in assuring that justice will be meted out" now had a backup strategy to an earlier petition from Diallo's parents for federal intervention: If Carroll, McMellon, Boss, and Murphy walked, they'd be heading straight toward a federal courthouse.

"In light of the passion and public outcry that has accompanied this case, the prosecutor's less than aggressive stance against the four accused officers has been an inferior denouement," Sharpton complained in the letter. "While justice has been swift in this case," he added, "it remained to be seen whether it will also be fair. It pains me to ponder that at some point, Mr. and Mrs. Diallo's introduction to American justice may only enhance rather than abate their grief." According to Sharpton, he and Holder talked later that day by phone, and Holder vowed that the Justice Department would closely monitor closing arguments, the judge's charge to the jury, and the panel's deliberation.

Driving back to New York City the day the last two defendants testified, Sharpton told aides he believed that blame for the bungled legal strategy lay squarely with Johnson. In the presence of two top lieutenants from his National Action Network, and his driver, Sharpton called Johnson from a cell phone and the two had a blowout. (Johnson denied he and Sharpton brawled. "The only conversations we had were civil conversations," said the D.A., whose insistence that his prosecutors did a good job in the Diallo case triggered calls for his resignation. "There were times when he didn't understand what our strategy was and we explained it to him.")

This is how and his aides reconstructed the verbal fisticuffs, blow by blow, with Johnson:

Sharpton: "All I wanna know, are y'all trying to throw this case or not? Because I'm tellin' you that there is no way we're gonna sit by and let y'all do this."

Johnson: "Reverend Sharpton, are you accusing me of throwing the case? Do you know who you're talking to?"

Sharpton: "Wait a minute! Not only do I know who I'm talkin' to, I'll be all the way up your ass if somebody doesn't turn this around!"

Johnson: "I am the Bronx District Attorney. I'm not going to be addressed like that!"

Sharpton: "I know who you are! I helped to get you elected Bronx D.A. The issue is not your title. The issue is the function of your office. You guys blew the Anthony Baez case [a federal jury convicted police officer Francis Livotti of civil rights violations in Baez's choking death after he was acquitted in Bronx Supreme Court] and we're not gonna let you blow the Diallo case!"

Johnson: "Let's calm down, reverend. We've gone far enough with this."

According to the aides, Sharpton took a deep breath. His massive torso heaved as he snorted from the Monday-morning quarterbacking. Johnson, who was soft-spoken, broke the silence.

"What exactly is your bone of contention?" he asked.

Sharpton: "This guy [Assistant District Attorney Eric Warner] never cross-examined Boss or Murphy on anything! He never laid a glove on them. He never asked Boss about the Patrick Bailey killing [on Halloween night in 1997, in Brooklyn, Boss shot and killed Bailey under controversial circumstances] when he and the other cops were allowed to go through their 'stellar' records. He never raised the contradiction."

Johnson: "What contradiction?"

Sharpton: "Sean Carroll testified that Amadou was standing up straight, erect, looked like he had on a bulletproof vest, and that's why he had to shoot at his legs. Boss testified that Amadou was in a combat position. That was the same thing he said about [Patrick] Bailey. All your prosecutor had to say to Boss was, 'Mr. Boss, are you sure Mr. Diallo was in a cramped position?' If Boss answered yes, then he should have asked, 'Were you sitting here in court when Sean Carroll said Mr. Diallo was erect?' If he answered in the affirmative, all your man had to say was, 'So you're contradicting Mr. Carroll's statement; isn't that the same thing you said happened in the Patrick Bailey shooting?' He could have crucified him on that. Again, 'Mr. Boss, you said that you looked in, saw Mr. Diallo, and shot—you thought you shot twice, it was five times—and then you jumped out of the line of fire, which means you didn't have to jump in the line of fire. You were not in danger, which means that you shot Mr. Diallo out of revenge, thinking that Officer McMellon had been shot when in fact he had not been shot. You were in no danger when you shot your five bullets.'"

This line of questioning would have guaranteed a murder conviction, Sharpton maintained. The aides and Sharpton said that at that point Johnson appeared to be taking notes, and recalled that they then had the following exchange:

Johnson: "Well, let me see what their explanation is as to why they didn't go into it. Maybe they think their case was so solid they didn't need it."

Sharpton: "So solid? How do you know when you've got a solid enough case? How do you know what a jury is thinking?"

Johnson: "I'll get back to you."

That was the last time Sharpton and Johnson spoke, an aide said. "He never took any more calls from Reverend Sharpton after that."

It was only on the second day of jury deliberation that Johnson finally showed his face in the Albany courtroom—a move his critics believed signaled that his strategy was in trouble.

On February 25, after deliberating for approximately 23 hours over a three-day period, the jury concluded that the four white cops were justified in their decision to shoot Amadou Diallo. They were acquitted of all criminal and lesser charges.

29

The Shooting of Dante Johnson

District Attorney Robert Johnson has never hesitated prosecuting anyone where there is evidence that a crime has been committed. Since 1995, charges alleging the use of excessive force while on duty have been filed against 20 police officers. Allegations of wrongdoing not involving excessive force have resulted in charges being filed against eight other police officers.

It is inappropriate for a district attorney to seek to influence a grand jury. The role of the D.A. is to serve as legal adviser to the grand jury and to instruct the panel on the law and the available evidence. [In the case of Dante Johnson], we submitted for the grand jury's consideration a felony charge of assault in the second degree, reckless assault. The panel, however, filed a lesser charge of assault in the third degree. We did not charge an intentional shooting because the forensic evidence did not bear that out.

—Steve Reed, spokesman for Bronx D.A. Robert Johnson

IN JUNE 2000, ON THE DAY A Bronx grand jury refused to file felony charges against a white police officer for shooting her unarmed 16-year-old son, Dante, Sharon Johnson sat in the office of D.A. Robert Johnson wringing her hands. She was listening in disbelief as the bumbling prosecutor added another of his shameful contributions to one of the saddest chapters in the history of New York's modern civil rights movement. Johnson was telling the mother what she'd already learned from news leaks: The grand jury had looked at the facts, listened to the witnesses, and determined that the May 26, 1999 shooting of Dante was not intentional.

The meaningful facts surrounding such controversial shootings all too often seemed lost on the stolid Johnson, who, tethered to the reins of his own political survival, apparently brushed aside the impact a cop's bullet wielded on a once promising future. In this case, the "criminal negligence" of Officer Mark Conway painted an indelible portrait of a victim's helplessness.

"He is feeling pain and he wants answers, and I can't give him any," Sharon Johnson told me the day I visited Dante and her in the hospital. "I thought that if he sees the cop being indicted, that would bring some closure and help with the nightmares and everything. But that is not so."

Dante was shot once in the left side of his lower abdomen.

"Dante's got a scar from the top part of his chest all the way down past his navel," the mother cried. "He has scars all over his neck. He can't take off any kind of clothing for anybody to see this—you would be in shock, you'd want to turn your face away. His legs are totally messed up. I'm not just talking about scars from stitches. They had to cut pieces of the muscles because they had decayed. Muscles don't grow back, so chunks of his legs are missing—both legs, inside and outside. I am trying to talk to him about positive things and [he is concerned about the fact that] he can't play ball. I said, 'Maybe you can coach ball.' And he is a skinny person. He said, 'Look at my arms; my arms are bigger than my legs.' He cannot lift up his foot to walk like you and I do."

Dante, she added "stays angry" about the outcome of the investigation into the shooting. "Sometimes he even gets angry with me," she intimated. "[In the past] if anything was wrong I was able to fix it or help him. [Now] here I am, completely helpless. Either he can't wear shorts in the summer or the braces are too tight rubbing into his foot if he walks a little distance."

SIX MONTHS LATER, AS DANTE JOHNSON battled his nightmares, Rudy Giuliani reignited bad feelings. In a meeting with Attorney General Janet Reno and federal prosecutors from Brooklyn at the Justice Department, Giuliani tried to drive another nail in the coffin of the anti-police-brutality movement. He hoped to bury charges that the cop who shot and critically injured Dante Johnson, the cop who blew Patrick Dorismond away at close range, and the cops who gunned down Amadou Diallo in a hail of 41 bullets, had targeted the victims because of their race. (All of the officers involved in those questionable shootings were acquitted or cleared of more serious charges by juries.)

The disgraced Republican mayor had been blocking a civil rights lawsuit, accusing the city of failing to discipline brutal cops. Reno sat through irksome exhibits of Giuliani's dubious charts and statistics, which he often used to defend the NYPD against charges of racial profiling.

Some black militants argued that if Reno had the guts some of her defenders insisted she had, she would have the FBI arrest Giuliani for inciting the police shootings, beatings, and criminalizing of his constituents. Reno's patience with Giuliani's stalling tactics, they asserted, should have run out by now. Recalling the lightning predawn raid to free Elián González, some black activists began to imagine the FBI breaking and entering pre 911 No. 7 World Trade Center (where they envisioned Giuliani would hide out to run his outlaw mayoralty in the event Reno appointed a federal monitor over the rogue NYPD) and snatching the "law and order" mayor from his high-tech bunker. But such fantasies about charging Giuliani with "war crimes" were shattered by the unnerving reality that his political influence extended further than they thought. Indeed, the "very attentive and very conscientious" Reno, as Giuliani described her after the meeting, was in no rush to embarrass the mayor.

The activists and other civil libertarians charged that the political pressure exerted on Giuliani would have been different had the victims of police misbehavior been mostly whites or Jews. Black blood was deemed cheap, they contended, and if blacks ever needed Reno it was now. Under Giuliani, the activists pointed out, the anti-police-brutality movement had been on the losing end in the highest-profile cases. They claimed that since wresting the mayoralty from David Dinkins in 1993, Giuliani—who was fighting to salvage his tarnished legacy—consistently encouraged police abuse of people of color.

Even as some blacks were beginning to express compassion for Giuliani because of his battle with prostate cancer, the mayor was setting them up to be victims of racial profiling. During a City Hall news conference in which he blasted a probe by the U.S. attorney in Manhattan—which found that the NYPD's Street Crime Unit had engaged in racial profiling while conducting random street searches—Giuliani declared that if police were searching for a hypothetical black suspect, as many as two in every five black men questioned could be arrested for some other crime.

In Giuliani's example of a hypothetical search for a black rape suspect, police are searching the Upper West Side for a male the mayor described as a "six-foot-two African American, roughly 35 years old." He added: "What is going to happen in order to find that person is a lot of people are going to be approached. You are going to have to search for people, you are going to have to interview people, you are going to have to ask them questions. When you approach some of them to ask questions, you may be frightened about the fact that maybe they have a gun, maybe they don't have a gun. So you frisk them. Sometimes you do find a gun. In the course of looking for that one rapist, you may arrest 30, 40 people. You may approach 100 people. But who are you going to be focusing on? You are not going to be focusing on a 70-year-old white male—if in fact the report is that the rapist is a 35-year-old African American male. And that happens in large percentages, and that is what drives what's been going on."

Janet Reno must have been aware that Giuliani's comments contradicted the NYPD's own statistics. In 1998, the Street Crime Unit made 45,000 stop-and-frisk searches—although 35,000 of those stops, or about 78 percent, did not result in arrests. About 90 percent of those stopped were blacks and Latinos, and the conviction rate of those arrested by the Street Crime Unit has not been a factor in Giuliani's slide shows. Even when given the chance to clarify his remarks later, the mayor stood by his numbers, saying that the arrests of black men would not necessarily be for the hypothetical rape, but for a variety of criminal activity, much of which fell under what the mayor called "quality-of-life" offenses—for example, drug possession, graffiti, or outstanding warrants.

In addition to considering whether to seize control of the NYPD, Reno, some activists suggested, should launch a far-reaching probe into the offices of the city's most controversial district attorneys. This investigation would focus on how Bronx D.A. Robert Johnson, Manhattan D.A. Robert Morgenthau, and Brooklyn D.A. Charles Hynes—in the face of overwhelming evidence—conducted flawed investigations that led to the exoneration of police officers in such cases as the maiming of Dante Johnson and the slayings of Amadou Diallo, Patrick Dorismond, and Patrick Bailey.

The federal overhaul must begin with Johnson, who wound up losing the Diallo case—at the time the most notorious allegation of police brutality in the city's criminal justice history. "One does not struggle to elect a black D.A. for cops to feel they can go to that borough and not worry about being prosecuted," said Sharpton, perhaps Johnson's most vocal critic. "We expect a black D.A. not to break rules in our favor but we also expect him not to break rules against us either." Johnson, he added, quickly was becoming a symbol of black betrayal in this city. He should be trying to be even more aggressive to show the community that he is not giving police a pass."

After Johnson, Reno should immediately focus on D.A. Morgenthau's office, one with a deplorable record of prosecuting brutal cops. In July, an announcement by the aging criminal justice czar that undercover cop Anthony Vasquez would not face criminal charges in the killing of Patrick Dorismond intensified anger, disgust, and fear in the black community. Asked whether the black victim of a police shooting could receive justice from a grand jury, Morgenthau replied that the "racially mixed" panel "took its duties seriously and reached a fair result." Morgenthau allegedly gave a "pass" to Officer Craig Yokemick in the case some activists now refer to as "Robbing Banks." In 1999, a Manhattan grand jury found that Yokemick had used justifiable force and should not be charged in Kenneth Banks' death.

As for Brooklyn D.A. Charles Hynes, Reno does not have to look far. According to Charles Barron, he was the prosecutor with the worst record of all when it came to giving cops passes in instances of alleged brutality. In fact, Barron accused Hynes of contributing to the death of Amadou Diallo, arguing that had Hynes prosecuted Officer Kenneth Boss for the 1997 fatal shooting of Patrick Bailey, Diallo would be alive. Hynes declined to prosecute Boss in the Bailey slaying, saying "there is no credible view of the evidence which would support criminal charges." In July, in a $155 million wrongful-death lawsuit brought by the family, a federal jury found that Boss, another officer, and the Giuliani administration were not liable.

D.A. JOHNSON HAD REQUESTED that Sharon Johnson have her son present in his office on the afternoon of June 9 when he delivered the bad news. "It's a good thing Dante didn't go over there," she recalled. "I knew a lot of crazy things have been going on, and as far as justice goes, blacks didn't seem to be getting any. I expected him to tell me that based on the information that they had that this cop was going to be indicted on a decent charge." Instead of charging Officer Conway with a felony, the grand jury slapped the 14-year veteran on the wrist with one misdemeanor count of third-degree assault. Conway was a member of the Street Crime Unit.

This, according to police and prosecutors, is what happened: At about 12:20 a.m. on May 26 1999, Conway, who was in uniform at the time, as well as two other cops, Sergeant Terrence O'Toole and Officer Michael Fraterrigo, were in an unmarked car on routine patrol in the Morris Heights section of the Bronx. They approached Johnson and a friend for questioning in connection with a string of robberies. When O'Toole and Fraterrigo got out of the car, the teens fled. The two cops caught Johnson's friend on the overpass of the Major Deegan Expressway. Conway chased Johnson in the car. According to a statement released by the D.A.'s office, "Conway pulled alongside Johnson, reached outside his moving vehicle and grabbed the sleeve of the boy's jacket. The gun discharged as the fleeing youth struggled to get away."

In Sharon Johnson's June meeting with the Bronx D.A., she and her attorney, Sanford Rubenstein, pressed the prosecutor for explanations that he seemed hesitant to give. According to Dante's mother, Johnson said that he did not pursue stiffer charges against Conway because of his failed strategy in the Diallo case. "He said that they [filed] many charges [in the Diallo case] but most of them were thrown out and he did not want to look stupid," she said. "I was rather upset. This was a different case." She added that Johnson tried to convince her that although the grand jury had viewed what happened to her son as an accident, the panel still held Conway responsible.

"No, no, it does not work like that," she remembered telling the prosecutor. "I served 30 days on a grand jury, right across the street. It depends on what you present to us."

She recalled the following exchange:

"I am not going to try to influence the grand jury," Johnson responded.

"That's what you come in there to do," asserted the mother who heard some 200 cases during her grand jury service. "That's what prosecutors do every day. They come in and present cases to us, trying to influence us with whatever information [is necessary] for us to make an informed decision. If you come in and ask for two misdemeanor charges and we give you one—that's what you asked for. We say, 'Ok, you don't believe you have a strong case; that's what you're gonna get.' So don't put that on the jury."

"I don't believe that the cop intentionally did the shooting," Johnson reiterated. Sharon Johnson expressed outrage at the prosecutor's stubbornness.

"It's an open window," she said, referring to the unmarked car in which Conway pursued her son. "He has to raise his hand. If the gun accidentally went off, the bullet had to hit something, the steering wheel, his lap, his elbow, something," added the boy's mother, a former soldier and computer technician who was training to be a police officer when Motorola lured her away. "You pull a gun, [aim] it through a window, and you tell me that you did not intend to shoot?" She described Johnson as "rather stunned" by her argument.

"It doesn't make sense going back and forth about this," the D.A. said.

"So in your opinion, this is the best you can do?" she asked.

"Yes," Johnson replied.

Sharon Johnson, Rubenstein, and Reverend Herbert Daughtry, who had joined them as an adviser, went to a nearby room where they consulted before facing a throng of reporters. "I was in shock," the mother said. "I think that he is weak. I think that the people in the Bronx need to know that you cannot take a case to this man and expect him to be fair about it."

At the news conference, Sharon Johnson again appealed to the prosecutor to rely on his common sense. "How can a cop pull a gun with one hand, aim it at a person, hold on to that person while driving a car, drive, and pull the trigger?" she asked, pleading, "Mr. Johnson, I need an explanation. My son needs an explanation. The city needs an explanation."

PART X

Race and Crime
(2000)

for
Carlene Nesbitt and
Danielle and Channel Warner

30

The Killing of Malcom F'

Fear covers the street like a sheet of ice.

—Bill Bradley (quoted in *Race, Crime, and the Law,* by Randall Kennedy)

ASKED TO IMAGINE A REPUTED HEROIN PUSHER getting high on black rage, friends of Malcolm Ferguson would conjure up the image of him going berserk after the acquittal of the four white cops who shot and killed Amadou Diallo.

Can't imagine that? Picture Mayor Rudy Giuliani—the "Butcher of Soundview," as protesters called him—standing before a bouquet of microphones, declaring in his trademark sneer that the 23-year-old Ferguson was no Diallo and that police officer Louis Rivera, who pumped a fatal bullet into the back of the unarmed man's head during a struggle allegedly witnessed by two people, was the true hero. Ferguson's eulogists predicted that an eerie twist of fate—that he was unarmed and slain just blocks from where Diallo was shot—would catapult him from ex-con to martyr of the civil rights movement. Such rhetoric worried Giuliani's backers, who asserted that the drug dealer some called "Malcolm F" did not have a political bone in his body.

But others who commemorated Malcolm Ferguson say they were not trying to clean up his image. How he died, and whether his alleged 11th-hour political awakening meant anything, should be of concern to all New Yorkers. Ferguson's mother, Juanita Young, said that her son had problems but was moving forward with his life. "We were straightening him out," she told WCBS-TV. "He was not a bad kid. What they say about him is a lie, it's a stone, barefaced lie. They abused him and they killed him."

If an allegedly brutal encounter with a cop did not convince him to join Al Sharpton's protest movement, the Diallo killing, friends insisted, was bound to have a profound impact on Ferguson. Friends weren't surprised that the five-foot-six "playa" with the disheveled Afro and goatee found himself on the front-lines protesting the outcome of the trial. Why not? they asked. If a jury had accepted the incredible explanation that Diallo's wallet morphed into a gun—causing cops to fire 41 shots at the street merchant, striking him 19 times—then anyone, they argued, even a "hardened criminal" like Malcolm Ferguson, could be politicized by an unjust verdict.

In the wake of the Diallo verdict, a multiracial crowd swooped down on Wheeler Avenue, the South Bronx neighborhood where Amadou Diallo lived and died. Among the swarm of demonstrators who taunted and badgered a phalanx of cops in riot gear was Malcolm Ferguson, who had every reason to be wary of police. He was one month shy of completing his parole for a heroin-selling conviction, and his attorney was about to file a $5 million brutality suit against the city, accusing police of breaking his hand when they handcuffed him during a March 9, 1999, drug arrest. As the protest began to wane, Ferguson and others tried to board a bus, according to a friend named Libby. "The bus driver just told him to get off," Libby recalled. That's when cops grabbed Ferguson. A Fox 5 TV camera captured the arrest and showed Ferguson grimacing, his face pressed against the roadway, as he was being handcuffed behind his back. Ferguson, whose jacket was unzipped and who wore baggy jeans that sagged to expose plaid boxer shorts, was then hoisted and escorted hurriedly by plainclothes cops to a police van. He was charged with disorderly conduct and resisting arrest.

"We were just speaking our minds like everybody else and we were just grabbed because they wanted to break the protest up," charged Josh S., a then 17-year-old member of the pressure group Refuse & Resist. "It was a strategy that the cops had set up. Actually, my arresting officer told me he was going to charge me with resisting arrest [but] he was going to be nice and not do this. I told him he wasn't supposed to arrest me in the first place. He said he knew that, but that's just the way it works."

Josh S. spent a night in the cell with Ferguson. "When we were there we were angry," he recalled. "We spent more time in jail than the cops who shot Diallo. They didn't even spend any time in jail, so you can imagine how we were feeling." Ferguson participated in the jailhouse discussion about eroding civil rights under the Giuliani administration. "Everybody in the cell was sharing the same sentiment of anger and rage [over] this whole situation," Josh S. added.

On March 1, five days after Ferguson was arrested, he wound up on Boynton Avenue, three blocks from where Diallo was shot. Chief of Patrol John Scanlon claimed that shortly before 6:30 p.m., five undercover housing cops on narcotics patrol saw someone lurking inside a building at 1045 Boynton Avenue. They entered the four-story building and confronted Ferguson and two other men in the lobby. They put the suspects up against a wall, but Ferguson suddenly bolted up a flight of stairs, and Officer Rivera gave chase with his 16-shot, 9-mm Smith & Wesson automatic drawn, Scanlon said.

"At some point, on the second-floor landing, there was a struggle," he added. "[The officer's] firearm discharged, and the individual succumbed." It wasn't immediately clear if Rivera fired intentionally or if the gun went off by accident, but Scanlon volunteered that Ferguson was shot at close range because blood was found on Rivera's gun. He added that six cellophane-wrapped packets of heroin were discovered rolled into the waistband of sweatpants Ferguson wore under his jeans. He was declared dead at the scene.

Josh S. learned about Ferguson's death while attending a benefit concert organized by Refuse & Resist. "I was paralyzed; I didn't know what to say," he recalled. "[T]hey just informed me that the same person I was in the cell with for 20 hours was shot in the back of the head. How do you respond to something like that?"

Within a couple of hours, scores of people had gathered behind police tape on the street, some carrying protest signs. One placard portrayed Mayor Giuliani as "The Butcher of Soundview," whose trigger-happy enforcers had shot another unarmed man. "Who Shot Rudy?" one protester shouted, his question a stark reference to a controversial rap similarly titled. Released in 1999 by a group called Screwball, the rap imagined Giuliani being gunned down at City Hall to the delight of the minority community: "Nobody cried—it was real like some Jews celebrating when the Pharaoh got killed." The lyrics could be traced to Giuliani's troubled relationship with the city's young blacks and Latinos, many of whom had been unlawfully stopped and frisked, brutalized, or killed by white cops.

Giuliani said the violent lyrics of "Who Shot Rudy?" were troubling, particularly if children heard the song. Kyron Jones, the 24-year-old rapper, who wrote the lyrics, said it came from his own troubles with the law, including a stint in jail. He added that he had a friend who was shot twice by police although he was not arrested. As for Giuliani, Jones said: "I don't want anybody to go out and shoot him. I'm just voicing the thoughts of my people."

The morning after the Ferguson shooting, Giuliani fired back at those who were comparing Ferguson to Diallo. Giuliani called the killing of Ferguson a completely different situation. He described Ferguson as a "career criminal" who had a long record of robbery, burglary, heroin trafficking, gun possession, and resisting-arrest charges, while Diallo had no rap sheet. "He'd been arrested several times while on parole, but somehow was never put back in prison, which is where people who violate parole should go," Giuliani scoffed.

"He was just a human being," said Josh S. "They didn't know he was an ex-con when they killed him." The night after Ferguson was killed, Josh S. went back to Soundview, protesting. "Everybody was obviously very angry," he said. "We were all feeling the same, fearing [for] our own safety from the people who are supposed to protect us and serve us."

Of course, no one expected Rudy Giuliani to embrace Malcolm Ferguson's grieving mother. Juanita Young's drug-dealing son—the scum of Soundview, Giuliani all but concluded—had it coming. (After what he called "a thorough and exhaustive investigation," D.A. Johnson refused to file criminal charges against Officer Rivera.)

31

The Killing of Patrick Dorismond

◆

Police Brutality, Rudy Giuliani, and Voodoo Justice

While the police officers on duty the day of Patrick M. Dorismond's funeral indeed showed restraint, Mr. Giuliani has not shown such restraint in his zeal to paint Mr. Dorismond as a petty hoodlum. The mayor's demonizing of the victim has added fuel to the simmering frustrations and pains felt by Haitians and others in New York. There are other actions Mayor Giuliani should take. One is to follow the lead of Detective Anthony Vasquez and directly offer his condolences to the Dorismond family.

—Jocelyn Mccalla, Executive Director, National Coalition for Haitian Rights, in a letter to the editor, *The New York Times*, March 29, 2000

FOR THREE MONTHS, LARRY PAGETT AGONIZED about going to prison. As the avowed Crips gang leader and aspiring rapper swaggered drunkenly one April morning, in 2000, into State Supreme Court in Brooklyn to seal a plea bargain deal for assault with a gun, he reminisced about the blustery winter night he bumped into his old dawg, Patrick Dorismond.

Pagett and Dorismond, the son of Haitian singer Andre Dorismond, became close friends in 1996 when Pagett, in his early teens, already was deeply entrenched in hardcore thug life. Pagett, who was 20 at the time we talked, was the head gangsta in G-Storm, a Flatbush-based set with strong ties to the Crips. But it was Dorismond, a burly figure nicknamed "Avalanche," who befriended

Pagett after learning of Pagett's gang affiliation and his cultural roots in Belize. In the early 1980s, Dorismond was a member of the U.K. Crew, a forerunner to groups like Killa Gangsta Crips. "It was based on Crips," recalled Pagett. "It was a little set. But by the time I met Avalanche, he was already calmed down. He was into some music shit."

Dorismond was an underground hip hop DJ who coined the phrase "Haitian Hop" while playing at the Caribbean Dome in Brooklyn. "He had the whole party talking Haitian. He used to say, 'Everybody say, 'Sak pasé [What's up]?' He was like a comedian, man," said Pagett. "He used to be buggin'. We'd be chillin', we'd all be talkin', and he'd just make an outburst, say some Haitian shit that had everybody laughin'. This is the same nigga whose mother used to call him out from her window, 'Patrick!' while we hangin' an' shit."

As they talked that cold night, Dorismond told Pagett he no longer hung out in the streets.

"I'm turnin' ma life around," he said in a sleepy ebonicized drawl. "I work now. I got ma own crib, and me and ma girl about to git married. I got ma li'l seed, ma li'l daughter."

Dorismond was 26 and working as a security guard with the Times Square Business Improvement District. Pagett wanted Dorismond to know that he too was at the crossroads in his life and was trying to make it as a hip hop artist. Pagett bragged about his rap group Brooknam Dodger—made up of "Me, dat Biz Loc, ma man Omega, ma man Relapse, and ma man Flatbush"—which was shooting a music video for their first single, "Brooklyn," in which Pagett goes off "on some gangsta shit."

Then Pagett told Dorismond he'd done something really criminal—a stickup—but that he'd fessed up and cut a deal with the Brooklyn D.A. to keep from doing 15-to-life. His surrender and sentencing had been set for April. Pagett asked the Haitian immigrant what he should do.

"He was mad at me 'cause I was gonna turn myself in," Pagett remembered. "He wanted me to run. He begged me to go to L.A. or somethin'."

It was the last time Pagett saw Dorismond.

On the night of March 16, during a break in the filming of the "Brooklyn" video, someone told Pagett, "Avalanche got kilt; the police kilt him."

Dorismond, the security guard who wanted to be a cop, was shot early on the morning of March 16 by detective Anthony Vasquez as the officer and two others were carrying out a "buy-and-bust" drug sting near Penn Station and Madison Square Garden. One of the officers approached Dorismond and another man in front of the Wakamba Cocktail Lounge and, in Police Commissioner Safir's words, "engaged them in a conversation relative to drugs." Mayor Giuliani added that the 29-year-old Vasquez then came to the aid of the officer and his gun discharged. (Giuliani said on the Fox News Channel that Vasquez had been wired, that words between him and Dorismond had been recorded, and that he thought a transcript of the exchange would be available—but his aides quickly backed away from the claim.) Dorismond, who was wounded in the chest, died at St. Clare's Hospital. No drugs or other contraband were found on his body. Police brushed aside witnesses' reports that Vasquez was pistol-whipping Dorismond when the gun went off.

It was the fourth shooting of an unarmed black civilian by undercover officers in the city in 13 months, and it occurred only a few weeks after an Albany jury had acquitted the four white undercover officers who shot and killed Amadou Diallo. There was a bitter irony to the shooting that haunted Pagett. He remembered Dorismond telling him shortly after Diallo had died, "You don't wanna catch 41."

SCORES OF MOURNFUL-EYED PEOPLE STREAMED in and out of Marie Dorismond's three-bedroom apartment in a four-story walk-up in the Flatbush section of Brooklyn, a couple days after the shooting. All hugged the inconsolable Haitian immigrant, trying to assure her that the police killing of her unarmed son, Patrick, finally would convince cautious federal prosecutors to seize control of the NYPD and file civil rights charges against the officer involved.

"I want to send a message to all mothers in the whole world!" the grieving pediatric nurse said in a hoarse voice while grasping the arms of Al Sharpton and Herbert Daughtry, the two civil rights leaders she had summoned to her side. "Every one of you that used to have a kid sick, coming to Kings County Hospital! Every nurses! Every doctors! Every lawyers! Stand up! This is Mrs. Dorismond from Pediatric D-72. They got my son now!"

They got her son because he said no to drugs. As the killings of unarmed black men became routine, it was easy for Giuliani to romanticize his ruthless rationales. The mayor said he personally ordered Dorismond's rap sheet unsealed to show that something in Dorismond's background instigated the struggle that led to his death. (As a teenager, Dorismond was arrested for robbery and assault. In 1993 he was arrested for attempted robbery and assault, and in 1996 for criminal possession of a weapon. The '93 and '96 charges were all misdemeanors. In both cases, Dorismond was allowed to plead guilty to disorderly conduct and perform community service. The juvenile case was dropped—and sealed by law.) "I'm sorry," Giuliani told reporters, "police officers are entitled to the benefit of the doubt."

Drug-policy watchdogs—while not commenting directly on the Smith case—contend that the pressure to make arrests and earn overtime (in Operation Condor, for which the NYPD has budgeted $24 million) had driven some officers to use aggressive tactics that led to incidents like the recent fatal shooting of Patrick Dorismond, who was unarmed. Although the plainclothes unit involved in the drug sting that led to the Dorismond shooting allegedly wasn't being paid with Condor money, critics have said it was operating under the same pressure to produce arrests that typifies the program.

From then on, nothing seemed to go right for the garrulous chief executive. Since Dorismond's death, Giuliani and his top cohort, Safir, had been diagnosed with prostate cancer; the mayor announced that he was separating from his wife of 16 years, Donna Hanover; and his U.S. Senate bid lay in ruins. Reaction in mostly black quarters was swift and brutally honest.

"What goes around comes around," one critic bragged.

"Never underestimate the power of an African God," said another.

Were Giuliani's health, marital, and political woes the perfect example of "the chickens coming home to roost?" What did an African God have to do with Giuliani-style justice? Once again smarmy operatives with close ties to Giuliani seized the opportunity to exploit the ignorance surrounding the voodoo religion for political reasons.

CLUTCHING A BLACK, LEATHER-CASED BIBLE, a grief-stricken Mrs. Dorismond, struggled to her feet following a rousing introduction by her adviser, Al Sharpton, one Saturday morning in June. An overflow crowd at Sharpton's House of Justice, which had welcomed the mother of Patrick Dorismond, was ululating with fervor akin to a mau-mau victory dance. Overnight, the scandal-scarred Giuliani had committed political suicide: He dropped out of the U.S. Senate race against Hillary Clinton. At long last, the spell cast by the city's famously ill-tempered leader appeared to be dissipating.

Many in the crowd seemed captivated by the stocky, church going Mrs. Dorismond, believing that the Haitian immigrant—who had named her slain son after Ireland's patron saint, and whose familiar, raspy-voiced complaint about Giuliani-style justice had touched New Yorkers—had something to do with the sudden turn of events in the mayor's life. Every time Mrs. Dorismond prayed, every time she tilted her head toward the heavens—her wide-set eyes rolled back—enraptured blacks felt that she had an inside track on Giuliani's destiny.

Whatever Mrs. Dorismond prayed for remained her secret. But Giuliani, she often predicted, had it coming for what he's done. "The Lord said, 'I put my child in the earth. Don't touch my child! You got no right to kill!'" she cried. "The Lord said, 'The time soon come. I am the Lord! You must respect me!'"

In Brooklyn's Little Haiti and on black talk-radio station WLIB, the so-called "Dorismond Curse" permeated discussions about police brutality and Haitian voodoo. In Little Haiti, it was not uncommon to walk into homes or apartments that had been converted into voodoo temples filled with dolls—"messengers" for spirits that help people probe the mysteries of life and death. Some were well-worn Barbies with notes that hung upside down by threads tied to their ankles. Doing "business" meant summoning the 11 principal voodoo divinities, or "Iwa," derived from benign West African spirits and aggressive Central African and Kréyòl ones. Rhythms beaten on drums and beaded rattles with bells woke the deities.

While some blacks, who adhered to the notion that voodoo was an "evil religion," envisioned zombies sticking pins in dolls resembling Giuliani and Safir, others wondered whether Mrs. Dorismond herself had done a little "business" to cajole the deity who would solve the mystery of her son's death. But Mrs. Dorismond would have no part of that, scoffing at rumors that voodoo was responsible for "who get hurt," a reference to Giuliani's and Safir's prostate cancer. "This is my voodoo! My Bible!" she said, hoisting the holy book and waving it around to accolades from supporters at the Sharpton rally. "I will never stop carry this!" she added. "It's in my hand! And everybody gonna hear this! The Lord said, *'If you touch my hair, you're gonna pay for it.'*"

FOR SOME BELIEVERS IN "EVIL VOODOO," the first Abner Louima police-brutality trial hinged on a handful of lavender rocks and holy water. During the explosive civil rights case in U.S. District Court in Brooklyn, Robert Volpe the father of Justin Volpe, who tortured Louima, told friends he was warned by Haitian spiritual healers that Louima was a wicked voodoo high priest bent on deadly revenge. Volpe reportedly carried around the kind of protection his spiritual advisers bragged would make Louima's evil bogeys suffer. The irony in Volpe's alleged fear that Louima—who wore a bulletproof vest—threatened his family with voodoo had not escaped some Haitians, who contended that Volpe's son brought a curse on himself. Some believed that Justin Volpe got the idea for the sadistic assault from the 1996 mutilation killing of popular Haitian family doctor Claude Michel.

Police found Michel's body slumped over in the passenger seat of his Nissan Pathfinder within the confines of the 70th Precinct. Someone had slashed Michel's throat and cut off his penis, placing it in his hand. The grisly slaying, which remains unsolved, had the hallmark of a Haitian voodoo sacrifice, said an East Flatbush specialist in ritualistic crimes who spoke to me on condition of anonymity. Asked why some Haitians saw a similarity in Michel's death and the sodomizing of Louima, the source replied, "We've seen these crimes before in Haiti and in the Haitian community in America; they're both crimes of passion. They are meant to kill." Volpe handcuffed and beat Louima, and rammed a broken broomstick into Louima's rectum and mouth in a fit of rage.

The phantoms Louima allegedly unleashed on the Volpes to avenge the attack on him were taken seriously, according to James Ridgway de Szigethy. The suspicion that Louima was heavily into devil worship developed in de Szigethy's mind when he began to assume the role of "Occult Cop." For three years, de Szigethy and a group of reporters investigated allegations that the killers of club kid Angel Melendez dealt in the netherworld. De Szigethy also had been looking into the Santeria religion "as spread by [Cuban refugees], who Castro dumped in this country" during the 1980 Mariel boatlift. "It was something that I'd suspected from the beginning about Louima," he said. "I suspected that he might be involved in the practice of voodoo." But de Szigethy could not find anyone in Little Haiti to confirm his wild hunches. He recalled Louima giving him the willies on the first day of testimony about a night of torture at the hands of Justin Volpe. "I looked at his appearances and I just got a funny feeling."

He said that after Louima testified, he approached Robert Volpe about Louima's alleged association with satanic voodoo. "I said, 'Bob, you're gonna think I'm crazy.'" The elder Volpe grabbed de Szigethy by the arm and led him out of the courtroom. "No, I don't think you're crazy," de Szigethy quoted Volpe's father as saying. According to de Szigethy, Volpe then pulled out "a little purple crystal and a little vial of holy water." The concerned father reportedly confided that Haitian spiritualists had urged him to carry the emblems of good over evil at all times.

What happened next would cause even Papa Doc to spin in his grave. "He took a sprinkling of the holy water and made the sign of the cross on his forehead," de Szigethy claimed. Convinced that Volpe's ritual somehow confirmed that Louima believed in the supernatural, de Szigethy contacted the Reverend William G. Kalaidjian, the controversial former NYPD chaplain who was forced to resign from the department after referring to a prosecutor as a "fag."

"I want you to come into this courtroom because there is evil here," de Szig-ethy told Kalaidjian, who also was a member of the National Police Defense Foundation. If Louima indeed had satanic powers with which to punish his ene-mies, why, some supporters argued, did he depend on a mostly white jury to give him justice? Wouldn't he have asked the evil spirits for the ultimate sacrifice?

32

Absence and Malice

✦

Policing Truants

What is the effect on a community's political influence when one quarter of the black men in some states cannot vote as a result of a felony conviction?

—*Race to Incarcerate*, Marc Mauer

AMID THE FUROR OVER THE DEADLY confrontational tactics of Operation Condor, high school truants became the next target of the Giuliani administration, seeking to boost arrest statistics. "African American and Latino parents are justifiably afraid for their children," asserted Deborah Small, director of public policy and community outreach at the Lindesmith Center, a leading drug policy research and advocacy group. "In the wake of the killing of Patrick Dorismond, the spotlight is on the policing policies of the NYPD, which is so focused on keeping arrest statistics high that it has taken to effecting pretext arrests of African American and Latino youths for offenses like truancy."

In addition to lurking in subway stations, Giuliani's police were being deployed outside some schools. And the outspoken public policy expert was worried that the police buildup would not be limited to high schools. "Officers have staked out areas in the vicinity of middle and high schools in 'high crime' areas," she pointed out. "Once the school day has begun, any young person hanging out on the street nearby without sufficient justification is subject to arrest as a truant. In recent months hundreds of minority youths have fallen prey to these tactics and have been swept up in the clutches of Operation Condor [officers] who are charged with one principal goal—keep up those arrest statistics."

According to Board of Education figures, on any given day about 121,000 youngsters—11 percent of the city's 1.1 million students—are absent from school. In 1999, the board disciplined 16,000 students at its truancy centers. The alleged upsurge in truancy arrests was linked to the undercover drug-sting initiative known as Operation Condor, which had netted more than 20,000 drug-related arrests. No NYPD or Board of Education spokespersons returned my persistent calls for comment. According to some students and parents, cops pounced on latecomers—even when the students seemed to be making an effort to get to their classes—and charged them with disorderly conduct or resisting arrest when they challenged stops and refused to hand over their ID cards.

That allegedly was what happened to Janell Boyd, the 17-year-old daughter of a black detective, when she and another student showed up late at Springfield High School in Queens on the morning of February 17, 2000. Shortly after nine o'clock, two officers sitting in a parked police van called out to Janell and her 14-year-old friend Tenyae, as they headed toward the entrance. The girls ignored the cops, who then jumped out of the van and ordered them to hand over their ID cards.

"What for?" Janell asked testily.

"You're late!" one of the cops retorted. Janell said she told the officer that her mother knew she'd be late, but he didn't buy it. She then argued that the doors to her school were still open. She and Tenyae could make it.

"Give me your ID card!" Janell remembered the officer demanding. When she flashed the card, the cop said the picture didn't look like her. She insisted it was. After ordering her to display the card so he could have a good look, he snatched it and started to write her up.

"What's your name?" Janell demanded. "What's your badge number?"

The officer identified himself but was silent as Janell and Tenyae kept asking why he was being so tough on them. Suddenly, the cop started "screaming in our faces, and spit got on us," Janell said.

"Move out the way!" the other officer shouted. The students refused, and according to Janell, he "pushed us out of the way and said that we pushed him." The cop told Janell she "had an attitude and was being rude." He tried to handcuff her. She resisted.

"Shut up or we're gonna throw you on the ground!" the cop allegedly barked. At that point, Janell said, she calmed down and asked to call her mother, but the cop refused—saying he was taking her to Central Booking. She then told the cop that her mother was a detective assigned to the 88th Precinct stationhouse in Brooklyn. The cop responded that if she showed him a PBA card (which was distributed to relatives and friends of police officers), he would believe her and let her go. Because Boyd did not have a PBA card, she was hauled off to the 113th

Precinct in Queens. "I was crying [because] the cops were treating me like I was a criminal," she recalled.

The arresting officer, Andrew Turano, had reached Detective Evi Boyd at home and told her that he was charging her daughter with disorderly conduct because she had an attitude. In a sworn complaint, Turano, a truant cop, claimed that at about 10 a.m.—when Janell was supposed to be attending classes—he saw her at the corner of 144th Avenue and Springfield Boulevard. According to the complaint, when he asked her for identification, she shouted, "Get the fuck away from me! I'm not getting in no fucking van." Turano added that Janell "did resist arrest by swinging her arms and punching."

Detective Boyd said Turano told her to get to the station house as fast as she could because a female lieutenant was pressuring him to process Janell's arrest at Central Booking. When Boyd, an 18-year veteran of the department, protested, saying that disorderly conduct was not a crime and Janell should not be taken to Central Booking, the officer told her that she, too, seemed to have an attitude. "He said that he had also charged her with resisting arrest," Boyd said, "and I said that you need a crime to charge resisting arrest."

At the station house, Turano told Boyd her daughter had been fingerprinted and assigned an arrest number and that, on orders of the lieutenant, Janell would be taken to Central Booking. A PBA delegate to whom Boyd complained shot back that Janell had an attitude and "gave them a hard time," but the lieutenant was willing to overlook that if Janell apologized. "I told him we would not apologize and that having an attitude was not a crime," Boyd recalled. Boyd demanded a meeting with the lieutenant, who claimed that her daughter had "some attitude" when she was brought in. "The lieutenant said that when asked questions, Janell did not answer right away and was rolling her eyes. She said Janell was disrespectful but never claimed that Janell was violent or used foul language."

Detective Boyd said the lieutenant then told her she would be allowed to see Janell—who was in a holding cell handcuffed to one of the bars—only if the girl showed remorse. "I asked what she meant by 'remorse.' I said my daughter is not a street kid. She is not used to being stopped and questioned by the police, handcuffed, detained, and arrested. I said this arrest would be very upsetting to her and frightening."

Finally, she recalled, the lieutenant had a change of heart and brought her daughter out. "Janell was crying, shaking, and telling me she was afraid of the cops who arrested her. She said that the officers had threatened her. I tried to comfort her and told her we would sort everything out. I then told her that she should not say anything more, and only answer questions that required her to give her name, address, and pedigree."

Detective Boyd's determination not to let her daughter further experience the rigors of the Giuliani-style criminal justice system paid off. The lieutenant said that because Boyd was a member of the department—"on the job"—Janell would be issued a desk-appearance ticket (DAT) and sent home. But the arresting officer hinted he would not let her off that easy. "He made the snide remark that I should let her go to Central Booking because the DAT could take several hours. At Central Booking she would be released more quickly." Six hours after she was arrested, Janell was issued a DAT and released in the custody of her mother.

The next day, Evi Boyd sat in her car near Janell's school observing her daughter's arresting officer and others as they confronted students who got off the school bus. "The officers appeared to ask for and receive ID cards from the students," Boyd claimed. "Although they did not put any of the students in the van, it looked like the officers held on to their ID cards. They went inside the school." After monitoring the cops' activities, Boyd and about five other parents met with the principal, who explained that it was Board of Education policy that a student be given a 10-minute grace period after classes officially began. Then the student was considered truant.

"He further said that if the student is going to be late, the student should walk with a note from a parent to show if stopped by the police," Boyd recalled. "Myself and the other parents never heard of such a policy. But the principal did agree with us that if a student—despite being late—is still making an effort to make it to school, that student should not be harassed by the police."

IN HIS STATE OF THE CITY ADDRESS IN JANUARY, Mayor Giuliani proposed an $18 million truancy-crackdown program. Under the plan—which the mayor said was designed to hold parents more accountable for their children's behavior—parents would pick up wayward students at 27 truancy centers across the city. Giuliani's proposal piggybacked on TRACK (Truancy Reduction Alliance to Contact Kids), a pilot program started by the Brooklyn D.A.'s office, the NYPD, and the Board of Education. "While wandering the streets unsupervised, truants naturally fall into petty criminal activity such as shoplifting, purse-snatching, and extortion of small sums from other children," TRACK's originators contended. "As many residences are vacant during school hours, truants have good opportunities for vandalism and burglary. More violent crimes are also committed; these are increasingly gang-related."

Offering some street-savvy advice, Deborah Small cautioned students who cut school not to hang out in public housing developments because cops were beefing up arrests for trespassing. She said the NYPD initiative worked like this: "Officers get lists from the Housing Authority with the names of registered tenants in buildings owned by the city. They then stake out the buildings, either in the lobby or just outside. They question individuals entering or leaving about whom they are visiting. If the person is not listed as a tenant or visiting someone listed as a tenant, that individual is then subject to arrest. Of course, once they are arrested and booked, if they should ever be involved with the police again—no matter what the reason—the prior arrest will be used to demonstrate their propensity to criminality, as was done in the Patrick Dorismond case."

33

Giuliani Storm Troopers

What about our humiliation, anguish, and mental stress? Why are we left to pick up the pieces?

—Charmaine Thornhill

AFTER HEAVILY ARMED IMMIGRATION OFFICERS forced their way into the Miami home of Elián González's relatives, Mayor Rudy Giuliani compared the INS officers to "storm troopers," saying he "couldn't imagine that something like this could happen in America." The suddenly civil libertarian mayor called the raid "unprecedented and unconscionable." Giuliani's statements provoked a strong response from an expert at the Lindesmith Center, a drug-policy institute, who noted that excessive use of force had been the hallmark of NYPD drug raids in homes.

"It's not just violent drug dealers who are targeted, but hundreds of thousands of Americans suspected of some involvement with drugs," said Ethan Nadelmann, founder and director of the Center. "The pictures we don't see are those of the tens of thousands of children exposed to paramilitary police tactics in their homes because some family member is a suspect."

Five cases, three in 1997, one in 1998, and the other in 2000, illustrate Nadelmann's point. In 1998, Sandra Soto of Brooklyn filed a $20 million lawsuit against the city, claiming that she and two of her four children—aged one and six—had been terrorized by cops who raided their apartment for drugs and guns by mistake. Attorney Susan Karten said that in June 1997, 15 narcotics detectives stormed Soto's apartment, dragged the nearly naked woman from her bed, and held a gun to her head, demanding to know where her stash of guns and drugs was. When her baby began screaming, Karten said, police refused to let Soto comfort the child. She added that while some detectives spent almost two hours ransacking the apartment, others interrogated the six-year-old, asking for information about Soto and her boyfriend. Karten said that when Soto asked the officers for a search warrant, they ordered her to "shut up."

The lawyer charged that after the cops realized they had the wrong apartment, they refused to apologize. Karten showed me photos of the ransacked apartment and a copy of the search warrant, which authorized the Brooklyn Narcotics SWAT Team to search Apartment 2M at 396 New Jersey Avenue for drugs and guns. The Soto family lived in Apartment 2L at that address. "You can't suspend the rights of minorities in the name of a drug crackdown," Karten told *United Press International*. She alleged that the NYPD blocked her attempts to obtain evidence that bolstered Soto's case. "They stonewalled our efforts and refused to turn over documents," Karten said.

In a similar, unrelated incident in 1998, Bronx narcotics cops mistakenly broke down the door of a wrong apartment and pumped 24 bullets into it after a terrified Ellis Elliot fired one shot at the officers when he thought he was being robbed. Elliot filed a multimillion-dollar lawsuit against the city. "The resort to such tactics in arresting nonviolent suspects, and more generally the growing practice of making the act of arrest as humiliating as possible, needs to be reversed," Nadelmann said.

ALONG 120TH AVENUE—A WIDE, tidy street in the South Ozone Park section of Queens lined with weather beaten maple trees and detached single-family three-bedroom homes—is a house well-known to some residents as a haven for gunrunners, drug dealers and "extreme fighting" pit bulls. But on March 21, 1997, police looking for a cache of guns burst into a different house, at 147-07 120th Avenue. In the words of one of the home owners, they "didn't find as much as a firecracker."

Officers from the Brooklyn North Street Crime Unit, acting on a tip from a "reliable" CF (confidential informant) had raided the wrong house. It was the first of two botched police raids of private homes in Queens and Brooklyn within 14 days. But the Giuliani administration's tight control of basic information makes it impossible to say conclusively how much higher the numbers are.

According to the department's own figures, police officers executed more than 5300 search warrants in 1996. These figures include more than 1,200 so-called "no-knocks," most of which were executed during raids for guns and drugs. "There is no breakdown on what was productive or what wasn't," claimed Marilyn Mode, the department's chief spokesperson.

In the March 21 raid, the confidential informant who told Officer Clifford Pacheco a sensational story about a gunrunning operation in Queens could be dubbed either blundering crime-watchdog of the month or a hoaxer like the character in the movie *Liar Liar.*

According to one law enforcement account, the informant told Officer Pacheco he would find a shipment of arms hidden in the boiler room in the basement of the house owned by Francisco and Charmaine Thornhill, West Indian immigrants who lived the American dream of homeownership.

The informant swore that he had been to the house before and gave Officer Pacheco a layout of the kitchen, next to which was an adjoining room with a pool table. In the driveway, he said, investigators also would find four cars and a vicious Rottweiler. The informant said he had observed the shipment of guns being delivered to the Thornhill residence, and warned Pacheco to act quickly because the contraband was supposed to be moved out on March 22.

Pacheco paraded his informant before Brooklyn Criminal Court Judge Lila Gold, who signed a search warrant at 5:10 or the morning of March 21. The Thornhills faced charges of conspiracy to possess and deal in illegal firearms, and long prison sentences if convicted.

The couple awoke that morning prepared for another uneventful day. Charmaine, then a 35-year-old native of Trinidad who emigrated from Canada in 1985, left early for her job as a hospital patient service clerk at Downstate Medical Center in Brooklyn. Francisco, who was 46, emigrated from Grenada in 1979 and ran the family's refrigeration and air-conditioning repair business from their home. He left shortly before noon with the couple's seven-year-old daughter to run an errand.

According to the account provided to the Thornhills by a member of the raiding party, between 1 and 2 p.m. the informant drove by with his handlers in an unmarked car and pointed out the house with the white vinyl shingles, yellow aluminum siding, and abutted skylight that made it look like a two-tier wedding cake. "Of course it was our house," Charmaine fumed. Francisco was returning home shortly after 2 p.m. when he ran into a roadblock that cordoned off his block between Sutphin Boulevard and 147th Street. The street was cluttered with ambulances, fire trucks, police cars, and about 50 heavily-armed uniformed as well as plainclothes officers who had guns strapped to their chests with Velcro strips.

"It was an army," recalled Francisco who lived on the block since 1986. "They came prepared to kill."

From a short distance on 147th Street, Francisco watched as the army marched in and out of his house. "That's my house," he protested after cops barred him from entering the secured area. He showed them his driver's license and was escorted begrudgingly to the house. Lying in a twisted heap on the front stoop was the Thornhill's stylized wrought-iron storm gate and their antique, wooden front door, smashed to pieces by the cops' battering ram.

An officer from the elite anticrime unit pulled Francisco to the side and told him they had a warrant to search for contraband.

"What contraband?" snapped Francisco, who did not have a criminal record.

"Anything like arms," the cop said coolly.

"We are not terrorists," Francisco said.

"Do you have a dog?"

"No," the homeowner replied.

"Five cars?"

Thornhill inventoried an old Chevy van and a Hyundai car that were moth-balled in his backyard. His wife owned a brown Mercury Sable and he drove the company vans, a Dodge Caravan and a Chevy. And although there was a refurbished Madison billiards table in the Thornhill's converted dining room, it still didn't add up. (In 1991, thieves broke into the house in broad daylight and moved out furniture appliances, and electronic equipment.)

"We have the wrong place," a cop he would later identify as Lieutenant Cantwell finally admitted. "You have a decent home," he reportedly told Francisco.

"We are sorry," interjected another high-ranking law-enforcement officer after his men had combed the basement for another 45 minutes, peered under beds, and ransacked closets.

"But who is going to fix my door?" Francisco balked. Lieutenant Cantwell, who left behind a copy of the warrant, told Francisco that the City Comptroller's Office would foot the bill for the damages.

Three days after the raid, Charmaine called the Street Crime Unit (which operated out of the 77th Precinct in Brooklyn) and spoke to Captain Barry Galfano, its commander. He told me that a confidential informant came into the Precinct at 4 a.m. on March 21 and that he had cut a deal with the D.A. Captain Galfano did not respond to my repeated requests for an interview. Charmaine accused police of accepting too readily the informant's claim. "Why didn't they set up a sting and catch everybody in the act; those coming, those going?" she asked Galfano, who, she said, did not answer.

"What about our humiliation, anguish, and mental stress? she continued. "Why are we left to pick up the pieces?" According to Charmaine, Galfano apologized effusively, but she was far from satisfied.

On March 31, after calling Galfano again to verify the registration number on a police report, Charmaine angrily inquired, 'What about the informant? What are you going to do with him?"

The cops allegedly changed their story.

"Between me and you, there was no informant, Mrs. Thornhill," Charmaine quoted Galfano as saying. "A guy came in and he was very upset. He said the person who had the shipment of guns had beat up his wife. I think the man was looking for revenge."

"My husband never beat up anybody's wife," Charmaine screamed. "I don t know how this guy could convince anybody that we had something to do with that."

Mode declined to comment on the officer's alleged statements. But she said Judge Gold had interrogated the informant thoroughly before signing the search warrant. "Something could have changed," Mode surmised. "Maybe the guns were diverted or maybe the guns didn't get there that day. Maybe they were there on Thursday and were already gone." Judge Gold did not return my phone calls.

ON APRIL FOOLS DAY, just as they had done in the Thornhill case, narcotics officers assigned to the Brooklyn district attorney's office appeared before Queens Supreme Court Justice James Starkey with an informant who had been vetted by the department, and applied for a search warrant to look for drugs at 226 Barbey Street in the East New York section of Brooklyn.

At 5:45 a.m. on April 2, cops stormed into the home of Jeremias and Ana Roman.

"Where is your bodega?" a cop asked Ana Roman, who along with her husband, a shipping clerk, and their three sons, one who was just nine years old, had been forced into a police van during the home invasion.

"They handcuffed us—all of us," Roman told the *New York Post*. "They kept us locked up for three hours [in the van]. We never put up a fight. We never saw a warrant. Everybody had a gun to their head." No drugs were found.

"We made a mistake," a cop reportedly told the family.

"That doesn't mean there wasn't narcotics there before," Mode said.

Can the informant's be charged with making false statements? "Not necessarily," Mode argued. "The NYPD felt they were reliable and the judges believed the probable cause."

But even Mode agreed that an informant's word was not a rubber stamp for a search warrant. (Around the time of the raid, the Supreme Court had ruled police do not have a blanket right to burst into a residence without knocking while serving a drug warrant, unless they face danger or fear that evidence may be destroyed.)

"Judges have said, 'I think you need more,'" Mode declared.

According to Mode, the department has stringent procedures for vetting confidential information brokers, as well as corroborating their information from other sources. "But I am not going to compromise the informants by saying what they are."

Sometimes an informant, usually a persistent felon seeking to have time shaved from a sentence, would plea bargain his way out by implicating people he suspected were lawbreakers. Asked if the informants in the Thornhill and Roman cases were bargaining criminals registered with the department or personally motivated crime busters, Mode refused to elaborate.

"It doesn't mean the informants showed bad faith," she said. "They went to the addresses and had negative results. All the proper procedures were followed," she insisted.

Despite the blunders, Mode said there would be no departmental review of procedures for vetting confidential informants. Norman Siegel, who represented a Queens family involved in a similar situation several years ago, said the raids were "a serious violation" of the Thornhills' and Romans' civil rights and constitutional guarantee against unreasonable search and seizure. "The NYPD had misinformation," asserted Siegel. "Their defense is that they got it from the informant, but the point is they still got it wrong. They are not immunized from the error."

A VIOLENT BANGING JOLTED SHAMEKA SMITH from her midday snooze on April 19, 2000. To the frightened 23-year-old onetime engineering major, it sounded like a roto-rooter snake being drilled into one of the day-glo orange steel doors in the Riverside Park Community Apartments, the sprawling high-rise at 3333 Broadway in upper Harlem where she lived. As smith was jarred awake, the bedlam seemed to be occurring right outside of the three-bedroom apartment on the 23rd floor that she shared with her grandmother, Viola. Her grandmother was not at home at the time. As Smith dashed toward her front door, it became clear that someone was using a power drill to rip into the bottom lock. And the banging was the sound of a battering ram crashing against the door.

"Who is it?" asked Smith, trying to quell a nauseating feeling. No one answered. She peered through the peephole and saw about 15 people—mostly white men—wearing what appeared to be bulletproof vests, scurrying about in the hallway.

"Who is it?" Smith demanded again.

"Police!" responded a chorus of voices.

Smith said the confusion left her dazed. Instead of opening the door, she ran back to her bedroom. "I had on a T-shirt and my panties," she recalled. "I was going back to my room to put on some shorts." But Smith didn't reach for her shorts. Instead, she grabbed a cordless phone and called her father, Kenneth Smith.

"Daddy! Daddy!" she screamed over the continuing racket at her now bulging and crumpling front door. "Somebody is trying to break in!"

"Who's trying to break in?" he asked.

"I don't know!" she cried. "I guess it's the police, and I don't know why they're trying to break down the door." She was hysterical.

"Cops?" her old man inquired. "Breaking in? For what?"

Suddenly the door swung open, and the intruders barged in with guns drawn, barking commands. They found Smith trembling in her bedroom, still pleading with her father to come to her apartment. Someone snatched the phone from Smith and threw it on the bed.

"Put your hands in the air!" he snarled. "Get on the floor!"

Only then did Smith believe that the men were cops. Four of them surrounded her, aiming their weapons at her menacingly. One stuck his 9mm Glock at the back of her head while another jammed the muzzle of his handgun in her back. The plainclothes cops wrenched Smith's arms behind her back, and ordered her to lie on the floor. "It was hard because I had cuffs on, so they pushed me down," she remembered. Smith lay face down, at times tossing her head, trying to see what was going on. At that point one of the cops, using a tactic adopted by SWAT teams to prevent suspects from observing controversial aspects of illegal searches, threw a bedspread over Smith's head.

"Shut up and lay down!" he yelled. "This is a drug bust!"

(Although absolutely no drugs were found during the raid, the NYPD, which rarely admits that it has gotten a bad tip and smashed down the wrong door, was combative in its response. "You know, there is no guarantee that there is going to be a recovery of any kind of material there," said Detective Walter Burnes, a police spokesman. "And we all know that materials—anything that could be put in a house—can easily be moved." Burnes insisted that Smith's apartment was the cops' target. "I'm telling you," he argued, "the apartment the search warrant was executed in is the apartment the search warrant was got for.")

Smith struggled on the floor like Houdini trying to escape from a body bag. The declaration that the cops had broken in to search for drugs resounded in her mind. "A drug bust? A drug bust? Where? What apartment are you looking for?"

Smith started crying. She was hoping it was a nightmare that soon would be over, if only she could wake up. Then the cops grabbed her from the floor, took her into the kitchen, and cuffed her to a chair. "I could hear them breaking things up, throwing the beds around, turning them upside down, going through the closets," she recalled. Smith said she tried to tell the cops she had no criminal record and that no drugs were being dealt out of her apartment.

"Shut up!" a cop shouted. "We have a warrant to search this apartment. There're drugs here!"

Another officer explained that an undercover cop had bought drugs from an individual selling out of Smith's apartment. The cop said the suspect wore a leather jacket with the initials "J.D." emblazoned on it. "I told him no one with that jacket lives here, but they just kept looking at me like I'm lying—like I'm trying to cover myself. They said the drugs were in a plastic bag, maybe it was weed or cocaine," Smith adds. "They never told me [what it was]."

(Detective Burnes told me, "It doesn't really matter what the police told [Smith]," adding that he would neither confirm nor deny the raiding party's story about the mysterious J.D. "That is information that has been gathered by the department, which we are not at liberty to [disclose]—information that is gathered in an undercover operation is not going to be revealed." Burnes also refused to say whether 3333 Broadway had been on the department's list of drug locations to watch. "I'm not gonna tell you about the location because you're trying to get into what we're doing in terms of our operation," he scoffed. "We're not gonna talk about that nor are we gonna thrash this out in the media.")

The cops ransacked the apartment. "I guess after they realized they wouldn't find anything, they got angry," Smith asserted. "They felt stupid because there were no drugs in here. And that's what I was trying to tell them point-blank when they came in." As Smith flailed about, she began to feel claustrophobic. In her tight T-shirt and silk underwear, she grew paranoid about sleazy cops ogling her body. "I wasn't properly dressed," she reflected.

Finally, a female cop asked Smith if there were some pants she could put on. But a male cop countered, "No, leave her the way she is!" The female cop persisted. "I think we should put something on her," she said. Eventually, she found Smith's shorts and slipped them on her. The cops continued to search the apartment. "They kept asking me the same question: 'Who lives here with you?'"

Smith continually responded: "Me and my grandmother stay here." (At one point she mouthed off, "Who's selling drugs? Me or my grandmother?")

After searching the apartment for two and a half hours, the cops gave up.

"Did you find anything?" Smith asked.

A cop told Smith the team had found a pair of brass knuckles, which Smith said belonged to an uncle who died in 1999. Having them constituted a felony. But the cops weren't interested in the brass knuckles. They threw them back like unwanted fish.

When Smith's father arrived, the police took him into a back room and showed him the warrant they had. He insisted that the cops had been given bogus information—that they had the wrong apartment. "Watch your daughter and who she hangs out with," one officer warned the father. "I think she is innocent, but somebody is selling drugs out of the apartment and she just doesn't know." Upon leaving the apartment, another officer asked Smith if she had any questions.

"Why?" she responded.

"Just cause!" was the gruff reply. The cops, Smith realized, were "being themselves—Rude."

According to Smith, when the cops uncuffed her, one said he was sorry. Later that night, Smith, her grandmother, her father, and an aunt tried to file a complaint at the 30th Precinct station house. "I saw the cops who were in my apartment, and I froze," Smith said. At the time, Smith planned to file a lawsuit to force the NYPD to review its procedures and pay for damages and civil rights violations. "If that young lady is interested in pursuing something, she [should not] do that through you," Burnes told me. "She needs to ... get the Department of Buildings [to] seal up her door [or] the police department would come and do that. *The Village Voice* doesn't do that. You're not the person that she needs to be talking with."

34

The Racist Factor

Consider the police officer who detains the young black man disembarking from an airplane because the officer believes that the young man's race is one of the signals indicating that he is probably engaged in drug trafficking. Consider, too, the lone pedestrian who perceives the blackness of an oncoming teenager as part of a reason to cross the street, shift the position of a handbag, or touch the grip of a hidden handgun.

—*Race, Crime, and the Law*, Randall Kennedy

ON THE AFTERNOON OF JUNE 14, 2000, as Al Sharpton prepared to introduce reporters to two new victims of a so-called "wild out" in Central Park, Bill O'Reilly, the alarmist host of the trash-TV talk show *The O'Reilly Factor* on the Fox News Channel, simultaneously began taping an interview about the incident for broadcast that evening. That interview would come to symbolize the exploitation of the hysteria and racial politics surrounding the alleged sex attacks.

It would not have mattered to O'Reilly that Sharpton—whom he had repeatedly criticized for not speaking out about crimes committed by blacks and Latinos—had rallied to the side of Josina Lawrence and Ashanna Cover, two New Jersey college students, both 21 and black, who claimed that attackers surrounded them, stripped off their blouses, and put their hands in their shorts. O'Reilly launched into another vicious attack on the favorite whipping boy of the extremist right, suggesting that the civil rights activist, who brought to the federal government's attention alleged abuses of blacks and Latinos by the NYPD in the wake of the Diallo shooting, was largely responsible for unleashing the assailants who moved about Central Park in, as one news report put it, "a wild, roving pack"—stripping, fondling, and robbing scores of girls and women.

It was as if O'Reilly had sensed that Sharpton would align himself only with those victims who charged that cops rebuffed them when they asked for help. At Sharpton's news conference, Lawrence and Cover said they planned to sue the city for $5 million each because police had failed to protect them. Sharpton, O'Reilly would imply, tied cops' hands.

"In the 'Impact' segment tonight," O'Reilly intoned in his set-up piece, "the tragedy of Amadou Diallo is now being compounded over and over. As I told you a few months ago, the pressure brought by Al Sharpton and others in the aftermath of the killing of Mr. Diallo has resulted in a less aggressive police force here in New York City, and other cities, like Los Angeles, and Louisville, Kentucky, [that] have similar problems. Now, you may have seen this terrible tape of dozens of thugs sexually assaulting young women in Central Park in broad daylight. Some of the victims say they pleaded with police to help, and some officers refused to do anything. NYPD officials deny it, but the rise in violent crime in the city after the Diallo shooting and the kind of terrible display in Central Park point to a far less aggressive police department. And where is Al Sharpton? Isn't he outraged over all this?"

O'Reilly's guest that evening was Eli Silverman, a professor of political science at John Jay College of Criminal Justice, who was hawking his book *NYPD Battles Crime: Innovative Strategies in Policing*. But for the most part, O'Reilly, whose phony "objectivity" highlighted the unfair and unbalanced reporting at Fox, tried to keep the subject on Sharpton.

"You know what ... you know what angers me?" fumed O'Reilly. "You have a demagogue like Al Sharpton who almost single-handedly, with the help of some Hollywood people like Susan Sarandon and other high-profile people—you have this man coming out selectively, in selective cases—and I feel bad for Amadou Diallo's family, believe me—putting pressure on the whole police department, and destroying aggressive policing in the city. And we see what is happening now."

Silverman initially refused to jump on O'Reilly's anti-Sharpton bandwagon, contending instead that there is a decline in morale among cops because "their pay is abysmally low."

O'Reilly went on to pander to white New Yorkers' fears that crime was on the rise once again in the city Rudy Giuliani had rescued from members of a suspect class. "[I]sn't it interesting that right after the Diallo situation, violent crime starts to rise?" he asked. "Murder's up 22 percent, the cabbies are getting knocked off like crazy, and this Central Park thing, in my opinion, never would have happened before the Amadou Diallo situation because most of the men involved in sexually assaulting these women in Central Park, in broad daylight, are minorities. They are minorities. And the cops surrounding the park knew something was going on, yet failed to stop it. Explain that to me."

To Silverman's credit, he corrected O'Reilly's trumped-up crime statistics, pointing out that homicides had gone up only "seven percent this [year] compared to the same [time] last year." O'Reilly's race-baiting quickly gave way to his yearning for the return of the Street Crime Unit, the rogue undercover force to which the four acquitted white cops who blew Diallo away in a barrage of 41 bullets were assigned. "[F]or people who don't live in New York, what they had was a unit called the Street Crime Unit, which were plainclothes guys who would go out and confront suspicious people in the streets, and pat them down for weapons …" he said. "That's gone. That's gone."

"Right," Silverman acknowledged.

"So the aggressive policing, which some people call racial profiling, all right, is over," lamented O'Reilly. "Now, how long did it take for the thugs to figure out that the streets are now a lot safer for them? What? About 15 minutes?"

The suspects in the Central Park attacks clearly had gotten under O'Reilly's skin. "[T]hat thing in Central Park bothers me," he sneered. "That thing bothers me."

"I think it's one of the worst events we've had in many years, and it destroys the hard work and the image of New York City and what people have done," Silverman chimed in. "What we need to do is get the police and the community on the same page …"

"That's never going to happen with guys like Al Sharpton, because he whips it up," O'Reilly declared. "Us against them. Us against them." Never mind that, Silverman argued, there were many untold stories about harmony between cops and people of color.

"I know there's good policemen," snorted O'Reilly. "Then why when Sharpton gets out there, as buffoonish and as demagoguish as he is—you know it and I know it—does he get such a big crowd?" Silverman maintained that "anyone who speaks very extremely will get attention by others and the media."

One New Yorker who may have watched *The O'Reilly Factor* wrote "very extremely" about the Central Park incident in the context of race, crime, and black activist politics. In an unsigned letter to me, Anonymous, who I assumed was white, had the suspects tried and convicted. "The Black and Hispanic men went on a rampage and attacked all of these women," the accuser charged. "Why isn't this a bias crime? Now there is outrage that the police did nothing. Could you imagine if the police tried to help? I'm sure there would be brutality claims then, and there would be more marches."

In analyzing the letter, I found that the only difference between Anonymous' extremist views surrounding the Central Park "rampage" and black criminality and Bill O'Reilly's was that the writer was overtly racist while O'Reilly presented himself as a reasonable racist. "Due to all of the utter nonsense, the racial climate in the United States will never change," Anonymous asserted. "Blacks will always be treated like criminals until they get their act together. When you behave like humans you will be treated like humans."

MY SIN WAS THAT I HAD DECLARED in the April 11 *Voice* that in the wake of recent shootings of unarmed black men, if a cop unjustifiably killed my son, I would kill that cop. Anonymous had seen me on *NY1* debating *New York Post* editorial writer Robert George, who was black. "You and the rest of the famous liberal minorities are outraged over the couple of incidents where black men were killed," wrote Anonymous. "Never mind that the numbers are much lower than when Dinkins the incompetent jerk was in charge. There was no outrage then. Why? Since you appeared on *NY1*, we have had an explosion of attacks on livery cab drivers. All of the victims were minorities, and all of the assailants were minorities. Why no outrage?

"The Wendy's massacre. All minorities again. No outrage? The two killers were black men. Is that really a surprise to anyone? If the police did not pick them up as quickly as they did, and they had to look for the killers, they would have had to stop black men and question them. How else would they find the killers? Just like in the other incidents, the police were looking for criminals based on solid descriptions. It is not their fault that the criminals are always black. Incidentally, the families of the victims now want the death penalty. I'm sure they did not want the death penalty before members of their families were killed."

Anonymous chose to ignore the unbridled outrage in black and Latino communities over the livery cabbie murders, the massacre at Wendy's, and the assaults in Central Park. It was Reverend Herbert Daughtry who appealed to blacks and Latinos in all of the cases not to protect those who were responsible. Daughtry condemned what occurred in Central Park as "inexcusable and savage," adding that the women should be supported and protected. But in the same breath, he blasted songs and rap music laced with profanity and references to anal intercourse and ejaculation. "We are saturated with sex songs and stimulants by rappers who sing of 'whores' and 'bitches,'" said the minister. "Most disturbing is when young ladies start shaking and grinding to their own humiliation. I believe that our young people see our hypocrisy and they manifest the extreme acts of that hypocrisy. Adults may not go wildin' in Central Park, but they will make a million dollars enticing a woman to take her clothes off in the movies."

Anonymous' opinions, which was shared by many whites in this city, only buttressed the argument that there was still a great racial divide on the vexing issue of criminal justice. "A football player [Reggie Lewis] and O.J. are free, yet poor Justin Volpe [the cop who confessed to beating and sodomizing Abner Louima] is in jail," noted Anonymous. "That is a crying shame. By the way, the Haitian community disregarded the family's plea for calm at the Dorismond funeral and they went on a rampage. Twenty-three cops were injured. If they cannot even respect the members of the Haitian community, how do you expect them to respect a white man in a uniform?"

In solidarity with police officers, who, as the *Post* reported, were saying they felt "caught in a catch-22 every day—damned if they do and damned if they don't take action," Anonymous signed off with a fantasy. "If I were a cop, I would carry an extra gun. I would kill every suspect and plant a gun on him. Hopefully they will start doing that and the thugs will get the message."

Among the white-hot rumors swirling about the Central Park fiasco was that Mayor Giuliani, who anticipated a new round of condemnation from the U.S. Commission on Civil Rights (which released its final report that June, accusing the NYPD of practicing racial profiling), had ordered the department not to harass revelers at the Puerto Rican Day Parade. The thinking among some Giuliani supporters was that in keeping with the "new Rudy" image, the mayor did not want to appear to be insensitive to an ethnic group that had been a target of his overly aggressive law-and-order campaigns.

But that's not how some hard-line critics of the Giuliani administration viewed such a scenario. They believed that the Central Park suspects walked into a classic Giuliani trap: The mayor, they hypothesized, lowered his guard in order to justify a crackdown and the reinstatement of some of his more ruthless policing tactics, shelved after the Diallo shooting. In any event, some Giuliani backers contended, Giuliani would reap political rewards for having devised a master plan plan to make Giuliani Land safe again. "Wanted" posters of the suspects, masquerading as banner headlines in the *Post* and the *Daily News*, more than hinted that such a plan should be immediately implemented.

35

Giuliani Declares War on Carnival

We have insisted and continue to insist that the uniqueness of the West Indian kar-na-val is one that has to be understood in its own cultural context. This is not a parade. We're not marching. This is not a festival. We don't put on cultural dances. This is kar-na-val.

—Rebel steelband advocate Dawad W. Philip

PLAYING TO FEARMONGERING BY BILL O'RILEY and his ilk, the Giuliani administration unleashed an army of police, firefighters, and building inspectors who consistently raided a Brooklyn lot occupied by steelband players and masquerade designers preparing for Carnival 2000. The crackdown coincided with borough-wide raids, which disrupted or completely shut down some pan yards, mas' camps, and backyard parties, and the Giuliani administration's ban on the sale of alcohol during the nation's largest ethnic gathering. "Why do we have to take medicine for someone else's fever?" asked an irate Dawad W. Philip, a steelband advocate. "If people at the Puerto Rican Day Parade got out of hand, why clamp down on us? That's not the way we behave."

One week before Carnival, a lawyer for the Pan Rebels, Metro, and Nu-Tones steel orchestras, acting on information obtained from Philip, filed a complaint in U.S. District Court in Brooklyn seeking to bar the NYPD from "proceeding with the threatened closure of their assembly and rehearsal location" at 660, 670, and 680 Parkside Avenue in Flatbush. According to the complaint, Philip and steelband captains Anthony Joseph and Anthony Trebuse allegedly had been "informed and instructed by high-ranking officers" that August 24 would be "the last night to practice and rehearse ... since [cops] would be closing down the block" between Rogers and Nostrand avenues. The complaint also named Mayor

Giuliani, newly appointed Police Commissioner Bernard Kerik, the fire department, and the Department of Buildings as defendants.

Although the Parkside Avenue steelband players and masqueraders had grown accustomed to sporadic harassment from the Giuliani administration over the years, it was an unusual collusion between cops and Klyn Properties Inc., owners of the lot, that sparked a 10-night, tension-riddled standoff with authorities. Shortly before the new spate of raids, the landlord—bypassing legal proceedings in which he might have obtained a warrant for eviction—filed an affidavit at the 71st Precinct stationhouse, complaining that the steelbands, which occupied three buildings on the lot rent free since 1994, were trespassing. Instead of marshals and sheriffs, the revelers suddenly had to contend with the stationhouse's private eviction squad. "The cops acted as surrogate marshals," recalled Philip. "Once the landlord made the call, it became convenient for the police. More than likely they viewed the nightly congestion on the block as a nuisance—these natives running wild—and ordered the place shut."

Stephan Gleich, the attorney who represented Klyn Properties, acknowledged that he filed the affidavit that "authorized the police to make arrests." He likened the occupation by the steelband players to "a criminal attack," adding, "It's no less than burglary." But Edward A. Roberts, the attorney who filed the federal complaint on behalf of the steelband players, questioned the relationship between Gleich and the 71st Precinct. "You can't get cops to evict people even when the marshal has a warrant," Roberts says with a smirk. "How can you get them to respond so quickly to an abandoned building without a court proceeding? Any rookie officer can walk across the street and say, 'Cut off the music. Everybody go home!' That's how bad it is. Totally whimsical."

For a short period, prior to the filing of the federal complaint, it seemed as though Giuliani would respond in favor of the steelband players. On August 22, as the mayor left a funeral service for the wife of Carlos Lezama, he was confronted by Brooklyn Assemblyman Nick Perry. "I informed him that there was a potential crisis situation on Parkside Avenue that needed some understanding and sensitivity in order to arrive at an appropriate solution," remembered Perry, who along with State Senator John Sampson, City Councilmember Una Clarke, and Congressman Major Owens had thwarted several illegal attempts to evict the steelbands.

Perry said that Giuliani "did not appear to be aware" of the controversy but promised to look into it and get back to him. As the deadline drew near for the cop-led eviction, Perry said he tried to contact Giuliani but was told that the mayor was traveling upstate. He was contacted later by Deputy Mayor Rudy

Washington, who is black and was the mayor's point man for Carnival. "Rudy called me with a solution that he apparently had thought up without taking the time to listen to the facts about the situation," Perry told me.

Washington put Perry in contact with an official at the New York City Housing Authority, who offered to relocate the steelbands to an abandoned warehouse in Long Island City. Perry recoiled at the "absurd suggestion," saying it was not a compromise he could take back to the steelband leaders. "I said, 'If you have any idea at all about what this is about, you'll know that if you take these guys to Long Island City you're effectively eliminating them from the carnival because they would never make it back to Brooklyn for Labor Day.'" The official's smug response was, essentially, "Take it or leave it."

"You guys aren't listening," Perry said he told the official.

"If you need shelter, that's all you can get," the official allegedly retorted.

That kind of dismissive attitude worried Philip, who had long suspected that the Giuliani administration, in cahoots with greedy developers and some ethnic groups, was instigating resentment of Carnival. "But why?" asked the dreadlocked activist, who was affiliated with Pan Rebels, a steelband vying for the championship in the 2000 Panorama competition. "Why would they resent us when we pump nearly $300 million into the city's economy every year?"

Among a series of changes for the September 4 Carnival was a ban on alcohol sales and consumption, and the requirement that the drivers of vehicles pulling floats pass a police department safety review. Further, the city mandated that the vehicles have a police officer riding in the passenger seat and required Carnival marshals to undergo training by the department. A mayoral task force said the safety measures were mandatory after two children and an adult were struck and killed in 1999 by floats.

But Philip, who also was editor in chief of *The Daily Challenge*, the city's only black daily newspaper, argued the ban on alcohol sales could hurt the event financially, since it was underwritten in part through alcohol sales during the five-day celebration that encompassed Carnival. Philip blasted the double standard that punished the West Indian Carnival but exempted the Festival of San Genaro in Little Italy from the alcohol prohibition. He added that West Indians unfairly were singled out as the city continued its crackdown on drunken mobs at parades. "[W]hy would you give preferential treatment to organizers of the Feast of San Genaro to sell liquor?" Philip asked.

Comparing Carnival under the Koch administration to how it was being treated by the Giuliani regime, Philip asserted that "Koch comes across as benevolent in light of what we're dealing with now to keep this culture alive." This was not a controversial claim; Philip was not a reckless blabbermouth. He had devoted his life to promoting tolerance of a culture that some in the Giuliani administration regarded as nothing more than the annoying din of "bottle and spoon" and steel drums.

That was the ignorance a phalanx of cops from the 71st Precinct might have been armed with when they swooped down on the Parkside Avenue steelband players at about 8 p.m. on August 16. According to the players' complaint, the raid occurred while they were "assembled and assiduously engaged in the practice and rehearsal of the art form of steelband music." When the players demanded to see a warrant, one cop allegedly replied, "You are being evicted because we are police officers and we say so. You must leave or you will be arrested." The players watched helplessly as the cops removed their expensive instruments, dumped them on the sidewalk, and padlocked the premises.

Philip arrived as police were taking Metro Steel Orchestra captain Anthony Joseph away in handcuffs. He contacted Assemblyman Perry, and they went to the 71st Precinct stationhouse, where Joseph was booked and charged with criminal trespassing. Like attorney Roberts, Perry felt it was inappropriate for the police to act as the landlord's enforcer. The cops confirmed they had an affidavit from Gleich. Said Perry: "So I asked the lieutenant, 'If I have tenants I need to get rid of, should I just sign an affidavit and you'd come and evict them?'" The cops were no swayed by that reasoning. A law-enforcement source said cops targeted Joseph because Gleich had accused him of impersonating the landlord and collecting money from the steelbands and other businesses who had illegally set up shop on the property. Gleich denied he knew Joseph.

"He is a liar," said Philip. "Stephan Gleich had a relationship with Tony Joseph for almost six years. Apparently, their relationship soured. What exactly happened when Tony and the landlord fell out, I'm not clear, but what I do know is that all the bands have suffered."

The next day—just as a judge was hearing the charges against Joseph—Philip, Perry, and two other concerned West Indian Americans were meeting with Joseph Fox, commander of patrol borough Brooklyn South, and other high-ranking officers at Perry's district office. The upshot of the meeting was that Fox would work to put an end to the "heavy-handed police action," both Philip and Perry recalled. After the meeting, Philip went back to Parkside Avenue. He was shocked to see four high-ranking officers from the 71st Precinct poised to eject the players from the sidewalk. "I mean, they're angry, in your face," he remembered.

Philip said he told the cops about his meeting with Chief Fox and advised them to consult him about changes in tactics that were being considered. "They were ready to go into gestapo mode," he charged. "One of them told me it doesn't matter who I talked to because tomorrow morning the buildings department was coming to shut this place down." Philip raced to Una Clarke's office. "While I was there, one of the guys called me and said the fire department was trying to close us down," he said. "Every time we tried to plug a hole, somebody opened one." Philip talked with a ranking firefighter and passed him on to a furious Clarke.

"I just opened your new firehouse," Clarke reminded the firefighter. Suddenly, he said, "We don't see a fire," and ordered his men to pull back. With elected officials like Clarke, Perry, Sampson, and Owens applying pressure, the steelband players were allowed back into the buildings temporarily.

On August 18, just as the cops promised, Department of Buildings inspector Anthony Carbone showed up at the premises. In the presence of the police, Carbone declared 670 Parkside Avenue "hazardous" due to a "failure to maintain [the] building." He found that the "roof joists at various locations [were] cracked and water-rotted." The roof itself was "collapsed in several locations." In his summons, Carbone recommended that the steelband players "make conditions safe immediately" and "upon completion [they were to] submit a letter of stability from a professional engineer." Despite the violations, Carbone declared that the building "essentially" was structurally sound, according to the players' complaint.

"Unfortunately for us, when the inspector came it was raining and the roof was indeed leaking," said Philip. "He gave us some time to pull out the instruments and then told the police to close us down. It would have been that or the instruments would be locked up in the building." Later that evening, a crew of building inspectors returned in the company of Chief Fox. The inspectors ordered the buildings vacated and again locked out the players.

"We brought in an engineer but then the landlord changed his rules," Philip charged. "He began to ask for rent, repairs, and liability insurance. Then he said he didn't want any activity in the building. He told me, 'We need our building.' He stacked the deck to make it impossible for us to do repairs." On August 21, the sanitation department hit the players with a $250 summons for having "steelband floats, steel drums, [and] wooden platforms … completely blocking [the] sidewalk." Said Philip, "We received at least three more citations."

PART XI
Killer Cop Excuses
(2001)

for
Annmarie Sookoo & the girls, Akilah, Crystal, and Cherise

36

"Death Reflex"

[W]ith my left hand, I grabbed his hair to try to get him out from under the car. I pulled, he pulled back. I pulled him again. I got him out of the car ... up to his shoulders. He pulled back again the third time; that's when I grabbed him with my right hand. I grabbed his hair and I pulled him back. I had him about halfway out. He pulled back, and that's when I heard a pop.

—From the deposition of police officer Jaime Palermo, April 19, 2001

[Police officer Lawrence] Ursitti stated that based on accidental discharge reports, which he has occasion to review as part of his duties, the most dangerous and accident-prone situations occur when an officer is in close contact with a suspect. In the close-combat course offered by his unit, officers are taught to beware of unholstering their weapon in close-contact situations because pulling on a suspect with the free hand produces a grip reflex in the gun hand to make a fist, creating a danger of accidental discharge.

—Josefina Martinez, NYPD assistant deputy commissioner of trials, after the departmental trial of police officer Jaime Palermo, July 6, 2000

ONCE AGAIN, THE NEW YORK POLICE DEPARTMENT had proven that cops should not police cops. Once again, at a sham trial, the NYPD had come up with a shameful hypothesis—the "grip reflex"—to explain how one of its so-called "Finest" could justifiably gun down an unarmed black man he found hiding under a car. Once again, it had sanctioned the notion among some white cops enforcing Giuliani law that black blood was cheap.

In July 2000, after a one-day departmental trial, Josefina Martinez, the assistant deputy commissioner of trials, ruled that police officer Jaime Palermo "did negligently and/or carelessly discharge his service firearm," resulting in the 1996 fatal shooting of Steve Excell, a devout Rasta. The punishment, Martinez concluded, fits the crime. Palermo lost 30 vacation days, was "retrained," given his gun back, and, according to one irate law-enforcement source, was "somewhere in the city policing the 'hood." Sharon Excell, the victim's widow, sued the NYPD and Palermo in a wrongful-death action that once again attempted to hold Palermo and the force behind him responsible.

But Martinez had crafted the ultimate excuse for Palermo's deadly behavior. "I realize that [Palermo] was involved in a fast-moving situation and that the period of time between each of his attempts to physically extricate the suspect was less than a few seconds," she wrote. "I am likewise cognizant of the ease with which one can evaluate the facts of an event after it has unfolded and I recognize that [Palermo], in the heat of the moment, did not have this luxury."

Sharon Excell did not have the luxury of explaining the situation to the eight officers who were summoned to her home in Jamaica, Queens, in the early morning hours of June 19, 1996. According to Martinez's summary of the trial, the cops, including Palermo, found Sharon hysterical and screaming. She told Sergeant Timothy Curley of the 103rd Precinct that she "had been beaten with an electrical cord" by her husband. She showed the officers "the marks on her back from the beating and told them that her husband would kill her if they left."

Curley and the contingent of cops searched the apartment "room by room" until one officer discovered that Steve Excell had "fled" through a closet staircase leading to the roof. Curley, Palermo, and another cop, Edward Monahan, bolted out the front door where Curley spotted the dreadlocks climbing down a tree and then a fence onto the sidewalk. Excell sprinted along 90th Avenue, heading toward Jamaica Avenue. Palermo led the chase. "By the time they reached Jamaica Avenue, about two blocks away, they had lost sight of the suspect," Martinez wrote. "Curley and Monahan turned left on Jamaica and walked toward a small grocery store.... [Palermo] walked into the street and approached a lone car parked near the front of the store."

During a deposition at the Greenwich Village office of attorney Ron Kuby, who was representing the Excell family, Palermo described in grim detail how he snuffed out Steve Excell's life:

> I saw a white car, like in the middle of the block, and I just walked up to it and, still looking into the doorways of the buildings, I stopped in front of the driver's side door and just stood there. As I was looking into the doorways of the buildings, for no apparent reason, I just ended up looking down on the ground and I saw his hair sticking out from under the car. So immediately after that, I mean that split second, right there, I kind of froze and maybe a second or two, that's when I stepped back, withdrew my weapon, pointed it at

the direction of where I saw the hair and yelled at him repeatedly, "Police, let me see your hands! Let me see your hands! Come out from under the car!" I said it at least three times, very loud. He didn't move. At that point, with my left hand, I grabbed his hair to try to get him from under the car. I pulled, he pulled back. I pulled him again. I got him out of the car ... up to his shoulders. He pulled back again the third time; that's when I grabbed him with my right hand. I grabbed his hair and I pulled him back. I had him about halfway out. He pulled back, and that's when I heard a pop.

At that point, I dropped him, and I thought he fired a weapon. So I told him, "Let me see your hands! Let me see your hands!" 'Cause I still couldn't see his hands. I kept yelling at him, "Let me see your hands! Let me see your hands!" He wouldn't move. So at that time, I holstered my weapon and I straddled him. As he was laying down, face down, I stepped over him and kept telling him [to] put his hand behind his back, and that's when I saw his right hand next to his head, and it had a little bit of blood on his hand. At that point, I thought I shot him in the hand but he still wouldn't move. So at that point, I went over and I moved his head and that's when his hair parted and I saw a hole in the back of his head. Right then and there, I knew that my gun went off. Right there. All I can remember is the sergeant and the other officer were standing to my right, they were saying something but I couldn't hear what they were saying and I just couldn't breathe.

At Jaime Palermo's departmental trial, Timothy Curley, Martinez's report noted, testified that as he approached the store, "he did not hear" Palermo say anything from where he was, about 15 feet away on the street side of the car. Then Curley heard a gunshot.

Martinez stated:

Curley went around the car to find [Palermo] bent over, shaking and pale. Curley saw the suspect lying face down, the lower half of his body under the car. He did not see any blood on the suspect's body. The suspect was handcuffed, and [Palermo] was immediately taken to the hospital by another officer. An ambulance arrived for the suspect in two to three minutes.

The department called Police Officer Lawrence Ursitti, a 19-year veteran and a master firearms instructor. Martinez wrote:

Ursitti testified that as a general practice, when apprehending a suspect who has hidden, the first thing an officer should do is get behind cover and command the suspect to do something: 'Stop! Come out! Show hands! Turn around!' As the suspect is complying, the apprehending officer should call for backup. If the suspect refuses to emerge after backup has arrived, and does not present an immediate threat to anyone, the officers should use tools such as pepper spray, dogs, or water cannons to assist in the extrication.

Ursitti, however, said that he knew of "no lesson plan" that instructed cops how to extract a suspect from under a car. That is when he advanced the "grip reflex" theory. Martinez wrote:

> Ursitti stated that based on accidental discharge reports, which he has occasion to review as part of his duties, the most dangerous and accident-prone situations occur when an officer is in close contact with a suspect. In the close-combat course offered by his unit, officers are taught to beware of unholstering their weapon in close-contact situations because pulling on a suspect with the free hand produces a grip reflex in the gun hand to make a fist, creating a danger of accidental discharge. In addition, unholstering a weapon in close proximity to a perpetrator alerts him of the weapon's exact location and increases the likelihood that he will attempt to take it away.

Should an officer, who was not in danger, put his finger on the trigger after drawing his gun? According to Martinez:

> Ursitti also stated that he was unaware of any tactical training instruction that an officer should have his or her finger on the trigger when the gun is drawn and the officer is within six feet of a suspect. He noted, however, that the propriety of this action is not based merely on distance but on the individual circumstances of each case.

Cross-examined by Mitchell Garber, Palermo's attorney, Ursitti disclosed that his only preparation for testimony consisted of speaking with the department advocate, the firearms-range instructor who testified before the grand jury, and reading a report about the incident, which, according to Martinez, "he found to be vague." Ursitti also never talked to Palermo or read a transcript of Palermo's official departmental interview.

Ursitti cracked.

But was he supposed to?

Prior to Ursitti's testimony, cops argued among themselves whether Palermo had run afoul of the guidelines.

In a January 1997 report, before an investigation into the shooting could be concluded, Captain Kevin Sheerin, commanding officer of the Queens South inspections unit, offered that Palermo had not violated department guidelines. But one month later, the Patrol Borough Queens South Firearms Discharge

Review Board found "that the accidental discharge" indeed was a violation and "recommended additional firearms instructions [and] retraining in tactics on apprehending a perpetrator."

"Ursitti admitted that, when he testified as to procedures for apprehending a suspect, he was speaking to a general hypothetical and not necessarily the specifics of the incident at issue," Martinez wrote.

Suddenly, the expert seemed to change his opinion about police procedure gone bad. "Given details of the assault and suspect's flight, Ursitti opined that the pursuing officers were in danger," according to Martinez. "He had not been told prior to his testimony that the fleeing suspect in the incident at issue had ingested marijuana on the night of the incident. He stated that tactics instruction is meant to give guidance rather than mandates because of unforeseen variables in situations."

In her "findings and analysis," Martinez set forth every reason why Jaime Palermo should have been thrown out of the force. She argued:

> I am further persuaded by the fact that [Palermo] had several opportunities to call for backup at points in time in which one would expect a reasonable, clear minded person to do so. Even if he initially believed that he could handle the suspect's apprehension alone, the latter's noncompliance to his repeated orders should have related a signal of at least potential difficulties which dictated a call for assistance. Thereafter, with the suspect's resistance to each of [Palermo's] next two attempts to extricate him by pulling his hair, [Palermo] became aware of information that the suspect was not going to go peacefully, which should reasonably have alerted him to the need to call for assistance. I note that this was not a situation in which [Palermo] had no sense of when or how backup would arrive.

Martinez pointed out that Palermo was aware that Sergeant Timothy Curley and Officer Edward Monahan were already nearby:

> Simply put, common sense dictates, given the circumstances, that the call for assistance should have been made. Moreover, [Palermo's] actions placed him, the suspect, and other officers, pedestrians, and passing motorists in harm's way. Not having a view of the suspect's hands, [Palermo] risked the former having shot or stabbed him as he stood close to the vehicle. Second, by holding the gun in such close proximity to the suspect whose hands he still could not see, [Palermo] risked an attempt by the suspect to remove the gun from him. Finally, the motion of pulling a suspect by the hair necessarily requires the making of a fist. In using the hand that is holding your weapon to make this motion, an accidental discharge was foreseeable. I note that [Palermo's]

firearm was found to be operable when tested shortly after the incident occurred and that an inspection of the weapon by the Firearms and Tactics Section revealed that no defects were found, all factory installed safeties were in place and working properly, and the weapon was found to meet all Department and factory specifications.

In concluding her recommendation that Palermo not be fired, Martinez contended that "his testimonial demeanor demonstrated that he is genuinely remorseful and places value on human life," adding that since the shooting Palermo had "done a better than average job." But could the public ever again trust Palermo with a gun?

"Although some penalty is appropriate to apprise [Palermo] of the importance of following the dictates of the Department's tactical training, I have no basis on which to conclude that [Palermo] is no longer qualified to carry out the duties of a police officer," Martinez ruled. "I have considered the possibility of placing [Palermo] on dismissal probation. However, given the fact that he continued to carry out patrol duties while remaining on full-duty status in the nearly four years since this incident occurred, such a penalty would serve no realistic purpose."

On August 18, 2000, then police commissioner Howard Safir (Giuliani had appointed Bernard Kerik after Safir resigned), who was under fire for failing to corral trigger-happy cops, rubber-stamped Martinez's recommendation.

37

Fall Guy

We believe that Curtis was beaten before he either fell or was pushed off the roof....
When I saw the pictures I felt he was beaten. He looked like someone who was banged
up. His face was swollen and his nose looked dislocated. Was this all from the fall?

—Pamela Jacobs, aunt of alleged police brutality victim Curtis Harmon

As the men were being questioned, one of them fled. The officers pursued. He ran up
the stairs. They followed but lost sight of him. When they get to the roof, they don't see
him. As they are searching the roof for him, they see a hand hanging off the side of the
building. Then he slipped and he went down, falling to the courtyard below.

—NYPD spokesperson Tom Antenen

IN JUNE 2001, THE INTERNAL AFFAIRS BUREAU of the NYPD and the
Civilian Complaint Review Board launched separate investigations into the
alleged death in police custody of a mildly retarded black man. The family of
Curtis Harmon Jr. had challenged a police claim that the 35-year-old Harmon
"slipped" and fell off a building on May 22 after he ran from cops. Police were
investigating a report about a stabbing in the University Heights section of the
Bronx. The medical examiner classified Harmon's death as an accident due to a
"fall from [a] height while fleeing police."

"I feel in my heart that he was beaten by the cops," said Pamela Jacobs, one of
Harmon's aunts, who was a registered nurse at New York Hospital in Queens.
"We need to know the truth about what happened on that roof. The police chase
after someone who just drops off a roof? I don't get it. How did he slip?"

According to Jacobs, an unidentified cop at the 46th Precinct station house
seemed to have all the answers, but told her family "next to nothing" about an
investigation that had been conducted. The day after Harmon died, said Jacobs,
who was a spokesperson for the family, two relatives went to the station house,

demanding an explanation. She said the officer read from a report. "He said the cops had received a report of a stabbing, and as two officers were walking past a building, one man ran into the building," Jacobs claimed. "He said the cops chased the man, who ran up several flights of stairs. It was raining. It was slippery. The man fell five stories and died of his injuries. End of story."

Jacobs felt uneasy about the police version setting forth such an abrupt end to her nephew's life. She believed that the cops had the missing chapters with all the gory details, and she couldn't—at least not yet—let them close the book. Her persistence finally prompted a phone call from a 46th Precinct cop identified only as Detective Tierney. She said he invited the family to a meeting at the station house, but she insisted that he tell her on the phone how Harmon died. Tierney reportedly told Jacobs that Harmon's death was "an unfortunate accident" and apologized on behalf of the NYPD. "He also read from a report; but one thing stuck in my mind," she recalled. "The EMS states that one of his arms was broken 'seemingly by a baseball bat.'"

She said that Tierney refused to divulge the names of the officers involved in the fatal chase. And when she asked if the cops were black or white, he allegedly replied, "Right now, it does not matter. We have investigated it, and it is just an unfortunate accident." When the detective asked Jacobs if Harmon wore dentures, she told him she wasn't sure. But Jacobs recalled an unnerving conversation she had with two alleged witnesses. They told her that after authorities left the scene they found several bloodied teeth on the roof. "We believe that Curtis was beaten before he either fell or was pushed off the roof," Jacobs said. I made several unsuccessful attempts to contact Detective Tierney. In fact, a detective at the station house refused to confirm that there was a Detective Tierney assigned there. For that kind of information, he scoffed, "you will have to go through channels."

Initially, according to the family, police classified Harmon as a John Doe but later matched his fingerprints with a set they had on file from a turnstile-jumping offense when he was a teenager. Investigators then went to Rikers Island, where Harmon's brother, Gregory, was being held, showed him a medical examiner's photo of a bloated and bloodied face, and asked him to make a positive ID. "When I saw the pictures I felt he was beaten," said Jacobs. "He looked like someone who was banged up. His face was swollen and his nose looked dislocated. Was this all from the fall?"

Harmon's family questioned the police theory that Harmon may have gotten into a fight with someone before fleeing from the cops. Jacobs claimed that a man told them that he was "hanging out" with Harmon when the cops approached, and Harmon had not been fighting. "I don't know if he was really involved in a fight before he died," said Jacobs, sobbing. "But how was his arm broken if it wasn't as a result of the so-called 'fall?' People are telling us that he wasn't in a fight."

On May 31, Jacobs filed a grievance with the CCRB. She said she was later contacted by Lieutenant Ray Daniels of the NYPD's Internal Affairs division, who told her he was looking into the circumstances surrounding her nephew's alleged death in police custody. Jacobs said her family was perplexed by Harmon's violent end. She described the son of a deceased Panamanian immigrant and U.S.-born father as a "simple-minded, gentle man" who held down a steady job as a security guard at a Duane Reade pharmacy in Brooklyn. "Uncle Butch" or "Butchy Boy," as some called Harmon, was "very muscular and strong when he was young," according to an obituary. This "quiet and humble person," who was "very easygoing and willing to help in any way he could," played high school football.

"Although he never married or had any kids, he would have been a great husband and father," the obituary stated. "He loved kids and was very good with them. His favorite pastime was television and taking his nieces and nephews to the movies."

Police maintained there was no foul play in Harmon's death. "The deceased fell in an attempt to elude police personnel," insisted NYPD spokesperson Tom Antenen. He said three cops responded to an anonymous call about a stabbing in a fight involving three men at 1715 Walton Avenue. But the officers only found two men in the lobby of the building. "As the men were being questioned, one of them fled," Antenen claimed. "The officers pursued. He ran up the stairs. They followed but lost sight of him. When they get to the roof, they don't see him. As they are searching the roof for him, they see a hand hanging off the side of the building. Then he slipped and he went down, falling to the courtyard below."

Antenen said that at the time of the chase "it was raining steadily," implying that inclement weather may have contributed to the fall. He would neither confirm nor deny a claim by a law-enforcement source that Harmon ran because he "had a small quantity of marijuana on him." He refused to name the officers. Ellen Borakove, a spokesperson for the medical examiner, said an autopsy concluded that Harmon died of "multiple fractures and visceral injuries due to blunt impact to head, torso, and extremities." Antenen could not ascertain whether the report of a stabbing was accurate, adding that the investigation by Internal Affairs "is routine."

What was routine about this "accident" was that another unarmed black man had died under suspicious circumstances. And again, the police made the victim the fall guy. "All Detective Tierney kept telling me is that the police were sorry for what happened," said Pamela Jacobs. "Sorry for what? Sorry won't bring him back."

38

"I Thought He Had A Gun"

'I saw the glint of metal' is the easiest, most common set up in the world. If you don't know whether or not the person has a gun then you can't shoot him. That's just common sense. Saying, 'I thought it was a gun' is the cousin and often the replacement of 'the gun went off by accident.' A police officer is trained and must be trained to know the difference between a gun, a set of keys, a package of cigarettes, a hand in the pocket, a penis, or, for Christ's sake, a candy bar.

—An NYPD Law Enforcement Source

IT LOOKED GOOD ON PAPER: "Do not be a victim of the 'SYMBOLIC OPPONENT SYNDROME,'" the NYPD urged in its guidelines regarding the use of deadly force by undercover officers, defining that syndrome as a "preconceived notion that places suspects into a 'BAD GUY' category because of race, nationality, grooming, or mode of dress." The guidelines directed officers not to "reach any definite conclusions that may lead to irreversible police action because of a suspect's appearance. Looks can be deceiving and should not form the basis for action."

But on the streets of Harlem, Flatbush, Bedford-Stuyvesant, East New York, and Canarsie, the only guideline concerning black male suspects was: When in doubt, shoot 'em.

William Whitfield, an unarmed 22-year-old black man who was gunned down on Christmas Day 1997 by a white cop, was "a victim of the 'symbolic opponent syndrome'"—triggered when police responding to a radio call of a rooftop sniper in a Canarsie public housing project were alerted that "a black man was crossing the street."

"What's disturbing about that is that there was no description: height, weight, type of hair, shade of black man—nothing," a high-ranking law enforcement source close to the investigation into the shooting told me. "He [Whitfield's shooter] automatically put the kid into a bad guy category because he was black."

Although many details of the shooting remained unclear, Officer Michael Davitt was among a backup team of cops from the Brooklyn South Task Force responding to a report of a domestic dispute. They began to search the area around the housing project after hearing gunshots nearby. According to one report, Davitt and his partner Michael Dugan saw Whitfield use a pay telephone then run from the scene. Sources told the *New York Post* that "cops believed Whitfield might be the rooftop sniper because they saw him running at full speed past them with a long dark object up his sleeve that appeared to be a gun barrel." An EMS ambulance driver passing by claimed to have rolled down his window and heard Davitt shout, "Stop!" to which Whitfield replied, "Not today," and sprinted into the Milky Way supermarket at 1669 Ralph Avenue.

"Drop it! Drop it! Drop it! Drop it!" Davitt repeatedly ordered Whitfield after Whitfield hid behind an aisle of groceries in the back of the supermarket, "a close friend of the officer," told the *Post.*

"Show us your hands! Show us your hands!" another cop allegedly demanded as customers cowered on the floor.

According to the account provided by Davitt's friend, "Whitfield suddenly emerged clutching something in his hand that Davitt feared was a gun. The veteran officer then fired one shot from his 15-round Glock service revolver" point blank into Whitfield's chest. No gun was found.

In fact, Whitfield was carrying a leather strap with a set of keys. Police said that might have been mistaken for a gun.

"'I saw the glint of metal' is the easiest, most common set up in the world," my law-enforcement source said. "If you don't know whether or not the person has a gun then you can't shoot him. That's just common sense." Saying, 'I thought it was a gun' is the cousin and often the replacement of 'the gun went off by accident,'" my source added. "A police officer is trained and must be trained to know the difference between a gun, a set of keys, a package of cigarettes, a hand in the pocket, a penis, or, for Christ's sake, a candy bar."

That last reference involved one of the more outrageous examples of renegade law enforcement tactics applied to black men in New York.

On November 6, 1997, an undercover federal agent shot 17-year-old Andre Burgess after apparently mistaking the Three Musketeers candy bar in his hand for a gun. Burgess, was walking down 138th Street in the Laurelton section of Queens at about 7 P.M. chomping on the confectionary when he passed a car full of undercover law enforcement officers who were hunting for a drug dealer suspected of killing a Customs agent.

One of the marshals reportedly mistook the silver wrapper of the candy bar for a pistol. "U.S. Marshal! Drop the gun!" the marshal yelled, jumping out of the car and pulling his gun. He shot Burgess once in the thigh and handcuffed him.

"I'm laying there, bleeding, waiting to go the hospital, and he's shaking hands with the other cops, or agents, or whatever they were," Burgess later recalled. "He asked one of them, 'Don't I know you from some other case?' And I'm still lying there." The teenager turned out to be the goaltender and captain on the Hillcrest High School soccer team.

Shootings of black suspects by police—who mistook an object a suspect was carrying for a gun or that police believed that the suspect was reaching for one—was, as Kafka put it, "a common experience, resulting in a common confusion."

These incidents include:

- The April 6, 1997 killing of 16-year-old Kevin Cedeno.

- The January, 20, 1996 killing of Leonard Lawton. (Police Officer Francisco Vargas shot the 24-year-old Lawton once in the head while looking for armed robbery suspects in the Polo Grounds housing project in Harlem.) Prosecutors said police had confronted a group of black men who were possible suspects and that the men ran away. Vargas caught one man and was handcuffing him when Lawton suddenly appeared running toward Vargas and "reaching toward his belt," prosecutors said. Lawton reportedly fit the description of a man who allegedly pulled a .38-caliber gun in the robbery. Vargas ordered Lawton to stop and when he believed Lawton was reaching for a gun he shot him. Relatives and friends charged that Vargas shot Lawton, an aspiring rap and rhythm and blues songwriter, "in cold blood." One witness told the *Amsterdam News* that Vargas, who was not involved in the robbery, had ordered Lawton to leave the scene, then demanded him to walk toward him. Suddenly Vargas yelled, "If you move, I'll shoot you," according to the witness. A Manhattan grand jury refused to indict Vargas partly on grounds that 23 witnesses offered conflicting accounts of what happened.

- The June 13, 1996 killing of Aswon Watson.

- The February 4, 1999 killing of Amadou Diallo.

There seemed to be no limit to the excuses a jury would buy when the victim was a black man and the perp was a cop. As far back as 1974, sociologist Kenneth

Clark began to take notice of police shooting cases that were filled with incredible stories cops had concocted in their attempt to get away with murder. Among the cases Clark cited:

- November 28, 1965: George Foley (race not stated), about 18, shot dead by Patrolman Octavio Alvarez (race not stated) after chase on foot, following Foley's failure to stop after a traffic violation in the Bronx. The youth allegedly came toward the patrolman with a hand in one pocket.

- September 7, 1971: Lawrence Blaylock (black), 16, shot dead by Nassau County Patrolman Frank Parisi (white) after chase in stolen auto. Police say Parisi shot Blaylock after youth whirled around as if he was about to shoot; youth was unarmed.

- December 5, 1971: Jerome Good (race not stated), 18, was shot and killed in the Bronx by Patrolmen Thomas Ward (race not stated), and Enrico Caponi (race not stated) after seen running from a gas station where an attendant had been robbed; Good's gun turned out to be a toy pistol.

- August 15, 1972: Ricky Bodden (black), was shot and killed by Patrolman Francis P. Ortolano (white) on Staten Island after Bodden allegedly turned toward the patrolman in a "crouching position" and appeared armed and dangerous. The shooting followed a chase in an allegedly stolen auto and an escape attempt on foot.

- March 29, 1973: Philip Sadler (black), 17, shot dead by Detective James Madden (white) after an alleged assault upon the patrolman in an attempt to escape an arrest for robbery. Police claimed that Madden's gun discharged accidentally during the tussle. Members of the dead youth's family, present at the time of the shooting, said that he was shot in the back without warning.

- April 29, 1973: Clifford Glover (black), 10, was shot and killed by Patrolman Thomas J. Shea (white) in Queens after fleeing when approached for questioning by the officers who were in plainclothes. Glover allegedly pointed a gun (which was never recovered) at Shea and his partner, Walter Scott (white).

"Black and Puerto Rican children are not expendable," Clark complained to Mayor Abraham D. Beame and Police Commissioner Michael J. Codd. "The New York City police must be taught to pay them the respect as human beings which whites ordinarily receive."

Two years later, on Thanksgiving night in 1976, Robert Torsney, a white cop, gunned down 15-year-year-old Randolph Evans after responding to a call of an armed man in a housing project in East New York.

"Did you just come from apartment 7-D?" Evans asked Torsney as he left the building.

"You're damn right I did," replied Torsney who then pulled his gun and shot Evans pointblank in the head. Torsney claimed the youth pointed a gun at him, but investigators found no gun.

Psychiatrist Dr. Herbert Spiegel, testifying for the prosecution at the murder trial, said Torsney acted in panic when he killed Evans and was not suffering from mental defect or disease. But Torsney was found not guilty by reason of insanity.

One expert testified that Torsney's insanity was organically caused and was described as a rare form of "epileptic psychomotor seizure." Another said Torsney was never aware of the crime he had committed and had engaged in involuntary "retrospective falsification." (I could find only one case in which a black officer shot an unarmed white suspect. In 1971, off-duty Patrolman Wayne Bolt fatally shot 21-year-old Leslie Kempler after Kempler's car hit a bus in Brooklyn. There was controversy over whether a tussle preceded the shooting.)

WITHIN DAYS OF THE KILLING OF WILLIAM WHITFIELD, the FBI released statistics showing that New York City cops actually shoot civilians far less frequently than their counterparts in other major cities. It found that the NYPD had the lowest per capita shooting rates of any large police department in the country.

New York had an average of less than one killing per 1,000 officers per year from 1985 to 1989, compared with four per 1,000 officers in San Diego, and three per 1,000 officers each in Los Angeles, St. Louis and Dallas. That was according to the most recent national study on deadly force by officers, published in 1991. The report also showed that 93.6 percent of the city's 38,000 officers had never fired their weapons while fighting crime. "We need to be looking at those numbers," urged Norman Siegel, "because they raise serious questions regarding the issue of racial overtones in the discharge of weapons."

Anti-police brutality monitors insisted that the FBI statistics could not obscure the "pattern and practice" of police shooting unarmed black males. That contention easily could be substantiated by statistics showing just how many of these incidents involve suspects who happened to be black. But the NYPD never compiled such data. "We don't have them," admitted the NYPD's Marilyn Mode.

Officer Davitt, who shot Whitfield, had fired his gun once too many times. According to the NYPD's own statistics, Davitt discharged his weapon eight times in his 14-year career. He also had been the subject of 12 civilian complaints. At Whitfield's open-casket funeral, Sharpton presided over a scene he knew all too well. "This is the ninth time this cop shot his gun," Sharpton said in his eulogy. "Let's talk about this cop's record. "Twelve complaints in 14 years," he emphasized. "Let's talk about this cop's record." Addressing the "mistaken stereotype that young black men are to be feared," Sharpton thundered, "They've mistaken all of us for a long time."

Sharpton was hardly the only black activist to have noticed this deadly trend. In his unpublished manuscript, *Book of Genocide*, a look at police brutality in America's inner cities, Sonny Carson conjures a scenario, which eerily resembled the circumstances surrounding the shooting of Whitfield. Wrote Carson in the chapter, *Up Against The Wall*:

> The sound of a shotgun blast disturbs the night in the Bushwick section of Brooklyn "There has been trouble in a disco, not unheard of in ghetto areas on weekend nights, where built up frustrations and hopelessness tend to make tempers short and men unreasonable. Shortly, police arrive at the scene. They come out of their cars like commandos on a raid, guns at the ready, eyes searching for any sign of movement. There. Over the curb. A car with some black youths in it. That must be the deal.
> "You! Out of the car! Hand where we can see 'em. Move it!" A young black man climbs cautiously out of the car, his hands high in plain view and he is shot down for his trouble. He has no weapon. That young man is dead today, his life terminated by the bullets of trigger-happy, nervous policemen. A vivid example of how those paid to protect us execute their influence in the black community.... You may ask, "Why is the black community so inherently dangerous that the only safe cop is the cop that shoots first and ask questions later?"

Over the years, black activists urged the NYPD to weed out and keep out officers who were unstable and potentially uncontrollable. The Department issued strict guidelines for the use of deadly force, stressing that "firearms be used as a last resort, and then only to protect life."

Officer Davitt had his 48 hours—and then some—to come up with a novel defense. But Candy Williams could not imagine what Davitt was thinking when he gunned down her fiancé. On New Years' Day, 1998, she sat on a bench outside of One Police Plaza in the freezing cold. She was the guest of Al Sharpton who was conducting an "anti-inauguration" rally to protest against police brutality at the same time Mayor Giuliani was being sworn in for his second term.

In her first interview since the shooting, the 28-year-old Williams told me that Whitfield would not challenge police. For one, he feared being arrested on three outstanding warrants—two for assault and one for possession of marijuana. He had dreams of enlisting in the army or playing in the NBA. Around 1 p.m. on that fateful Christmas Day, Whitfield decided to surprise his mother. "B'u (a black term of endearment), I'm going outside to call my mother to let her know we're coming over for dinner," she recalled Whitfield telling her. The pay telephone was across the street from William's apartment. William's two children from another relationship, Laquannia, 9, and Colin, 6, watched eagerly from the window as Whitfield hurried over to the phone. The next thing she knew she was trying to explain to them that Whitfield would not be coming back. She said she did not know what happened. "I have heard 50 million stories but the one thing I know is that a cop killed him," she cried. "There are more questions than answers."

Sonny Carson posed yet another question that Mayor Giuliani could not answer: "What type of system is it that places policemen, totally unfamiliar with the mores of blacks, on duty in the black community?"

THE NYPD'S CLOSELY KEPT INTERNAL GUIDELINES to officers who are challenged by other officers could be the key to stopping mistaken shootings of black suspects. "Authoritatively state, 'Police! Don't move!' as the initial challenge," the NYPD urged officers in a training manual I had obtained. "Try to discourage the challenged person from turning around. If this person intends to escape or retaliate in any manner he may be able to establish the challenging officer's exact location and the number of backup officers.... Remember, if you are being challenged you are a suspect until properly identified. Act accordingly—as you would have a suspect act if you were challenging them."

In March 1998, Sergeant Dexter Brown, an undercover narcotics officer, accused the NYPD of "conspiring to cover up his unlawful shooting." The shooting occurred on February 27 after a team of undercover cops, including Brown, moved in to arrest drug dealers during a predawn buy-and-bust operation in a crack house in the Fort Greene section of Brooklyn. As Brown struggled for his revolver with one of four suspects, three shots were fired from it. Detective Kenneth Cullen fired a single shot, killing the suspect, Steven Service. But one undercover cop, who is Latino, and whose name police withheld because of the nature of his job, fired nine shots. A bulletproof vest stopped a slug from penetrating Brown's back, possibly saving his life. Two other bullets struck him in the buttocks.

But earlier versions of the shooting trotted out by the department claimed that Brown was shot by a sniper, according to attorney Bonita Zelman who filed a $50 million lawsuit against the city on behalf of Brown. The suit alleged that authorities gave "a false account of the shooting to the public, and failed to conduct and insure a full, thorough, and complete investigation, and hold the shooting officer accountable for the crime." Deputy Inspector Michael Collins told me that the report that Brown was shot by a sniper—published in an early edition of the *Daily News*—may have been transmitted over a police radio as events surrounding the shooting unfolded. He denied that "the department issued a statement saying that the officer was possibly shot by a sniper."

Informed by top law enforcement sources that the NYPD kept never before released records of "classic confrontation" situations—violent cop-on-cop encounters—I successfully filed a Freedom of Information Law request to obtain them. The records showed that white cops either could not, or refused to tell the difference between black criminals and plainclothes cops. There were 21 "mistaken identity" cop-on-cop shootings from August 1972 to August 1994. During that period, 16 white cops fired at fellow officers: seven blacks, five Latinos, and four whites. Of the 21 documented incidents, one Latino cop fired on a black colleague, and blacks fired four times at black officers.

There are no reported incidents of blacks firing at whites.

So-called "classic confrontation situations" were a "major concern to this Department," according to the documents. When I asked the NYPD for more recent statistics of cop-on-cop shootings, the department said it had not compiled any statistics "relative to mistaken shootings" since 1994, the year Rudy Giuliani took office. "We've had 10 similar cases in recent years," said retired detective Roger L. Abel, a former president of the Guardians Association, a black fraternal officers group. Abel, author of *The Black Shields*, a controversial history of black cops in the NYPD, kept impeccable records. "Since 1941, we have had a total of 28 cases of blacks who have been shot at, shot, or killed by white police officers," Abel disclosed. "Black officers have never shot at, shot, or killed white officers." Countered NYPD spokesperson Marilyn Mode: "I can tell you, however, that less than 1 per cent of the entire force have fired their guns. That's really pretty staggering." Equally staggering was the assertion by black law enforcement activists that the inability to distinguish criminals from cops—usually a white officer's problem—began to affect black and Latino cops as well. It remained a contentious issue in the shooting of Sergeant Brown.

The shooting evoked an outcry from *100 Blacks*, which questioned whether the Latino cop assumed that Brown was a criminal because he is black. "It is important that we point out that he is Hispanic," said then Sergeant Eric Adams, who long had alleged that accepted notions about the "color of crime" among white officers led to "mistaken identity" shootings of black and Latino cops. "Black and Hispanic officers fall into the same dangerous pattern," Adams added.

Brown's shooting rekindled charges by Adams's group that the NYPD had failed to assure the safety of black and Latino cops, who dominate the ranks of undercover officers. Less than 24 hours after Brown was shot, the group made sure the Giuliani administration was listening. *100 Blacks* appeared on the steps of City Hall brandishing bloodstained, bullet-riddled shirts, which, it said, symbolized the peril that black undercover officers face from fellow officers as well as criminals. Speakers alleged that in an attempt to muzzle the group's complaints of racism in assignments and "grave concern" over "friendly fire" incidents, the department "failed to report" the circumstances surrounding the shooting of Brown "in a timely and accurate manner." It gave the department one day to come up with "the true account."

The department, however, remained adamant about its version of the shooting, and did not invoked the usual explanation that it was "a terrible but understandable mistake." It insisted that the Latino cop and other backup officers did not think that Brown was a criminal and used justifiable force in coming to his aid. "There is no mistaken identity here," stressed Mode, who accused Adams' group of making "irresponsible comments" to "forward their political agenda." Mode said the officers fired their weapons after the sergeant was grabbed in a chokehold from behind and was struggling with Service, the suspect. "They saw their sergeant in grave danger and they had to make a decision how best to save him," Mode said.

She denied that the department delayed making the shooting public, adding, "We had to wait for ballistics." Mode emphasized that Brown worked with the Latino cop and other members of the backup team for more than a year, "so it wasn't mistaking Brown in any fashion."

However, some sociologists theorize that "classic confrontations" may be a result of "reasonable racism" or "rational discrimination," which trigger racial fears in a white cop when he believes he is about to be attacked by a black man with a gun—even though that black man is an officer with whom he has worked side by side for six months or a year. "This is not 'reasonable' or 'rational'—it is pure, ingrained racism nurtured by negative stereotypes," asserted Roger Abel. "White men are afraid of black men with guns. Period! The perception that all black men with guns are dangerous has been reinforced on the six o'clock news with a constant parade of black men who are accused of committing crimes. These white cops rarely see white males as criminals and therefore can't, or refuse to, differentiate between a black police officer and a criminal. We are victims of their racial fears."

DESPITE THEIR ALLEGED familiarity with Sergeant Brown, both the Latino cop and Detective Cullen could have mistaken Brown for a criminal. In January 1998, attorney Zelman introduced a black narcotics cop who claimed he was assaulted by Detective Edward Hughes, a white member of his undercover team who he alleged mistook him for a drug dealer during a buy-and-bust operation in Brooklyn in December 1997. Zelman filed a $10 million suit against the Giuliani administration alleging that the undercover cop "was assaulted and battered by … Hughes … who grabbed the undercover and violently threw him onto a car face down striking him in the left side of his head three times with a portable radio." The NYPD refused to talk to me about that allegation. The suit claimed that after the attack, "supervising officials conspired to cover up the misconduct by destroying" an original report, "which gave a false account of the incident." That account alleged that the undercover officer fell while running, causing his own injuries.

In *Tragic Mistakes*, a chapter in Roger Abel's book, a similar situation was recounted. A black undercover narcotics cop working out of the 50th Precinct in the Bronx allegedly was accosted and beaten in 1989 by four white backup officers during a buy-and-bust operation. "You open up his face and his head with a radio. When he turns around you didn't stop the beating," said Abel. Zelman also represented Latino detective Jerry Ortiz, who was severely wounded by drug suspects in 1989 during a buy-and-bust. According to published reports, Ortiz was shot when he brought $9000 to a drug den in the Bronx and attempted to buy a half kilo of cocaine. A group of gunmen robbed Ortiz, ordered him to lie on the floor, and fired at least two shots into him.

One bullet went through Ortiz's heart, and he was declared dead on the operating table. But doctors revived him, removing his spleen, liver, and part of his pancreas. Ortiz sued the city, claiming that police were warned beforehand that he was going to be robbed but failed to call off the purchase. Ortiz filed a $40 million suit against the Giuliani administration and the NYPD. Again, Mode said she could not comment on a case that was in litigation.

The NYPD Hispanic Society, a Latino officers' group, called for a criminal investigation of the department's handling of the undercover operation, accusing commanders of recklessly ordering inexperienced and outgunned undercovers into dangerous buy-and-bust operations to pump up arrest statistics, *Newsday* reported. Even black beat officers faced such dangers. "It has been brought to our attention that, on occasion, uniformed police officers have been challenged from behind by other members of the service," according to an NYPD document.

In 1993, following accusations that the department was not doing enough to sensitize officers involved in "challenge and confrontation" situations, a training exercise was devised to help cops identify other cops. At the time, according to a training manual a law enforcement source handed to me, "over one thousand N.Y.P.D. shields were missing or unaccounted for" and the department feared that a badge offered as a sole means of identification during tense encounters would not be adequate verification. It is unknown whether former officer Peter DelDebbio, who shot undercover cop Desmond Robinson four times in the back in 1994, had participated in the department's 30-minute training program. DelDebbio subsequently was convicted of second-degree assault and sentenced to five years probation and 200 hours of community service. He was fired from the force. (In 1997, a judge threw out a lawsuit by Robinson alleging that Giuliani and the NYPD had violated his privacy by staging the widely publicized bedside meeting with DelDebbio.)

AFTER THE UPROAR OVER THE SHOOTING of Desmond Robinson, retired detective Eddie Singleton broke his 23-year-long silence about a day in April 1971 when a white officer shot him down like a common criminal. Singleton and his partner were on duty in the Bronx when a drug dealer burst into the 41st Precinct station house, claiming he'd been robbed. The plainclothes officers put the man in their unmarked car and drove to Vice Avenue, where the dealer pointed out a suspect. The cops chased the suspect, but lost him in a nearby building.

A knock on an apartment door was answered by a barrage of bullets. Singleton, who had been on the force for 11 years, called for backup. While waiting for the officers to arrive, he anticipated that the suspect might jump out a window. On his way down the stairs, Singleton came face-to-face with a white officer. "He saw me with a gun in my hand," recalled Singleton, who burst into tears. "I put my gun down and I was cowering against the wall because I knew he was gonna shoot me. He was in full uniform. I was wearing a turtleneck sweater. "He was gonna shoot me. He wasn't terrified that I was gonna harm him. No way! I could have killed him. But if I did, other white cops would have executed me right then and there."

Singleton shouted, "Hey! I'm a cop!" But there was no place for him to take cover.

"I had my shield on, but he didn't see that," Singleton remembered. "He only saw a black man with a gun. He let two go. One missed and the other hit me in the left arm. After that, I hit the floor. They saw my ID around my neck, put me in a car, and took me to the hospital."

While he was recuperating, Singleton said, someone in the Bronx borough president's office warned him that the department was going to blame him for causing his own injuries. "Nobody from the PBA or the Guardians came to see me," Singleton charged. "The PBA automatically took care of that white boy who shot me. The Guardians never did anything for me."

On a sun-drenched September afternoon, Singleton sat on the stoop of his brownstone in Bedford-Stuyvesant. He rolled back his shirt sleeve to show the scar from the bullet, which shattered a bone in his arm. "To this day, I can't straighten out my arm," he said. "It is killing me. Oh man, every time I think about it, it brings tears to my eyes. I still have bad dreams about it."

Singleton also had bad memories of becoming a member of the NYPD in 1959, a time when black officers were not deemed fit to join the white fraternity in blue—and a time when many of the racial attitudes in the present-day NYPD were being formed. He was assigned to the 90th Precinct, manned mostly by Irish and Italian officers. "I remember the white old-timers would scrawl 'Hey, nigger' on my locker door. They wouldn't speak to me. You had to have a sound mind. I needed the job, which paid only $6000 a year. I was married and had a kid. I swallowed a whole lotta pride."

Singleton's fellow officers often baited him, hoping that he wouldn't be able to bear the taunts and leave the force. "There was this guy they called 'The Basher' who was in another precinct," he recalled. "He was a prejudiced son of a gun, a German dude. When they needed an officer over there, they would send me to work with him, knowing that he hated black people. When you rode with him, you couldn't touch the radio, you couldn't do nothing. That's another time that I kept my mouth shut because I could have easily gotten in trouble with this guy. I could fight him and lose my job." Singleton resigned from the force in 1973 and sued the city and the NYPD for the injuries he sustained in his "classic confrontation." He would spend the next 10 years battling city lawyers for a settlement. In 1981, he said, he settled for $275,000. "None of these people have ever gone to jail," said Roger Abel, referring to the white cops who killed or injured black officers like Eddie Singleton and Desmond Robinson. "The strongest punishment was termination from the service."

PART XII
Blacks, Giuliani, and Police in the Aftermath of 911 (2001)

in memory of
Letnie English

and for
Dr. Bernard W. Ben, Norma Greaves, Horace James, Roslyn Haynes, Bernice James, James Phillip, Ricardo Achan, Herbert "Power" Benta, William "Stretch" McPherson, Joy Pierre, Zanelia Chevalier, Donalis "Fish" Alleyene, Irwin "Goliath" Bruno, Mervyn "Gyaller" Alexander, Steve Creft, Alexander "TTT" Davis, Silburn Callender, Gordoness "Pops" St. Hillaire Lloyd "Flatter" Chapman Anthony "Mesh" Walcott Charles Walcott, Michael "Snake" Paul, Taramattie Balkaran, Denise Howell, Stafford Byers, Dennis Garraway, Irwin Pinney, William Felix, Paul Serrette
Derek "Nigs" Quanchan, Kazim Ali, Derek Pascal, Wyneth Charles Emmonds, Pretter St. Hillaire, Charmaine Ovid, Adina Rodriguez, George Jessop, Aldwyn Charles, Oriel Thomas, Horatius Gittens, Jim Baptise, Anthony Johnson, Percy, Willis, and Sharon Wilson, and Edmund "Frustration" Anthony

39

Ground Hog

Too many Negroes are jealous of other Negroes' successes and progress. Too many Negro organizations are warring against each other with a claim to absolute truth. The Pharoahs had a favorite and effective strategy to keep their slaves in bondage: keep them fighting among themselves. The divide-and-conquer technique has been a potent weapon in the arsenal of oppression.

—Martin Luther King, Jr., (Quoted in *There Is A Balm In Gilead,*
by Lewis V. Baldwin)

SEIZING THE OPPORTUNITY TO ECLIPSE political rival Al Sharpton, Jesse Jackson, once scorned by Rudy Giuliani, stood shoulder to shoulder with the lame duck mayor at Ground Zero on September 25, 2001, wiping out in 15 minutes of "shameful grandstanding" Sharpton's eight-year battle to portray the mayor as hostile to blacks.

Jackson's audacious show of solidarity with Giuliani, arch-rival of the city's black-led civil rights movement, had inflamed his already combustible relationship with Sharpton. Jackson denied his trip to the site of the 911 terrorist attack was political. "Eighty of my friends, waiters who worked for Windows on the World, perished," he said. "My grief transcends everything else. My feelings for my lost friends were the issue. It had nothing to do with the mayor." Jackson said that an American Red Cross board member invited him to inspect Ground Zero. "They offered to escort me to the site, but when I got there the mayor was conducting the tours, just as he had done for others," Jackson insisted.

It happened on Sharpton's watch, a sneak political attack executed in the waning hours of the Democratic primary—on the very day that Sharpton was preoccupied with the goal of electing Bronx Borough President Fernando Ferrer the city's first Latino mayor. Ever since hijackers crashed two jumbo jets into the twin towers, Giuliani stood guard at the entrance to the world's most notorious graveyard, waving through friends and political allies while allegedly denying entry to foes. Manhattan Borough President C. Virginia Fields watched from the sidelines as Giuliani escorted a parade of high-profile national and foreign dignitaries into Ground Zero. One by one, they congratulated Giuliani for his "strength" and "compassion" in the aftermath of the attacks.

On primary night, as black and Latino leaders and prominent businesspeople flocked to the Puck Building in Greenwich Village to celebrate Ferrer's victory—he won 36 percent of the vote, forcing a runoff with Public Advocate Mark Green—political gadflies overheard a torrent of complaints and questions about Jackson. "I talked to Jesse yesterday, and he never told me he was going down there with Giuliani," Sharpton videographer Eddie Harris quoted a top black elected state official as saying. "We are not going to be disrespected," the politician fumed. "Why would he come into town and do this?" But there were more questions than answers. "Why didn't Jesse touch base?" Harris then heard a wealthy black businessman ask. "Who did he talk to? Who agreed to this?"

"How could he come to town on the day we're trying to get Ferrer elected mayor and stand with Giuliani?" queried one well-known Latino community activist.

According to several campaign workers that night, Sharpton and the other black and Latino leaders were equally troubled by Jackson's blatant snub of Bill Thompson, the former Board of Education president who won the Democratic primary to become the city's first black comptroller. "Jesse Jackson, the creator of the Wall Street Project, didn't endorse Bill Thompson for such a powerful position," a contributor to Jackson's project lamented. "He did not pass out a flyer, did not go to a subway stop. But he rushes to Ground Zero with Rudy Giuliani. On the day that a Rainbow ticket is winning in New York, he is totally uninvolved. He is standing with the anti-Rainbow mayor. What is wrong with this guy?" (Jackson asked me to remind his critics that he'd promoted Ferrer's candidacy in several radio interviews. In the search for answers, a Ferrer campaign contributor, who spoke to me on condition of anonymity, asserted that maybe Jackson had lost so much ground in black New York political circles that he did not even bother to volunteer to campaign for the Rainbow candidates. "Maybe he did this in desperation, to get some attention from us," the Ferrer supporter surmised.

Dedrick Muhammad, the former field director of Sharpton's National Action Network, said he heard a black political analyst pepper a Jackson defender with these questions:

- In the eight years Rudy Giuliani has been in office, did he invite Jesse to Gracie Mansion?

- Did he invite Jesse to City Hall?

- Has Giuliani ever attended Jesse's annual convention of the Wall Street Project?

- Is it not true that when David Dinkins was mayor Jesse was given police security and treated like a V.I.P. when he came to town?

- Don't you think that Giuliani is using Jesse?

- How does he explain not endorsing the Rainbow slate?

- How could he come to town and not campaign for them?"

According to Muhammad, the analyst contended that if Giuliani was trying to unite his city he certainly missed a unique opportunity to do so. "He said, 'Giuliani did not want to reach out to people like Sharpton, Carl McCall, or C. Virginia Fields,'" Muhammad recalled. "He said, 'This is a fraud that Giuliani has orchestrated for his own political ends,' that Giuliani 'choreographed the visits to Ground Zero so that only certain people would get maximum PR,' making it appear that his black political opponents like Reverend Sharpton didn't care."

Sharpton swore that Jackson's foray into New York for a detente with Giuliani caught him by surprise. He said that the day before the primary, his mentor called him. Sharpton aide J.D. Livingstone, who hooked up a three-way conversation told me Jackson said he was coming to the city and wanted to "touch base" with Sharpton when he arrived. After Jackson inquired about the well-being of the activist's wife, Cathy, and teenage daughters, Dominique and Ashley, Sharpton told him that the girls had been consoling a survivor, 12-year-old Travis Boyd, whose mother was presumed dead in the World Trade Center rubble. Livingstone recalled Sharpton suggesting that Jackson reach out to some black aid workers who were toiling near Ground Zero or engaged in a range of relief efforts in mostly black neighborhoods. Again, Jackson promised to reach out to his protégé.

At about eleven o'clock on the morning of the primary, Livingstone put through a call from Jackson to Sharpton on his cell phone. Livingstone said Jackson seemed eager to let Sharpton in on his New York itinerary. He allegedly told Sharpton he was scheduled to speak at an elementary school and afterward would swing by the Red Cross to meet some of its officials. He then asked where Sharpton would be that afternoon. "Sharpton said he would be in the streets campaigning for Ferrer and Thompson, and later he would tape a show for the Fox network," Livingstone recalled.

Upon leaving the Fox studios in downtown Manhattan, Sharpton was confronted by a reporter who pointed out that while Sharpton was accusing Giuliani of exploiting the World Trade Center tragedy by seeking to extend his term in office, Jackson was at Ground Zero, standing next to Giuliani and praising his leadership.

"Doesn't this smack of Rudy being accepted by a lot of people in the civil rights community?" the reporter asked.

Sharpton expressed surprise. "He was in shock," an aide recalled. Sharpton told the reporter that Giuliani should be commended but that he was not prepared to sweep eight years of the mayor's ironfisted rule over his black constituents under the wreckage of the twin towers. "I remember saying, 'Rudy seems sensitive now because he has been insensitive to our community for eight long years,'" Sharpton confirmed. "I said, 'We had gotten so used to the mean and insensitive Rudy.'"

As a disgruntled Sharpton resumed campaigning, Livingstone again connected one of Jackson's aides to Sharpton. This is how Livingstone recalled the conversation:

"You know that Reverend Jackson is still trying to touch base with you later today?" the unidentified aide said.

"Get in touch with me?" Sharpton screamed. "He just left Ground Zero with Rudy Giuliani! How could y'all do this?"

"What do you mean?" the Jackson aide shot back. "He got involved with the American Red Cross. They brought him there."

"Do you realize that Giuliani has snubbed Carl McCall, C. Virginia Fields, and other people that were critical of him? They were not allowed to speak at the memorial at Yankee Stadium. He knows that Giuliani is under attack by me. This only gives Giuliani cover. Is Jesse mindful of the fact that Giuliani is trying to use us, one against the other?"

The Jackson aide, according to Livingstone, said Jackson would contact Sharpton later to offer an explanation. Jackson called as Sharpton sped to the Puck Building to revel in Ferrer's win. According to Dedrick Muhammad, who was traveling with Sharpton, the two Baptist preachers argued bitterly. Sharpton aides reconstructed the following details of that showdown:

"I think you absolutely violated our territorial integrity by being there with Giuliani," Sharpton said.

"Al, everybody's coming to see him, heads of nations," Jackson explained.

"That's not the point!" Sharpton shouted. "I think this is an absolute outrage. I'm going to deal with both of y'all!"

"We don't need to get into a spat over this," Jackson replied.

Sharpton, the aide recalled, was inconsolable.

"You always do this thing," Sharpton charged. "You come in here and screw us and then turn around and act like you don't understand. I feel absolutely violated by this. Why would you give cover to Rudy Giuliani on a day like this?"

"I'll call you later," Jackson pleaded. "That's not the way it is. You need to defend me."

"Defend you?" Sharpton bellowed. "I'm the one out there telling people that Giuliani did us wrong."

"We'll talk later," Jackson said.

Muhammad recalled that Ferrer's supporters sensed the rage in Sharpton as he entered the ballroom of the Puck Building. "One by one, they came up to Reverend Sharpton, asking him, 'What was that all about?' and 'Is Jesse Jackson crazy?'"

Jackson may have believed that he had pulled off a public relations coup by being the first prominent black leader to visit Ground Zero. But unbeknownst to Jackson and many in the media, Sharpton, absent the fanfare, beat Jackson to the tragic scene.

On September 16, the first Sunday after the attack, police officers sympathetic to Sharpton guided him and attorney Michael Hardy through several checkpoints for an hour-long visit to Ground Zero. "Police officers and firefighters were surprised," recalled Sharpton, who organized blood drives and counseling. "Some asked for my autograph and took pictures with me to show their families that I was concerned about them."

Sharpton told me that none of his previous visits to strife-torn regions in Africa and Haiti prepared him for what he saw at Ground Zero. "I went to the killing fields of Rwanda, witnessed slavery in Sudan, and saw abject poverty in the slums of Haiti, but there was something haunting about Ground Zero," he said. "I never thought I would see something like this. It is an eerie feeling that you cannot get out of you."

As Sharpton stared at the twisted remains of the once majestic twin towers, he remarked in the presence of a high-ranking white NYPD cop that he had been to Ground Zero before, the Ground Zero that became known as as the African Burial Ground in lower Manhattan.

Until the burial ground was closed just before the turn of the 19th century, it served as the final resting place for tens of thousands of free blacks and slaves. The cemetery was forgotten as the city expanded above and around it, eventually burying the site more than 20 feet underground. It was rediscovered—along with more than 400 sets of remains—during excavations for a federal building in 1991. The burial ground, most of which still lies deep beneath sidewalks, buildings and streets, was designated a national historic landmark in 1993.The site was declared a national monument in 2006. A memorial, a 20-foot-high chamber of gray stone with water elements running beside it, was dedicated in October 2007 (*The Associated Press*).

"Three hundred years ago my ancestors went to Ground Zero, and we've been fighting for a final resting place, an African burial ground, for years," Sharpton explained to the mystified cop. "No one cares that they are still under that rubble. No one hears their cry. We can't even reclaim their bones. Three hundred years later, the government is doing to us what they did to my ancestors: They're trying to make us invisible in lower Manhattan."

The next morning, a shaken Sharpton called Secretary of State Colin Powell. During their 10-minute conversation, Sharpton expressed reservations about the Bush administration's warmongering. "I told him I was concerned about the war, but that I felt that terrorism must be fought at all costs, and that I was willing to lead a fact-finding trip to Israel and Palestine," Sharpton said. Powell, he claimed, promised to give him a full briefing on the Middle East, similar to the one he got before visiting the Sudan. But he warned Sharpton to be extremely careful in that region.

Later that day, Sharpton contacted Governor George Pataki and Assembly Speaker Sheldon Silver. "I called them to object to calls for the Democratic primary to be postponed," said Sharpton, who rebuffed suggestions from aides that he ask Pataki to escort him to Ground Zero. "I could have asked the governor to take me there in front of all the cameras, but I didn't," he said.

If he had, that's where the *New York Post*'s Steve Dunleavy—combing "through white-hot shock, tears of mourning, and steel anger of revenge"—might have found the minister. Instead Dunleavy later asked, "Where the hell is our great community leader, the Rev. Al Sharpton?"

"I'd been all over the place," Sharpton declared. "The media ignored the black presence and now condemns us for being ignored." Unlike Jackson, Sharpton refused to upstage top black state and city officials for a photo op. "I felt that Carl McCall and C. Virginia Fields should be respected."

40

Police Brutality Is Back

We thought we were done with these things but we were wrong ...

—From *Litany for Dictatorships* by Stephen Vincent Benet

AFTER POLICE OFFICERS WERE MURDERED in the terrorist attacks on the twin towers, the outpouring of solidarity with the NYPD—even in black neighborhoods where cops were reviled for brutal conduct—seemed unbreakable. Gangbangers, blow dealers, skeezers, and stragglers openly bonded with the Five-O. Some drank from the same beer cans as the undercover DTs, and snitched voluntarily on their counterparts in the name of fighting crime. Outcries against racial profiling—echoes from protests over the torture of Abner Louima and the killing of Amadou Diallo—were smothered in the glad-handing and warm embraces.

But some officers were exploiting the hero worship of the NYPD by waging vicious attacks on members of the suspect class. Civil rights watchdogs claimed that complaints about menacing cops, beatings, and wrongful arrests began to mount once again. "Our files [bulged] with charges of police brutality that occurred after September 11," said Sharpton aide J.D. Livingstone.

"Courtesy, Professionalism, and Respect"—the watchwords of the NYPD initiative to win back the trust of African Americans—allegedly were ignored by cops when they responded to a report about noise coming from the basement of a Flatbush home in the early morning hours of October 7, 2001. Indeed, the birthday party that Trinidadian immigrant Rayanne Thompson and her friends had organized at the San Cosa All Fours Club at 347 Lincoln Road in Brooklyn had been going nonstop. Around 3 a.m., according to Thompson, an officer assigned to the 71st Precinct stationhouse confronted her in front of the building. He asked Thompson, who was 30, if she was the owner of the premises.

"No, I'm not, but hold on," she remembered replying. "Let me get the owner."

"Get the fuck away from the door before I arrest your ass!" the cop allegedly shouted, pushing Thompson out of the way.

"You just assaulted me!" said Thompson, a member of the Rastafari, who began walking behind the officer. Edwin Dick, who was attending the party, told the cop that the building belonged to him, and raced into the basement to turn off the music. Meanwhile, several other officers had responded.

"Get out!" the officer told the celebrants. "The party is over." Thompson said that as she and others began to leave, she heard a commotion and looked back. She said she saw about five police officers restraining her 45-year-old husband, Devon Thompson, who was also a member of the Rastafari, and pushing him against a cupboard. When Thompson asked a female officer why her husband was being arrested, the cop replied, "He touched a cop, and you are not supposed to touch a police officer."

Thompson said she hugged Devon and would not let go. "But four male cops grabbed me, threw me to the floor, and dragged me by my dreadlocks," she charged. "When I looked over to my right I saw the officers slam my husband's head into the cupboard, then they threw him to the floor and started stomping him in his face and head. Two other cops beat him on his back with nightsticks, and they kicked him in his left side several times."

Thompson recalled that when Dick tried to determine what was going on he was jumped by about five cops. "They threw him to the floor and started stomping on his wrist," she said. "I could hear him begging them to stop." While some cops escorted Thompson's husband and Dick out of the building, leaving her on the floor handcuffed, others "smashed up the basement and took the music and drinks." After an hour, Thompson claimed, paramedics removed her from the basement. "I came outside and saw helicopters hovering above and the road blocked off with a lot of police cars."

According to attorney Sanford Rubenstein, a judge in Criminal Court in Brooklyn dismissed resisting arrest and assault charges against Dick and Devon Thompson on November 15, 2001. Rayanne Thompson was not charged. "The behavior of the police in this case [was] outrageous," contended Rubenstein, who filed an $8 million notice of claim against the city on behalf of the Thompsons, and $3 million on Dick's behalf. "These were innocent people who were doing nothing wrong." The preamble to the lawsuit alleged "false arrest, false imprisonment, and malicious prosecution" by "police officers from the 71st Precinct whose identities have not been discovered." The suit also claimed—in addition to "emotional distress and psychological overlay"—that Rayanne Thompson suffered injuries to her head, back, left shoulder, chest, left leg, and left hip; that her husband, Devon, suffered injuries to his head, ribs, back, left shoulder, face, and hands; and that Edwin Dick sustained injuries to his shoulders, ribs, right arm, right hand, and back.

TO THE WHITE COP who had participated in a raid on a Flatbush home across the street from where Sheretha Anderson and her friend Kelsey Jones were standing on the morning of October 30, both 23-year-old women looked like truants cutting classes.

"Aren't you ladies supposed to be in school?" the bike-riding, uniformed cop who Anderson and Jones would come to know as Officer Bello allegedly barked.

"How old are you?" they said he asked. "You look like truant students."

The women insisted they were not students, gave their ages, and explained that they were on their way to a doctor's office. When the officer turned his attention to another pedestrian, Anderson and Jones continued walking toward a bus stop.

"Didn't I tell you bitches to show me some identification?" Anderson and Jones said Bello shouted on approaching them. Anderson said that she and Jones were surprised by the cop's outburst.

"In disbelief, we started cursing, telling him that he was disrespectful," Anderson recalled.

"Now you're resisting arrest," she quoted Bello as saying. "You're going to jail." According to Anderson, Bello "grabbed Kelsey by the arm and twisted it, and threw her" against an iron gate. Anderson said she and Bello got into a tug of war over Jones. "I tried to free Kelsey, but he was being too aggressive with her." Anderson let go of her friend, and whipped out her cell phone. As she headed back to her apartment to notify her stepfather, Bello radioed for backup.

Anderson said when she turned around she saw several police vehicles converging at the scene. While some cops blocked off the street, two others raced toward her. One of them, Anderson claimed, ripped the phone from her hand. Then both of the officers shoved her into a phone booth and "started to handcuff me with a lot of hostility.

"I told them to stop being aggressive with me because I am pregnant," Anderson recalled. But the cops allegedly ignored Anderson and forced her into the back seat of a squad car. She began vomiting. "One of the officers told me to vomit out the window and not in the car," she claimed. Upon their arrival at the 69th Precinct station house, Anderson and Jones once more were challenged on their claims that they were in their twenties. A check revealed they had no criminal records.

"When Officer Bello realized we didn't have any criminal charges against us, he took the cuffs off, and apologized for the misunderstanding," Anderson said. "But I felt that the damage was already done, and that an apology was unacceptable. My best friend and I were traumatized by the incident. My wounds will heal quicker, but Kelsey has a sprained wrist and she pulled two muscles in her leg. The 69th Precinct will never heal the emotional pain of two young black women who were assaulted in the street by their cops."

41

How Giuliani and the NYPD Got Away With Murder

The moral argument is that although the past cannot be undone ... the effect of this historical injustice constitutes a continuing violation.

—Elazar Barkan

IN THE END, BOTH THE CLINTON AND BUSH ADMINISTRATIONS failed to take control of the New York Police Department under Republican Mayor Rudy Giuliani. The Department was never held accountable for violating the civil rights of black citizens and the acquitted killers of Amadou Diallo, Patrick Dorismond, Malcolm Ferguson, and other victims of police lawlessness escaped federal indictment.

The fault to some extent lay with an allegedly ambitious black prosecutor, according to former U.S. Attorney General Janet Reno.

Saying he no longer felt bound by a vow of confidentiality, Sharpton told me that during a meeting he and other civil rights leaders had with Reno in August 2000, he demanded to know why she seemed to be dragging her feet on their call to shackle the allegedly abusive NYPD. Reno, he recalled, attributed part of the blame for the holdup to Loretta Lynch, the black then acting U.S. Attorney for the Eastern District, whom some activists had accused of kowtowing to Giuliani by not pushing for the federal takeover of the nation's largest police force.

"Miss Reno's response was that there had been no request from the Eastern District [which covers Brooklyn, Queens, Staten Island, and Long Island] that the Justice Department proceed with a federal takeover," said Sharpton. "We were shocked because our position was that they'd already found that there was a 'pattern and practice' of police brutality. I said, 'How many atrocities do you need before you see a pattern to intervene?' Clearly we felt there was a pattern."

381

(Alan Vinegrad, who was a spokesman for Lynch, declined to discuss Sharpton's claims with me.)

Attorney Carl Thomas blamed Lynch "for not aggressively pursuing blatant police misconduct." But Charles Barron rejected Reno's and Thomas' explanation. "I am not saying that the local U.S. attorney did all that she could have done, but Janet Reno[had] the power and the authority to stop anyone below her from standing in her way of putting the NYPD into receivership," he said. He added that if Reno and President Clinton had "the real will to do it" they would have pursued the takeover.

At the close of 2000—as the activists scrambled to assess the impact an incoming Bush Administration would have on high-profile civil rights cases stagnating in U.S. Department of Justice files—Giuliani exhaled: The curse of Abner Louima finally appeared to be lifting.

In November, Giuliani practically was on bended knee, pleading with Reno not to appoint a federal monitor to oversee the NYPD. There were several ongoing federal inquiries into racial profiling tactics that allegedly led to fatal shootings and beatings of blacks. Unable to wrangle concessions from Giuliani and then Police Commissioner Safir, Lynch had threatened to file a lawsuit against the city, charging it with civil rights violations and demanding broad changes, including the dreaded federal oversight.

After Giuliani protested and stonewalled, Lynch allegedly backed off. By following the rules of engagement as dictated by Giuliani, black activists charged, Lynch set back efforts to break the stranglehold that the mayor's paramilitary cops had on black communities. These activists feared that a Bush Administration would be more sympathetic to Giuliani's claim that the investigations were politically inspired by the Clinton Administration and would pull back on federal intervention that began after Louima was torture.

That Lynch had not, at that late stage in her investigation, sought authorization from Reno to sue the city provoked a more radical response from some in the legal community. Thomas angrily accuses Lynch of shielding the NYPD. He charged that Lynch was not gung-ho about "arresting the force" because she wanted to impress conservatives in the Senate who were considering whether to elevate her to U.S. attorney. After U.S. Attorney Zachary Carter resigned in 1999, Senator Charles Schumer asked Clinton to nominate Lynch for the plum assignment, saying that she "proven throughout her career that she is tough, fair, and honest." Lynch, who had been Carter's chief assistant, was appointed interim U.S. attorney pending a confirmation by the Senate. As president-elect George

W. Bush inched closer to the White House, the Senate confirmed Lynch's appointment.

"She was trying to placate Giuliani conservatives, who it [was] clear [were] against the appointment of a federal monitor," Thomas insisted. "Giuliani and his cohorts believed that the police department [was] doing a fine job, that the Abner Louima case was an aberration. Lynch bowed to conservatives who [were] not going to allow Giuliani's legacy to be soiled by a takeover of the NYPD."

Thomas emphasized that Lynch should have filed her lawsuit as soon as Giuliani balked at federal oversight. "Racial profiling and police brutality [was] dealt a knockout blow because of Loretta Lynch's failure as a prosecutor," the attorney asserted.

When reminded that Lynch had presided successfully over the prosecution of some of the officers involved in the attack on Louima, Thomas argued that accomplishment was tainted after Lynch allegedly showed her soft side for one of Louima's torturers. In all, four officers were convicted in three trials and two pleaded guilty. Officer Justin Volpe was sentenced 30 years in prison. Before Officer Charles Schwarz was sentenced in June 2000 to 15 years for holding down Louima and then conspiring to cover up the attack, powerful right-wing pols like Staten Island Borough President Guy Molinari loudly proclaimed Schwarz's innocence. In a shocking move, Lynch's office asked Judge Eugene Nickerson to go easy on Schwarz. (Again, Lynch's office declined to talk to me.)

According to Thomas, Lynch should have asked for the maximum sentence. "She disregarded the jury's decision, giving credence to the claim that Schwarz was innocent," he charged. "Schwarz spat in their faces by claiming that he was absolutely innocent. They turned around and still joined in a motion for the judge to depart downward at his sentencing. This, to me, shows tremendous weakness on Loretta Lynch's part."

Schwarz filed an appeal, accusing prosecutors of intimidating and coaching witnesses. Sharpton recalled that after Patrick Dorismond was gunned down by an undercover cop in March, he and Reverend Daughtry met with Lynch, who told them that she was vigorously pursuing plans to monitor the NYPD, despite reports that negotiations with the city had been deadlocked. Lynch, Sharpton said, assured them that she was doing everything she could.

Some activists had given up. They said it was a waste of time appealing to Lynch; the takeover would be short-lived anyway. They envisioned Giuliani scurrying back to a friendlier Department of Justice armed with more fuzzy cop statistics, a new plan to crack down on his permanent suspects, and the racist declaration by Heather Mac Donald (controversial analyst for the right-wing

Manhattan Institute for Policy Research) that "the NYPD is—to its detriment—awash in the spurious 'diversity' ideology." Lynch, Thomas offered, had contributed to this nightmare scenario by giving the NYPD a stay of execution: Under Bush, he predicted, the Department would get away with murder. "Justice for Amadou Diallo, Patrick Dorismond, and other victims is doomed," he swore.

Although a Manhattan grand jury was investigating the circumstances surrounding the Dorismond shooting, Sharpton expressed no confidence in D.A. Morgenthau. In May, a grand jury ruled that Officer Craig Yokemick had used justifiable force when he hurled his police radio at Kenneth Banks, fatally injuring him. Morgenthau claimed witnesses' accounts differed as to whether the radio struck Banks' head or shoulder, and whether Banks fell as a result of the radio hitting him or because Yokemick jumped on him. Sharpton told the Dorismond family he had bypassed the D.A. and asked Lynch for a meeting (because Dorismond had lived in Brooklyn).

THE JUSTICE DEPARTMENT HAD BEEN SUCCESSFUL in prosecuting several high-profile police-brutality cases by intervening after local district attorneys refused to present them to grand juries, or failed to secure indictments, or win convictions. After the Diallo verdict, advocates like Sharpton and Daughtry clamored for officers Sean Carroll, Kenneth Boss, Edward McMellon, and Richard Murphy to be tried for violating Diallo's civil rights. Sharpton even suggested that D.A. Robert Johnson threw the case after a racially mixed jury indicated that it had been incompetently presented. (A former investigator who worked for the prosecution team agreed. "It was the most incompetent prosecution that I have ever seen," he said.)

Some legal watchdogs pointed fingers at Johnnie Cochran, the former lead attorney for the Diallo family's battery of lawyers, who relied on the indictment secured by Johnson and did not call on the Justice Department to take over the case. "The Diallo lawyers were so involved in the protest hype that they forgot their role as lawyers," said a critic of Cochran, who spoke to me on condition of anonymity. "The Diallo legal team," he added, "should have learned the lesson of the original Abner Louima legal team."

That team—Thomas, Brian Figeroux, and Casilda Roper-Simpson—contacted Ken Thompson (then an upcoming assistant U.S. attorney in Brooklyn) within hours after Justin Volpe and other cops took Louima to Coney Island Hospital, handcuffed him to a bed, and told doctors that their suspect, who was bleeding from his rectum, was a homosexual who had engaged in consensual rough sex. Louima lived to tell a tale of unbridled torture that rivaled abuse in a medieval dungeon. Had Louima died, some argued, Giuliani and his supporters would have defended Volpe and his fellow officers, just as he defended Boss, Carroll, Murphy, and McMellon. Louima's original legal team pleaded with Zachary Carter to wrest the case from D.A. Hynes. They launched a media campaign, calling on New Yorkers to flood Carter's office with demands that he intervene. In addition, the lawyers placed strategic calls to influential elected officials, such as then Congressman Chuck Schumer, Senator Alfonse D'Amato, and Congressman Jerry Nadler.

These same politicians, including D.A. Hynes and other Jewish community activists, provided the impetus that forced Janet Reno to launch an investigation into the racially motivated murder of Yankel Rosenbaum. In September 1993, on the eve of Reno's announcement that she would not file civil rights charges in the Rosenbaum case for lack of evidence, Schumer and other members of the New York congressional delegation went over her head to White House counsel Bernard Nussbaum and other high administration officials close to the Jewish community. In a legal brief, Schumer asserted that the FBI and a grand jury could "shake evidence out of the trees." Reno canceled her news conference, and deputy attorney general Webster Hubbell relieved her as the point person in the Justice Department's investigation.

Schumer led the charge in Congress, D'Amato agitated in the Senate, and from his Brooklyn office Hynes hawked a 17-page brief arguing for federal involvement. Senator Robert Dole chimed in, arguing that federal civil rights statutes had been successfully invoked to try the white police officers in the Rodney King case. According to black political analysts, all the efforts were calculated to bring about a federal indictment of Lemrick Nelson, the black teenager who had been acquitted in state supreme court of killing Rosenbaum. After bowing to pressure from this powerful lobby, the feds used an obscure 1960 statute to charge Nelson. Under that law, it was illegal to injure or intimidate a person while that person was enjoying a federally protected activity because of race, color, religion, or national origin.

Many lawyers familiar with the Rosenbaum case counter-argued that prosecuting Nelson under the controversial statute was specious because Rosenbaum was not engaging in any federally protected activity that Nelson had conspired to deny. Apart from that contention, there were no allegations of prosecutorial incompetence. Fortunately for those who mourned for Rosenbaum, federal prosecutors presented new evidence, and Nelson was convicted.

Despite a lack of similar support from the Crown Heights advocacy group, Abner Louima's lawyers were able to convince Janet Reno to prosecute his attackers.

The decision to go straight to the federal government was further vindicated when police officer Antonio Valasquez was acquitted—in spite of overwhelming evidence—after an inexperienced state supreme court judge, Francois A. Rivera, deliberated for only 15 minutes. After allegedly beating yet another Haitian immigrant, Duken Kernisant, at the Department of Motor Vehicles in Coney Island, fracturing his eye socket, Valasquez claimed that Kernisant had assaulted him—a charge that was later dropped.

The Department of Justice has certain guidelines it must follow in weighing the viability of a state criminal case being considered for civil rights review. Two of the main issues that apply to the Diallo killing were prosecutorial incompetence and the feds' ability to introduce new evidence. Civil rights advocates argued that it was time for federal prosecutors to recognize the inability of local district attorneys to effectively prosecute sophisticated, well-funded cases of police misconduct. Thus, acquittal of police officers in state prosecutions should not automatically close the books.

But too often that was not the case.

In 1995, D.A. Johnson indicted 16 officers from the 48th Precinct. Most of the cases were dismissed and Johnson chose to prosecute the remaining officers on misdemeanor charges. One cop, John Lowe, was tried unsuccessfully three times on a misdemeanor charge. If Johnson had recommended that the officers be charged with federal civil rights violations, no one heard about it. One year later, a state supreme court judge acquitted Officer Francis Livoti in the 1994 choking death of Anthony Baez. The feds stepped in. During closing arguments in the 1997 civil rights trial, assistant U.S. Attorney Andrew Dember criticized the D.A.'s office for gross incompetence.

Fast forward to 2000. D.A. Johnson's prosecutors came under fire again—this time for botching the Diallo trial. Eric Warner, Johnson's lead prosecutor, had not tried a major case since the Happyland Social Club inferno trial nine years earlier. In some legal circles, Warner's opening argument was considered weak. Others felt he neglected to develop a clear theory of the case, and then made a grave omission when he failed to proffer expert witnesses on police training and procedures.

When the defense provided an expert on police practices, Warner and his team seemed surprised. The prosecution did not refute any information or cross-examine Dr. James Fyfe, a former NYPD cop who is a professor at Temple University in Philadelphia. Fyfe was the only authority on police practices and proce-dures in the entire case: The jury had no choice but to accept Fyfe's testimony as an accurate representation of acceptable police procedures. Schrrie Elliott wound up in the clutches of the defense team—a crucial mistake. Even if prosecutors were uncomfortable with Elliott, they should have called her, explaining any problems in her testimony while keeping the offensive.

The prosecution's incompetence stretched further with the mishandling of the key defense witnesses. Officer Sean Carroll testified that Amadou Diallo fit the description of an armed rapist they had been searching for on that tragic night. When Carroll further stated that he could not see Diallo's face clearly as he made that determination, that was the very moment that the officer admitted to violat-ing Diallo's constitutionally guaranteed right of equal protection under the law. Carroll and his Street Crime Unit buddies allegedly had profiled Diallo as a crim-inal, and were confronting the unarmed man on a fallacious, inarticulable suspi-cion. These four white cops, who seem to have had a rabid predisposition to criminalize a black man, inappropriately approached Diallo for reasons that can-not be soundly articulated, and killed him when there was no evidence that he had any connection to a crime. That approach, some argued, demonstrated intent to deny Diallo his federally protected rights.

A police officer can hold whatever prejudicial views he or she chooses, but that officer is not legally free to interfere with the freedom of a citizen based on fear, instinct, or stereotypical views about black people. To act upon fear and per-ceived criminality—even in "high-crime" areas—without some type of articula-ble, reasonable suspicion that an individual is connected to the commission of a crime is a violation of the 14th Amendment's Equal Protection clause. Racial profiling and stopping and questioning are closely related. Cops arguably are spe-cial citizens who have rights that are not available to John and Jane Doe. But fed-eral prosecutors should closely examine the notorious "48-hour rule"—a police union policy that forbids the questioning of officers in the immediate aftermath of a serious incident.

This prophylactic insulates cops from criminal liability by inhibiting the timely investigation of incidents in which they are suspects. They are allowed a "cooling-off" period, and during this time they are not required to make any statements or speak to investigators. Crimes often are solved in the embryonic stage of an investigation, when suspects are questioned, and written, oral, and videotaped statements are taken. When detectives investigate a non-police shoot-ing, they question perpetrators immediately and make their statements part of the permanent trial record. Instead of enjoying the right not to immediately report their involvement in alleged criminal misconduct or controversy, police officers should be obligated to give their version of events—without undue delay.

D.A. Johnson, searching for a way out of the political maelstrom after the Diallo verdict, argued that Diallo's killers frustrated prosecutors when they invoked the 48-hour rule. Johnson bristled at the criticism he was receiving from Sharpton and other observers, but he certainly deserved it. That the cops refused to talk to his investigators was not an excuse. His prosecutors never shook the trees to bring down evidence, much less racist cops. They clearly failed to properly investigate, anticipate defense strategies, and litigate the Diallo case.

I believed there was redemption for beleaguered prosecutors like Johnson. He should have taken a page out of D.A. Hynes' book and prepared a brief for Janet Reno as she considered whether to file civil rights charges against Carroll, Boss, McMellon, and Murphy. But Johnson didn't do that. From all appearances, the D.A. was too busy dawdling with the politics of damage control.

Epilogue

✦

If A Cop Kills My Son

Had a dream last night that I was dead
Had a dream last night that I was dead
Evil spirits all around my bed.

The Devil came and grabbed my hand
The Devil came and grabbed my hand
Took me way down to the red hot land.

Mean blue spirits stuck they forks in me
Mean blue spirits stuck they forks in me
Made me moan and groan in misery.

Fairies and dragons spittin' out blue flames
Fairies and dragons spittin' out blue flames
Showin' their teeth, for they was glad I came.

Demons with their eyelids drippin' blood
Demons with their eyelids drippin' blood
Draggin' sinners through that brimstone flood.

"This is hell," I cried, cried with all my might
"This is hell," I cried, cried with all my might
Oh, my soul, I can't bear the sight.

Started runnin' cause it is my cup
Started runnin' cause it is my cup
Run so fast 'til someone woke me up.

—Bessie Smith, "Blues Spirit Blues" (1930),
quoted in *Seems Like Murder Here*, by Adam Gussow

*I MUST HAVE DOZED OFF ON APRIL FOOL'S DAY, 2000, with the radio set
to* 1010 WINS News. *During my mid-day slumber, the gutsy street reporting of Lisa
Evers, regarding the latest fatal shootings of young black men in Brooklyn, played out
in my psyche in melodramatic bulletins. I remember hearing snippets of news about a
robbery, toy guns that looked real, three suspects who got away, and soundbites from
police brass calling the shootings of two allegedly armed teenagers by Operation Condor cops justifiable killings.*

*In and out of my snooze, I thought the police version of what happened could only
bolster Rudy Giuliani's contention that his private Ton Ton Macoutes are all that
stand between law-abiding New Yorkers and violent young black men. With the
breaking news on my mind, I fell into a deep sleep and my worst nightmare. I
dreamed I was in the office of Father Edward Durkin, the principal of the Catholic
school my then 13-year-old son, Peter Jr., attended. I had come with tears welling in
my eyes to tell Father Durkin that Little Peter, the taciturn, six-foot center on the
school's basketball team, was one of the stickup kids involved in the Brooklyn robbery.*

*In my dream, Father Durkin put his arms around me and led this former wan-
nabe altar boy in reciting the 14 Stations of the Cross. I woke up suddenly. Disoriented. Flailing my arms. Grasping. How could this happen? Little Peter, who wears a
fake diamond stud earring in his left ear and is grooming a Kobe Bryant Afro, is not
some street kid. Was he among the three suspects who got away? Had some trigger-
happy cop shot and killed my boy? Why, in the name of the Father and of the Son, am
I not on death row? My dream was incomplete.*

*In my family of West Indian immigrants, however, the women dream with horri-
fying accuracy. The night before an unarmed Patrick Dorismond was gunned down
by an undercover cop, my mother left a message on my voice mail regarding my close
relationship with Little Peter.*

*"Boy," she sobbed, almost choking, "I keep getting these bad dreams about you and
Little Peter. I keep seeing you and him struggling. He's pulling away from you, but
you keep crying out, 'My son! My son! I can't let you go!'"*

*Ma paused. But that only meant that she was perusing her blue, large-text Bible,
the one that has the names of her six boys written all over her favorite chapters and*

stuffed in white prayer envelopes dipped in the special anointing oil some televangelist sold her.

"Peter!" she bawled, as if she sensed I was on the other end silently listening to her. "Peter Noel! You don't listen! I am warning you not to leave your job today without saying the 119th Psalm. Don't tell me, 'Ma, it's too long!' Read it! Son, this is your protection! It will guard you and that beautiful, big-eye boy!"

I read all 176 verses of the Psalm and called my mother. "You made a mistake, Ma," I said. "You always tell me to read the 70th Psalm. (The five verses of the 70th Psalm are short and to the point, but I always read the second verse: "Let them be ashamed and confounded that seek after my soul: let them be turned backward, and put to confusion, that desire my hurt.") Ma cut me off. She said she'd figured out the dream that kept haunting her in the wake of the uproar over the Amadou Diallo verdict and the subsequent police killing of Malcolm Ferguson.

"Little Peter was trying to get away," she said. "He was frightened, and if he'd only run, if you'd only let go of him, the people—the big white people who was chasing him—would have caught him."

I felt my mother was holding something back. "Did Peter die in this dream?" I asked.

"It could be you. It could be him," she said. "Talk to Little Peter," she advised. "Tell him that Grandma Alice say, 'Never talk back to police! Don't fight! Don't struggle!' He's just like you, Peter Noel. He has your spirit."

I slumped back in my chair. I am afraid of my mother's dreams. In 1998, two days before my younger brother, Derrick, was fatally shot by a white cop in Montgomery County, Maryland, my mother had dreamed she was attending the wedding of one of her sons. "Marriage is death," she predicted. "This is bad news for somebody in the family." On the night of March 30, my brother Seaver called. A cop had killed Derrick. Two bullets to the back of his head, allegedly during a struggle over the cop's gun. Derrick was unarmed.

This reminiscence was broken when the phone rang. Ma again. This time she brought up the unpleasant subject of a spiritual struggle between Little Peter and me. In a West Indian ritual, when a "boy chile" is the "spitting image" of his father, the father must pay his son—put a dollar or more in his hand—or the son's spirit may wind up vanquishing the father's. "Pay the boy!" she demanded. "Ole people say that you killed your father because he never paid you. You look like him, walk like him, and talk like him—and you're just as pigheaded."

Despite our strong resemblance, I don't believe Little Peter's spirit would kill mine so that he could live. If anything, I would be the one to give my life for him. I told Ma that the recent killings of young, unarmed black men by police have crept into her dreams and my own fears.

"Peter might die before me," I said. "What if a cop killed him?"

"What can you do?" she asked angrily.

"Ma, you'd have to bury me," I replied.

"Killing yourself is not the answer," she shot back.

"It's homicide I'm talking about, Ma. The 'Vengeance of Moko' [a Trinidadian phrase meaning all-out revenge against your tormentor] will fall on him. I'll beg God to forgive me, and kill the cop who killed my son."

"Did I kill anybody when Derrick died?" she asked. "Look at those African people [Amadou Diallo's parents]; are they talking about killing and killing and shooting the police who killed their son? You're crazy if you start thinking like that."

Maybe I had gone over the edge, I thought later. But it was a vow born of rage and sorrow. There are thousands of black fathers like me who are having the same thoughts and dreams—not from feelings of retribution, but out of a desperation born of the belief that justice for them and their sons is impossible in Rudy Giuliani's New York.

William H. Grier and Price M. Cobbs, the authors of the book Black Rage, say we can't be blamed for such "copicidal" fantasies. "Black people, to a degree that approaches paranoia, must be ever alert to danger from their white fellow citizens," they write. "It is a cultural phenomenon peculiar to black Americans. And it is a posture so close to paranoid thinking that the mental disorder into which black people most frequently fall is paranoid psychosis. Can we say that white men have driven black men mad?"

On the afternoon of March 16, I learned that Patrick Dorismond had been shot to death by an undercover narcotics officer. Another young black man had died, and I lashed out in anger. It could have been Peter, I said on the several talk shows to which I subsequently was invited to comment about, as Grier and Cobbs put it, "the depth of the grief for slain sons."

Except for my mother, and Paula, Little Peter's Mom, I had never told anyone about the rage that I feel would overwhelm me if a cop unjustifiably murdered my son. But, after a white man almost drove me mad, my secret got out. During a heated debate with New York Post columnist Steve Dunleavy on The Alan Colmes Show on WEVD radio, Colmes questioned the decency of demonstrators, at Patrick Dorismond's funeral, who carried posters declaring: "IF MY SON WERE KILLED BY THE COPS, I'D GO AFTER MAYOR GIULIANI'S SON." Colmes said the signs threatened the life of the mayor's then 14-year-old son, Andrew. I responded, and, in the ensuing acrimonious exchange, bared a black father's pent-up rage.

"*I have a 13-year-old son, and any police officer who kills my son, he's dead! Period!*" *I bellowed. "I'm going after him! That's how I feel! I'm not waiting for this system to give up any justice. I am going after that police officer! … If a police officer kills my son in this city, I am not waiting for Rudy Giuliani to do anything. I'm going after that cop. I'm just as dead!*"

Dunleavy argued that I had created an implausible scenario—that he could not imagine my son being shot by a cop. But then he turned. "[L]et's talk about circumstances," he said. "You've come outright and [said] if any cop killed your son, the cop's dead. What would happen if that 15-year-old son of yours—which I'm sure would not happen—had a gun in his hand, was shooting at a cop?"

"*No! No! No!*" *I replied. "My son will not have a gun in his hand. I'm gonna tell you like it is. I raise my son with proper values, Ok? My son is an endangered species when he walks outside. Your son is not an endangered species … if you have sons.… You don't understand the black experience in this city at all! Whenever my son or my daughter, who is 19 years old, step out of their apartment in this city, I don't know if they're gonna come back home because some police officer might mistake their cell phone, might mistake their wallet, or their set of keys, for a gun, and then shoot them down because he profiles them! You don't understand that experience, Steve, because you don't live it! You live in your own nice world where … you protect the status quo, protect people like Rudy Giuliani.*"

Just as I felt Dunleavy might be sympathizing a bit with what I had to say, he began to question my standards. "You keep on talking about how you bring up your children with proper values, and they wouldn't have a gun in their hand, and I quite agree with you. I'm sure they wouldn't.… But if you say you bring your children up with proper values and you talk like this, I think you better readjust what you call values."

I stuck to my declaration: "Any police officer [who] kills my son; I'm taking him out because I'm just as good as dead!"

Colmes interjected: "But you're talking about taking justice in your own hands.…"

"*Yes!*" *I emphasized. "[The cop] took justice in [his] own hands. There has to be some kind of response, Alan. There are … grieving mothers and fathers.… I come from a totally different culture. My culture tells me 'an eye for an eye, and a tooth for a tooth.' You kill my son and you want to say that he had some gun in his hand when he didn't have one! I am dead. You guys are gonna write my story for me. I am coming after that police officer."*

Dunleavy invoked an argument popular with Giuliani conservatives and far-right talking heads. "I think you should take your activism down to Washington, where the

394 Why Blacks Fear 'America's Mayor'

Washington cops have a frightening record [of killing black men]," he said. (If Dunleavy was suggesting that I tolerated black cops killing black people, he was sadly mistaken.)

"I [live] in New York," I reminded him. Dunleavy pressed the point, hinting that the civil libertarian's theory—that police brutality would be almost nonexistent if black cops patrolled mostly black neighborhoods—does not work. "It just so happens the majority of Washington cops are black," he said.

But my beef is with Giuliani's terror squad. "Any cop in this city, black or white, who attacks and brutalizes people ... should be punished....," I said.

"But you're talking about vigilante justice, Peter," said Colmes. "You're talking about going after them yourself." I wanted to make it clear that my fight with the cop who killed my son would be personal. If there were four cops, like in the case of Amadou Diallo, I'd go after them all—but I wouldn't be avenging every alleged police killing.

"I'm speaking about me!" I explained. "I'm speaking about what would happen to me if a white police officer, a black police officer, a Latino police officer, kills my son. I'm gone. I'm dead!"

The liberal Colmes attempted to link my views to those of some of the radical protesters at Patrick Dorismond's funeral who, according to Colmes, advocated killing Andrew Giuliani.

"I think a sign at this rally threatening Giuliani's son [was] way out of line," he declared. "It was really inappropriate."

"There is something called righteous indignation," I asserted. "People are angry! The only thing that they have ... is freedom of speech, regardless of whether ... they are fighting words."

Dunleavy interjected: "Is that what you call righteous indignation? You're talking about righteous indignation when you talk about killing the mayor's son? Are you out of your freaking mind?"

".... The mayor has killed the sons and daughters of African Americans in this city," I retorted. "He has sanctioned it! And if people feel that they have to send a message back to him ... let them do that." (In no way was I calling for the life of the Pharoah's first-born son.)

"Oh, come on, for God's sake," Dunleavy fumed. "You better stop taking those stupid pills you've been taking."

Pills? Much like the undercover cops who assumed Patrick Dorismond was a pothead, Steve Dunleavy was not above inferring that I might be a drug abuser who popped pills. News flash, Steve: I don't need pills. I get high on black rage, which makes African American fathers like me consider homicide when Giuliani justice is not enuf.

On the second anniversary of my brother's death, Little Peter's mother summoned me to their home. I told Paula that if she was going to talk to me about another one of her "Stephen King nightmares," I didn't want to hear it.

"It's about Peter!" she snapped. "No dream could predict what I am about to do to your son."

I raced over to the apartment. Little Peter, who is always at the door to greet me, remained in a back room. Paula was sitting on a chair in the kitchen gritting her teeth, trying to calm her erupting nerves.

"His pants is hanging off his ass these days, and he's not listening to me!" she complained.

"Take him!" offered Paula, "because if the cops don't kill Peter for looking like a thug, I will."

I called Little Peter from his hiding place, rapped him a couple of times in the back of his head ("Kid, what wuz you thinkin'?"), and thrust a $10 bill in his hand.

"What's that for?" he asked, still wincing from the thumps.

"This," I said, staring at Grandma Alice's beautiful big-eye boy, "ensures that both of us will live."

978-0-595-71621-0
0-595-71621-0

CPSIA information can be obtained
at www.ICGtesting.com
Printed in the USA
LVOW11*2339070717

540642LV00017B/470/P

9 780595 716210